New Thinking About Strategy and International Security

Titles of Related Interest

New Thinking About Strategy and International Security

Edited by
KEN BOOTH
University College of Wales

HarperCollins*Academic*
An imprint of HarperCollins*Publishers*

Published by
HarperCollinsAcademic

77-85 Fulham Palace Road
Hammersmith
London W6 8JB
UK

First published in 1991

British Library Cataloguing in Publication Data

New thinking about strategy and international security.
1. International security
I. Booth, Ken
327.116
ISBN 0-04-445414-7
ISBN 0-04-445415-5

Library of Congress Cataloging-in-Publication Data

New thinking about strategy and international security /
edited by Ken Booth.
p. cm.
Includes bibliographical references and index.
ISBN 0-04-445414-7 (alk.).
ISBN 0-04-445415-5 (pbk. : alk. paper)
1. National security – Congresses. 2. Strategy – Congresses.
3. World politics – 1985 – 1995 – Congresses. 4. Security,
International – Congresses. I. Booth, Ken.
UA10.5.N48 1991
355'.03–dc20
90–44099
CIP

Typeset in 10 on 12 point Bembo
Printed in Great Britain by
Billing and Sons, London and Worcester

This book is dedicated to

JAMES E. KING
(1914–1988)

Jim King was one of the wisest yet least
acclaimed strategic analysts of the first
generation of the nuclear age. His *The
New Strategy* is the best strategy book
never published.

Preface

Since the mid-1980s 'new thinking' of one sort or another has begun to set the agenda of the defence debate in both East and West. Just as the 'old thinking' so influentially represented by the Committee for the Present Danger in the United States came to dominate the defence agenda in the second half of the 1970s, so, a decade later, dominant attitudes came to be challenged and to some extent replaced, this time by new thinking about notions such as common security, reasonable sufficiency, denuclearization, arms control and disarmament, non-provocative defence, stability, dealignment and the role of military power. There is presently a sense of change in international politics which is as profound as any this century. We are living the unthinkable and it is almost becoming normal. Not surprisingly, there is some turmoil about the way we should think about strategy and international security. Whether we move ahead to a more satisfactory international order or revert to the habits and attitudes of the pre-1939 world will in part depend on the outcome of the debate between new and old thinking.

New thinking achieved political salience in the second half of the 1980s, but it remained surrounded by uncertainties and scepticism, and its further development faces many obstacles. Anything in this field brash enough to describe itself as 'new' immediately attracts criticism. In the West the policies advocated by 'alternative' security specialists have attracted official censure in some countries, while a critical mass of favourable public opinion has not built up to enable sympathetic political parties to achieve office. The main power structures in the West have argued that many if not all the alternative security ideas are neither practical nor desirable. In the Soviet Union President Gorbachev's new political and defence thinking became the state's declaratory policy and also achieved some measure of practical implementation, but resistance has been shown from within the military establishment and among conservatives. Sceptical observers in the West were for too long unconvinced that what Gorbachev offered was more than window-dressing or a rationalization of weakness. By the time scepticism had weakened, many were then doubtful whether Soviet new thinking could be sustained beyond Gorbachev's own finite political life.

Whatever happens in the future, we are undoubtedly witnessing a new wave in thinking about strategy and international security (the fourth of the nuclear era if we accept Colin Gray's identification of three earlier waves). But this wave is different: it promises to be the most radical of any since Bernard Brodie announced, at the beginning of the nuclear age, that the main aim of armed forces would not be to fight wars, but to deter them. Unlike the earlier ones the fourth wave promises a radically different philosophy of security.

The theory and practice of strategy and international security are at a turning point. Some argue that we can move into a radically new and improved security environment whereas others, who believe that nothing has fundamentally changed in the world, argue that new thinking should be resisted and well-trodden paths continued. Almost everybody, however, agrees that the 1990s will be a time of opportunity and danger in international politics, though there is disagreement about what constitutes the dangers and what the opportunities. Which old ideas should be jettisoned? Which new thinking should be operationalized?

A book which is sensitive to the dynamic situation we find ourselves in, which provides a survey of the new thinking and offers a basis for answering these questions, should therefore be both timely and useful for all those interested in the theory and practice of strategy and international security.

Most of the papers contained in this volume were originally presented at the joint BISA/ISA Annual Conference in London in March 1989. It was a testimony to their astuteness that little or no changes were necessitated by the revolution which took place in European affairs and East–West relations in the autumn of 1989. Thanks are due to the conference organizers for providing the opportunities for discussion, and to many typists and other helpers in numerous academic institutions, particularly Marian Davies at UCW, Aberystwyth. I want also to thank Richard Wyn Jones for compiling the index.

Ken Booth

Note. During the final preparation of this book, in August 1990, a major international crisis broke out in the Middle East, the first of the post-cold war world. Four weeks into the crisis, war now seems a distinct possibility, though not an inevitability, as the major contending powers dig themselves into entrenched military, political and psychological positions. With the passage of time the initial emotions are subsiding, but other factors (impatience and the momentum of the US military build-up) are creating a different calculus for war. In the light of the Iraqi aggression and its immediate aftermath, readers might ask themselves about the relevance of a book about 'new thinking' about strategy and international security. Is it not premature? Does the crisis not show that we live in a Hobbesian world in which it is only realistic to stick by the old lesson of meeting power with power? Is not Saddam Hussein the Hitler figure who has once again punctured any hopes that we might be entering a more co-operative and peaceful era?

The temptation to think that nothing has changed, and that nothing can change, is strong, but a rush back to traditional Realism now would be as unwise as was giving into the temptation at the end of 1989 to believe that everything had changed in world politics. Whatever happens next, the Gulf crisis underlines many themes in this book, and offers a test-tube experiment on the relative strengths – and more important on the validity – of 'new' as opposed to 'old' thinking.

The Iraqi aggression has confirmed the theme of the Introduction that many 'morbid symptoms' persist in an international situation which is undergoing considerable change. Some of the reactions of the other powers also demonstrate traditional attitudes. In contrast, there have also been signs of new thinking. The most noteworthy have been the almost universal condemnation of the aggression; the call for unconditional Iraqi withdrawal, the release of the hostages and an economic embargo; the unprecedented degree of co-operation at the United Nations, including between the formerly adversarial superpowers; the practical multilateral efforts to negate the aggression; the search for alternatives to military responses; the growing appreciation that the crisis cannot be compartmentalized from other issues in the region; and the wide (if not universal) understanding that a war could have incalculable consequences. There has also been, in some Western circles, a realization that the West is not without culpability in the flow

of events, and that the Iraqi population belong to the victims of
Saddam Hussein, as well as the Kuwaitis and the Western hostages.
Already, the crisis has proved much more complex than the great
simplifiers in the main governments have portrayed it in order to
garner sympathy and support for their own positions. Saddam
Hussein blundered badly by his crude assessments of the likely
response to Iraqi aggression on the part of regional countries and
others, while those Western leaders who want to make policy by
national loyalty tests (as in the early 1980s) do not understand that
to recognize that Arab standpoints are affected by a deep sense of
grievance against the West does not by one jot weaken one's belief
in the rightness of confronting aggression.

Kuwait was a defenceless small state living next to a regional
military power. Its rapid conquest by Iraq does not say anything
significant about the offensive utility of military force, which in
several points of the book is said to be in historical decline. It is not a
vindication of the effectiveness of the offensive use of military force
when there is no contest. All the authors below accept that the logic
of military power has to be attended to, but most would point out
that the conditions are significantly changing, and so, in parallel,
must the manner in which force is exercised. In particular, restraint
of a qualitative and quantitative type should be employed, and there
should be a shift from the idea that attack is the best form of defence
to the idea that defence is the best form of defence. Early in the
crisis Saddam Hussein explicitly recognized the failure of his earlier
aggression against Iran. This vindicated the latter's bitter defensive
struggle. Meanwhile, for the moment, the defensive utility of military power has been underlined by Saddam Hussein's unwillingness
to extend his aggression to Saudi Arabia or other Gulf states
following the build-up of the multilateral defensive arrangements.
Nor is the United States rushing to attack Kuwait to drive out
Iraqi forces, which in turn would probably escalate, inadvertently
or otherwise, into a general attack on Iraq itself. Despite the size of
the US military build-up, the degree of international support it has
received, the government's determination to uphold US interests
in the region, and the desire of the administration to counter talk
of 'declinism', the White House is being cautious about offensive
military operations. Some if not all Americans know that a conflict
against war-bloodied Iraq is not likely to be a 'three-day turkey
shoot' in the manner of the attacks on Grenada and Panama.

While the crisis shows the continuing importance in international affairs of the United States and the Soviet Union, it also gives evidence of their declining authority. Until recently it is unlikely that an ambitious but vulnerable regional leader like Saddam Hussein would have acted against the wishes of the superpowers in a region in which they both have major interests. Any talk of terminal US decline is premature, since it remains the foremost economy and still leading military power, but it is in relative decline. In countering talk of declinism it is actually showing how much it has declined: by invading Kuwait Saddam indicated his disregard of possible US responses; US projection forces, which for over a decade have been in the Indian Ocean to deter major regional instability, once again failed in that mission; and the relative economic decline of the United States has been reflected in the call for financial support from its allies (which logically should give them a bigger say in what happens next). In such ways the United States has proved to be neither as independent nor as authoritative an actor as hitherto. If a major war does break out, instigated at the decision of either Iraq or the United States, it will be the clearest signal yet of the decline of US power in the region; the use of force will demonstrate that US power lacks persuasive credibility.

If US power is not what it was, the decline of the Soviet Union as a superpower has been precipitous. In no major international crisis since the late 1940s has it been such a passive actor.

The Gulf crisis proves beyond doubt the argument made later that crisis prevention is better than crisis management. So far in the crisis the dangers of crisis mismanagement have been all too evident: the perceptual tunnels of governments, unhelpful statements by supposedly experienced leaders, the danger of the military instrument shaping the will to use it, the risks of misperception and misinformation, the possibility that policy-makers will become the victims of their own propaganda, and the considerable danger that an accidental or fabricated incident will lead to a general escalation. In the first weeks of the crisis there have been worrying hints that in the nuclear context, governments had quickly forgotten in the Third World what they believed they had learned from Sarajevo.

Whether the Gulf crisis could actually have been 'prevented' obviously depends upon the time-scale allowed for different policies to have worked. What should be uncontroversial is the proposition that alternative policies over decades could have shaped the regional situation in a markedly more benign pattern. Without in any way condoning Saddam Hussein's behaviour, it must be accepted that important problems in the region have their roots in the West's own imperialism in the Middle East in the distant past, and in its geopolitical ambitions more recently; policy-making has not been helped by the general depth of Western cultural and religious incomprehension about the Arab world and Islam; the strategic practicalities of the crisis have been dangerously complicated by the huge arms sales into the region by all the major powers; tensions have been exacerbated by the failure of the regional actors and the relevant external powers to have made more progress towards the settlement of the Arab–Israeli conflict; the West is seen to have done little against other countries which march into neighbouring territory (notably Israel) or to have engaged enthusiastically in comprehensive sanctions against pariah states (notably South Africa), with the consequence that the West is seen as calling on universal principles only when it is geopolitically or otherwise convenient; Western policy within the Arab world has been hampered by its identification with some reactionary leaders, and by its failure to do much to support the growth of the more liberal and democratic elements in the Arab world. Finally, the external powers cannot avoid the charge that they bear some responsibility for creating the ambitious and dictatorial Iraqi leader by provoking Arab nationalism in his early days, by supporting him against Khomeni, by failing to criticize adequately his earlier brutality against his own population, by their arms sales, and by giving commercial interests too high a priority. The crisis has not only re-confirmed the brutal image of Saddam Hussein, but it has also exposed double standards and weaknesses in Western policy. Double standards are not solely a moral issue: those who adopt them perpetuate what they claim to want to change – the lack of law in the jungle. It is not surprising, therefore, if Arabs and others look on cynically as the United States and others drape the geopolitics of oil with the language of international law.

The arguments above underline one of the major themes of the Conclusion, namely that it is desirable for states to adopt a 'holistic' or comprehensive approach to security. In this as in other respects we are witnessing in the Gulf crisis a struggle, of which we shall see others in the years ahead, between the advocates of old and new ways of thinking about strategy and international security.

One victory will not settle the debate either way. The main point,
new thinkers argue, is that if we want a different and more secure
world, then decisions in this crisis, as in other security issues that
arise, should be taken with a forward-looking, global and comprehensive perspective. In practice, this favours international action
rather than the pursuit of unilateral advantage; the containment of
Saddam Hussein not the roll-back of Iraq; defensive deterrence not
offensive intervention (even to right a wrong); holistic security
policies not double standards; the strengthening of international
norms not the primacy of national interests; the appreciation of
the interconnectedness of events and their complexity rather than
demonizing and simplifying; empathy not ethnocentrism; and an
appreciation of the human dimension of the situation (in Palestine
and Iraq and not just the homes of Western hostages) instead of a
crude state-dominated mindset. Would this crisis have arisen had
policies been pursued over the years seeking to create democracies
in Iraq, Kuwait and elsewhere in the Middle East, had greater
mutual understanding been encouraged between the Arab/Islamic
world and the West and had dependence on oil been reduced?

If there is a major war in the Gulf, either as a result of further
Iraqi aggression or US-led forces moving from defensive positions
into an offensive strategy – or by an escalation leading to a war
'nobody wants' – the consequences could be incalculable. An
ensuing war would obviously be costly in human and material
terms, but also in its long-term political, economic, religious and
moral implications. It could consolidate Arab nationalism and
Islamic fundamentalism into an uncompromising force, destroy
whatever support there is for the Western (and general international) position on the Kuwait issue; create economic chaos in
the region; make long-term access to oil more uncertain than
it is now; and ensure that for years the Middle East will be
more rather than less unstable. Even a war sanctioned by the
United Nations would not automatically be right, let alone prudent. Defensive military precautions and vigorous non-military
sanctions is one thing; an international offensive force is another
entirely. Would similar international offensive action be advocated
in other conflicts (such as that between India and Pakistan) where
territory might be occupied 'unlawfully' following an outbreak of
violence? If not, why not, if 'international law' is the transcend-
ent value?

Essentially defenceless states such as Kuwait can only be made secure by the creation of a world order based not on the principle that might is right, but on the creation of an effective political-legal security regime – what is later described as a 'non-violent conflict culture'. This will best be achieved by the adoption of a holistic approach to security.

International society, as is argued in Chapter 1, is in good shape. The political divisions in the crisis are not as crude as the Realists would claim. Many Arabs oppose Iraqi aggression, while many in the West urge restraint as the military build-up moves beyond simply defensive capabilities to offensive options. It is encouraging to date that there are no simple cleavages between Arabs and non-Arabs, or between Islam and Christendom. If the temptations of old thinking are resisted, and a determination is shown to pursue a different course, then the crisis might be resolved without further violence and with the strengthening of international order. It is difficult to imagine that Iraq will be successful in its invasion of Kuwait if the major powers have patience and create the conditions for Saddam Hussein's power to collapse from within. The simple choice is to surrender to aggression or risk a terrible war. But it is possible to avoid both these extremes, as was proved in Europe after the late 1940s.

We are now at a cross-roads in this crisis, as in so many other matters in world politics. There is no road that will lead simply to Utopia, but there is always one which, however little, is more progressive than any other available. Some roads offer the prospect of merely travelling in circles (replicating past behaviour); but one road has always some promise of advancing the idea of global community-building and limiting the role of force. We can choose.

Contents

Introduction
The interregnum: world politics in transition

KEN BOOTH

> The old is dying and the new cannot be born; in this inter-regnum there arises a great diversity of morbid symptoms.
>
> Antonio Gramsci,
> *Prison Notebooks*[1]

Whether we are thinking of particular situations or world politics as a whole, these words of Gramsci speak pertinently to the condition of international politics at the start of the last decade of the twentieth century. This is a time of manifold change. Established structures of international politics are collapsing, while within and between nations and groups of nations there are tensions between old and new ways of thought and action. This is a time of opportunity, but also one of both familiar and unfamiliar dangers. Despite the latter, as the 1990s begin, many people are suffused by a sense of expectation that is nearly without equal in the twentieth century. Those earlier springtimes of hope turned out, in the end, to be dreams. Morbid symptoms spread, and hope was crushed by world wars or lost peaces. Today, morbid symptoms exist in plenty, but there are sound reasons for thinking that our new springtime might last. But it is not certain. Human behaviour comes without guarantees.

TREND AND TRANSITION

The 1980s began with a Cold War, and an image of history going into reverse. This was personified by the leaders of the superpowers: Ronald Reagan and Leonid Brezhnev were yesterday's men in every sense of the term. In remarkable contrast, the decade ended with history going into fast forward.

Change was everywhere in the air in the late 1980s. The biggest revolution was in East–West relations, as the first postwar era ran its course, but important changes were taking place elsewhere. Across the world the bipolar confrontation which had structured so much of international politics was in decline, and in its place a multipolar multidimensional pattern of relations was emerging, with major new actors such as Japan, Germany and the European Community. Previously, many states had determined their security, economic, ideological and political positions according to the superpower relationship, but as power in world affairs diffused, and the leverage of the superpowers declined, so did the significance of bipolarity in the daily business of the world.

The new Cold War of the early 1980s witnessed the final flaunting of US–Soviet pre-eminence in world affairs. Both superpowers overstretched their military and political power. The US humiliation in Vietnam was matched by that of the Soviet Union in Afghanistan. The superpowers even proved decreasingly influential in what had always been regarded as their own geopolitical backyards: uncomfortable neighbours like the Sandinistas survived the Reagan doctrine and Solidarity the Brezhnev doctrine. Whether they would later survive elections and economic distress remained to be seen.

The economies of the superpowers came under increasing pressure, though not to the same extent. While the United States simply lost its former pre-eminence, the crisis in the Soviet Union was systemic. Both superpowers became overburdened by military spending; at the same time they could see that who gets what in today's world is more often determined by economic power than by the somewhat declining currency of military strength. For both superpowers the rise of Japan and Western Europe as economic superpowers marked major milestones in international politics. Western Europe would clearly grow more politically influential, in parallel with its economic strength, while a significant shift was taking place in the international political economy towards the Pacific Basin. Here as elsewhere, new actors were appearing, and the regimentation of international affairs that had characterized the Cold War was eroding. This proved most spectacular in Eastern Europe, however, as countries moved Westwards in their economic and political orientation. The military implications were enormous.

The stimulus for so much of the recent change was the second Russian revolution, presided over by Mikhail Gorbachev but with roots going back years. The Soviet Union has been striving to emerge not just from Stalinism but from even deeper habits: an economic, strategic and political culture is being challenged to change itself. In the course of attempting to bring about the political reforms necessary for economic progress, deep problems in the Soviet state and in its relationships with Eastern Europe were opened up. Future economic prospects are uncertain, and the lack of progress in the short run threatens to undermine Gorbachev's efforts in the long run. But change there had to be, whatever the risks. As Gorbachev told Erich Honecker, another of yesterday's men, in October 1989: 'Those who delay are punished by life.' Together, *perestroika* and *glasnost* have put the Soviet Union on the road to becoming a more 'normal' country, defined broadly in Western terms (multi-party and market-oriented), though the Soviet Union is holding on to the trappings of communism far longer than its former Eastern European satellites. The changes in the USSR have been marked by important mental leaps: a more objective analysis of Soviet history; a more realistic assessment of the country's position in the world; a better understanding of the effect of Soviet behaviour on other nations; and a less doctrinaire attitude towards the West. The changes have also been accompanied by an understanding that progress requires the winding down of the inflated military burden the Soviet Union has carried since the late 1940s – an overinsurance that only inflated Western suspicion and increased the risk of war. Predictably, the second Russian revolution stimulated change throughout the Soviet bloc. For nationalists in Eastern Europe and increasingly within Soviet republics, openness did not stop with words. They also wanted it to apply to borders. The unity of the Soviet empire not only collapsed on its periphery, but was also being threatened at its heart.

Communism was everywhere in collapse towards the end of the 1980s. The countries of the Warsaw Treaty Organization (WTO) had run out of steam in everything except military power. Their economies did not meet the needs of their consumers, their political systems lacked legitimacy and their ideology lost appeal.

On the face of it capitalism had won the war of the systems, but Third World poverty, alienation, an impoverished underclass and environment-threatening levels of consumption indicated that capitalism had not succeeded at a more fundamental level. Soviet-style 'socialism' had failed because, although it could meet basic needs, it could not satisfy wants. Meanwhile, capitalism flourished; it could not satisfy all basic needs, but it could meet the wants of the powerful.

Change across Europe has been intoxicating. In the summer of 1989 history began to accelerate more quickly than anybody had predicted, as we witnessed the peaceful installation of a democratic non-communist government in Poland; the taking down of the iron curtain in Hungary as that country moved towards pluralism; the non-interference by the Soviet Union in the radical developments in Eastern Europe, thus signalling that the Brezhnev doctrine was dead; the gathering momentum of the Gorbachev revolution at home, though in *glasnost* rather than *perestroika*; the growing expressions of nationalism in the Soviet Union; the perceptible progress in disarmament at the talks on Conventional Forces in Europe (CFE) after years of disappointment; the promise of deep cuts in the Strategic Arms Reduction Talks (START); the acceleration of Western reciprocation to developments in the East instead of mere spectator status; the exodus of large numbers of citizens from the GDR to the West; the widespread expressions of discontent in the Soviet Union and other parts of the communist world based on appeals for greater democracy and better living standards; and the surprising speed, after years of hibernation, with which the issue of German unification had again to be contemplated if not actually confronted. Before these trends could be fully assimilated, there occurred the most dramatic breakthrough of all, the opening up of the borders of the GDR and the promise of political reform. The most potent symbol of this historical moment was the breaching of the Berlin Wall. Radical changes quickly followed in Czechoslovakia and Bulgaria, the two East European members of the WTO apart from the Ceaucescu regime in Romania which had hitherto set their face against reform. Until that moment, the revolutions in the East had been remarkably peaceful. Finally, at the very end of a miraculous year, the Stalinist dynasty of the Ceaucescus was challenged, and quickly fell in bloody revolution. 1989 had proved to be a springtime of democracy and freedom in

Eastern Europe, but it left every country with enormous problems of reconstruction, while confronting the West with the need for difficult mental and material readjustments.

The geopolitical map of Europe is therefore changing. The stark postwar division of Europe is being transformed into a more fluid pattern which will involve a reduced role for the superpowers, the disappearance or reform of the military blocs, several national claims for self-determination, the rise of new pan-European structures and new political and economic associations. Boundary changes will take place, including the unification of the two Germanys and possibly the redefining of the Soviet state. Others could come on the agenda, as the 'daily plebiscite' of nations challenges the established pattern of states.

A notable feature of European affairs in particular but world affairs in general through the 1980s was the role played by non-state actors: peace movements, opposition parties and political movements, ethnic groups, religious bodies, environmental activists, and large groups of citizens acting as refugees, consumers or protesters have helped to determine the international agenda. Left exclusively to yesterday's men (and women) in power at the start of the 1980s, the agenda today would look markedly different to the one we are now addressing. In the West, the peace movements of the early 1980s helped to prevent Reagan being Reagan on arms control, intervention and other issues, and helped to develop alternative security ideas which became superpower business in the late 1980s through their support by Gorbachev. In the East, more dramatically, people marched and helped to bring about the promise of reform in hitherto repressive and unsuccessful systems. Above all, the looming issue of German unity was thrust to the forefront of affairs not because governments wanted it – they did not – but because enough citizens of the GDR did. Together, a popular front of non-state actors brought an end to the Cold War, though the extraordinary part played by President Gorbachev cannot be underestimated.

As 'détente from below' flourished, some international institutions, such as NATO, provided a framework in a continent where structures were crumbling. But NATO would have to evolve or become irrelevant. One international body, the European Community (EC), developed into a major force in its own right, and in political as well as economic matters. 1992, the year of the integrated single market, loomed larger on the horizon and became an urgent matter in the political and business life both of countries which are EC members and of those who want to be. Across Europe, the state is being eroded from above and from below. Borders matter less than ever before in recent times. Similar trends are evident elsewhere, as non-state actors increasingly shape public affairs. Multinational corporations and financial organizations have globalized economic activity while being relatively immune from the control of governments; at the same time alliances and inter-state economic institutions constrain national governments. States are still the main actors in international politics, but they are more constrained. Interdependence is now the dominant theme. A steadily growing density of interaction between the world's economic, political, social and military actors has produced a web of 'complex interdependence' (Keohane and Nye, 1977). By increasing mutual interaction and dependency new possibilities are created for peace and security, though the danger of new strains is also raised.

Bipolarity has declined, as the 'realities' (actual and imagined) of the Cold War have changed; this is a process that began in the early 1960s. The unravelling of the knot of the Cold War in Europe was prolonged by the continent's central involvement in the superpower confrontation. The two halves of Europe always wanted détente to a greater extent than the superpowers. The idea that Danes might fight Poles, or Bulgarians fight British in a nuclear war was always an outrageous possibility. The black comedy of the superpower confrontation in the early 1980s helped convince a growing body that cold war posturing was both irrational and anachronistic. The behaviour associated with the Cold War (mutual threat inflation, overinsurance in military power, intra-bloc discipline, implicit enemy imagining) is out of touch with a world of complex interdependence, where military force is unusable between industrialized societies. In such circumstances, maintaining massive military strength is not only wasteful, it is also dangerous, since it becomes an independent cause of mistrust. Although plenty of old thinking remains, the realization is growing that security interdependence is a fact of life.

Along with the changes in the economic and political order, there have also been new trends in military affairs. In the West in particular there has been a 'crisis of nuclearism': strategies of flexible response and limited nuclear options have increasingly been seen to be both dangerous and incredible, while extended deterrence has faced growing pressures. As a result, the strength (and value) of the US security guarantee to Western Europe has become a matter of lively debate. On the US side shedding some defence burden has become a major issue, as has worry about the EC. The experience of the Reagan years left only a handful in Western Europe whose confidence in US leadership was unconditional: later, not even the decline of the Soviet Union could compensate for the shrinking authority of the United States, suggested by President Bush's caution. The loyalty of the NATO allies to the defence of the West remains, but how this will be translated into practice remains to be seen, as the decline of the WTO threat undermines NATO's main rationale. Through the 1980s the economies of the WTO allies ran into the ground, and this had a serious effect on their military potential. More significantly, the traditional military overinsurance of the Soviet Union proved by the early 1980s to be counterproductive in economic and foreign policy terms. In the East, as well as the West, the accumulation of nuclear overkill has increasingly come to be seen, by a growing number of experts as well as the public at large, as an obstacle to more security rather than a panacea for East–West relations.

While the risk of nuclear war has been much reduced as a result of the amelioration of the superpower conflict, it has not been eliminated. Nuclear proliferation is a particular danger, especially if it takes place in unstable regions (where it is obviously most likely), while recent superpower trends could be reversed, and the mutually targeted cold war nuclear infrastructures still remain. The nuclear threat exists but seems less urgent; this makes clearer the extent to which the daily lives of people in the West are threatened by drugs, terrorism, refugees and the spread of modern weaponry (especially ballistic missiles and chemical weapons) to the Third World. Security is no longer just military security. As time passes it will be conceived more broadly: threats to economic and environmental wellbeing will demand more attention.

Military power certainly has not become unimportant, but its utility has become more circumscribed. This was evident in the 1980s with the declining clout of the muscle-bound superpowers. Their experience suggested the increasingly restricted usability of military force, the growing economic liability of big defence spending, the waste and irrelevance of nuclear overkill and the decreased value of large-scale projection forces. Some Third World countries continue to entertain military aspirations, despite the lessons offered by the superpowers. At the highest level, the nuclear extravagance of the Reagan years failed to produce political leverage; it only hurt US economic prospects. The Soviet Union was in much worse trouble economically. The prolonged conventional war in Afghanistan failed to secure a satisfactory outcome, but was at the cost of a 'bleeding wound' to the Soviet Union itself. Meanwhile, the build-up of Soviet projection forces feared in the 1970s quickly peaked, and then declined. In the light of the US experience in Vietnam and the Soviet experience in Afghanistan, and the decreasing utility of military threats by both superpowers against backyard nationalist irritants, the usefulness of large-scale and long-range conventional projection forces and interventionist strategies is clearly declining. When a US President can describe the fly-swatting war in Grenada as 'our finest hour', the days of offensive superpower military intervention are numbered.

Power in world affairs is increasingly determined by economic success rather than military statistics. The rise of new centres of power such as Japan and the Federal Republic of Germany attest to this. Their emergence took place behind the shield of US military power during the uncertainties of the Cold War. By the time they had become economic superpowers the need to translate economic strength into military statistics appeared to be less pressing. The dynamic economies of the Pacific basin suggest that power in international politics decreasingly grows out of the barrel of a gun. This could change, but it does not seem likely as the costs both of war and of breaking the links of interdependence continue to increase.

The accelerating technological revolution, mainly in electronics and communication systems, is accelerating the development of a world society, the 'global village' that has long been foreseen. This technological revolution is having and will continue to have profound implications. In addition to promoting the globalization of economics and politics, it will create both opportunities and problems in the security realm. At the interstate level it will assist the interpenetration of states, and so reduce the risks of irrational mistrust developing. For individual states, however, the technological revolution could be disturbing. The growth of productivity at lower employment levels threatens employment and therefore life-support prospects, and this could obviously have violent repercussions in countries where the mass of people already have little to lose. This is the case in much of the Third World, where there is a crisis of development. Burdened by debt, environmental problems, ineffective administrative structures, ethnic divisions and weak economies, the systems of many Third World countries are overloaded. The future threatens to be one of yet further poverty, economic and political instability, social dislocation, and the ever-present possibility of internal violence. The latter increases the dangers at the international level.

Relations between the Third World and the industrialized north will, in the years ahead, be much more concerned with environmental issues than hitherto. The destruction of nature is global and the problems can only be mitigated by appropriately global co-operation. There is a wider consciousness of the interconnectedness of environmental issues, and even some consensus about what needs to be done: but who will pay is a matter destined to cause considerable disagreement. Until solutions are agreed internationally, hard decisions taken nationally, and the bills picked up, the degradation of the physical environment will continue. At best, it will take many years before adverse trends can be reversed since creating a sustainable and habitable environment will involve achieving widespread agreement about philosophies and policies relating to such fundamental issues as population growth, economic management and the global maldistribution of wealth. Exacerbating all the environmental problems is the simple fact that we have a world with too many people with too many wants.

We are therefore living in a world of rapid transformation, in which old power structures will disappear, new associations will arise, complex interdependence will evolve, and new problems and opportunities will open up. The international landscape in the decades ahead will be shaped by the interreacting trends discussed above, namely:

- the end of the Cold War
- the decline of bipolarity
- the collapse of communism
- the rise of new powers
- the changing map of Europe

- the new significance of non-state actors
- the growth of interdependence
- the declining significance of military power
- the revised security challenges
- the shifting international political economy
- the accelerating technological evolution
- the crisis of development in the Third World
- the increased salience of environmental issues.

Whether the new post-postwar era will prove to be more or less secure than the past remains to be seen. It will depend on the way governments and peoples respond to the challenges and opportunities they face. In terms of the subject of this book, it will depend upon whether they practise 'old' or 'new' thinking about strategy and international security. The prospects from the vantage point of the very start of the 1990s are mixed, though in the heartwarming afterglow of the breaching of the Berlin Wall and the possible termination of several long-running and bloody wars in the Third World, there is cause for more optimism than for many years. But the new always has to be built on the foundations of the old and there remain many morbid symptoms which threaten to repeat familiar patterns of fear and turmoil.

MORBID SYMPTOMS

Change, in many cases in a benevolent direction, has charged the atmosphere of international politics. But amid the hopes there are many morbid symptoms. If these multiply out of control, the outcome could merely be a perpetuation of the traditional vicious circle of the past, when periods of hope and co-operation collapsed into conflict and sometimes catastrophe. The list of morbid symptoms that follows includes only those that are most threatening to the development of more benevolent processes and structures.

(1)   East–West relations
- The record of the past is discouraging. Cold wars have been more normal than prolonged détentes. Confrontational

posturing and point-scoring dies hard. Some vested interests are served by perpetuating the old struggle. Periods of co-operation in international politics have often collapsed.

- Features of superpower domestic politics militate against pre-dictable co-operation. The four-yearly electoral succession struggles in Washington, the influence of military-industrial complexes, and the scope for rapid changes of direction by the Communist Party of the Soviet Union decrease one's confidence in the prospects for long-term coexistence. People in the West are particularly concerned about Gorbachev's political future, and the character of the Soviet Union that might follow.
- The influence of strategic fundamentalists in both superpowers continues. They will try and delay if not disrupt the arms control process and ensure that defence is equated with high levels of nuclear weapons, state-of-the-art technology, and conventional forces with offensive (or major counter-offensive) potential. As the WTO fades and Germany rises, the scope for military fundamentalism will grow in many countries.
- As long as the infrastructure of nuclear deterrence remains, so will the risk of a cataclysmic war. As long as countries target each other with weapons of mass destruction the dynamic of the security dilemma will threaten the success of efforts to transform the political relationship.
- There is danger of instability in Eastern Europe. Were a serious outbreak of violence to occur, perhaps over minority rights, it could set back overnight the positive mood of the late 1980s and early 1990s. If domestic unrest resulting from shortages or nationalist aspirations provokes brutal counter-measures, the outcome could poison international relations and (illogically) be used to justify a return to cold war posturing.
- Although superpower influence in Europe is waning, the pos-sibility of future competition cannot be ruled out between a United States seeking leverage over what President Bush hopes will be a 'free and united Europe' and a Soviet Union seeking leverage over what President Gorbachev hopes will be a 'Common European home'.
- There is a danger that the political and military agendas in Europe will not be synchronized. There are warnings here from the 1970s when uncontrolled military innovation contributed to

the undermining of political efforts to pursue détente. Military innovation can of itself provoke mutual suspicion, which in turn will feed into the political process. Armaments competition is pushed along by many factors, and hence is difficult to control.

- The enormity of the task facing the former communist states weighs against the orderly development of a European peace structure. Success requires nothing less than political, economic and in some senses cultural revolutions. While the potential for failure is considerable, the prospects for overnight success are nil.

- The future development of the Soviet Union will be one of the keys to the character of the European security problem. President Gorbachev faces serious difficulties in his pursuit of *perestroika*. The collapse of the Soviet state might occur, as nationalities (including the Russians, the most powerful of all) seek independence from the USSR. This could obviously create massive instabilities, which would feed dangerously into the international arena. While other potential Soviet leaders share Gorbachev's diagnoses and prescriptions, some do not. Under a different leadership constructive engagement with the West might be slowed or reversed; this would play into the hands of congenital anti–Soviets in the West. Traditional Russophobia has recently been evident in the triumphalism witnessed in some quarters.

- In 1989 the German question was catapulted to the forefront of the international agenda before any of the states concerned were ready for it. It is a subject which causes nervousness throughout Europe. The prospect of the unification of the two Germanys raises fundamental questions and fears about such issues as the continent's postwar boundaries, the deployment of the forces of the superpowers and the role and membership of the alliances. These are all issues that had been thought to be indefinitely settled. The German question will throw many spanners into the complex workings of multilateral arms control.

- The Cold War is over, but not cold war thinking, and certainly not its structures. Decades of short-term vigilance, exacerbated by fear and mistrust, had created by the early 1980s a quite irrational and obsolete Cold War. It will take time to dismantle all its machinery and reorient all its mindsets. Such has been the bewildering pace of recent change that it is not surprising that some prefer the simplicities and apparent certainties of the past. For some the Cold War has become a habit of mind, as well as a vested interest.

- The Cold War, for all its dangers, did help to suppress some traditional nationalist conflicts, particularly in Eastern Europe. The lifting of the structures of the Cold War may encourage their revival, while future socio-economic patterns in Europe (possibly a split between a rich West and a poor and exploited East) could create social strains within and between countries. The international politics of Europe have entered a more, not less, complex phase.

(2) Third World developments

- There are many trouble spots in the Third World, and although the superpowers began in the second half of the 1980s to adopt a much lower profile than hitherto, the possibility remains of their being drawn into some conflicts – notably in the Middle East – in ways that could have far reaching consequences. On the other hand, the lifting of superpower interest could in itself encourage some local instabilities. Persistent civil disorder exists in several Third World countries, while old international conflicts, such as in Kashmir and the Middle East, rumble on and occasionally threaten to erupt.
- There has been a worrying spread of advanced military technology, notably ballistic missiles and chemical weapons (the 'poor man's bomb'), to the Third World. Chemical weapons have already been used. A Missile Technology Control Regime was established in 1987 by seven industrial countries, but this was another case – like the nuclear non-proliferation regime – of those that possess weapons trying to impose limits on those that do not possess them. The spread of such weaponry in some regions might not be stabilizing.
- Traditional rivalries and new ambitions will stimulate appetites for weaponry. Where this occurs, it will tighten the knot of local security dilemmas. In addition to external suppliers, the rise of indigenous arms suppliers will help give the conflicts of the Third World an increasingly costly and dangerous high-tech dimension.

- None of the familiar problems of the Third World have been widely solved, and some have grown worse. The debt problem holds back progress while contributing to new issues such as environmental destruction. Capitalism triumphed over Stalinism in Europe, but connives in dreadful poverty in the Third World. The continuing crisis of development will lead to social injustice, political strife and possibly violent internal conflict. The latter always contains within it the risk of international ramifications.
- While the number of states with nuclear weapons by the end of the century is still likely to be below that feared and predicted by analysts in the 1960s, the possibility of further proliferation cannot be ruled out. If it occurs it will increase the risks of nuclear war both locally and more generally, and of pre-emptive attacks to try to prevent the further progress of near-nuclear states.

(3) General

- The 'system-induced' dimension of international conflict militates against predictable peace. The pressures of the game of nations create difficulties, suspicions and threats to progress towards a stable peace order.
- In the superpowers and elsewhere there exist bodies of opinion which have traditionally seen security in terms of military strength and unilateral action rather than the result of co-operation and reassurance. There may be some regimes which are beyond reassurance.
- The military cultures of the armed forces of the major powers have typically favoured offensive action. It is often extremely difficult to change deeply held doctrines. But improved stability requires the replacement of old ideas about attack being the best form of defence with ideas emphasizing mutual defensive supremacy. Resistance to policies emphasizing defensiveness has already been shown by military establishments.
- Peace remains an undeveloped concept compared with the sophistication with which military strategy has been developed since the late 1940s. Ideas about peace tend to be vague, while security has usually been seen in a narrowly military perspective. We cannot expect peace and security until we better understand what we are seeking.

- Environmental issues are in most important cases transnational, and difficult to solve. They offer an arena for international co-operation, but they also give scope for conflict over sovereignty, rights, responsibility and money. Ecological interventionism (together with drugs) may become future justifications for conventional projection forces on the part of larger states. The global Cold War has ended, but the politics of a hotter earth threaten to be no less troublesome.

- The globalization of daily life continues apace, from stock markets to T-shirts, and quick transportation to ever-present television. Some differences between peoples are breaking down, but we still live in a multi-cultural world; nationalism, fundamentalism and sheer cultural incomprehension divide people. Ignorance and lack of interest are also widespread. A recent survey showed that many American schoolchildren believed that the United States had fought the Second World War against the Soviet Union, and that Winston Churchill had been a US President (*Listener*, 13 April 1989). Such a low level of knowledge is not the basis on which to build a world community.

- Demographic trends increase strain. The continuing expansion of the world's population exacerbates long-term environmental and development problems. Meanwhile the North faces the social and economic problem of deciding how to cope with an ageing population, the South with the problem of a declining average age. Unemployment and urbanization problems will be increased by the multiplying young in the Third World, and will add to the risks of internal strife. The young South will find it easier to man armed forces than the ageing North.

- New security issues are arising on the agenda, and although they are unlikely to lead to the catastrophic international explosions of the past, their presence could tear holes in the fabric of international society. Governments will have to pay attention to such problems as drug trafficking, refugees, terrorists, and contamination (be it of disease, such as AIDS, or religious and political ideas).

- Benevolent change, even where it occurs, does not happen at the same rate and its survival chances vary. One of the crucial obstacles to the development of stable peace in the years ahead will arise at the interface of countries and regions at different stages of development – cultural, economic, social, political and strategic.

If the world community is thought of as a convoy, there will always be pressures to move at the pace of the slowest country or region. This will particularly be the case on military matters.

● Finally, there is the phenomenon of 'old thinking' itself, which must be explained and examined before we can assess what is helpful about new thinking. This will be discussed in the next section.

OLD THINKING IN A CHANGING WORLD

Even in a world of rapid change some things are slow to alter, and among these are the way people think. For shorthand purposes, old thinking about international politics can be taken to be synonymous with a dogmatic interpretation of the philosophy of political Realism.

Realism is the mode of thinking which purports to see world affairs 'as they are' as opposed to 'as they ought to be'. The latter is said to be the failing of liberals and idealists, who are criticized for placing unwarranted faith in the role of reason, law and morality in human relations. Realists play down or ignore these dimensions and stress that politics is about preserving or increasing power in the pursuit of group interests. Realism is synonymous with a 'power-political' view of the world. In international politics this perspective offers a static and rather pessimistic picture of the states system and its processes. Realists stress the primacy of states as actors in the system, the importance of sovereignty, the inevitability of crises and war, the dominance of the pursuit of self-interest, the prevalence of expediency rather than principle and the absence of progress in history. In such a setting security is seen as essentially deriving from military strength, and in the postwar era that has meant a high priority being given to nuclear deterrence. Realists are cautious (favouring multilateral not unilateral arms reduction); they believe that governments and their expert advisers always know best; they reject disarmament as an effective way to achieve peace; and they take an entirely national view of security matters. Nuclear strategy in particular and strategic studies in general were created in the likeness of the Realists who dominated the theory and practice of US national security between the late 1940s and early 1960s.

Realists captured the semantic high ground when they tied to their philosophical flagstaff a designation ('Realism') which connotes common sense, concreteness and objectivity. But the semantic flag should not cloak the fact that Realism is not necessarily realistic. Realism is a set of ideas which have hardened into an ideology, and a growing body of opinion does not think that it has kept pace with all the changes in the world over the past twenty years. Like other ideologies, Realism has sought to legitimize and naturalize the status quo; it portrays as natural and immutable what are believed to be the prevailing characteristics in the system. Thus Realists tell us that this is the best of all possible worlds. It must be so since their static view of the world does not allow that what is possible can expand. Realists are as much prisoners of their preconceptions as the doctrinaire idealists they scorn.

There are too many Realists in contemporary strategy, but there is not enough actual realism. Paradoxically, while Realists stress the conflictual side of human history, they above all seem to believe that more of the same will work for evermore. But as both Hans J. Morgenthau and E. H. Carr, the masters of Realism, knew, Realism is not enough. Towards the end of his life Morgenthau warned of the great dangers of Realism, while Carr had earlier stressed the need for diplomacy to be based on 'elements of both utopia and reality' (Boyle, 1985, pp. 70–4; Carr, 1940, pp. 89, 94). And this is never likely to be more so than in the next few difficult decades. As we contemplate the new challenges ahead, the question we have to ask ourselves is: who are the 'real' realists and who are the real 'non-realists'? (Fox, 1985, p. 12). The static quality of Realism marks it out as a regressive doctrine, because it has stressed what is not possible and it has pointed to futures which are out of reach. But as William T. R. Fox has argued, we now need to devote as much effort to 'determining what can be done as what cannot'. He then made an important distinction, between what he called 'empirical realists' and 'doctrinal realists', and he suggested that it is the empirical realist rather than the doctrinal kind who is best equipped to meet the new challenges.

The distinction between the two kinds of realist is fundamental to understanding how changeable is future change. The doctrinal realist asserts the basically rapacious character of contending great powers in a Hobbesian world. Eternal conflict, he says, is structurally determined; there is, he maintains, no escape from the security dilemma, and the quest for national security foments all round insecurity in a gigantic and unending negative-sum game. The doctrinal realist does not need to examine how nation-state actors really behave because he has already posited how they *must* behave by virtue of their nation-stateness in a multi-state world system. The empirical realist by contrast looks to see how they actually behave and perhaps beyond that to examining the possibilities for tolerable coexistence. (Fox, 1985, p. 12).

Doctrinal Realism is regressive; empirical Realism is a necessary element of new thinking.

These criticisms of Realism should not be read to mean that everything is and always was wrong with its analyses and prescriptions. What is being criticized is doctrinal Realism, that is, Realism without any utopianism, without a theory of change and without a sense of the open-endedness of politics. The time for Realism was the Nazi period and the Cold War; international life then did indeed threaten to be 'nasty, brutish and short'. Realism during that period was, as Joseph Nye has suggested, 'the most promising and useful first approximation' of international theory, though he did quickly add that 'it does not take us very far' (quoted in George, 1988, p. 6). But Realism's claim to rule international politics has diminished in explanatory and prescriptive strength. It is not now pertinent to many of today's problems. The times have changed more quickly than the once dominant philosophy of international politics.

Realism helped to get us through the militarized first three-quarters of the century, but is has been on the run since the 1970s. Strategic studies, academically speaking, has been its last laager. There is much that Realism cannot explain or cope with, and security co-operation is one (George, 1988, introduction); this is a critical shortcoming in a world determined to live indefinitely only half an hour from nuclear catastrophe. Realism needs reconceptualizing, and the aim of this book is to show that the real realism these days is 'new thinking', not old Realism. The thrust of new thinking about strategy and international security is not that military power is irrelevant and that war is impossible. On the contrary, one of the characteristics of new thinking in comparison with old idealism is that today's utopianism requires sophisticated thinking about defence.

The morbid symptoms listed earlier are disturbing. At the same time, some of the more positive developments in international relations discussed at the start of this introduction are recent phenomena and critics would say may well be merely transitory. History suggests that we must always reserve the right to be sceptical about the permanence of benevolent change. Even if they have the best will in the world, we must be concerned about the ability of governments to carry out their programmes, especially if they fly in the face of national strategic cultures. Trends pointing towards a new and more peaceful security order do not guarantee the outcome, though some developments encourage the hope that we are not doomed in a permanent cycle of Cold War and nuclear arms racing, with the possibility of a civilization-shattering war in the background.

Progress in reconceptualizing East–West relations, in devising new structures and also in creating a more stable world order beyond will be slow, though less so in some periods than others. In seeking these ends mistakes will surely be made and history will toss into the arena its share of unpleasant surprises. But future failures will not be a justification for rejecting new thinking and wrapping ourselves in the threadbare security blanket of the past. We must move on as we witness the building up of a web of interrelationships, rules, institutions, processes and habits that promise for the East–West relationship at least the glimmer of hope of producing the stability that has developed among the countries of Western Europe over the past forty years. Among the nations of Western Europe deeply entrenched rivalries have been ameliorated, and old thinking about the role of force in their interrelationships has been dramatically reversed. It is now possible that we could create comparable changes in East–West relations. Stable peace might yet evolve out of a perilous century of nationalism and ideology.

For the benevolent trends discussed earlier to develop and bear fruit, and not merely be part of the old cycle of war, Cold War and détente, we require a new definition of realism and a good dose of luck. The former we can do something about, the latter not. The images we have about the nature of the game of nations will play a crucial part in shaping the reality of that future. Regressive mindsets such as ethnocentrism need to be overcome. In their place, what is required are varieties of new thinking about fundamental aspects of politics and economics. The rest of this book consists of a discussion of one important dimension of the problematic, namely new thinking about strategy and international security.

NEW THINKING FOR THE INTERREGNUM

It is useful, at this stage, to provide a snapshot of the book by summarizing the individual chapters addressing the issue of what is new and what is valuable in thinking about strategy and international security.

At the outset, Barry Buzan's answer is optimistic to the central question 'Is international security possible?' While absolute security is not attainable in an 'anarchical society', he argues that relative security is, and that the international system already provides relatively high levels of security for many states. 'Security', it is suggested, is an ambiguous and multidimensional concept, in which the military factor has attracted disproportionate attention. Security should be approached from a holistic perspective, though the context for contemplating it is the 'anarchical' international system. In this respect it is important to appreciate that the anarchy of the state system is significantly different from the Hobbesian implications of anarchy at the level of individuals. International anarchy certainly imposes competitive (self-help) pressures on states, and creates the pervasive unease of the 'power–security dilemma', but the structures of this anarchy are highly durable. Furthermore, at present many trends are improving the prospects for security, particularly those leading towards interdependence and multipolarity. Anarchy can therefore be seen as the framework for solutions to the problem of insecurity. Economic and other forms of competition will continue, but this need not result in that form of competition known as war: anarchy can be synonymous with international politics without violence. Important in this regard has been the development of the idea of common security, including the strategy of non-provocative defence; such ideas seek to deal with the military problem which lies at the heart of the security dilemma.

Various academic traditions involved in thinking about security are the subject of David Dunn's chapter. The 1980s are identified as a period in which there was an emerging dissensus within strategic studies about the direction that was being followed, whereas peace research enjoyed a renaissance. The latter's progress was related to increased public concern about nuclear war and scepticism about the utility of traditional approaches to security problems. Both strategic studies and peace research had recognizable prehistories which reflected certain assumptions. In particular, there had been a close affinity between the Realist approach to international relations and the study of strategy, whereas peace research had derived from the rationalist tradition in which the perfectibility of man was not beyond question and which did not accept that we live in an inescapable reality. As a result, strategic studies has been concerned with managing the situation, peace research with trying to change it. Through the 1980s peace research came to redefine the nature of security in an interdependent world. It could claim to be realistic in its emphasis on the multidimensional nature of security, which included issues such as human rights, the environment and the economy as well as nuclear matters. The traditional strategic studies approach to the study of security, meanwhile, has been under pressure because of its narrowness. At present we are witnessing degrees of convergence between the two schools; their concerns are more alike, but their approaches remain different. Convergence is not an end in itself but the relationship between the two schools is now less one of confrontation and more one of symbiosis.

The next four chapters examine aspects of the various dimensions of security. Lawrence Freedman discusses the difficulties involved in thinking about nuclear weapons in today's rapidly changing world, since the international situation is now so much more complex than the one which existed when the original nuclear theorists set out their ideas. It is suggested that there is now a widely held and wholly understandable belief that nuclear strategy has reached the dead end first proclaimed by Bernard Brodie in 1955. There is a crisis for nuclear specialists, with deterrence under threat and nuclear weapons being discredited as a military means. The experience of the Reagan administration underlines the difficulty of devising a strategy based on nuclear threats other than that of mutual and massive destruction. What is called 'existential deterrence' might describe how deterrence works, but it leaves some difficult questions. One obvious way to reduce the risk of nuclear war, for example, would be to remove nuclear weapons from likely points of confrontation: however, such an act of control, involving the detaching of nuclear risk, also implies a redefinition of the removing state's (vital) interests. In the more fluid situation of present-day Europe, interrelated questions will therefore be raised about the definition of security interests and the role of nuclear weapons. This will challenge NATO's established nuclear strategy. Nevertheless, nuclear weapons will remain, and before we an assume they no longer serve any strategic purpose, we need to understand better the strategic environment of the post-cold war world.

Despite early postwar fears about the political utility of nuclear threats, Eric Herring argues that nuclear diplomacy ('blackmail' at its worst) has not shaped the evolution of international politics. He shows that there have been some attempts at manipulating nuclear weapons for political gain: twenty-one nuclear threats issued by the superpowers are indicated. However the record shows that the threats were mostly vague, and their occurrence has declined since the 1950s. The potential obviously remains for the use of nuclear threats in the future, but it seems unlikely that they will play a role between the superpowers or between a superpower and a third party. Fear of nuclear escalation has generated both a tradition of nuclear non-use and a taboo against nuclear blackmail. Nuclear threats have therefore greatly diminished in significance as a factor in strategic affairs.

Turning from unsuccessful nuclear strategy to unsuccessful arms control, Jane Sharp points out that for most of the twentieth century the effort to impose formal limitations on military forces has failed. This was more than ever the case in the early 1980s. Recently, however, arms control has become unexpectedly dynamic, with agreements involving intrusive inspection and the actual destruction of advanced weaponry. President Gorbachev's role was crucial in this change; his arms control diplomacy successfully created the image of the Soviet Union as a co-operative security partner. The most important determinants of the success or failure of negotiations are the political climate, the distribution of power between the parties and their political relations with their allies. A future period of instability could complicate the arms control efforts of both sides. The Western response to Gorbachev has been mixed, though NATO governments did eventually react to public criticism of their complacency. At the start of the 1990s a spirit of co-operation is replacing that of confrontation, though there are important domestic impediments to arms control, such as the respective military establishments. One paradoxical danger for the future is the possibility that traditional arms control policies could hold back progress that might otherwise be expected from the positive changes in East–West relations.

International crises are moments of great insecurity, and Phil Williams shows that crisis management has been a controversial topic. It was in vogue in the aftermath of the Cuban missile crisis, but subsequently a reaction set in as a second wave of writers placed the experience of Sarajevo at the centre of their concern, and stressed the dangers and scope for irrationality inherent in intense situations. Although successful crisis prevention is obviously preferable to crisis management, the latter deserves serious attention since the former cannot be guaranteed. To date, tacit rules of conduct for crisis management have been developed regarding bargaining, decision-making procedures and operational conduct. These were developed in the conduct of US–Soviet relations, but they may not be relevant elsewhere, for example between Third World states. In the early 1970s there was an attempt by the superpowers to develop a semi-formal crisis prevention regime, but it was seriously deficient. There is still interest in moving in this direction and several ideas have been discussed, notably crisis centres and stable force postures. The 1990s promise a more peaceful world but they also threaten danger; there are reasons for hoping that progress will be made in the theory and practice of crisis prevention, but parallel efforts are also advisable in crisis management.

The change in East–West relations have major implications for the doctrinal aspects of recent military policy, the subject of Colin McInnes's chapter. The traditional gap is exposed between the formal agreement among the NATO allies about the conventional defence of their territory and their actual commitment to put the agreed policies into practice. In place of a satisfactory conventional strategy there has been an emphasis on deterring war by the threat of nuclear escalation. Through the 1980s, however, growing dissatisfaction with the alliance's inflexible escalatory posture led to changes in NATO's thinking, equipment and morale; this led to greater confidence among NATO commanders in the conventional component of NATO strategy. Doubts still existed about its potential effectiveness, but less so than the alternative, and hope increased that the gamble was justified. But then a new problem arose; concern is now expressed whether the earlier changes in military doctrine are compatible with the radical political developments in Europe. NATO's military doctrine and force structures now appear ill-suited to the radical shift in such basic assumptions as the Soviet threat. For NATO, concepts such as non-offensive defence and common security do not currently dominate the defence agenda, but there are indications that the future of existing doctrines and force structures may be numbered.

Alternative defence ideas are now being taken seriously, and Michael Clarke's chapter looks specifically at this school of thought in the West; its aim has been to devise feasible non-nuclear defence postures, including the concept of non-provocative defence. It is believed that the latter promises a more secure basis for the pursuit of détente and co-operation between East and West than the existing posture. The chapter suggests that there has been a certain amount of uneven convergence between many of the premisses of the alternative school and official thinking, as both have adopted more pragmatic positions. Among the main points of convergence have been calculations about the military balance, NATO's military and command deficiencies, and thinking about emerging technology and new battle plans. Despite such trends there remain important points where the two schools of thought do not agree. The chief divergence is over three fundamental assumptions: that security is an end product rather than a process, that the Soviet threat is synonymous with the structural threat, and that retaliation is necessary. In contrast with establishment thinking, the alternative security school believes that security is a process, that the arms competition is a bigger threat than the Soviet Union and that states do not have to adopt nuclear deterrent postures just because they have the capability.

Three chapters then address regional issues. The examination of the future of European security by Adrian Hyde-Price and John Roper begins by pointing out that the assumptions underpinning the postwar European security system can no longer be taken for granted. This has led some to fear that Europe has entered its most unstable period since the war; others see the changes as holding out the prospect of finally overcoming the great postwar dangers. In the opinion of the authors, the changes that are in train give good reason for believing that the current period is not a brief interlude in a perennial Cold War, though the 1970s should warn us against being over-optimistic. The postwar division of the continent created a logic from which it is hard to escape. The formal structures of European security are likely to remain in place, but their content and the context are gradually being transformed. As a result, some of the basic assumptions of the postwar European security system are being eroded, while the prospects have improved for expanding pan-European co-operation and interdependence. While the former blocs are likely to retain certain distinctive characteristics, positive peace is now on the agenda, as is evident with such notions as a 'Common European Home', a 'European Peace Order' and the development of a 'culture of political strife' in place of that of military confrontation.

At the heart of the problem of European security, from a Western viewpoint, has been the Soviet military threat. However, as Roy Allison shows, Soviet military doctrine under Gorbachev is in a period of transition which may fundamentally alter the character of Soviet defence policy. A major debate has been taking place, involving a wider body of participants than hitherto. The outcome has been a set of new principles; these offer a more sophisticated assessment of the role of military power in national security and present a direct challenge to the orthodoxies of the Brezhnev era. Among the principles of new thinking are reasonable sufficiency, non-offensive defence and the rejection of nuclear war as an instrument of policy. Opposition to the changes has been evident, notably from the General Staff, and there are inherent difficulties in implementation, for example in determining the offensive–defensive ratio. Although the debate is continuing and important matters have not been settled, certain steps have been promised and adopted. The changing military doctrine appears to be part of a broad political strategy aimed at producing a more effective external policy at reduced cost. It may happen that new military thinking will transform the Soviet defence agenda only for the latter to fall victim to the collapse of *perestroika*. If the latter fails, the shift to a truly defensive posture will be halted, and a defensive–offensive mix based on military-technical criteria will develop. However, a reversion to the militarist excesses of old thinking is unlikely as long as there are thought to be positive results from better relations with the West.

East–West issues have naturally dominated the security debate, but Caroline Thomas shows that security issues in the Third World are both important and different. She argues that the traditional approach to security matters, based on the Realist conception of international relations, fails to identify the most pressing security concerns of the world's poorer states. The primary physical threats to the security of most of the latter are internal not external, and result from the granting of international legitimacy to states that lack domestic legitimacy; many Third World states exist juridically but not as social facts. Some physical threats of a non-military nature exist which are of international proportions, notably the debt and ecological crises; these threaten not only Third World states but also the security of the rest of the world. The debt problem undermines the domestic stability of states and therefore increases the danger of external intervention, while ecological damage physically threatens the Northern industrialized world. The two crises are intimately interrelated. Consequently, development and international co-operation are vital components of any strategy aimed at greater security in the Third World or elsewhere. Military strategy is a necessary but not sufficient factor for security; in the Third World the fundamental problem is the need for socio-economic development because of the poor quality of life. A realistic security strategy will be a holistic one, and must take care of people and not just governments. Even if correct diagnoses are made, agreeing upon and implementing solutions will be politically inflammatory in both the North and South.

In the final section of the book, two authors address various political questions. Hugh Miall argues that what has come to be called 'new thinking' offers a new departure in the way we conceive international security. Instead of being designed for states, like traditional national security thinking, it is designed for the world. Such ideas as common security are a timely response to world challenges and the emergence of a world society. It is suggested that the new ideas have growing support, though those who occupy power structures in the West have not been won over. The chapter illustrates the clash between traditional and common security approaches by comparing the ideas of new thinkers with those of nuclear decision-makers in Britain. Two very different outlooks emerge. Even so, there are signs that old thinking is showing evidence of signs of cracking. The implications of new thinking are described as enormous, both for the way international security is conceived and for the way the domestic affairs of states are organized. The pursuit of national security in the traditional manner is considered obsolescent, as new thinkers shift their concern from the security of states to the security of peoples. Overall, there should be a broadening of the conception of security, with new thinking suggesting an escape from the trap into which unilateral conceptions of security have traditionally led us.

Finally, the theme of Mary Kaldor's chapter is that the roots of the Cold War and the arms race were not simply to be found in the international arena, in the interaction of mutual threat, but rather in the domestic political and socio-economic conflicts within states in the East and West. The Cold War was a mechanism for managing those conflicts. Thus the postwar East–West confrontation could be described as an 'imaginary war'. It imposed a kind of symmetry on both East and West, with Atlanticism and Stalinism being mutually reinforcing. Today these ideas are undergoing profound transformation, and it may be that their benevolent alternatives might also be mutually reinforcing. But so far new thinking has hardly penetrated Western policy-making; a degree of complacency has been induced which is related to the mistaken belief that new thinking came about in the Soviet Union because of Western toughness as opposed to internal reasons. Further positive changes in the old socialist countries are neither inevitable nor irreversible. Western complacency is not just dangerous for the future evolution of the former socialist countries, but also for the West itself. New thinking is needed in both societies.

In the book's conclusion the editor attempts both to synthesize and draw out the ideas being discussed under the label of new thinking, and to suggest what they might mean in theory and practice for security, war and strategy.

It should be clear from this overview that the new thinking being addressed is not simply an updating of the old utopianism of the interwar years. Although in most respects the adversary of new thinking is old doctrinal Realism, we are not simply engaging in a rerun of the interwar Idealism versus Realism debate. Some readers may be disappointed that what is called new thinking is not as radical or utopian as they would have hoped; but that is its strength. While still being progressive the new thinking of the present is more sophisticated, strategically literate and in tune with the times than was the case with the visionary ideas about international relations in the interwar years. As will be seen later, whereas Realism has become a shop-worn ideology posing as timeless wisdom and practical common sense, the normative concerns which informed Idealism have evolved into the contemporary realism of new thinking; this new thinking is both empirical and forward-looking, realistic and utopian. It aims, in this intellectual and behavioural interregnum, to introduce a different and objectively necessary bias into the conceptions and practice of world politics. Although many morbid symptoms persist in international relations, it is not too soon to proclaim that utopian realism is an idea whose time has come. One of its essential tasks is to elaborate the new agenda for thinking about security, war and strategy – the traditional problematic of all students of international politics.

NOTE

1 The Gramsci quotation was the appropriate beginning of Nadine Gordimer's exploration of black–white relations in South Africa: *July's People* (London: Jonathan Cape, 1981).

REFERENCES

Boyle, Francis Anthony (1985), *World Politics and International Law* (Durham, NC: Duke University Press).

Carr, Edward Hallett (1946), *The Twenty Years' Crisis* (London: Macmillan).

Fox, W. R. T. (1985), 'E. H. Carr and political vision: vision and revision', *Review of International Studies*, vol. 11, pp. 1–16.

George, Alexander L. *et al.* (eds) (1988) *US–Soviet Security Cooperation. Achievements, Failures, Lessons* (New York: Oxford University Press).

Keohane, Robert O., and Nye, Joseph S. (1977), *Power and Interdependence: World Politics in Transition* (Boston, Mass.: Little, Brown).

PART ONE

Rethinking security and anarchy

1

Is international security possible?

BARRY BUZAN

THE CONCEPT OF SECURITY

Security is a complex concept. In order to get to grips with it one needs, at a minimum, to be aware of three things: (1) the political context of the term; (2) the several dimensions – political, military, economic, societal, environmental – within which it operates; and (3) the logical contradictions and ambiguities that are inherent in any attempt to apply the concept to international relations.

Anarchy as the context for international security

The main political context for international security is the anarchic structure of the international system. In this usage anarchy means the absence of *central* government. In the international system, anarchy does not mean the absence of government *per se*, but rather that government resides in the units of the system. If those units are states, then they will claim sovereignty, which is the right to treat themselves as the ultimate source of governing authority within the territorial limits of their jurisdiction. Since the claim of sovereignty automatically denies recognition of any higher political authority, a system of sovereign states is by definition politically structured as an anarchy.

In the international system, anarchy is thus a decentralized form of political order. It does not necessarily, or even probably, merit

the Hobbesian implications of disorder and chaos that attach to
the concept of anarchy as applied to relations among individual
human beings. On the individual level, anarchy means the absence
of *all* government. A political system structured in that way could
only avoid chaos if human society had evolved to far higher
levels of cohesion and responsibility than any yet attained. Indeed,
no greater indication of the difference between anarchy at the
individual and international levels is possible than the fact that
the former requires the abolition of the state, whereas the latter
finds its clearest and most perfect expression in the state.

The anarchic context sets the elemental political conditions in
which all meanings of international security have to be constructed.
Anarchy can be seen fatalistically as a product of history, representing either the current limit of the ongoing human attempt
to create stable political units on an ever larger scale, or the
natural political expression of an ethnically and culturally diverse
population. It can also be seen as a preferred form of political order,
representing values of ideological and cultural diversity, decentralization, independence and self-reliance. Either way, the structure of
anarchy is highly durable, because the actions states take to preserve
their independence and sovereignty automatically perpetuate the
anarchic system. In turn, that structure generates system-wide
effects on relations among states (Buzan, 1989a; Waltz, 1979).
An anarchic structure imposes competitive, self-help conditions
of existence on the states within the system. To say this is not
to say either that relations between states are inevitably, or even
probably, violently conflictual under anarchy, or that international
anarchy makes co-operation unlikely or impossible (Axelrod and
Keohane, 1985; Jervis, 1985; Keohane, 1984; Oye, 1985). Violent
conflict is possible, and in some circumstances likely. Competition,
however, is pervasive, and takes political, economic and societal
forms as well as military ones.

Some analysts make a potent link here between anarchic political structures and capitalist economic ones (Chase-Dunn, 1981;
Kennedy, 1988; McNeil, 1982; Wallerstein, 1974). The argument
is that the fragmentation of political authority in a system of states
is both a necessary condition for the emergence of capitalism,
and/or the natural political expression of an operating capitalist
world economy. Suggestive historical evidence for this view can
be drawn from the contrast between the fragmented, anarchical

political experience of Europe, which generated capitalism, and the much more centralized, hierarchic tradition of China, which did not, despite similar, or even superior, levels of science and technology on the Chinese side.

This link between political and economic structure makes competition under anarchy double-edged. On one side, international political fragmentation supports the competition of the market, in which producers are forced to vie with each other in terms of innovation, quality and price in order to pursue their own economic welfare. The political structure of anarchy creates more freedom for economic actors, both because they can move from less to more congenial governments and because at least some governments will come to see the power advantages of hosting them. Insulated imperiums like that in China can more easily decide to suppress the disruptive challenge from rising economic classes. On the other side, international anarchy creates the pervasive unease of the power–security dilemma, in which the measures states take to preserve their security are easily, and often rightly, seen by others as threatening to their own security (Buzan, 1983, ch. 7). Competition for strength in the qualities of survival thus has to be added to competition for wealth in the market. Both types of competition stimulate technological innovation, which in turn continuously redefines the requirements for successful (and unsuccessful) behaviour (Buzan, 1978b, chs 2–4).

Competition under anarchy, as Waltz (1979, pp. 76, 128) argues, tends to produce units that are similar in function. Successful states have a demonstration effect on those seeking to emulate their success. If differential rates of success, and therefore of power, grow very large, as they did in the eighteenth and even more in the nineteenth centuries, then the processes of alignment become more forceful. The strong simply take over the weak, reconstructing them in their own image. The European states did this to most of the world, in the process expanding the anarchic structure from one continent to the entire system. As well as encouraging (though never reaching) functional homogeneity, the 'showing and shaping' influence of anarchic structure generates balance of power behaviour. In seeking to preserve their own sovereignty and security, states will behave in such a way as to prevent threats from any one expansionist centre of power from dominating the system (or subsystem). This behaviour preserves the overarching

structure of anarchy even though it may fail to preserve a particular state (Austria-Hungary, Tibet) or lead to a variety of local
mergers between states (Italy, the Soviet Union, the European
Community).

The context of anarchy thus imposes three major conditions on
the concept of international security.

(1) States are the principal referent object of security because
     they are both the framework of order and the highest source
     of governing authority. This explains the dominating policy
     concern with 'national' security.
(2) Although states are the principal objects of security, the dynam-
     ics of national security are highly relational and interdependent
     between states. Domestic insecurities may or may not dominate
     the national security agenda, but external threats will almost
     always comprise a major element of the national security
     problem. The idea of 'international' security is therefore
     best used to refer to the systemic conditions that influence
     the ways in which states make each other feel more or less
     secure. With this usage, individual national securities can only
     be fully understood when considered in relation both to each
     other, and to larger patterns of relations in the system as a
     whole (Buzan, 1983, chs 8 and 9).
(3) Given the durability of anarchy, the practical meaning of
     security can only be constructed sensibly if it can be made
     operational within an environment in which competitive rela-
     tions are inescapable. If security depends on either harmony
     or hegemony, then it cannot be lastingly achieved within
     anarchy. Among other things, this means that under anarchy,
     security can only be relative, never absolute.

So long as anarchy holds, these conditions will obtain. If there
is a structural shift out of anarchy, then the entire framework of
the security problematic would have to be redefined.

Dimensions of security

International security embraces at least five dimensions: military,
political, economic, societal and environmental. Military security concerns the two-level interplay of the armed offensive and

defensive capabilities of states, and states' perceptions of each other's intentions. Political security concerns the organizational stability of states, systems of government, and the ideologies that give them legitimacy. Economic security concerns access to the resources, finance and markets necessary to sustain acceptable levels of welfare and state power. Societal security concerns the sustainability, within acceptable conditions for evolution, of traditional patterns of language, culture, and both religious and national identity and custom. Environmental security concerns the maintenance of the planetary biosphere as the essential support system on which all other human enterprises depend. It is well understood that these dimensions do not operate in isolation from each other. They interact in myriad complex and often contradictory ways.

Of these five dimensions, the military one attracts disproportionate attention in thinking about security. This is partly because an expensive, politically potent, and highly visible sector of state behaviour is generated by the need to respond to the possibility of armed threat, attack or invasion. Mostly, however, it is because military means can dominate outcomes in all the other sectors. A state and its society can be, in their own terms, secure in the political, economic, societal and environmental dimensions, and yet all of these accomplishments can be undone by military failure. In one sense, this primacy justifies the amount of attention paid to military security. But the cost of a military-dominated view is too often that the other elements of security end up playing too small a role in both analysis and policy. This tendency becomes increasingly regrettable as the rising tide of communication, interaction and interdependence in the international system gives some states very potent economic, societal and political levers over the affairs of others.

One consequence of military primacy is that thinking about international security is excessively concentrated in the sub-field of strategic studies. This is unwelcome for two reasons. Firstly, strategic studies does not contain the breadth of expertise necessary for security analysis. The field is mostly, and rightly, populated by people who know about military technology, military relations between states, and the interplay between these two. As a result the study of security gets skewed towards the military dimension, leaving the other dimensions inadequately developed. Secondly, because it has immediate policy linkages, strategic studies contains strong ethnocentric tendencies (Booth, 1979). This pushes its analysis towards national security perspectives, where competitive self-interest dominates perceptions, and consequently discourages analysis of security interdependence and the systemic aspects of the concept. Identification with strategic studies has thus doubly curtailed development of the concept. The proper home of security is in the much broader field of international relations. Only there can be found the range of expertise and the scope of interest necessary for its full development.

It is not my aim in this chapter to dispute the centrality of military factors in security. Instead, it is to set these military factors into the broader context of a holistic security perspective. The logic behind this exercise can be illustrated by the cold war security problem in Europe, where the interplay of military and non-military aspects of security is conspicuous and well understood. The longstanding armed tension in Europe makes it impossible to deny the importance of military security. But although the military dimension carries the urgency of its potential for massive and rapid transformations of relationships across the board, and the threat of extremely high costs, it is not necessarily the only, or even the principal, driving cause of insecurity. That military factors are not, by themselves, determining forces is evident from the major role that ideological hostilities played in both the Cold War and the run-up to the Second World War (Jahn, Lemaitre and Waever, 1987, ch. 3). This point can also be illustrated by the way in which armed states can avoid the power–security dilemma if their relationships are secure in the other dimensions. Britain did not find it necessary to respond to the rise of the United States Navy during the late nineteenth century. Sweden and Finland have made their self-defence mutually supportive because of the political harmony of their neutrality. France and Britain do not fear military attack from each other's nuclear arsenals.

Nevertheless, when they do get established, the reciprocal interactions of the arms dynamic are almost always *partly* autonomous: that is, self-driving within the military dimension. As in the Anglo-German naval race before the First World War, and the post-1945 military rivalry between NATO and the WTO, arms levels on one side become a key referent for research, acquisitions and deployments on the other. But the insecurities of the military dimension seldom, if ever, arise without being driven by more fundamental insecurities in the other dimensions. In the case of Europe, the military confrontation was called into being, and sustained by, a host of non-military insecurities. The clash of incompatible ideologies provided a framework in which many kinds of political, economic and societal insecurities were linked together.

As with India's secular federal constitution, and Pakistan's Islamic one (Buzan and Rizvi, 1986) the basic construction of government on either side of the cold war lines in Europe stood as a permanent challenge to the political legitimacy of the other side. The organizing philosophy and political practice of Marxist-Leninist and democratic pluralist states were in such profound contrast as inevitably to make each feel uncomfortable and insecure in the presence of the other, a fact already evident in Western–Soviet relations during the interwar years. In such conditions, it can become nearly impossible for principled opposition within either system to escape identification with the rival system.

These basic political incompatibilities extended into the economic and societal dimensions. The imposition of cold war boundaries not only cut off longstanding trade and financial links between Eastern and Western Europe, but also created another sector of rivalry to multiply the political insecurities. The Cold War was in large part about a socio-economic challenge as to which system could most efficiently produce and distribute the conditions for material welfare. Khrushchev's much quoted line 'we will bury you' was a reference to Soviet production aspirations, not to its capacity for nuclear destruction. This politicization of economic performance drove a rivalry, which in turn amplified the fears and obstructions that the two economic systems placed in each other's way.

For the capitalists, the communist system denied access to both markets and resources. In so doing, it identified itself with the militaristic neo-mercantilism of the 1930s (of which the Soviet Union was the only survivor) as posing a threat to both prosperity (and therefore domestic political stability) and peace. By enclosing their economies, the communist states threatened the liberal capitalist project of constructing a global market economy as a means of promoting not only peace and prosperity, but also pluralist democracy. Any success for communism restricted the potential of the capitalist project, so creating the deep insecurity of a zero-sum game.

For the communists, capitalism was also hostile by definition, and also threatened a project for global peace and prosperity. Marxist-Leninist ideology emphasized this opposition and, until revised by Khrushchev, officially expected it to result in war. Capitalist practice was self-evidently contradictory to the maintenance of communist government – or at least to the type of totalitarian bureaucratic rule that Stalin and his heirs defined as communism. The operation of capitalism could not but penetrate state and society, creating both conceptual and administrative challenges to the commanding control of the communist party. This politicization of economics on both sides made significant economic interaction between them extremely problematic. Each feared that dealing with the other would worsen its own position in the political and strategic rivalry.

In the societal dimension the overall ideological rivalry between East and West heightened the contradictions already inherent between the overarching cosmopolitan ideologies on both sides, and the more parochial religious and ethnic identities of the indigenous societies in Europe. In the East, homogenizing communism faced resistance from both local religious forces, as in Poland and Georgia, and local national ones, as in Hungary and Estonia. In the West, France perhaps best exemplified the widespread national level of resistance to the equally homogenizing effects of liberal capitalism in terms of universal product brands, financial systems, cultural styles, music and language. In the East, societal insecurities linked directly to the Soviet-dominated political and military structures. In the West, the picture was and is more complex and less fraught, because the homogenizing ideology is not almost solely, as it was in the East, an imposition of the dominant superpower, but also stems powerfully from the indigenously driven forces that are constructing the European Community. In between the two systems lay the German problem, where a powerful national identity was riven into two states lying uncomfortably on opposite sides of the ideological divide.

In Europe, the military confrontation was substantially sustained by the political, economic and societal insecurities that underlay it. In the late 1980s, however, quite massive changes in non-military factors began to break down the fixtures of the Cold War, in the process redefining the conditions of European security across all dimensions. In the East, Gorbachev's twin revolutions of *glasnost* and *perestroika* seemed to open up real possibilities of defining economic and political relations in other than zero-sum game terms (Lemaitre, 1989). By the end of 1989, oldstyle communism had either collapsed or was in headlong retreat all across Eastern Europe. The Berlin Wall was broken, and there was open and serious talk about German reunification. In the face of these sweeping political and economic changes, decades of military tension melted away with such astonishing rapidity that the two alliances had to cast about to find reasons to keep themselves in existence. In the West, the European Community gained both political and economic momentum with its 1992 project, becoming a major magnet for the newly liberated states in Eastern Europe. At the global level both superpowers weakened in will and capability to sustain their global rivalry. The system as a whole moved increasingly swiftly away from the rigid bipolar structure of the post-Second World War era, and towards the more fluid multipolar structure of the twenty-first century. What the consequences of all this are for security in Europe is one of the foremost questions for the coming decade. What is certain is that the old military arrangements are deeply inappropriate to the new political conditions, and that major rethinking and restructuring will be necessary.

The European case illustrates not only the many dimensions of security, but also the way in which the non-military dimensions interweave both with each other and with the military dimension. This complex interweaving is characteristic of security in all parts of the international system, although the composition of the mixture naturally varies.

The ambiguities of security

Like many of the major concepts used to discuss the human condition – justice, equality, love, power – security is plagued with ambiguities. The idea of 'international security' embraces many different types of units ranging from individuals, through states, nations and firms, to coalitions such as alliances and blocs. This diversity requires that care be taken to specify the referent object to which security analysis is being applied, often a difficult task given that some referent objects, such as states, are far less concrete and more metaphysical than they might at first appear. In quite different ways the recent histories of Poland and Lebanon exemplify this problem, pointing to the conclusion that the stability and security of the whole state is vitally dependent, *inter alia*, on the security of all the major political forces in play within it. Whatever units are chosen, there is still the problem of working out how an essentially preservative idea like security can be applied to entities that undergo many types of change as a result of their natural interaction with their environment. There is also the difficulty of distinguishing between objective and subjective security (is one secure versus does one feel secure). Those who wish to apply the idea of security systematically need to be aware of its ambiguous quality if they are to make any useful progress.

One such ambiguity that is particularly relevant to the question under consideration here is: if the anarchic environment is irretrievably competitive, then how can any units within it ever be meaningfully secure? Competition implies an ever-present danger of becoming a loser. For states as for individuals, being subjected to continuous assessment of relative performance in a highly dynamic economic, military and political environment means living with continuous insecurity.

This conundrum is most evident in the realm of economic security under capitalism, though it applies more subtly to many other dimensions of international security. A capitalist economy only works if market competition is allowed to shape behaviour. Individuals and firms within it prosper only if they can compete, and the overall productivity and prosperity of the system depends on the less efficient and less innovative producers being driven out of business by the more efficient and more innovative ones. In one sense, capitalism is founded on the permanent insecurity of producers, making the idea of economic security within capitalism seem a contradiction in terms. But inasmuch as capitalism can claim to be overall an effective generator of wealth, it offers a kind of macro-security in the prospect of ever-expanding growth, and ever-unfolding opportunity. To the extent that growth alleviates both the economic and the political problems of shortage and uneven distribution, capitalism can be seen to offer a trade-off in which a measure of insecurity on the unit level is endured in return for a measure of security on the level of the economic system as a whole.

This type of logic points to the inescapable relativity of security under anarchy. In a capitalist economy, absolute security requires monopoly, which is undesirable. In the political and military sectors, absolute security is conceivable for any one unit, but only at the cost of making all the other units in the system absolutely insecure. In the previous section it was shown how the zero-sum logic of the power–security dilemma operated politically, militarily and economically in Europe. The measures that each side took to make itself secure made other units within the system feel less secure. The resultant competition itself becomes part of everyone's insecurity, both because of the continuous threat of losing (the power–security dilemma), and because of the overall threat to survival posed by some of the military means with which the competition is pursued (the defence dilemma) (Buzan, 1983, chs 6–7).

The many ambiguities and contradictions inherent in the concept of security reinforce the argument made above that the idea of international security is best deployed to focus on the systemic conditions that influence the way in which states make each other feel more or less secure. If international security can only be relative, never absolute, the necessity is to identify the factors and conditions that might ameliorate the insecurities that arise naturally out of the inherently divided and competitive structure of the anarchy. The most obvious place to begin such a search is the still fashionable idea of interdependence.

INTERDEPENDENCE, ANARCHY, AND INTERNATIONAL SECURITY

The principal driving force behind interdependence is the rising density of the interaction networks that tie the international system together. In raw physical terms, rising density is driven by a combination of increasing population, and increasing technological, organizational and financial capabilities and incentives for action. Given the sustained pace of an apparently open-ended technological revolution, density could be expected to increase even if the human population became static in numbers. Because of the age/fertility structure of the population, this event is still several decades distant at the earliest. Density, then, is about more people doing more things. It means that people's activities are more likely to impinge on the conditions of other people's existence, both intentionally and unintentionally, and positively as well as negatively. Inasmuch as the whole idea of an international system depends on interaction (without interaction there are parts, but no system), increasing density raises the importance of the whole in relation to the parts.

In concrete terms, rising density is measurable across all of the dimensions of security. Military capabilities have reached levels where it is possible for the major powers both to involve the whole planet in conflict, and to inflict levels of destruction that could well eliminate the human species. In the political sphere, ideas now circulate globally, many issues are discussed in global or semi-global forums as a matter of routine, and the model of the industrial democracies has emerged as a kind of universal holy grail of development, albeit by very different routes (Von Laue, 1987). Economically, the world is increasingly tied into a global market of production, trade and finance, whose circulation system is an ever more efficient transportation network by land, sea and air, and whose nervous system is a worldwide web of electronic communication and data processing facilities. Societally, the international system is still profoundly parochial, although superficial elements of a global society are emergent in such things as the use of English as a common language, and in the spread of common materialist values and styles. Environmentally, the collective impact of human activity is producing effects of a regional and global scale, in the process creating both common fates and a need for collective action. Should global warming produce a significant (over one metre) rise in sea level, as seems far from impossible, the environmental sector may well confront humankind with its first truly systemic challenge some time in the next century. Barring massive global disasters the pattern of density can be expected to continue its relentless increase.

The major theoretical question arising from density is how its increase affects the general character of international relations within an anarchic structure. The principal political impact of rising density is to increase the levels of interdependence among states across a broad spectrum. In the military sphere, the dominance of long-range strike weapons means that states depend for their survival on the restraint of their rivals, nowhere more so than in the context of mutual nuclear deterrence. In the economic sphere, they depend for their prosperity and development on complex patterns of access to external markets, resources and credit. In the environmental sphere, they increasingly depend on each other to adopt restraint towards ecologically damaging activities.

Interdependence is unlikely to reduce conflict, and may increase it by giving states a broader agenda of issues over which their interests and circumstances will differ. But where interdependence is strong, it should reduce incentives to resort to armed force. Interdependence makes relationships costly to disrupt. It also gives states an expanded repertoire of instruments with which they can influence each other's behaviour. Force is increasingly costly not only in itself, but also in its consequences. This is true regardless of whether the motive for using force is greed or justice. Force is best used to determine control of territory, but in an interdependent and technologically sophisticated world, control of territory is not an attractive solution, as it once was to a wide range of problems. Armed force is a poorly tuned instrument for many interdependence issues (Keohane and Nye, 1977, 1987).

This line of reasoning points towards the conclusion that rising density will, other things being equal, tend to have a mitigating effect on the possibility of violent international relations under anarchy. The natural pressure of rising density is away from the security-driven anarchic imperative of 'look after yourself', and towards the more economic imperative 'specialize!'. This logic is apparent in the current diffusion away from advanced industrial countries of basic industries such as steel and shipbuilding, and in the international stratification of production for major goods such as computers, aircraft, cars, and even armaments. Both movements work powerfully against the logic that states should seek security by retaining a broad-spectrum capability for self-reliant military production.

The divergent logics of anarchy and interdependence are both powerfully at work in the contemporary international system. The tension and interplay between them are major elements in the conditions that define international security. Among other things, rising density makes it more difficult for states to pursue national security in the traditionally preferred fashion of seeking unilaterally to reduce their vulnerabilities to outside pressure. Instead, states are pressured by circumstances into relying more and more on collaborative measures to reduce threats by dealing with them as multilateral international issues. Even the superpowers are now accepting that their security is interdependent, and that arms control is a serious alternative to arms racing as a national security strategy.

The interplay between anarchy and interdependence thus sets the major framework within which thinking about international security has to take place. Anarchy tells us important things not only about the international system (that it has no central government, and that relationships within it are competitive), but also about the units (that security is a high policy priority for them, that they have to look after themselves, and that consequently they are likely to be functionally similar). Interdependence directs our attention to the specific conditions that shape the way states interact with each other. In part it points to issues where either the scale of problems transcends the abilities of individual actors to make effective policy by themselves, or where the linkages are so strong that independent action by any unit cannot avoid engaging the concerns of others. Interdependence also points to the general conditions of interaction, especially the capacity of the communication, transportation and organizational networks that not only tie the system together, but also determine the speed and volume of everything from trade and finance to military attack. The prospects for international security have to be located within the complex dialectic that results from the dividing tendencies of anarchy interacting with the binding ones of interdependence.

One idea to emerge from this interplay has been 'common security' (Buzan, 1987a; Møller, 1988; Independent Commission on Disarmament and Security Issues, 1982; SIPRI, 1985; Vayrynen, 1988; Waever, 1988; Windass, 1985), which seeks to combine the self-reliance, self-preservation imperatives of anarchy with the idea that the only rational approach to security under contemporary political, military, economic and environmental conditions is through the logic of interdependence. Common security emphasizes both the relational and the relative character of security in the international system. Its advocates are realist in that they accept the need to work within the existing anarchic political framework, and idealist in that they see plenty of room for improving international security within the limits set by prevailing conditions in the system.

Common security invites us to consider what military, economic, political, societal and ecological conditions in the international system might work to ameliorate (or exacerbate) the power–security dilemma. How, in other words, can the international anarchy be made more 'mature'? (Buzan, 1983; 1984) This question leads down two paths of inquiry. The first requires identification of the apparent trends in the system, and assessment of whether they promote or vitiate the operation of the power–security dilemma. The second path focuses on the level of state policy, and requires identification of options that are both helpful in improving international security conditions, and 'realistic' (in the sense of (a) capable of being implemented without the necessity of a political transformation, and (b) not obviously counter-productive in effect). This approach opens up an agenda much too large to be fully explored, or even fully outlined, in this chapter. It is, however, possible to indicate a few highlights, and to suggest the flavour and direction of the arguments. Three crucial areas of inquiry are the characteristics of states, the strength of international society, and the shape of the international system structure.

CONDITIONS FOR COMMON SECURITY

The characteristics of states

It is obvious that the character of states is a major factor in shaping international security. The many traditional theories linking the domestic political structure of states – whether monarchical, autocratic, fascist, communist, capitalist or theocratic – to propensity for aggression clearly make this link. In the contemporary system, three state characteristics stand out as centrally important to security relations: the political cohesion of states, the nature of their military policy, and their transparency to observation by others.

THE POLITICAL COHESION OF STATES
Whether states are *weak* or *strong* (Buzan 1983, ch. 4; 1988a, pp. 17–27) in terms of their degree of socio-political cohesion is crucial both to their own security and to that of the regions within which they are embedded. Whether a state is weak or strong by this definition has little to do with whether it is weak or strong as a power. Strong states can be weak powers (Denmark) and weak states can be quite strong powers (Argentina, Pakistan, even the Soviet Union in some ways). The international anarchy is a decentralized system

of order, and therefore depends for its stability on the robustness
of its component units. Weak states are like holes in the fabric
of international order. Their internal politics are often violent,
and their domestic insecurity frequently spills over to disrupt the
security of neighbours (South Africa, Kampuchea, Afghanistan,
Pakistan in 1971). Weak states easily draw in competitive outside
interventions (Angola, Chad, Cambodia, El Salvador, Grenada,
Lebanon, Nicaragua, Panama), and they may offer tempting targets to opportunistic neighbours (Afghanistan, Lebanon, Chad,
Mozambique).

In an international anarchy, strong states are a necessary but not
sufficient condition for international security. They are necessary
because without them the insecurity of political fragility and disorder prevail almost by definition. They are not sufficient, because
as the recent history of the European states in the first half of this
century shows all too clearly, strong states can easily generate an
environment of exceptional insecurity. The present international
system contains more states on the weak than on the strong end
of the spectrum, and thus has a massive element of international
insecurity built into itself. Rectifying this problem will be a long
job, in which the stronger states can only intervene up to a limit
without being charged with neo-colonialism. It is not yet clear
whether the momentum of decolonization will tend naturally, if
slowly, towards the emergence of stronger states, or whether it
will, in some places, result in stagnation or even a collapse of local
self-government. The Brandt Report (Independent Commission on
International Development Issues, 1980) is clearly right to argue that
international security depends in part on strengthening the political
economies of the weak states. Whether its prescription is an effective
way to proceed is much more arguable. Existing strong states are
gifts of history, and as yet we have little knowledge about how to
create others like them where it has not happened naturally.

THE NATURE OF MILITARY POLICY

The nature of military policy lies at the heart of the power–
security dilemma. The problem is how to bring domestic and
foreign perceptions of reasonable defence needs into some sort of
balance. If states are seen by others to be inadequately defended,
like China was during the period of Western and Japanese imperialism, they run the risk of inviting aggression from opportunistic

expansionists. If they are seen by others to be over-defended, like the Soviet Union has been since 1945, they risk appearing threatening, and so triggering fruitless and insecurity-generating cycles of arms racing. The inherent ambiguity of military means (whether given weapons can be designated as offensive or defensive), and the strategic advantages of surprise attack (Pearl Harbor, Barbarossa, Falklands) have always made it difficult to find a balance between legitimate military defence and a militarily threatening posture legitimately seen by others as aggressive.

During the 1980s, a useful school of thought has emerged which has tried to tackle this dilemma with the idea of non-provocative (or non-offensive) defence (Agrell, 1987; Buzan, 1987a, pp. 271–8; Galtung, 1984; Møller, 1987; Windass, 1985). Inspiration for this work has been drawn from several sources. In part it comes from the practice of some states, most notably the European neutrals, Japan, and in some ways China. In part it comes from so-called 'emergent technologies', which offer the prospect of extremely accurate and 'intelligent' munitions married to powerful systems of observation and control. The hope is that these technologies will restore advantage to the defender by making any large, moving object highly vulnerable to destruction. Since invaders (though not always attackers) depend on a host of large moving objects, these new weapons may tip the balance in favour of well-prepared defenders – and do so without necessarily giving the defenders a significant counter-invasion capability. In part it comes from the desire to reduce military tensions and capabilities in Europe, and it is no accident that much the biggest and best developed literature exploring 'structural incapability for attack' has been produced in West Germany. Judging by the promises of Mikhail Gorbachev's December 1988 speech to the UN, and subsequent Soviet actions and proposals, non-provocative defence has also made significant converts in the Soviet Union (MccGwire, 1988). There are, of course, sceptics (Freedman, 1987; Gates, 1987). Non-provocative defence is far from being an orthodoxy, though it does have a firm historical record of practice, and looks set to play a major role in the defence debates of the 1990s and beyond.

The basic principles of non-provocative defence are:

(1) that national defence is necessary in an anarchic international system;

(2) that under modern conditions national securities are highly interdependent, and that rational national security policy must therefore balance the legitimate needs of the state with the legitimate security concerns of other states;

(3) that all countries have the right to live free from the fear of either invasion or disarming first strikes, and national security policies must therefore be designed to minimize these capabilities.

To the extent that these principles can be put into operation without unacceptable costs in vulnerability, the power–security dilemma could be broken, and international security thereby improved very markedly.

TRANSPARENCY TO OBSERVATION

Transparency to observation is part of what makes non-provocative defence feasible. In this respect, improvements in space-based observation since the early 1960s have worked a remarkable and under-recognized, transformation on security relations. Using national technical means, states can now observe each other's military dispositions and behaviours much more accurately and continuously than ever before. These capabilities make surprise attacks, especially those requiring the mass mobilization and movement of military and naval forces, much more difficult to achieve than in the recent past. Where there is the political will, these national technical means can be bolstered by agreed confidence-building measures (CBMs). CBMs of the kind that have developed in Europe involve increasing transparency by a system of agreed reporting and inspection measures that give each side the ability to reassure itself about the other's military deployments.

Transparency also has a broad political–economy dimension that parallels, and interacts with, the military one. The Soviet Union, for example, traditionally sought advantage in its vigorously promoted non-transparency. Being a closed state enabled the Soviet leadership to hide everything, from the size of its nuclear forces (Khrushchev 1957–62) to the extent of its military budget. This closedness greatly exacerbated the power–security dilemma for the West, and therefore subsequently for the Soviet Union, by forcing NATO to react to worst-case assessments about Soviet military capability.

It is also obvious that one of the advantages of capitalist (or at least market-based) political economies is that their very operation generates high levels of transparency. Extensive trade and investment naturally make societies relatively open to each other. Because extensive interaction forces adherence to standard units of account, reliable and comparable statistics are readily available on a wide variety of activities within and between such states. This socio-economic interoperability avoids serious problems of opacity like those that the West has had in trying to estimate Soviet and Chinese defence expenditure. The lack of tradeable currencies in the communist powers, added to their governments' more than usually self-serving way with statistics, has been an impediment to broadly based transparency, and thus an obstacle to international security. The apparent triumph of market over centrally planned economies in the late twentieth century would seem to be a powerful stimulus to greater transparency, and therefore to the easier achievement of international security.

The strength of international society

The condition of international society is an important element of international security. To the extent that an international society exists, it not only makes it easier for states to accept each other's legitimacy, but also facilitates civilized (that is, non-violent) interaction among them. Anarchical society, in other words, is capable of generating order only if the units within it can adopt norms against which their own and others' behaviour can be communicated, regulated and judged. This is especially so when the density of the system is high enough that the units cannot ignore each other's presence and activity. Hedley Bull (1977, pp. 38–40, 257–60, 315–17) worried that the common norms underlying international society had been seriously weakened by the expansion of a culturally cohesive European system into an incoherent multi-civilizational global one. It can be argued that Bull's portrait was an excessively gloomy one, and that, even to the extent that he was right, his analysis is now dated.

There are several reasons for thinking that international society is in fairly good shape by the standards of most of this century, and that the trends are improving ones. Most basic is the near-universal acceptance of the territorial state as the fundamental unit of political legitimacy. Except for Islam, all of the universalizing political ideologies have been firmly nationalized. As the Iran–Iraq war demonstrated, even Islam is heading in that direction. Mutual recognition of sovereignty is the system norm, and the number of serious boundary disputes – perhaps the major source of international insecurity in an anarchic system – is declining as the now universal state system settles down.

In theory, the state system can be a stable depository for the natural diversity of human culture. Provided that there is general agreement on boundaries, the system of sovereign states is well designed to handle the legitimization of relations among diverse social and political cultures. Indeed, given the range and intensity of that diversity as an undeniably dominant historical reality, a system of sovereign states may be the only way of constructing a stable international political order for many decades to come. In such a system, peace can be conceived in terms of 'non-violent conflict culture' (Jahn, Lemaitre and Waever, 1987, p. 55). In this conception, peace does not require harmony. Disagreement and conflict are assumed to be part of the human political condition both within and between states, but war is ruled out as a legitimate instrument of policy except for the purpose of defence against a military attack. If international society is strong enough to support legitimate mechanisms for change, then anarchy can become a framework within which international disputes and conflicts can be both carried on or settled without large-scale violence.

In addition to the basic consensus on the state system, it could be argued that three other norms are emerging as major elements of international society. The first is the consensus amongst the major powers that wars between them are no longer a desirable or fruitful way of settling differences. In some of the great powers – most notably the major sufferers of the last war in Europe and Japan – this norm is quite deeply embedded in their societies. In others, it is more a function of nuclear deterrence, and the fear that victory and defeat will be indistinguishable. This norm has emerged with exceptional strength in some regions, notably North America and Western Europe, and for rather different reasons among the ASEAN states (Buzan, 1988b, pp. 12–13). In these regions, the existence of security communities offers micro-demonstrations of what mature anarchy looks like. To the extent that this norm depends on nuclear weapons, however, it raises the divisive and unresolved question of whether or not nuclear proliferation is desirable as a way of spreading the constraint on the resort to war. The role of nuclear weapons in non-provocative defence is also a matter of controversy (Buzan, 1987a).

The second norm concerns the desirability of market-based economies both within and between states. When Bull wrote, the international system was so deeply divided on this question as to make it the major cause of threats of war involving superpower rivalry. But during the 1980s, market economies moved decisively into a position of intellectual and practical dominance over centrally planned ones, and this took much of the heat out of the Cold War. As the twenty-first century approaches, the international community – or at least the group of major powers at its apex – is beginning to look less ideologically divided than at any time since 1914. As this new norm consolidates, it will spread the benefits of transparency discussed above. It will also weaken, and perhaps even eliminate, the zero-sum ideological divide that was such a powerful driver of the power–security dilemma during the post-Second World War era.

The third norm arises from increasing concern over ecological issues. Because of the nature of the issues, this concern carries with it a strong global consciousness. Changes in the planetary atmosphere affect everyone in a way that distributes burdens and concerns much more evenly than is the case with the longer-running issue of overpopulation. This is an exceptionally useful counter-weight to the deeply ingrained societal parochialness that almost everywhere still dominates the human condition. Ecological, or 'green', consciousness is by no means universal. But its rise has been dramatic, and it looks well set to be ever more widely promoted as the issues on its agenda begin to impact on people everywhere in their daily lives.

All of these norms both reflect and promote interdependence, and on balance might be taken as useful developments towards greater international security.

The shape of international system structure

Historically, power is always very unevenly distributed in the international system. In particular the number of great powers is always measurable in single figures. Great powers, almost by definition, dominate life in the anarchy because they control the bulk of the capability necessary for action in the system. The number of great powers, usually between two and seven, defines the degree of polarity in the system. Variations in the degree of polarity, especially when the numbers are low, make a big difference to the overall character of relations in the system (Waltz, 1979, chs 5–6). It can be argued that a structural change of this type is fundamentally altering the political conditions of international security as we approach the end of the twentieth century.

There can be no doubt that the bipolar structure is evolving towards a multipolar one. For those European and Asian centres of power temporarily knocked out by the Second World War, the process of recovery has long been complete in the economic sector. As living memory of the war fades away, there is good reason to think that political recovery is now moving into its final stages. The post-colonial rise of new centres of power such as China, India and Brazil is, of course, an open-ended process that will not peak and fade from significance. There is much room for argument about the precise degree to which the system has already become multipolar. Some still think of it as bipolar because of the military superiority of the superpowers. Others see it as tripolar because of the rise of China as a centre of military and political power independent of both superpower camps (Bull, 1977, pp. 200–5). Yet others see it as already multipolar, though mostly in the economic sector where Japan and the European Community play roles in the top rank.

Strong supporters of bipolarity, such as Waltz (1979, chs 7–9), and those who worry about the difficulties of managing a polycentric political economy, will see this development as negative for international security. Others might argue that the merits of bipolarity are more than offset by the intense and immovable hostility that it generates between the two rival superpowers, and that consequently a move towards multipolarity should create an easier international security environment (Buzan, 1987b, ch. 12; 1989b). Among other things, a multipolar system should exhibit lower levels of hostility among the great powers, more flexibility in international relations, more locally based security management, and consequently less competitive intervention in regional affairs and fewer problems with extended deterrence. This debate is not as well developed as it should be, but in my view the trend towards multipolarity will yield large net gains for international security.

CONCLUSIONS

Is international security possible? In absolute terms, the answer has to be no. There are plenty of facts available to point to the enduring presence of insecurity in the international system, ranging from the threat of accidental nuclear war, and the existence of many local wars, through the wealth of religious and ethnic hatreds, and political instabilities, to the dismal array of economic and environmental catastrophes that afflict many peoples.

In relative terms, the answer is yes. The international system already provides historically high levels of security for many of its states and vast numbers of its people. Many of its main trends are improving ones. There are certainly no grounds for complacency about international security, and given the many contradictions within the concept, some improvements will carry negative side effects. Socialists, for example, might see the triumph of market economies as exacerbating some kinds of security problems whatever other benefits it might have. But there are compelling grounds for optimism that in some vitally important respects the conditions for international security are improving. Anarchy can increasingly be seen not as the source of the security problem, but as the framework for solutions to it.

REFERENCES

Agrell, W. (1987), 'Offensive versus defensive: military strategy and alternative defence', *Journal of Peace Research*, vol. 24, no. 1, pp. 75–85.

Axelrod, R., and Keohane, R. (1985), 'Achieving cooperation under anarchy', *World Politics*, vol. 38, no. 1, pp. 226–54.

Booth, K. (1979), *Strategy and Ethnocentrism* (London: Croom Helm).

Bull, H. (1977), *The Anarchical Society* (London: Macmillan).

Buzan, B. (1983), *People, States and Fear: The National Security Problem in International Relations* (Brighton: Wheatsheaf).

Buzan, B. (1984), 'Peace, power and security: contending concepts in the study of international relations', *Journal of Peace Research*, vol. 21, no. 2, pp. 109–25.

Buzan, B. (1987a), 'Common security, non-provocative defence, and the future of Western Europe', *Review of International Studies*, vol. 13, pp. 265–79.

Buzan, B. (1987b), *An Introduction to Strategic Studies: Military Technology and International Relations* (London: Macmillan).

Buzan, B. (1988a), 'People, states and fear: the national security problem in the Third World', in E. Azar and C. Moon (eds), *National Security in the Third World: The Management of Internal and External Threats* (Aldershot: Edward Elgar), pp. 14–43.

Buzan, B. (1988b), 'The Southeast Asian security complex', *Contemporary Southeast Asia*, vol. 10, no. 1, pp. 1–16.

Buzan, B. (1989a), 'Systems, structures and units: reconstructing Waltz's theory of international politics', paper given at the BISA/ISA conference, March/April.

Buzan, B. (1989b), 'The future of European security', in O. Waever, P. Lemaitre and E. Tromer (eds), *European Polyphony: Perspectives Beyond East–West Confrontation* (London: Macmillan), ch. 1.

Buzan, B., and Rizvi, G. (1986), *South Asian Insecurity and the Great Powers* (London: Macmillan).

Chase-Dunn, C. (1981), 'Interstate system and capitalist world economy: one logic or two?', *International Studies Quarterly*, vol. 25, no. 1, pp. 19–42.

Freedman, L. (1987), *Strategic Defence in the Nuclear Age*, Adelphi Paper No. 224 (London: International Institute for Strategic Studies).

Galtung, J. (1984), 'Transarmament: from offensive to defensive defence', *Journal of Peace Research*, vol. 21, no. 2, pp. 127–39.

Gates, D. (1987), *Non-Offensive Defence: A Strategic Contradiction?* Occasional Paper No. 29 (London: Institute for European Defence and Strategic Studies).

Independent Commission on International Development Issues (1980), *North–South: A Programme for Survival* (London: Pan).

Independent Commission on Disarmament and Security Issues (1982), *Common Security: A Programme for Disarmament* (London: Pan).

Jahn, E., Lemaitre, P., and Waever, O. (1987), *European Security: Problems of Research on Non-Military Aspects*, Copenhagen Papers No. 1 (Copenhagen: Centre for Peace and Conflict Research, University of Copenhagen).

Jervis, R. (1985), 'From balance to concert: a study of international security cooperation', *World Politics*, vol. 38, no. 1, pp. 58–79.

Kennedy, P. (1988), *The Rise and Fall of the Great Powers* (London: Unwin Hyman).

Keohane, R. (1984), *After Hegemony: Cooperation and Discord in the World Political Economy* (Princeton, NJ: Princeton University Press).

Keohane, R., and Nye J. S. (1977), *Power and Interdependence* (Boston, Mass.: Little, Brown).

Keohane, R., and Nye, J. S. (1987), '*Power and Interdependence* revisited', *International Organization*, vol. 41, no. 4, pp. 725–53.

Lemaitre, P. (1989), 'Krise und Reform in den Socialistischen Staaten und das Sicherheitssystem Europas', in C. Wellmann (ed.), *Frieden in und mit Osteuropa – Osteuropa in den Neunziger Jahren* (Suhrkamp).

MccGwire, M. (1988), 'A mutual security regime for Europe?', *International Affairs*, vol. 64, no. 3, pp. 361–80.

McNeill, W. H. (1982), *The Pursuit of Power* (Chicago: Chicago University Press).

Møller, B. (1987), 'The need for an alternative NATO strategy', *Journal of Peace Research*, vol. 24, no. 1, pp. 61–74.

Møller, B. (1988), 'Common security: some military and non-military aspects', paper given at the East–West Workshop on Common Security.

Oye, K. (1985), 'Explaining cooperation under anarchy', *World Politics*, vol. 38, no. 1, pp. 1–24.

SIPRI (1985), *Politics for Common Security* (London: Taylor & Francis).

Vayrynen, R. (1988), 'Common security and the state system', unpublished manuscript.

Von Laue, T. H. (1987), *The World Revolution of Westernization: The Twentieth Century in Global Perspective* (New York: Oxford University Press).

Waever, O. (1988), *A few, somewhat critical, notes on the concept of common security* (Copenhagen: Centre for Peace and Conflict Research, University of Copenhagen).

Wallerstein, I. (1974), 'The rise and future demise of the world capitalist system', *Comparative Studies in Society and History*, vol. 16, no. 4, pp. 387–415.

Waltz, K. (1979), *Theory of International Politics* (Reading, Mass.: Addison-Wesley).

Windass, Stan (ed.) (1985), *Avoiding Nuclear War: Common Security as a Strategy for the Defence of the West* (London: Brassey).

2

Peace research versus strategic studies

DAVID J. DUNN

Although much studied, especially in Western Europe and Scandinavia, in the 1980s peace became a much more salient issue in political, social and intellectual debate. More directly, it has become more public and for a variety of reasons. For many Americans this might be ascribed to a process of coming to terms with the legacy of the war in Indo-China. For many Britons the debate focused, in part, on the decision to replace the Polaris weapons system. For the Germans, self-evidently, peace has been rather more of a public, political concern, as well as a subject for academic debate. For the Scandinavian states, peace has long been a component of the public political philosophy, consistent with their established status in international politics. But to explain the importance of the discussion of peace and security in the 1980s we need to go beyond these issues, important as they were.

There was in the early 1980s a sense of fear allied to protest: fear at the prospect of nuclear war, which many saw as increasing rather than receding, and protest at the increase in nuclear weapons, particularly with respect to the deployment of cruise missiles in Europe but also with respect to the sheer quantity of nuclear warheads deployed by the nuclear powers. The concern found expression in many ways. Films such as *Threads* and *The Day After*, both depicting nuclear attacks, were shown on television to large audiences and prompted debate. Likewise, *The China Syndrome*, depicting a fictional melt-down in a nuclear power station, was shown in cinemas, and later the Chernobyl disaster demonstrated that things could indeed go wrong and that, furthermore, nuclear plumes were no respecters of national sovereignties. In the United States the 'Freeze' movement became active in an attempt to halt the nuclear arms race, and the statement of the American bishops on nuclear deterrence became a central focus for the US nuclear debate. In the UK the Campaign for Nuclear Disarmament rapidly grew in membership and activity (stimulated by both cruise missile deployments and the Polaris replacement question) and the traditional bipartisan political consensus on defence collapsed. In Europe, END (European Nuclear Disarmament) activities spread and much political debate centred on the nature of peace and security in Europe after the détente of the 1970s, as well as on the role of the European theatre in any future (limited) war scenarios. However, conspicuous and novel though these efforts were, concentration on them should not obscure or neglect the existence of peace concerns and movements in many countries which served to add momentum when public concern became more focused and organized.

In summary, we can see many indicators of public concern and protest throughout the 1980s. (There was also the development of a significant literature of nuclear concern, manifested in novels and stories: this literature is important to note, and it certainly demands a full treatment which cannot be given here, though Bernard Malamud's 1982 work *God's Grace* and *Einstein's Monsters* by Martin Amis, which appeared in 1987, represent respectively American and British contributions. (This was not all. There was a significant broadening of participation in the intellectual debate about peace and security and the role of nuclear weapons as means to those ends. The moral basis of deterrence engaged a much wider nexus of philosophers and clerics alike, and what had once been the sometimes arcane concerns of the strategists alone now became the subject of wider debate (see, for example, Blake and Pole, 1983 and 1984; Hardin, Mearsheimer, Dworkin and Goodwin, 1985). And this occurred at a time when some of the basic assumptions started to be questioned from within the strategic studies community itself. For example, the collection of essays edited by Gwyn Prins (Prins, 1984) was entitled *The Choice: Nuclear Weapons Versus Security*; note *versus*, not 'as a means to'. Moreover, many of the contributors to the Prins collection were former military men. The implication to be taken from this was quite clear: there was an emerging dissensus within the strategic community about the direction that was being followed and we shall refer to it in what follows.

At the same time there were significant developments in peace research, a field of study which had emerged years earlier but which apparently enjoyed, in the circumstances of the 1980s, something of a renaissance. Writing in 1985, Andrew Mack observed a significant renewal of interest in peace research and suggested that

> this upsurge of support for peace research, and the parallel proliferation of peace studies courses in colleges and universities, is related to the increased public concern about nuclear war and scepticism about the utility of traditional approaches to national security in the nuclear age. (Mack, 1985, p. 1)

It is clear, therefore, that the 1980s represented, if not a turning point (this may or may not become clearer with the passage of time and the nature of current and future debate), then a period of increased concern in intellectual and public debate. There were evident novelties, but there were also extant forces and movements which often facilitated the public and new debates. In light of these introductory remarks and observations, the aims of this chapter are twofold. First, to put into context the recent appearance of the public discussions of the peace issue by demonstrating that peace research can be traced back to the 1950s and that, in its third decade, when the issue became public, work done in previous years could underpin the new debate. Second, to compare and contrast the development of peace research and strategic studies with a view to establishing the extent to which the 'versus' in the title might better be replaced with 'and', so stressing complementarity rather than difference.

PREHISTORIES

Both strategic studies and peace research have recognizable prehistories, generally reflecting certain assumptions or approaches to the understanding of human behaviour. The study of war is a central concern of each (as well as the more formally established field of international relations), and, as we might expect, has a long history. Clausewitz dominates the intellectual landscape, less for what he tells us about how to win battles (for the traditional view of strategy was that it was concerned with the art of generalship) than for how he informs us about the political and philosophical aspects of war. Strategy, in its more modern guise, has become more concerned with the political role and function of war and threats than about soldiering *per se*.

In the traditional analyses of war and peace, there is an implicit assumption which represents a starting point: we accept as a given that war and force are important makers of our political and cultural landscape. Or, as John Garnett puts it in outlining the intellectual underpinnings of strategic studies, it 'is concerned with the darker side of human nature, in that it examines the way in which military power is used by governments in pursuit of their interests' (1975, p. 3). Such a focus is due in no small part to the nature of the international system of states. This system is devoid of any central authority capable of presiding over the conduct of affairs and mediating interests, so that, in essence, it is a system of self-help, wherein the states comprising the system must retain for themselves the right to use force in order to enhance, if not guarantee, their own security. In these terms, we are not being too pessimistic in stressing the darker side of human nature, but rather 'Realist' in accepting that, in the absence of a central authority, it is an inescapable, and for some perhaps even fatalistic, principle of conduct of international politics that war and force will be central. Some may find this regrettable and deplorable, seeming only to stress the worst aspects of humanity. Others see it as inescapable given the organization of international politics. All of this suggests that there is a close affinity between the Realist approach to international politics and the study of strategy.

Peace research finds its prehistory in the more rationalist tradition, where the perfectibility of men and women is not beyond question and where reform of institutions and norms of behaviour is more than a remote possibility. The tradition is long established and comprises, amongst others, the writings of Kant, Grotius, the Abbé de Saint Pierre and Penn. The impulse here is to change the way men and women act and not to accept that we live in some inescapable, immutable reality. In these terms, there is no enduring reality of international politics which assumes that the darker side of human nature must always out: rather, the reality can be changed by using scientific and rationalist modes of inquiry, by discovering and implementing aspects of belief and behaviour which make resort to war and force less likely, through the pursuit of peaceful means and more collaborative mechanisms of social and political choice.

STRATEGIC STUDIES

What changed these diverse traditions in the study of war into marked intellectual movements after 1945 was the appearance of the nuclear weapon and the transition to nuclear deterrence; deterrence in itself was not new, but the nuclear component added an extra, decisive twist to the notion of executing a threat should deterrence fail. What marked out Bernard Brodie as one of the fathers of modern strategy was his recognition, in 1945, that the primary function of military force was to be devoted to deterrence rather than pursuit of victory in the traditional sense. As Brodie put it: 'Thus far the chief purpose of our military establishment has been to win wars. From now on its chief purpose must be to avert them. It can have almost no other useful purpose' (Brodie, 1946, p. 76). Brodie was also one of the new breed of strategists, namely civilians, often from within universities, who contributed to the study of deterrence and found rationales for, and limits to, force in the new nuclear environment. Their aim was to proceed from where they were: the atomic bomb existed and the vastly more destructive hydrogen bomb soon followed; the Soviet Union acquired the nuclear weapon and a situation of mutuality obtained, although what some saw as mutuality, others saw as a balance of terror. These were the 'realities' of the situation and the situation had to be managed. In these circumstances, the strategists had to examine what conditions could contribute to successful military policies which achieved goals and minimized risks. How might stability obtain such as to prevent war on a global scale, but still permit options in foreign and military policy? How might foreign policy be conducted within an acceptable limit of risk? What types of military forces were required, how might they be defended and how much would they cost? These were the sorts of questions the new strategists addressed.

The new modes of strategic analysis soon became institutionalized and established. Throughout the 1950s institutes and departments were founded in the United States and elsewhere, though the task was not necessarily easy. A notable milestone – in the sense that it marked the formal organization of the international strategic community – was the foundation, in 1958, of the (International) Institute for Strategic Studies.

There were also significant problems. At first it appeared that the US possession of the atomic bomb was a strategy in itself: as long as the Soviet Union did not have a nuclear capability the US task was relatively simple. But once the Soviet Union acquired such a capability, in 1949, the search for nuclear strategies on both sides led to the acceleration and development of an approach well known today. Recall that the strategists had to accept the situation as they found it: an opponent had a certain number and type of forces in the military inventory; 'hardware' became, for the many, a key concern. But what were the intentions of an opponent? Did force structures belie intentions? In taking account of capabilities, how was this to be influenced by declared or tacit intentions? Thus, much of strategic thinking focused on threat estimation and often took on a psychological dimension, not only with respect to what the opponent's intentions might be, but also how one might respond to what one presumed were the intentions of an adversary. These questions would have been difficult enough, but given the changes in technology which saw the appearance of long-range and accurate missiles allied to smaller and very powerful warheads, the degrees of difficulty were compounded.

This is not the place to recount in detail the evolution of strategies, not least because it has been done elsewhere (Freedman, 1989; Herken 1985; Kaplan 1984; Newhouse, 1989; Paret, 1986 all stand as excellent surveys). Nevertheless, three significant issues need to be identified and discussed briefly if we are to understand the public and professional concerns of the 1980s: these are flexibility, survivability of forces and extended deterrence.

The operational strategy for the United States through much of the 1950s was massive retaliation but doubts as to its credibility precipitated a search for an alternative strategy. This appeared, in the 1960s, as mutual assured destruction (MAD) and flexible response. The key here was to retain a secure second-strike capability which could survive the opponent's first strike and still inflict unacceptable pain and damage; this, it was believed, would deter a first strike. Securing a second strike led to the development of a nuclear triad, with forces based on land, under the sea and in the air;

if one or two legs were destroyed, at least one could strike back. In addition, it was thought that flexibility, having the option to meet an opponent's thrust like for like, and therefore more credibly, enhanced deterrence. Such strategies seemed sensible, but their development led to an enormous proliferation in the quantities of delivery systems and, later, warheads. More were acquired as a means to deter more, and enhance the prospects for strategic stability. But to the critics flexible response constituted matching forces for forces, with actions prompting reactions and thus fuelling an arms race.

Subsequent evolutions to these strategies appeared to many to strain credibility. An extreme example was the proposal to enhance the survivability of the MX missile by putting it in a loop within which several silos were to be located; the Soviet Union, if contemplating an attack, would have to guess which one it was in, after the logic of the fairground 'shell game'. Earlier, arms control had fallen into disrepute when the Strategic Arms Limitation Talks (SALT) produced an agreement which allowed the United States and the Soviet Union to build up to agreed limits. Of course, the logic of arms control is such that even restrained growth constitutes arms control, but nonetheless the SALT experience, allied to the dispiriting experiences in European arms control forums, pejoratively described as 'bean counting', raised serious questions about the value of the exercise.

In terms of extended deterrence, the relationship of the United States to its European allies, and more particularly how the United States could make credible its commitment to Europe in an age of bilateral superpower arms control, raised other serious questions. In part, the cruise missile was a solution (for some at least), but it produced monumental problems for the European allies. Sections of European public opinion saw the missiles as evidence of the Americans foisting not only more but also more dangerous weapons on the allies. More was not always thought to be better. Moreover, arms control was at a standstill and the relationship between the United States and its European allies was a cause for concern. Later, with the development of smaller nuclear weapons and the prospect that they might actually have utility in a limited land battle in Europe, the problems were exacerbated: limited war in Europe for the Americans was one thing, but quite another for the Europeans.

All of this suggests that throughout the 1980s the strategic theorists have been in some difficulty, at the very least, and perhaps even in crisis. There probably never was a golden age of strategy, but many of the new strategists must have thought that the problems of the 1980s were more difficult than most. Lawrence Freedman sums up their problem thus:

> By the mid 1980s, therefore. . .the nuclear strategists had still failed to come up with any convincing methods of employing nuclear weapons should deterrence fail that did not wholly offend common sense, nor had they even reached a consensus on whether or not the discovery of such methods was essential if deterrence was to endure. The fundamental dilemma of nuclear strategy remained as intractable as ever. (Freedman, 1986, p. 778)

Yet there is a fundamental irony here, and it ought not to go unnoticed, especially in a book dedicated to assessing new ways of thinking. If there is a theme that runs through much of strategic thinking since 1945, it is the coming to terms with novelty and searching for novelty. Brodie first saw the new world as it presented itself and if there is a recurrent theme in reading Kaplan, Herken and Newhouse, amongst others, it is the search for new options; options that will give the President more than an 'allout attack or do nothing' choice, options that seek to make this strategy more credible to opponents and allies alike, as opposed to this option, and so on. Nevertheless, the net result has been a massive proliferation in the quantities of weaponry – stability at very high levels of armament. Hence, the implicit message from the Prins volume: that by the 1980s, the weapons were the problem, not the solution, and that they were making many feel very insecure.

PEACE RESEARCH

What distinguished the peace researchers from the strategists, in broad terms, was their refusal to accept the management of nuclear weapons as the realistic option; a new one had to be found and it could be found, with enough of the right kinds of effort. Several

initiatives were underway in the 1950s (Dunn, 1978). Pioneering
work had already been done by Lewis Richardson in Great Britain
and by Quincy Wright in the United States. Theodore Lenz,
another 'father of peace research', contributed further pioneering
work in the early 1950s. The critical point in the development of
peace research came in 1954–5, with the meeting of several like
minds at the Center for the Advanced Study in the Behavioral
Sciences based at Stanford University. Kenneth Boulding, Harold
Lasswell, Anatol Rapoport and Herbert Kelman, among others,
as well as Lewis Richardson's son, Stephen, met together. What
they did was to shift peace research out of the realm of the possible
into the probable and practical, taking steps to ensure its early
institutional foundation. From the perspective of the 1990s, this
meeting appears as a beginning.

Initially there was a small-scale bulletin; this was followed by the
Journal of Conflict Resolution, based at the University of Michigan.
In 1964 the International Peace Research Association (IPRA) was
founded in London and at the same time the *Journal of Peace
Research* was founded at the International Peace Research Institute in
Oslo. In the United Kingdom, small-scale but significant activities
were giving rise to the foundation of a Peace Research Centre
at Lancaster, a recognizable precursor of the Richardson Institute
which followed in the 1970s.

At first, the subject matter of peace research was hardly different
from that studied by the strategists: deterrence, the functions of
armaments, game theoretical approaches to strategy, reductions
in tensions, stability conditions and so on. What mattered was
that the approach to the subject was different: the issue was less
one of managing the situation and more one of trying to change
it: this difference became even more accentuated in the 1960s and
1970s, with the so-called radical input into peace research. The
influence of the New Left in the 1960s was felt in the evolution
of peace research. Emphasis tended to switch away from the
nuclear dimensions of conflict and rather more to questions of
neo-colonialism, underdevelopment, structural violence, liberation
strategies and unconventional conflicts. Scandinavian influences
were important here in stressing perspectives from outside the
dominant framework of East–West bloc images, as was the effect
of Vietnam on American society and the radicalizing influences to
which it gave rise.

What was especially important in the development of peace research at this time was not so much the Scandinavian inputs or the radical inputs *per se*, but rather the more maximal approach to the definition of peace. What the maximal approach did was to go beyond force, war and armaments; they were not marginalized, nor displaced, but instead were seen in the context of the wider socio-economic processes of peace and war. Peace did not just mean the absence of war: peace also related to the existence of certain social conditions. Societies based on exploitation were deemed to be inherently 'unpeaceful': there could never be, in these terms, a happy slave, for slavery is inconsistent with happiness (Burton, 1962; Galtung, 1969).

Concern about armaments was not displaced: far from it. Instead there was some emphasis on the systemic consequences of, and the problems associated with, proliferation of arms, the arms trade, the motives behind weapons proliferation, the conversion of defence industries and so on. Moreover, in journals such as the *Bulletin of Peace Proposals*, as its title suggests, practical aspects of peace thinking were to be emphasized. In this regard, it is illuminating to compare and contrast the work of the International Institute for Strategic Studies and the Stockholm International Peace Research Institute, where there is a different approach to the subject matter. What is often clear is the complementarity of approaches, rather than competition. Over the course of thirty years, then, peace research has moved from a small-scale to a larger scale activity; it is now rather more of an alternative approach to questions of peace and security and less of an intellectual protest movement. It is not institutionally secure as a matter of routine and there are periodic reports of funding difficulties. Nevertheless, there is now an extensive network of journals, conferences and organizations (in the United States, for example, COPRED, the Consortium on Peace Research and Education, is very well developed) and the networks are global in their reach (Mack, 1985).

CURRENT ISSUES

What is particularly interesting about the recent development of peace research is the extent to which it has tended to redefine the nature of security in an interdependent world. Here the work of the World Order Models Project is important. Johan Galtung (Galtung, 1980) has been associated with the project, and the work done by Richard Falk (Falk, 1983) and Samuel Kim (Kim, 1984) is illustrative of the approach adopted, stressing the search for a regulating mechanism in the world politics beyond a state-centric system, while at the same time highlighting the multidimensional nature of security: apart from the nuclear threat, the security agenda encompasses the need for environmental quality and the enhancement of human rights and economic wellbeing. Clearly their work draws on much that had been done in peace research, and taken together might be described as a 'new realism' in the study of security and welfare. What they do is stress the immanence and imminence of threats to security: the ecological threat is 'real', the deprivation that is characteristic of much of the globe is 'real' in its consequences and, as analysts, we must perceive these issues for what they are. First, there is a clear relationship between rich and poor states and it is not always benign. Second, there is a link between armaments and (under)development, the pursuit of one perhaps prejudicing the other. Third, for many citizens of the world the real security dilemma is how to survive through today and into tomorrow: for them, nuclear weapons are not the most pressing threat. Fourth, the international system of sovereign states is deficient in terms of its capacity to enhance the security of many citizens; indeed, the logic of state-centric security might actually jeopardize security prospects. What these brief comments try to illustrate is that there is now an alternative approach to the study of world order which can claim to be 'realistic' in stressing the new problems and processes of security in an ecologically whole and complex interdependent system of human behaviour. It is alternative in the sense that it does not accept the traditional definitions of security, nor the self-help principle enshrined in the traditional logic of international politics.

Nor should we neglect the recent studies taking place in the context of a search for 'common security'. In this, the Palme Commission (1982) was especially important as a landmark, but there are continuing studies in this area, as for example the work done at the Foundation for International Security in the United Kingdom. Windass and Grove (1988) have recently reported on the deliberations of study groups which have explored the prospects for common security in Europe.

Many of the radical inputs from the 1960s left little by way of legacies, but of real significance was the need for a maximal interpretation of the social and economic underpinnings of the peace process and, with it, a wider definition of the meaning of security and meaningful, life-enhancing structures. In short, weapons were one means to peace, but not a sure guarantee, while at the same time 'peace' was more apparent than real, in so far as people were suffering in exploitative relationships, deprivation and so on. So a new stage has been reached in contemporary peace research; this has resulted in a haziness in some of the boundaries with associated areas, notably normative studies in international relations, development studies, radical strategies and so on.

Peace research in the early 1990s stands more securely than ever. First, it is well entrenched in institutional terms in the United States, Australia, Japan, Scandinavia, India, the Federal Republic of Germany and Great Britain, though the rates of development and the funding problems often vary. The development of these institutions has been very slow: acquiring and retaining finance has been a major problem in most cases. It is safe to say that if the search for finance to fund and run strategy and defence studies institutes was not easy, it was probably easier than the task faced by the peace researchers. Indeed, to have set up and run a peace research institute at the height of the Cold War was well nigh impossible in many places: this might help to explain why the name for the new journal of the movement was the *Journal of Conflict Resolution*. Second, peace research exists as a legitimate approach to the study of war and peace in the 1980s: despite some opposition and misunderstanding it is now clearer that peace research or peace studies were not novelties spawned by the resurgence of the peace movement after 1979 but represent the product of more than thirty years' intellectual development (Dunn, 1985). Third, some of the work done has filtered down into undergraduate texts and into schools: what was once radical research is now deemed to be a legitimate object of study in school and society and accepted as such, as, for example, is the study of arms control and arms races. Fourth, much of the content in contemporary peace research is convergent with the concerns in mainstream international relations – and strategic studies. Fifthly, there is now a huge body of work devoted to conflict dynamics (how conflicts originate, how they worsen, why some become violent and some do not) and conflict resolution strategies, involving mediators, third parties and so on. Much of this work has application in conflicts between states as well as between other human groups.

This shows that an approach which was once thought radical and beyond the bounds of the 'real' might one day become part of the conventional wisdom: such is the nature of paradigm change. It is challenging to consider that the traditional approach to the study of security exemplified in the Realist-strategic paradigm is under pressure and that part of the pressure is exemplified by the increased salience of what was referred to earlier as the 'new realism'. Clearly our conventional understandings are under pressure and we are embarking on new ways of thinking: how do we go about solving pollution problems, if part of the problem is that sovereign states are sole arbiters of their own interests and sovereignty? How can we enhance the prospects for global development if some states are manifestly unable or incapable of embarking on the process? Does development for the poor mean less for the rich?

CONCLUSION

It is surely beyond doubt by now that there are serious questions to be asked about the performance of the state-centric system in an interdependent environment, notwithstanding the rather more recent changes in the international environment which has seen a significant breakthrough in arms control with the agreement on intermediate nuclear forces (INF) and historic changes in the European security situation. Self-help is no certain solution to pollution and ecological decay: a me-first approach to resource management is hardly the most appropriate. When states seek to make themselves more secure through the acquisition of armaments, nuclear or conventional, the system as a whole may become less secure: hence the problems associated with the management of a situation where upwards of 50,000 nuclear warheads are deployed. Moreover, what is to be done when states charged with the obligations of self-help are manifestly incapable of helping themselves and their citizens? Is there then an obligation on the part of the well-fed and secure to assist those who are less well-fed and insecure, indeed dying? If there is not, should there be?

In the light of its often precarious past, peace research now appears much more authoritative and shows, perhaps, degrees of convergence with strategic studies. This thought is echoed by Joseph Nye in a recent comment which, though it does not displace the importance of war and force from the agenda of strategic studies, certainly puts it into a wider context. 'Security problems', says Nye, 'have become more complicated as threats to state automony have shifted from the simply military, in which the threat is defined largely in terms of territorial integrity, to the economic' (Nye, 1989, p. 24). Moreover: 'In a world where both goals and instruments have become more complex, a definition of strategic studies limited to issues of military operations would be severely deficient' (1989, p. 25). Convergence might be to overstate the case: but perhaps not. Overlap there almost certainly is. This is not to suggest that strategic studies and peace research are becoming one and the same: the subject matter may be similar, but the approach is different. Strategists have tended, by and large, to start from where we are and have tried to manage the situation: peace researchers have tended not to accept that constraint and to be more maximal in their approach. Because they have not been forced into the 'real', they have often been more exploratory, even creative. An excellent example of such an approach is a work of Johan Galtung, dating from the mid-1980s and written at a time when the so-called New Cold War was at its height. As Galtung put it in a book written, appropriately enough, in Berlin: 'There are alternatives' (Galtung, 1984); and he explored alternative routes to European security, informed by immediate concerns but motivated by an equally significant concern for realistic, possible secure futures. But there is surely room for a degree of complementarity. It can be taken as self-evident that, at the opposite ends of the spectrum, the peace researcher studying the optimal components of a just world order will find minimum commonality with a strategist seeking optimal roles for small nuclear weapons in a limited battle strategy. As we move away from these polar opposites we are likely to move to a situation where the 'versus' means less than 'and' in terms of the relationship between peace research and strategic studies. Put another way, the world of the late 1980s – with successes for arms control, progressive détente, evident interdependence, global problems, common security concerns for the superpowers and the causes of wars being found in the absence of peaceful conditions –

was complex and difficult enough as to be beyond the limits of one approach. If, for the strategist, arms control now heralds the change towards a less armed environment, work done in peace research on the nature of a warless or armamentless world is hardly irrelevant. If strategic studies is about the disposition and means of force in world politics and peace research is about the causes of war and the conditions of peace they are but different approaches, marked by different styles and different assumptions, but hardly a different language altogether. The overlap is growing. As time passes it is not always possible in conferences and seminars to identify immediately the peace researchers and the strategists.

Consideration of the new should not blind us to the value of the old. Novelty is not always a virtue, nor is age a fault. As we move into the 1990s and assess the interdependent world and the problems of security in it, we do not have to reinvent the wheel. There is, in the thirty years' work done in peace research, an effective library and store: many of the efforts undertaken in the 1960s and not taken seriously might be more relevant in the 1990s: after the events of 1989, contemporary debate about what security futures await in Europe might be usefully informed by work done in peace research on alternative security systems.

Yet in suggesting a new relationship between peace research and strategic studies, perhaps it is as well to state that convergence is not an end in itself and might not even be consciously pursued. Nor need it be. But it is happening as the strategists move out from narrower assumptions which now look like major problems in themselves, and impediments. It might be that the best way to perceive the relationship between the two approaches is as one of synergy or symbiosis.

Quincy Wright stands as one of the fathers of peace research, his *A Study of War* representing a landmark (Wright, 1942). Bernard Brodie first saw the implications of the atomic bomb in terms of the new requirements of strategy:

> Bernard Brodie was Quincy Wright's star student in his graduate-school days [and] Brodie absorbed from the University of Chicago two great lessons: that political change in international relations is likely, and so is war; that there are ways to reduce the chances of war, but short of drastic and unprecedented changes in the distribution of global power,

a world government is destined to remain a feckless and ephemeral vehicle. (Kaplan, 1983, pp. 14–16.)

It is a measure of progress that the study of peace has gone well beyond the study of world government; it is a measure of the progress of strategic studies that war is but one aspect of strategy. And the juxtaposition of Wright and Brodie in these terms might prompt the thought that the differences are not as fundamental as were thought then – or now.

REFERENCES

Blake, N., and Pole, K. (1983), *Dangers of Deterrence: Philosophers on Nuclear Strategy* (London: Routledge & Kegan Paul).

Blake, N., and Pole, K. (1984), *Objections to Nuclear Defence* (London: Routledge & Kegan Paul).

Brodie, B. (1946), *The Absolute Weapon: Atomic Power and World Order* (New York: Harcourt, Brace).

Burton, J. W. (1962), *Peace Theory* (New York: Knopf).

Dunn, D. J. (1978), 'Peace research', in T. Taylor (ed.), *Approaches and Theory in International Relations* (London: Longman), pp. 257–79.

Dunn, D. J. (1985), 'The peace studies debate', *Political Studies*, vol. 56, no. 1 (Jan.–Mar.) pp. 68–72.

Falk, R. A. (1983), *The End of World Order* (New York: Holmes & Meier).

Freedman, L. (1986), 'The first two generations of nuclear strategists', in P. Paret (ed.), *Makers of Modern Strategy* (Oxford: Clarendon), pp. 735–78.

Freedman, L. (1989), *The Evolution of Nuclear Strategy*, 2nd edn (London: Macmillan, in association with IISS).

Galtung, J. (1969), 'Violence, peace and peace research', *Journal of Peace Research*, vol. 6, No. 3, pp. 167–92.

Galtung, J. (1980), *The True Worlds* (New York: Free Press).

Galtung, J. (1984), *There Are Alternatives: Four Roads to Peace and Security* (Nottingham: Spokesman Books).

Garnett, J. (1975), 'Strategic studies and its assumptions', in J. Baylis, K. Booth, J. Garnett, P. Williams, *Contemporary Strategy: Theories and Policies* (London: Croom Helm), pp. 3–21.

Hardin, R., Mearsheimer, J. J., Dworkin, G. and Goodwin, R. E. (1985), *Nuclear Deterrence: Ethics and Strategy* (Chicago: University of Chicago Press).

Herken, G. (1985), *Counsels of War* (New York: Knopf).

Kaplan, F. (1984), *The Wizards of Armageddon* (New York: Simon & Schuster).

Kim, S. S. (1984), *The Quest for a Just World Order* (Boulder, Col.: Westview).

Mack, A. (1985), *Peace Research Around the World* (Canberra: Strategic and Defence Studies Centre, Australian National University).

Newhouse, J. (1989), *The Nuclear Age* (London: Michael Joseph).

Nye, J. S. (1989), 'The contribution of strategic studies: future challenges', in *The Changing Strategic Landscape*, Adelphi Paper No. 235 (London: International Institute for Strategic Studies).

Palme Commission (1982), *Common Security: A Programme for Disarmament* (London: Pan).

Paret, P. (ed.) (1986), *Makers of Modern Strategy* (Oxford: Clarendon).

Prins, G. (1984), *The Choice: Nuclear Weapons Versus Security* (London: Chatto & Windus/Hogarth Press).

Windass, S., and Grove, E. (1988), *A Study of War* (Chicago: University of Chicago Press).

PART TWO

The decline of
nuclear strategy

3

Whither nuclear strategy?

LAWRENCE FREEDMAN

THE END OF THE ROAD

There is a widely held and wholly understandable belief that
nuclear strategy has now reached the dead end that was first
predicted for it by Bernard Brodie in 1955. He questioned
whether nuclear weapons would still be used as an instrument
of national policy as both the United States and the Soviet
Union obtained the power to inflict thermonuclear destruction
on the other (Brodie, 1955). Part of the tension in his own
work thereafter was his recognition of the logic of this dead
end with his belief in NATO's dependence on credible nuclear
deterrence. The impact of the question was blunted because this
was still a time of US nuclear superiority and because all the
various permutations for resolving the tension had yet to be fully
explored. The 'golden age' of nuclear strategic thinking was in the
late 1950s and early 1960s.[1] During this period most of the various
options were identified and explored. The excitement of the period
stemmed from the real urgency in policy terms, at a time when
East–West antagonism was high, the military competition intense
and nuclear weapons prominent in both sides' arsenals and, as far
as was known, operational plans. There was also an intellectual
vitality resulting from the sheer novelty of many of the issues
and the variety of disciplines that were brought to bear upon
them. In the process of exploring the perplexities of nuclear

strategy many of the more general problems of strategy itself
were rediscovered.

Two decades after Brodie's article, when a weariness had set
in with much nuclear theorizing, James Schlesinger, as Secretary
of Defense, also asked whether a dead end had been reached.
His answer was qualified: 'As far as the massive attacks that
preoccupied us in the 1960s are concerned, that may well be
the case.' However he believed that it might still be necessary
to deter more limited contingencies and, he suggested, this could
be done by developing a capacity for selective strikes (Schlesinger,
1975).

Technological developments in data-processing and precision
guidance gave this effort a push. However, the revival of nuclear
strategy in the late 1970s and early 1980s was as much bound
up with a revival of East–West antagonism as any new insights
into problems of nuclear policy. The dogmatic statement of a
particular approach to nuclear strategy by the Reagan administration provoked the expected response from those who had long
opposed it, in its various previous manifestations. This 'second
wave' of nuclear strategy has now also run its course, without
demonstrating convincingly that the traditional problems are much
closer to resolution.

The current mood gives more encouragement to those who
believe that the dilemmas of nuclear strategy have become almost
irrelevant. The much-proclaimed 'end of the Cold War' reduces
concerns about a superpower nuclear confrontation and shifts
attention towards new controls on nuclear armaments and further
disarmament. Even those governments who remain committed to
the nostrums of nuclear deterrence are being undermined by the
steady dismantling of the established framework on the initiative
of President Gorbachev.

The objective of this chapter is to ask whether nuclear strategy
has at last come to the end of its road. The position taken was first
suggested a decade ago:

> If real innovation in strategic thought is to rely on technological
> change then it could well have reached a dead-end; if it starts
> to address the problems of nuclear arsenals in a world of
> political change then there remains much more work to be
> done (Freedman, 1979, p. 131).

At the time those words were written there was little prospect of a dramatic transformation of East–West relations. Now that transformation has already begun, the need to think through its nuclear implications is more urgent than ever.

CLASSICAL STRATEGISTS AND NUCLEAR SPECIALISTS

It is often tempting to distinguish 'schools' in the nuclear debate, such as the 'deterrence' and 'war-fighting' schools. Such a division begs the question of whether there really is a distinction to be made, and also encourages the identification of certain notorious individuals as representatives of a particular school of thought, thereby exaggerating their importance.

For the purposes of this chapter, the preferred distinction is between classical strategy and a nuclear specialism. Many of those described as nuclear strategists have been so because of their familiarity with the arcana of nuclear weaponry, targeting, doctrine, arms control and so on. Nuclear specialists can develop a particular strategic view revolving around their expertise, leading to a preoccupation with new weapons projects and tactics for either severe crises or full-scale wars.

However, rather than attribute a set of intellectual characteristics to what has been a diverse group, many of whose members have been quite unconcerned with the wider implications of their work or who have held heretical opinions, we can note that this knowledge by itself cannot be considered 'strategic', even though at times it has seemed a prerequisite for the formation of a strategic view.

Michael Howard has identified classical strategists in the following terms: 'the thinkers who assume that the element of force exists in international relations, that it can and must be intelligently controlled, but that it cannot be totally eliminated'. Such beliefs follow naturally from a study of history and the more traditional political science, and are therefore associated with such figures as Brodie, Kissinger, Aron and Howard himself – who was also happy to consider those from other disciplines, such as Schelling (Howard, 1970, p. 155). Because nuclear weapons have inevitably occupied a large part of the classical strategist's universe since 1945, many have been obliged to become nuclear specialists.

This was especially true during the golden age when everything appeared to turn on the nuances of the nuclear balance, so that even modest variations in nuclear policies could have major implications for international stability. From the perspective of classical strategy, that situation no longer obtains. There is now no longer such a dependence on nuclear specialism, because the nuances matter less. However, there remains a strategic role for nuclear weapons as an indicator of states' vital interests. If we are now moving into a period of political fluidity in which vital interests are being redefined this will raise a series of novel questions that have important implications for nuclear policies.

In classical terms, strategy is concerned with the relationship between military means and political ends. This is a broad definition, and covers the applied aspects (how to define ends in ways which can be realistically achieved and then employ available means to achieve them) and the theoretical (the study of how strategies are formulated and implemented). Although the prime focus in strategic studies is with military means, it is important to stress that the value and relevance of military means can only be judged by reference to other means – economic, diplomatic, political. This underlines the point that strategy concerns more than simply preparing for fighting wars, and must include all measures of peacetime deterrence and coercion.

The key features of strategic objectives are that, first, they are not fixed but must adjust to circumstances, and, second, that they contradict another's objectives. This second point is critical: the drama and uncertainty of strategy comes from the oppositional element. It should be noted that the interdependence of decision-making, which Schelling for example sees as the essence of the game of strategy, is not confined to adversary relations. Much of contemporary strategic studies is concerned with alliance relations. In terms of substance, the objectives of strategy concern the state – ultimately its security, but that term can refer to both internal and external challenges, to extending influence as well as resisting the influence of others.

Contemporary strategic studies is a creation of the nuclear age, and it has naturally focused on the special problems created by these extraordinarily powerful weapons. This encouraged the ultimate conceit of describing these weapons as *strategic* weapons, as if they could meet national objectives all by themselves. (This, of course, followed on from the prewar airmens' conceit over strategic airpower.)

Yet, to the classical strategists, however important nuclear weapons are to national strategy they can never be the whole story, and indeed over time they have become less important. In the end nuclear weapons are *one* means available to national policy-makers. Strategy itself should be driven not by weapons but by politics. To view nuclear weapons in isolation or to assume that they provide a satisfactory vantage point to discuss strategy as a whole distorts strategic studies.

So, for the classical strategist, strictly speaking there really is no such thing as nuclear strategy. The term can only be used as a shorthand way to describe a specialism in a particular military means, albeit one that will remain relevant so long as nuclear weapons remain part of military establishments.

The nuclear element in strategy has been summed up by the word 'deterrence'. This word itself has stimulated a large literature which properly explores deterrence in a non-nuclear as well as a nuclear context (Huth and Russett, 1988; Lebow and Stein, 1987). This literature, to some extent, overcomplicates our understanding of nuclear deterrence in that the range of cases embraced introduces far more political variables than have been in play since 1945 (at least up to now), and they are often studied in an ahistorical manner.

Nuclear specialists have tended to fall into a different sort of trap, overcomplicating the problem by exaggerating the importance of nuclear variables. The projected interaction of two nuclear and nuclear-related forces has been analysed in a search for areas of advantages that might shape broad international behaviour as well as responses to crises. Although the technical quality of this work is often high, the political grasp can leave a lot to be desired. This in itself reflects the tendency to focus on means and take questions of objectives for granted. The crisis for the nuclear specialists has resulted from their inability to provide even a compelling *technical* analysis of how nuclear weapons might be used.

THE CRISIS IN NUCLEAR STRATEGY

This crisis takes one of two – not exclusive – forms:

(a) *a* particular strategy based on nuclear weapons (that is, nuclear deterrence) is under threat;
(b) nuclear weapons are being discredited as *military* means.

Because one explanation of (a) may be (b) we can start with (b). When some talk of nuclear strategy they are in practice talking about nuclear operations or capabilities, including command and control, vulnerabilities to surprise attack and defences, and targeting. The difficulties for those who see the essence of the subject captured by these issues is that any particular proposals are overwhelmed by the dominant 'facts' of the horrific destructive capacity of nuclear weapons, which mean that for most objectives their use appears wholly disproportionate, and of the existence of an adversary arsenal of comparable capability, which means that any first use raises enormous risks.

The efforts of nuclear specialists have been devoted to rescuing nuclear means from these two facts. To limit destructive potential they have sought the development of low-yield/low-collateral-damage weapons which in themselves are not so destructive, and of strike plans which avoid centres of population. The trouble with this approach is that either the number of weapons required to destroy important targets ensures that the level of destruction remains high or else the weapons become indistinguishable in practice from conventional weapons. When this latter possibility has been raised concern is often expressed that blurring the nuclear/conventional distinction might lead policy-makers to step unwittingly into the nuclear sphere in a mistaken belief in limitations. Moreover, many of those advocating limiting strikes do so in recognition that they create the risk of something worse (such as escalation) and so should give the adversary pause for thought. It has thus become hard to develop confidence in limitations on nuclear use and almost impossible to rely upon them.

The possibility of eliminating the adversary's capacity for retaliation brings in the question of 'first-strike capability' which has been seen as *the only* limited strike which could make any military sense. All other strikes rely on paralysing or disrupting or in some way intimidating the enemy decision-makers, but they cannot physically prevent retaliation. However, the technical requirements of a true first strike have remained impossibly demanding, and even the more hawkish strategists have tended to discount it as a genuine option. President Reagan's personal odyssey through the countervailing strategy, star wars and Reykjavik, can be taken as an eloquent statement of this inability to come up with a strategy based on nuclear threats that can ensure a conclusion *other* than mutual and massive destruction.

If the only safe statement is that any nuclear exchanges will be disastrous for all concerned, then it is hard to see what political conclusions one can draw – other than the very large and important conclusion that such exchanges must be avoided.

In theory any readiness to run a risk of nuclear war might create an advantage in a confrontation with the side that is not. A further twist is provided by the twin assumptions – absorbed rather than created by the specialists – that (a) the anti-status-quo power is the Soviet Union and (b) NATO depends more on the nuclear threat. The logical conclusion would be that the declining credibility of the nuclear threat should have encouraged a Soviet challenge to the status quo.

In practice this has not happened. It is of course a familiar point that it is impossible to know the role that nuclear weapons have played in the development of postwar international politics, for it has been negative in ensuring that certain things do not happen, but they have played *some* role. Our greatest fears have not been realized and so nuclear deterrence in this sense has been quite successful. It is, however, extremely difficult to point to anything particular done in the name of nuclear doctrine or force planning and claim this as the key to stability.

EXISTENTIALISM

Developing this point further may help to get us closer to the strategic problem. The incredibility of a first-use threat might have been expected to discredit a strategy of nuclear deterrence, employing this threat to deter severe challenges (conventional as well as nuclear) to vital interests. This is widely believed to be the case.

Classical strategy suggests an alternative way of looking at nuclear deterrence by which its success does not depend on the credibility of a threat to initiate nuclear war as a 'rational' and deliberate act of policy. Instead it depends on the more credible proposition that in the chaos and passion of war, nuclear weapons might get used. All that is required is that the weapons exist; there is no need for elaborate plans for their use. This is now known, thanks to McGeorge Bundy, as 'existential deterrence' (Bundy, 1983; for a discussion see Freedman, 1988).

There is often a presumption that nuclear existentialism is synonymous with minimalism. Certainly existentialists have tended to be on the side of those arguing for less or against particular additions. However, it is in the nature of existentialist arguments that it really does not matter how many of these weapons exist or how it is proposed to operate them in war. The supposition is that deterrence is really so easy that force planning and targeting can be guided by other, secondary, criteria. The real issue with existentialism is not the minimal level of numbers but the minimal level of acceptable risk.

While existentialism might describe how deterrence works and might continue to work, it still leaves us with some difficult questions. It rests on two untested (and hopefully never tested) hypotheses. First, the consequences of nuclear war are so horrendous that policy-makers will not be prepared to run even the tiniest risk of becoming involved in such a war. Second, the risk is created so long as the weapons are likely to be touched in some way by the dynamics of conflict.

This second hypothesis has survived a tangible decline in the role of nuclear weapons in strategic planning. The natural presumption during the 1950s was that if war came these weapons would be used, almost immediately. Since then both sides have made it a policy goal to push back the point where the fateful decision to cross the threshold would need to be taken. The other, complementary tendency has been a declining confidence in the ability of central government to control the course and conduct of war. The Vietnam War undermined the previous confidence in the possibility of controlled escalation, and provided eloquent testimony of the confusion and unpredictability of war.

In recent years great nervousness has attached to any use of force by either superpower, especially if there was a prospect that the two might end up confronting each other. There are limits to this squeamishness over the use of force, but the limits are still far more restrictive than in previous periods. From this one might conclude that existential deterrence can work through the fear of conventional, almost as much as nuclear, war. To reinforce this point it can be noted that operational military experience is increasingly remote and/or irrelevant to any attempt to assess the character and consequences of a major clash in the centre of Europe.

The existentialist case has been further strengthened by the literature on the command and control problems associated with nuclear forces. Whatever the specific intent of contributions to this literature, the net effect has been to encourage the view that even moving into a period of tension carries with it some risk of inadvertent nuclear war.

There is a danger of taking these arguments too far. As with the misperception literature, which can soon lead one to assume that all diplomatic signals inevitably miss their targets and that threats and reassurance are figments of the recipients' imagination, it now tends to be assumed that any crisis or minor clash of arms will immediately spiral out of control and lead inexorably to a nuclear holocaust.

So strong is this view that many of those sympathetic to existentialism still believe that the risk of nuclear war is unacceptably high and can be reduced further without any serious impact on deterrence. It plays on uncertainty and the possibility of things getting out of control, but this is in itself a discomforting prospect when contemplating conflicts which might otherwise be settled without nuclear use. Existential deterrence depends on a residual risk, yet much of the energy in contemporary arms control has been put into ways to eliminate this risk.

The only certain way of removing this risk would be to remove all the weapons under a scheme of general and complete nuclear disarmament, and this raises all the problems of verification and enforcement, and the possibility of stockpiles being recreated during the course of a conventional conflict. Short of this, another obvious way of reducing risk is to remove the weapons from the most likely points of confrontation. But although this might be done as an act of control the consequence is to redefine strategic interests.

In practice, the nuclear element in strategy involves attaching the risk of massive nuclear exchanges to any challenge to vital interests. For a nuclear power to detach nuclear risk from an area of potential challenge might be taken as a redefinition of vital interests, unless it can be shown that those vital interests no longer depend on a nuclear guarantee. Thus, the most important political message conveyed by the external deployment of the weapons is that it identifies certain allies as ones for which a nuclear power is prepared to run the greatest of risks. The means by which existential deterrence can be shown to *exist* is by a close link between the instruments of deterrence and that which is being protected.

Throughout the recent decades of comparative political stability this has made nuclear strategy inactive, in that alliance commitments have not been redefined. The active period concluded in the early 1960s, by which time the superpowers had developed reasonably clear understandings of the extent of each other's vital interests. There was a blip on the screen at the end of the 1970s and early 1980s as a result of the apparent change in the rules following on the Soviet intervention in Afghanistan. As President Carter declared the Gulf area a vital US interest it was implicit that this added an extra risk of nuclear war to any superpower confrontation in the area.

In general the key question has been less the extension of vital interests than their contraction. The alliance system of the 1950s was created at a time when policy-makers East and West found it almost impossible to view international affairs in terms other than the conflict between the two blocs, and were concerned with building up the strength of the two blocs. The pronounced nuclear bias in US strategy reflected confidence – until well into the decade – in US nuclear superiority.

This alliance structure did not survive. In Europe there was a logic to the NATO–WTO division that did not apply elsewhere. The complexities of regional politics underlined the unwisdom of linking nuclear risks too closely with local turbulence, while potential allies saw clearly the limits of external support. The US nuclear guarantee is now largely confined to Europe, with the exception of Japan and South Korea (where it may not last for long) and, implicitly and very loosely, Israel. The limits to the Soviet nuclear guarantee were one of the factors making for the break-up of the Sino-Soviet bloc.

Within NATO the question of nuclear strategy revolved around what was required to reinforce confidence in Europe that it was still seen as a vital interest in Washington. There was concern that US commitments will be redefined through inadvertence, by not bothering to ensure that key nuclear systems are replaced at obsolescence, and so provide a physical 'coupling' between the US 'strategic' nuclear systems and the defence of Europe. The debates on various systems – ERW, INF, Lance – provided an opportunity for the US to reaffirm its commitment and insist that it did *not* depend on these particular systems. In the end West Europeans had little choice but to accept the symbols of commitment offered by the US however credible it honestly found them. The association of nuclear risk with European security could be represented by US conventional forces or even persistent declarations that Europe was a vital interest.

The reason why this was possible was because few expected – as time went on – that push would ever actually come to shove. If it did come to shove then it was by no means clear that *any* of the devices employed to 'couple' the two parts of the Atlantic would withstand the reassertions in the United States of the most obvious national interest of all – the avoidance of nuclear devastation.

This became a very familiar set of debates and eventually there was little new to be said. By and large the continuing discussion on deployment decisions was interesting as political commentary but it prompted little original conceptual thinking.

THE NEW CONTEXT

We are now at a historic turning point in postwar international affairs as European politics breaks out of the bipolar mould. Up until recently the predominant view within NATO has been that the established arrangements must be maintained while keeping a firm eye on developments on the other side. This position is becoming untenable as developments in the erstwhile Soviet camp take us well beyond what could ever be dismissed as some cosmetic ploy designed to lull the West into a false sense of security or even a genuine policy shift that might none the less be 'reversible'. Even a new hardline Soviet leadership could not return to the 'good old days' of stagnation.

We now have great diversity within Eastern Europe, with a far looser arrangement within the Warsaw Pact (if it survives at all) and severe challenges to the Soviet state itself with the Baltic Republics already seeking greater autonomy. In practice there is only one superpower – and the United States is becoming more particular in its concerns as the spectre of a global Soviet threat recedes. German unity is not only 'thinkable' but imminent. Arms control has moved forward at a spectacular pace but still risks being overtaken by events.

All this is removing the framework within which nuclear strategy was developed and implemented. If we are seeing the end of the NATO/Warsaw Pact confrontation then a whole range of issues that up until recently seemed absolutely criti-cal turn out to be of purely historical interest. Of course the disposition and structure of nuclear forces in Europe reflect the old order and until they are removed by one side then the other has a case for sustaining its position. But there is clearly not going to be very active modernization. Shortrange nuclear forces in particular appear as being completely anachronistic. One cannot imagine a West German agreeing to new systems that can threaten Walesa and Havel, never mind its provinces-in-waiting to the East. The strategic calculation that produced flexible response and the requirement of nuclear first use is no longer valid.

Residual nuclear arsenals still provide a very general reminder of the risk of conflict, but in the future they might barely be related to any particular conflict. Because nuclear weapons cannot be disinvented and because the number of nuclear powers may still grow in the future then the existing nuclear powers will wish to hold on to a portion of their existing stocks. The emphasis will be on long-range retaliatory capabilities rather than short-range warfighting.

If we are moving into a situation where states are redefining their vital interests what role will nuclear weapons play in this process? On recent experience the answer would be 'very little' in that the nuclear powers are likely to use the opportunity to either reduce their commitments or else argue that existing commitments can now be sustained at a lower – and possibly non-nuclear – level of risk. However this process itself can be difficult. Simply by raising long-dormant issues it can force a state to look anew at the nature of its security interests.

To take one example close to home, Britain's nuclear commitment to West Germany, which is quite substantial, made sense largely in the context of the American commitment. Reappraise the American commitment and questions which have never even appeared on either the British or German political agenda are pushed to the fore. An American withdrawal creates a case both for a British withdrawal and for giving British nuclear forces in Germany a higher profile at a time when there would be seen to be an urgent need to hold Western Europe together. But then what possible role can there be for nuclear forces in Germany if all stationed forces are preparing to leave? Then again, if Germany is going to be a major player in Europe, perhaps one day offering security guarantees of its own to some of the smaller European states, it will still want some nuclear cover. Either it can 'go nuclear' itself which might well make its neighbours nervous or else it can draw on the nuclear capability of another. It is not inconceivable that the British and French together could play this role.

The various links between nuclear deployments and the evolving structure of European security are going to provide a number of intriguing questions for the future. Consider just one awkward issue: if the Soviet Union begins to disintegrate who will control the nuclear weapons? What happens if some are controlled by one of the old republics and some by another, and the two become antagonistic to each other?

So post-cold war Europe could face new and disturbing elements of instability. So far the record of managing the processes of political transformation, which had been assumed in anticipation to be fraught with danger, is in itself encouraging. The objective generally in the current situation should be to keep the military aspects of European relations well to the background in the hope that it will make it easier to contain the effects of any future disturbance. The general objective should be to marginalize nuclear weapons.

The decline of the Cold War has been responsible for a number of generally benign developments outside Europe. This has been coincident with a process of sheer exhaustion in some of the familiar conflicts in the Third World, from the Iran–Iraq war to Afghanistan.

This has all encouraged an optimistic mood. But this has to be put side by side with the use of missiles in the Iran–Iraq war, the proliferation of chemical weapons and evidence of a number of states prepared to go nuclear. There are already some extremely complex interactions between nuclear and chemical threats (for example between Israel and Iraq) and these could expand, especially if the superpowers judge that it is no longer prudent to offer security guarantees of their own.

It is by no means inevitable that we will see a resurgence of interstate tension and violence or that if we do nuclear weapons will be judged all that relevant. But the weapons remain as instruments of strategy, and before we assume that they no longer serve any strategic purposes we need to understand better than we do at the moment the sort of strategic purposes that might arise in the post-Cold-War political environment.

Thus the context in which the nuclear element in strategy will need to be developed in the future is still evolving. A final question is whether classical strategy has been permanently strengthened by the intellectual legacy from the years in which nuclear weapons loomed much larger. Many of the concepts developed under the general heading of nuclear strategy – such as deterrence, escalation or such themes as the use of threats in bargaining and the role of uncertainty – are now regularly applied to conventional strategy and non-European conflicts. The care required in their future application results not so much from the connection with the ultimate horror of nuclear war, but with the uncomplicated bipolar world which simplified matters for the original conceptualizers that is so different from the extremely complex world into which we are now moving.

NOTE

1 Colin Gray has popularized this phrase (Gray, 1982, ch. 4), but it was first used by John Garnett in 1970 (Garnett, 1970, introduction, p. 24).

REFERENCES

Brodie, Bernard (1955), 'Strategy hits a dead-end', *Harpers*, October.

Bundy, McGeorge (1983), 'The bishops and the bomb', *New York Review*, 16 June.

Freedman, Lawrence (1979), 'Has strategy reached a dead-end?, *Futures*.

Freedman, Lawrence (1988), 'I exist: therefore I deter?', *International Security*, Summer, pp. 177–95.

Garnett, John (1970), *Theories of Peace and Security: A Reader in Contemporary Strategic Thought* (London: Macmillan).

Gray, Colin (1982), *Strategic Studies and Public Policy: The American Experience* (Lexington: Kentucky University Press).

Howard, Michael (1970), 'The classical strategists', in *Studies in War and Peace* (London: Temple Smith), pp. 154–83.

Huth, Paul, and Russett, Bruce (1988), 'Deterrence failure and crisis escalation', *International Studies Quarterly* vol. 32, no. 1 (March).

Lebow, Richard Ned, and Stein, Janice Gross (1987), 'Beyond deterrence', *Journal of Social Issues* vol. 43, no. 4, pp. 29–45.

Schlesinger, Secretary of Defense James R. (1975), *Annual Defense Department Report, FY 1976 and FY 1977* (Washington, DC: US GPO).

4

The decline of nuclear diplomacy

ERIC HERRING

Bernard Brodie is most widely known for the following statement made in 1946 regarding the impact of nuclear weapons on
international politics: 'Thus far the chief purpose of our military
establishment has been to win wars. From now on its chief purpose
must be to avert them. It can have almost no other purpose' (1946,
p. 76). Bodie's qualifier 'almost' and his reference to the avoidance
of war being the 'chief' rather than the sole purpose of a military
establishment is not normally noted. Later in the same chapter
of *The Absolute Weapon*, he suggests another purpose for which
nuclear weapons may be used:

> Hitler made a good many bloodless gains by mere blackmail,
> in which he relied heavily on the too obvious horror of modern
> war among the great nations which might have opposed him
> earlier. A comparable nuclear kind of blackmail in the future
> may actually find its encouragement in the existence of the
> atomic bomb. Horror of its implications is not likely to be
> spread evenly, at least not in the form of overt expression.
> The result may be a series of *faits accomplis* eventuating in
> that final deterioration of international affairs in which war,
> however terrible, can no longer be avoided. (1946, p. 85)

Over forty years later these fearful developments have not come
to pass. Instead, since the 1950s there has been a steady decline in

what will be called 'nuclear diplomacy' (in contrast to the more pejorative and emotive phrase 'nuclear blackmail'). This involves the threat to use nuclear weapons in order to influence the outcome of a crisis. The threat may be to initiate a nuclear attack deliberately, or it may be to escalate the crisis with the danger that control may somehow be lost and nuclear war begun.

The United States has routinely deployed and redeployed naval and air forces abroad equipped with nuclear weapons (Leitenberg, 1980). This has also been done. by the Soviet Union to a more limited extent. Movements which were not designed to influence crisis behaviour have not been categorized here as nuclear threats. Nikita Khrushchev issued many warnings between 1956 and 1961 that countries which had United States nuclear forces on their territory were certain to be completely destroyed in the event of a nuclear war. While Khrushchev sought to intimidate those countries, his threats-cum-warnings did not usually become the subject of crisis bargaining.

Twenty-one nuclear threats have been issued by the superpowers in order to influence bargaining in seventeen crises. These cases include the threats issued by the United States regarding Berlin in 1948, 1958 and 1961; Korea in 1950 and 1953; Guatemala in 1954; the Taiwan Straits in 1955 and 1958; Suez in 1956; Lebanon in 1958; Cuba in 1962; Vietnam in 1969; the Indo-Pakistan War in 1971; the Middle East in 1973; and the Persian Gulf in 1980. The Soviet Union issued nuclear threats regarding Suez in 1956; the Taiwan Straits in 1958; Berlin in 1958 and 1961; Cuba in 1960; and China in 1969.

The general character of these nuclear threats as indicated in the scholarly literature can only be noted in summary form here (Betts, 1987; Bundy, 1988; Fukuyama, 1981). Most nuclear threats were not very influential and were never put in terms of a clear-cut ultimatum. When issued, they were often intended as indicators of more general resolve, support for an ally, or disapproval of an adversary's actions. They were even used as a means of looking tough once the outcome of a crisis was already apparent. In spite of their vagueness, these threats should not simply be dismissed as bluffs because the attitude of decision-makers towards nuclear weapons has been one of essential ambivalence. From the historical record it appears that they did not decide what they would do if their demands were not met. And even if they were not inclined towards nuclear punishment, making a nuclear threat risks escalation which the threatener only partly controls.

The striking decline in the use of nuclear threats has been brought about by a number of mutually reinforcing factors. Decision-makers have increasingly found nuclear threats to be ineffective, politically costly, and irrelevant to the kinds of issue and crises which they face.

THE ABSENCE OF
SEVERE CRISES INVOLVING
THE SUPERPOWERS

The decline in the use of nuclear threats has been caused in part by the absence of severe crises involving the superpowers. The growth of nuclear arsenals has brought about a significant degree of caution on their part. This caution has not been equally present on both sides at all times, and conflicts of interest have induced both to take risks. However, other factors have helped to reduce the frequency and severity of these conflicts of interest.

First, both superpowers now seem to be essentially oriented to the status quo with regard to territorial control. Although the Soviets have often been identified with revisionism and the United States with the defence of the status quo, in practice each has been on both sides of the fence. For example, the Soviets have sought to defend the status quo in Eastern Europe while the United States attempted rollback in North Korea in the 1950s and in Nicaragua and elsewhere under the Reagan doctrine in the 1980s.

Second, some crises were induced to a great extent by uncertainty and disagreement as to what constituted the 'status quo'. Up to 1962, the crises involving nuclear threats were taking place in Europe, the Middle East, the Caribbean and Asia. Since then there have been no crises involving nuclear threats in Europe or the Caribbean. The crises over Berlin in 1948 and 1958–61 and over Cuba in 1962 led to the clarification of the status quo in these areas, at least in terms of the basic role of the superpowers.

Third, since 1973 there has been a change in the kinds of crises in which the superpowers have been involved. Territorial conquest is not the main concern of the superpowers, and problems such as international debt are not seen as amenable to influence by nuclear threats.

Fourth, the superpowers have become less willing to intervene militarily in Third World crises due to their recent unpleasant experiences. The United States failed in Vietnam in that the country soon fell under complete communist control after the United States' withdrawal. The Soviet intervention in Afghanistan was at best a partial and uncertain success. The government of President Najibullah is showing some signs of being able to retain power, but it may still fail, and much of the country remains under the control of the rebels.

It follows from this analysis that in future crises between the superpowers, or between a superpower and a third party, nuclear threats are unlikely to play a role. Nevertheless, despite this absence of crises involving nuclear threat in recent years, the potential remains for their use where actors prepared to challenge a nuclear power are territorially revisionist, where the status quo is not clear, and where the military instrument is seen as a useful tool in conflicts of interest.

MUTUAL VULNERABILITY AND STRATEGIC PARITY

The arrival of mutual vulnerability and strategic parity has discouraged the use of nuclear threats by the superpowers. The arrival of nuclear parity is not an event which suddenly took place one day in the early 1970s. Instead, the superpower nuclear balance developed in stages. Khrushchev's nuclear bluster was based on a pretence of nuclear superiority. Once the limitations of the Soviet nuclear arsenal were exposed, Khrushchev had the wind taken out of his sails. Richard Betts (1982; 1987) concludes that long before the arrival of parity in the 1970s, Soviet nuclear capabilities in the 1950s were making United States decision-makers more cautious. However, Betts shows that they took some comfort in being able to inflict higher casualties on the Soviet Union and destroy a higher proportion of Soviet stategic nuclear capabilities in comparison to what the Soviets could do to the United States.

A leading Soviet commentator, Genrikh Trofimenko of the Institute of US and Canada Studies of the USSR Academy of

Sciences, takes a similar position to that of Betts in arguing that the confidence American leaders had in nuclear threats declined gradually as the nuclear balance evolved. It is conventional wisdom among Soviet commentators that the United States has been restrained primarily by the Soviet attainment of nuclear parity. In the words of Politburo–member Alexander Yakovlev, 'The Soviet Union achieved strategic parity with the United States, which made a course of confrontation with the Soviet Union senseless' (1985, p. 375). Trofimenko does not take a simplistic approach: he also refers to the Vietnam syndrome and the emergence of global, non-military problems as contributing to the shift of the United States away from 'confrontation'. He explains the lack of United States success with nuclear threats before parity by saying that it was never able to develop a first-strike capability in which United States leaders had confidence. Furthermore, he argues that Kennedy realized that 'American nuclear threats addressed to Moscow could not check worldwide social change because this change was not Moscow-inspired but represented popular uprisings against unbearable living conditions' (1986, p. 96).

Mutual vulnerability reinforced by strategic parity still leaves open the possibility that a nuclear threat can be based on the possibility that one side will somehow lose control of the escalatory process rather than deliberately choose to go to war. This is what Thomas Schelling refers to as the threat which leaves something to chance (1966, pp. 92–125). In contrast, states which lack close ties to a superpower are still vulnerable, at least theoretically, to threats of deliberate nuclear use.

THE POLITICAL COSTS OF NUCLEAR DIPLOMACY

Leaders who resorted to nuclear threats feared nuclear war. However, they also felt the need to use those threats in order to achieve their political objectives. In contrast, observers relatively free of those perceived imperatives – whether allied leaders or the public at home and abroad – placed more of a priority on avoiding nuclear war. The development of enormous nuclear arsenals means that a nuclear war might not simply be a Third World War: it might be a global catastrophe which the majority of the human race might not survive. From this perspective, nuclear threats are unacceptable because they risk global destruction for the sake of what appear to be relatively unimportant objectives.

The hostile public reaction in the United States and in allied countries to the possibility of nuclear *use* under Harry Truman and Dwight Eisenhower was extended after the Cuban missile crisis to include open nuclear *threats*. Richard Nixon found this out with the negative public and allied reaction to his nuclear alert during the Middle East War of October 1973. In the Cuban missile crisis, the Kennedy administration worked hard to line up international opinion against Khrushchev's 'adventurism'. The international reaction to Khrushchev's nuclear bluster was a mixture of condemnation and dismissal from its targets, and contempt from the Chinese who felt that he was both 'adventurist' and yet not resolute enough. Attitudes within the Soviet bloc to Khrushchev's use of nuclear threats remain to be explored.

Statements of willingness to use nuclear weapons in response to nuclear attack are still acceptable only if they do not appear to be linked to crisis bargaining or appear to indicate that nuclear use is actually being considered. Governments usually present the argument that the public should support nuclear deterrence because it will prevent war and because it is unlikely to fail. Rocket-rattling unnerves the public by raising the prospect that nuclear war may happen – the feeling is 'if nuclear deterrence is so stable, why are nuclear threats flying back and forth?'. Furthermore, attitudes towards war are changing. In the 1950s memories of the Second World War were very fresh. These days, the use of a nuclear threat would seem more like a bizarre aberration from the normal course of events.

The fear of escalation has generated both a tradition of nuclear non-use and a taboo on nuclear use. Schelling suggested in 1960 in *The Strategy of Conflict* that there was a tradition of non-use of nuclear weapons – 'a jointly recognized expectation that they may not be used in spite of declaration of readiness, even in spite of tactical advantages in their use' (1980, pp. 260–1). This expectation has continued to the present. Similarly, the taboo may, in the mind of a particular individual, be based on this fear of escalation; on a moral abhorrence of the mass, indiscriminate destruction that would result if even one nuclear weapon is used and no escalation is expected; or on some mix of the two.

In his memoirs, Eisenhower asserted that he was prepared to use nuclear weapons if necessary to get a settlement at the Panmunjom peace talks during the Korean War and that he 'would not be limited by any world-wide gentleman's agreement' (1963, p. 181). This represents an awareness of the tradition and a desire to reject it. The idea of a nuclear taboo was also disliked in the Eisenhower administration. The records of a National Security Council meeting on 31 March 1953, which examined the deadlock in the war, note the following: 'the President and Secretary [of State John Foster] Dulles were in complete agreement that somehow or other the tabu which surrounds the use of atomic weapons would have to be destroyed'. Dulles stated that 'in the present state of world opinion, we could not use an A-bomb, [and] we should make every effort now to dissipate this feeling' (FRUS, 1984, p. 827). It seems that the gap between the decision-makers and the onlookers is closing. There are few decision-makers in the early 1990s who see the taboo as undesirable, and few amongst them who believe that the taboo can be overcome.

THE INEFFECTIVENESS OF NUCLEAR DIPLOMACY

Although there are differences in emphasis, an academic consensus is developing on the ineffectiveness of nuclear threats. The factors discussed above are all perceived to have undermined the value of the nuclear weapon as a diplomatic instrument (Betts, 1987; Bundy, 1988; Halperin, 1988). Outside the academic world, more weight is attached to the importance of nuclear threats in past crises. A number of factors promote this image of the success of nuclear threats. First, the country which has used them has often achieved its basic objectives (but for reasons other than the nuclear threat). Second, the simplicity of the idea is appealing: an enormously powerful weapon must be influential, and non-nuclear states must be 'wide open' to nuclear blackmail. Third, among a number of United States presidents there has been a combination of wishful thinking, a yearning for the good old days, and a desire to look tough. Truman claimed in 1952, falsely it seems, that a nuclear ultimatum forced Stalin to withdraw from Azerbaijan in 1946 (Bundy, 1988, pp. 232–3). Nixon asserted that the nuclear bomb was decisive in reaching a peace settlement over Korea in 1953, in calling Khrushchev's nuclear bluff and preventing Soviet conventional intervention over Suez in 1956, and in making Khrushchev 'back down' over Berlin in 1959 (*Time*, 29 July 1985). In an interview in 1980, Ronald Reagan claimed that nuclear threats could have been useful during the Vietnam War. He also volunteered the opinion that Eisenhower's vague nuclear threats had the following effect: 'it was almost immediately that the North Koreans said let's sit down and have armistice talks and that was when Panmunjom started' (Scheer, 1983, p. 253). These statements do not sit well with the following remarks which he made on 31 March 1983: 'In 1946, when the United States was the only country in the world possessing nuclear weapons, we did not blackmail others with threats to use them . . . Doesn't our record alone refute the charge that we seek superiority, that we represent a threat to peace?' (McNamara, 1987, p. 480). The reminiscences by United States decision-makers regarding the value of nuclear threats in the past have an air of nostalgia about them: they indicate a belief that nuclear threats are not what they used to be. The perception that they have declined in effectiveness has contributed to the decreased frequency of their use. Careful academic research which demonstrates their ineffectiveness may gradually become part of the climate of policy debate and influence future decisions on whether or not to use nuclear threats.

The likelihood of the serious or successful use of nuclear threats is minimal. But there are a number of obstacles to recognition of this.

Fear of nuclear 'blackmail' as a political instrument

The continuing fear of nuclear 'blackmail' is used for a number of political purposes. Reagan used it as an argument in favour of the Strategic Defence Initiative. Conservatives in the United States condemn the Soviet Union for its use of nuclear threats in the past, while liberals condemn United States leaders for their use of nuclear threats. The issue of nuclear blackmail was also central to the case of the Conservative Party and others in Britain against the Labour Party's non-nuclear defence policy (which Labour abandoned in May 1989). There are substantial gains to be made by manipulating concern over this issue, whether or not one shares the concern.

Fear of a ruthless, nuclear-armed opponent

The fear of nuclear blackmail gains its credibility from the fact that nuclear weapons exist. As long as they exist, the possibility that one will be subjected to nuclear threats cannot be ruled out. However unlikely it may be, someone – usually referred to as 'a' Hitler, Gaddaffi, or Ayatollah Khomeini – may buck the trend, and use nuclear threats ruthlessly. Two points can be made briefly. First, people of the kind referred to here are not absolutely unstoppable or undeterrable, and would be affected by many of the factors that have drained nuclear threats of their value. Second, this chapter is about adjusting to the realities of the nuclear age, not about abandoning nuclear weapons, as this will not happen in the foreseeable future. If someone with nuclear weapons *is* totally implacable and is unimpressed by your nuclear capability, then war seems almost unavoidable. And there are no proposals here which would make us worse off in such a situation compared to current strategies.

The lack of a shock to the system?

Robert Jervis, following up on a comment made by Herman Kahn with regard to how world government might emerge, suggests that perhaps a superpower security regime based on reciprocal restraint in pursuit of long-term interests 'could be formed only in the wake of a limited nuclear exchange or the accidental firing of a weapon'. He suggests that, however unlikely, 'it is hard to think of a more plausible shock that could provide the basis for the formation of a regime' (1983, p. 194).

Jervis may be right, but one could just as easily argue that slowly developing mutual confidence is more likely than a shock to produce such a regime. Will it really take a radioactive glow to make us see the light? If a limited nuclear exchange is survived, it may be taken as evidence that nuclear wars can be fought and even won. And the accidental firing of a nuclear weapon may provoke accident-prevention measures in the form of attacks on the nuclear capabilities of other countries.

Some writers believe that the shock has already taken place in the form of the use of nuclear weapons against Japan. Alvin Weinberg refers to the 'sanctification of Hiroshima', that is, 'the elevation of the Hiroshima event to the status of a profoundly mystical event, an event ultimately of the same religious force as biblical events' (1985, p. 34). Weinberg derives his argument from William Pollard who suggests that 'Hiroshima is becoming a myth deeply embedded in the psyche of all peoples on earth . . . the symbol of their conviction that nuclear warfare must never be allowed to occur' (Weinberg, 1985, p. 34). This may be so for some (although 'symbol' or 'event' would be a better word than 'myth') but for many Hiroshima also signifies the effectiveness of nuclear weapons. Whether or not it is true, many believe that the atomic attacks on Japan brought the war to a rapid halt and prevented the loss of millions of lives in the planned invasion of the main Japanese islands. The latest and most prominent example of this kind of thinking is the recent essay by Paul Fussell (1989), the title of which ('Thank God for the atom bomb') also has religious overtones. Furthermore, the religious interpretation put on nuclear weapons by one section of the right wing in the United States is that a nuclear holocaust will be the welcome means by which we reach God's Day of Judgement.

The lack of commitment to common security

The evidence to date suggest that Gorbachev and his supporters are serious about reasonable sufficiency and common security (that is, the view that increases in your own security cannot be attained at the expense of the security of others). The degree to which they will be able to pursue these principles will to a great extent be linked to the nature of the Western response: a 'wait and see' approach is not good enough. Jack Mendelsohn points out that Bush administration officials constantly talk of the need to be 'prudent' (1989, p. 14). Ironically, Western leaders such as George Bush and Margaret Thatcher have shown no enthusiasm for the idea of common security and, indeed, appear to feel threatened by it. They are even uncomfortable with the speed of Soviet unilateral military reductions, although these reductions have increased NATO's ability to provide for its own security *unilaterally*. And even if the Soviet military reductions were reversed, the recent rejection of communist rule in Eastern Europe has surely destroyed whatever remains of WTO capability to develop a coherent strategy for the invasion of Western Europe.

The NATO desire to retain a first-use option

Whereas the Soviet Union and China have both declared that they will never be the first to use nuclear weapons, United States and other NATO leaders continue to refuse to make such a declaration on the grounds that the first-use option is vital to the defence of their interests. During the negotiation of the bilateral Agreement on the Prevention of Nuclear War in 1973, the Soviets proposed a United States–Soviet renunciation of the use of nuclear weapons against each other. In response to questions asked by Henry Kissinger, the Soviets indicated that nuclear weapons could be used by the superpowers in a NATO–WTO war as long as that use was restricted to the soil of their allies. They also suggested that any nuclear use elsewhere should be banned and that 'the two parties "shall prevent" situations whereby actions of third countries might produce a nuclear war' (Kissinger, 1982, p. 274).

The United States rejected this proposal on the grounds that nuclear weapons were vital to NATO defences in the face of Soviet conventional superiority; that the United States wanted to be able to extend the first-use threat to the Middle East and even to the protection of China against the Soviet Union; and that the blunt requirement to prevent escalatory situations smacked of superpower condominium (Kissinger, 1982, pp. 274–5).

What might be done to end United States and NATO dependence on nuclear first use? The first possibility is to change the military balance in Europe so that NATO can defend itself without nuclear weapons. This is a real possibility for the first time due to the combination of NATO's modernization of its conventional forces and the Soviet Union's willingness to undertake unilateral and asymmetrical conventional force reductions. The problem is more difficult outside the European theatre. It is unlikely that the United States will ever field the kind of conventional forces which it would need to intervene in any significant independent way in, for example, the Middle East.

The second, more radical, approach is to reject the idea that first use can compensate for conventional weakness. The leading advocate for this point of view is Robert McNamara. McNamara observes that NATO strategy calls for early use of nuclear weapons in a conventional war with the Soviet Union in Europe, and that the West has 25,000 nuclear warheads ready to be used as part of that plan. His key point is that in spite of the existence of the plans and the weapons, 'no human mind has conceived of how to initiate the use of nuclear weapons with benefit to the initiator' (1987, p. 136). While there are plenty of theories around, none is worth trying because of the risk of escalation.

McNamara went even further in asserting that 'nuclear weapons serve no military purpose whatsoever. They are totally useless – except to deter one's opponent from using them' (1987, p. 139). He has been taken to task for this claim (although not by name) by Albert Carnesale, Joseph S. Nye Jr and Graham T. Allison, who note that 'The proposition that the *only* military purpose of nuclear weapons is to deter the adversary's use of nuclear weapons is gaining acceptance as a new conventional wisdom' (1985, p. 230). They say 'DON'T pretend that nuclear weapons deter only nuclear war' (1985, p. 230). Nuclear weapons can deter conventional war because there is always the possibility of deliberate or accidental nuclear escalation from a conventional conflict. This possibility is likely to influence the calculations of a potential attacker.

Actually, the two positions are reconcilable. There is a difference between the intended and unintended effects of the possession of nuclear weapons. The fact of possession of nuclear weapons may have some deterrent effect on an opponent at lower levels of conflict. McNamara appears to be proposing that the West should not have a *policy* of attempting to exploit this. For many, the idea of delinking conventional and nuclear weapons is not a good one because it will 'make the world safe for conventional war'. However, nuclear peace would not be given up for the certainty of conventional war. In adopting a policy of delinking conventional and nuclear forces, the question is whether or not the gains made in nuclear stability outweigh the possible losses in conventional stability. The irony now is that, as the Soviet Union dismantles what NATO has regarded as Soviet conventional superiority, NATO's main rationale for nuclear weapons such as the Lance missile is shifting from countering that superiority to symbolizing the strategic linkage between the United States and Western Europe.

The impossibility of nuclear strategy

The continuing fear of nuclear threats, the lack of commitment to common security, and the NATO desire to retain a first-use option have in common a basic characteristic, namely the failure to accept the impossiblity of nuclear strategy. Nuclear strategy is impossible because no one can know which nuclear response to a nuclear attack will prevent escalation to total devastation. Lawrence Freedman states near the end of his classic survey of nuclear strategy that 'the position we have now reached is more the antithesis of strategy than its apotheosis – on threats that things will get out of hand, that we may act irrationally'. His conclusion is that 'C'est magnifique, mais c'est ne pas la stratégie' (1981, p.400). Fred Kaplan is similarly damning in his assessment of the failure of nuclear strategists:

> They contrived their options because without them the bomb would appear too starkly as the thing that they had tried to prevent it from being but that it would ultimately become if it ever were used – a device of sheer mayhem, a weapon whose cataclysmic powers no one really had the faintest idea of how to control. The nuclear strategists had come to impose order – but in the end, chaos still prevailed. (1983, p. 391)

Some people have better judgement than others, but no one's judgement will ever be good enough to be the basis of a decision to use nuclear weapons in response to a nuclear attack. This implies the rejection of second, third or any use of nuclear weapons, not merely first use. No amount of cleverness, scenario-drawing, history, psychology or game theory can overcome this problem. It is inherently insoluble as long as uncertainty exists regarding human actions.

How have the main recent surveys of nuclear diplomacy and nuclear war avoidance approached the problem of what to do once the first nuclear warheads have begun to detonate?

Carnesale, Nye and Allison (1985) have much to say on which ideas they do not like in nuclear theory. They oppose a no-first-use declaration, a freeze on strategic arms, anti-ballistic-missile (ABM) defences for cities, launch on warning, a low nuclear threshold, first-strike capabilities, nuclear demonstration shots in Europe and reliance on short-range-theatre nuclear weapons. While they reject mutual assured destruction (MAD), they do not offer an alternative. Once the weapons start flying, they propose that 'war termination' (for conventional as well as nuclear war) should be sought:

> Planning for terminating a nuclear war is a taboo subject. To the left it implies toleration of limited nuclear war; to the right it smacks of surrender. We wish to avoid all nuclear war, but if war should break out, there still may be a chance to avoid total holocaust. If a nuclear war ever occurs, a top priority will be to stop it. (1985, p. 235)

Note that they refer to war termination as 'a' top priority rather than 'the' top priority. This suggests that other priorities must also be kept in mind: presumably this involves not sacrificing those values they hold dear. The further implication is that nuclear war is worth fighting to the degree that the danger of total holocaust can be kept to a tolerably low level. However, they offer no further guidance on this crucial issue.

McNamara's views are similarly opaque. Recall his comment that nuclear weapons are totally useless, except for the deterrence of nuclear attack (1987, p. 139). He argues that the superpowers and the other nuclear powers should adopt minimum deterrence based on MAD, that is, they should negotiate down to a few hundred nuclear weapons each in a force structure able to survive a surprise attack and then inflict unacceptable damage on the attacker (1987, pp. 122–4). However, if nuclear weapons are *only* useful for deterrence, it follows logically that they should not be used for retaliation once deterrence has failed. Is this what he thinks? He does not explain how this is compatible with his view that the United States must have a war plan based on inflicting unacceptable damage in retaliation. McNamara rejects first use for NATO because he cannot see how anything could be gained by it. But he does not explain how *any* nuclear use could be advantageous to NATO. There is a way to deal with these points, but McNamara does not attempt to do so.

The most explicit assessment of these questions has come from McGeorge Bundy (1988, pp. 604–6). He opposes decapitation in order to allow a negotiated end to the war, stresses the need for 'peace without victory', and poses the central question: 'What response or lack of response has the best chance of bringing such a war to an end?' His answer is that the United States should have the capacity to inflict assured destruction on the Soviet Union, but that the United States should respond to a nuclear attack 'at a level more moderate than that of the initial attack'. The idea here is that, in a world of thousands of nuclear weapons, 'a strategy that is visibly *not* one of escalation presents a clear-cut invitation to stop'. This he labels the 'less-than-equal reply'. The targets for this attack should be military and away from population centres. This is very imaginative, and is the least unattractive attempt at nuclear strategy presently on the agenda.

Bundy quotes Reagan as saying 'a nuclear war cannot be won' and indicates his agreement with him. To be exact, Reagan said 'a nuclear war cannot be won and must never be fought'. Yet what Bundy has proposed is still a way of fighting a nuclear war: it is war without victory rather than peace without victory. Bundy does contemplate the possibility of not responding to a nuclear attack:

> It is even conceivable that there could be an attack that should receive no nuclear reply at all. The president who chose not to reply with nuclear weapons to a single limited nuclear strike – a single warhead, perhaps, at a single strictly military target – might well be both wise and brave. It is well to remember that when Kennedy held back from instant reaction to an unauthorised Soviet attack on Rudolph Anderson's U-2, he turned out to be right. (1988, pp. 604–5)

This is the real taboo: not war termination, but the admission that the best thing may be to not respond. Bundy appears to be referring to a deliberate attack as well as unauthorized or accidental launch. Admissions like this are virtually unknown among prominent establishment figures. Another exception is Alexei Arbatov of the Institute for World Economy and International Relations of the USSR Academy of Sciences, who has made the same admission. In a conference presentation in 1988 he expressed the view that the Soviet Union should move, along with the West, towards minimum deterrence. On the question of who or what he would target for a retaliatory strike, he said that 'Nuclear weapons are for deterrence only. If an attack came, there would be no point in retaliating.'

The paradox of nuclear deterrence is that, in order to make nuclear attack less likely, decision-makers issue threats which may have disastrous consequences if they are carried out. No doubt many politicians have decided privately that they would not want to retaliate but have not dared to say so because they believe that the credibility of deterrence rests on the belief that they would retaliate if attacked. In effect, they have had to pretend that the paradox does not really exist and that nuclear strategy is possible. The nuclear warfighting approach springs partly from dissatisfaction with the failure of MAD doctrines to provide an alternative to 'suicide or surrender'. Warfighting doctrines rely on command and control systems and selective targeting to keep a nuclear war under control. However, warfighting doctrines are defeated by the inescapable uncertainty involved in a nuclear conflict.

NUCLEAR STRATEGIZING:
THE DELUSION OF KNOWING
THE UNKNOWABLE

Once nuclear weapons start to be used, escalation may be rapid, total and inevitable or it may be slow, partial and contingent. For any scenario, a counter-scenario can be developed. Yet these opposing positions are put forward with an absurd degree of confidence about what is credible or incredible. This will be referred to as nuclear 'strategizing', that is, the development of nuclear doctrine based on delusions of certainty and of knowing the unknowable. Nuclear strategizing is common to both MAD and warfighting doctrines. Although warfighting theories demand even more rationality, control and predictability than MAD doctrines, the shared tendency to exaggerate what is knowable is more important than what divides them.

The classic argument used by strategizers is that 'If an opponent believes it has an advantage in, say, nuclear warfighting capacity, even though it is illusory, then that becomes a real advantage because the opponent will feel emboldened and will act accordingly. Perceptions are what matter, and we are thus forced to produce weapons which cancel out those perceived advantages.' The rebuttal is simple: tell the opponent that the advantage is illusory, that *your* perceptions are what matter, and that you are therefore not intimidated. This is the kind of advantage that tends to be given to an opponent, not taken by one.

To go beyond the strategizing of the MAD versus warfighting debate, one must accept rather than try to overcome the paradoxical nature of nuclear deterrence. The adequacy of what Bundy (1984) calls 'existential deterrence' should be acknowledged. Existential deterrence is based on the view that 'Deterrence is inherent in what any nuclear power can do if it chooses, and also in the possibility that open warfare may drive one side or both to permit in anger what it would never consider in peace' (Bundy, 1988, pp. 593–4). A few hundred nuclear weapons would be enough to support this new form of minimum deterrence.

In explaining the ideas behind this approach, traditional scenarios need not be elaborated. On the contrary, the basic assumptions of nuclear strategizing must be rejected. No one can know what they would do if deterrence did fail, and leaders should cease to pretend that they do. This makes declaratory doctrine on targeting unnecessary. Leaders can point out that they have a whole range of options available to them, and the kinds of targets selected would depend on the specific circumstances. Uncertainty, keeping the opponent guessing, and refusing to be specific in order to prevent an opponent from being able to calculate risks with any confidence has been an important part of the NATO approach to flexible response. This could be applied to nuclear deterrence generally. As observers of the nuclear scene, academics, ex-policy-makers and other citizens are free to state their preferences, including the preference for non-retaliation. Leaders, for their part, can continue to use the stock formula 'a nuclear war can never be won and must never be fought' while allowing others to draw their own conclusions. Minimum deterrence based on uncertainty can help in de-emphasizing the importance of nuclear weapons in relations between states. The paradox of nuclear deterrence may be inescapable as long as nuclear weapons exist in large numbers but it does not have to occupy centre stage in the relations between states.

CONCLUSION

The use of nuclear threats has declined dramatically because the number and severity of crises involving the superpowers has declined. This in turn was caused by:

- an increase in the willingness of the superpowers to accept the status quo;
- clarification of the status quo in many areas important to the superpowers;
- a shift to crises which are less amenable to influence by military threats;
- a reduction in direct superpower involvement in limited wars;
- the emergence of the mutual vulnerability of the homelands of the superpowers;
- the development of roughly equal superpower nuclear warfighting capabilities;
- growing domestic and international opposition to the use of nuclear threats;
- the tradition of the non-use of nuclear weapons since 1945; and
- the strengthening taboo on the use of nuclear weapons.

Among these factors, the most important is undoubtedly the ability of both superpowers to destroy each other completely even after absorbing a first strike. The fear of nuclear blackmail is rooted in a mindset which is unable to accept the fact that nuclear weapons are too dangerous to be usable. This is the reality, even though decision-makers who realize this feel that they cannot admit it outright. An approach which takes this into account has the invaluable virtue of helping to reduce the danger that a deterrence failure will escalate to global catastrophe. It might also be seen as a recipe for surrender, and might be interpreted as creating opportunities for the exploitation of the fear of nuclear war. Brodie speculated about this possibility in the quotation given at the beginning of this chapter. But there are no risk-free strategies, and with nuclear weapons there are no strategies, only risks.

NOTE

This research was assisted by an award from the Social Science Research Council (SSRC) of an SSRC-MacArthur Fellowship in International Peace and Security.

REFERENCES

Betts, Richard K. (1982), 'Elusive equivalence: the political and military meaning of the nuclear balance', in Samuel P. Huntington (ed.), *The Strategic Imperative: New Policies for American Security* (Cambridge, Mass.: Ballinger), pp. 101–40.

Betts, Richard K. (1987), *Nuclear Blackmail and Nuclear Balance* (Washington, DC: Brookings).

Brodie, Bernard (1946) 'Implications for military policy', in Frederick S. Dunn, Bernard Brodie, Arnold Wolfers, Percy E. Corbett and William T. R. Fox, *The Absolute Weapon: Atomic Power and World Order* (New York: Harcourt, Brace), pp. 70–107.

Bundy, McGeorge (1984), 'Existential deterrence and its consequences', in Douglas Maclean (ed.), *The Security Gamble: Deterrence Dilemmas in the Nuclear Age* (Totowa, NJ: Rowman & Allenheld), pp. 3–13.

Bundy, McGeorge (1988), *Danger and Survival: Choices about the Bomb in the First Fifty Years* (New York: Random House).

Carnesale, Albert, Nye Jr, Joseph S., and Allison, Graham T. (1985), 'An agenda for action', in Graham T. Allison, Albert Carnesale and Joseph S. Nye Jr (eds), *Hawks, Doves and Owls: An Agenda for Avoiding Nuclear War* (New York: Norton), pp. 223–46.

Eisenhower, Dwight D. (1963), *Mandate for Change* (Garden City, NY: Doubleday).

Freedman, Lawrence (1981), *The Evolution of Nuclear Strategy* (New York: St Martin's).

FRUS (*Foreign Relations of the United States*) (1984), *Korea 1952–54*, Vol. 15, Pt 1 (Washington, DC: United States Government Printing Office).

Fukuyama, Francis (1981), 'Nuclear shadowboxing: Soviet intervention threats in the Middle East', *Orbis*, vol. 25, pp. 579–605.

Fussell, Paul (1989), 'Thank God for the atom bomb', *Guardian Weekly*, 5 February, pp. 9–11.

Halperin, Morton H. (1987), *Nuclear Fallacy: Dispelling the Myth of Nuclear Strategy* (Cambridge, Mass.: Ballinger).

Jervis, Robert (1983), 'Security regimes', in Stephen D. Krasner (ed.), *International Regimes* (Ithaca, NY: Cornell University Press), pp. 173–94.

Kaplan, Fred (1983), *The Wizards of Armageddon* (New York: Touchstone).

Kissinger, Henry A. (1982), *Years of Upheaval* (London: Weidenfeld & Nicolson/Michael Joseph).

Leitenberg, Milton (1980), 'Appendix 3: threats of the use of nuclear weapons since World War II: an introductory note', in Asbjorn Eide and Marek Thee (eds), *Problems of Contemporary Militarism* (London: Croom Helm), pp. 388–95.

McNamara, Robert S. (1987), *Blundering into Disaster. Surviving the First Century of the Nuclear Age* (New York: Pantheon).

Mendelsohn, Jack (1989), 'Gorbachev's pre-emptive concession', *Arms Control Today*, vol. 19, no. 2, pp. 10–15.

Scheer, Robert (1983), *With Enough Shovels: Reagan, Bush and Nuclear War* (New York: Vintage).

Schelling, Thomas C. (1966), *Arms and Influence* (New Haven, Conn.: Yale University Press).

Schelling Thomas C. (1980), *The Strategy of Conflict*, 2nd edn (Cambridge, Mass.: Harvard University Press).

Trofimenko, Genrikh (1986), *The US Military Doctrine* (Moscow: Progress).

Weinberg, Alvin M. (1985), 'The sanctification of Hiroshima', *Bulletin of the Atomic Scientists*, vol. 41, no. 11, p. 34.

Yakovlev, Alexander (1985), *On the Edge of an Abyss: From Truman to Reagan. The Doctrines and Realities of the Nuclear Age* (Moscow: Progress).

5

Disarmament and arms control: A new beginning?

JANE M. O. SHARP

INTRODUCTION

For most of the twentieth century, the effort to impose limits on military forces via international agreements has been a sterile and frustrating business. At the Hague Convention in 1897, the League of Nations and the Naval Disarmament conferences in the 1930s, the United Nations conferences in the aftermath of the Second World War, the bilateral and multilateral efforts to control nuclear and chemical weapons, and the inter-alliance talks on conventional forces, little was achieved beyond codifying some aspect of the status quo which the negotiating parties found acceptable (Madariaga, 1929; Miller, 1984; Tate, 1942; Tuchman, 1967).

Reductions of military forces were almost always unilateral measures, undertaken after wars or political settlements, when the forces in question were manifestly superfluous or obsolete. At best, arms control agreements reflected, and to some extent cemented, the improved relations already achieved between the negotiating partners. At worst, arms control talks exacerbated rather than eased tension and consumed rather than built trust (Carnesale and Haass, 1986; Sharp, 1981–2).

Yet in the latter half of the 1980s East–West arms control diplomacy took on a more dynamic quality with agreements that opened up each side's military force structures to inspection by the other, and involved destruction of the most modern weaponry. Moreover, arms control began to look like a vehicle to accomplish change rather than merely codify the status quo.

This chapter reviews arms control efforts during the 1980s between the USA and the USSR, and between the North Atlantic Treaty Organization (NATO) and the Warsaw Treaty Organization (WTO) to see what has changed, why, and whether the changes will last.

ARMS CONTROL IN THE 1980s:
A MIXED PICTURE

Two success stories: The Stockholm Document and the INF Treaty

The Stockholm Document on Confidence and Security Building Measures signed in September 1986 by the thirty-five states that participate in the Conference on Security and Co-operation in Europe (CSCE), and the bilateral treaty eliminating Soviet and American intermediate and shorter range missiles, the so-called INF treaty, signed in December 1987, both show a marked improvement over the achievements of the previous decade. After ratification of the Strategic Arms Limitation Agreements (The ABM Treaty and SALT I) in 1972, no major arms control agreement was concluded between the two superpowers. A threshold test ban treaty (TTBT), a peaceful nuclear explosions treaty (PNET), and a second strategic arms limitation treaty (SALT II) were all signed in this period but not ratified, in large part because of lack of confidence among Western conservatives that they could be adequately verified.

By contrast, both the Stockholm Document and the INF Treaty provide for on-site inspection and are notable for the co-operative way in which both routine and challenge inspections are being conducted by all parties concerned (Fieldhouse, 1988; Fieldhouse and Krohn, 1989; Griffiths, 1990). The INF Treaty is also notable because it mandates the destruction not of obsolete weapons but of modern technologically sophisticated systems, eliminating all US and Soviet land-based missiles between 500 and 5,000 km range (Dean, 1988).

Pressures on the INF Treaty

Not everyone, however, considered the INF agreement a success. Some Nato leaders argued that loss of cruise and Pershing II missiles undermined NATO's doctrine of flexible response and urged various measures to compensate. These included upgrading NATO's nuclear artillery as well as acquiring new air-to-ground nuclear systems, and a longer range follow-on to the Lance missile (FOTOL). Proposals for a longer range Lance that would bump up against the 1987 INF Treaty limits were particularly unsettling to Chancellor Kohl of West Germany, however, who faced an election in December 1990 and an increasingly anti-nuclear electorate. During 1988 and 1989, whether and how to modernize or to limit NATO's shortrange nuclear forces (SNF) was thus a matter of some dispute in NATO, particularly between Mrs Thatcher (anxious to deploy both a longer range FOTOL and new air-to-ground missiles) and Chancellor Kohl (anxious to negotiate SNF limits).

The MBFR failure and the potential CFE success

The 15-year-old inter-alliance talks on mutual and balanced force reductions in central Europe (MBFR) formally ended in Vienna on 3 February 1989 having failed to reach an agreement. But given that NATO initiated MBFR talks with WTO in the late 1960s precisely to stem the trickle of unilateral NATO reductions on the central front, MBFR was a success of sorts. After all, conventional force levels remained remarkably stable for the duration of the talks. Mikhail Gorbachev's proposals for radical reductions in conventional forces, which first emerged in the spring of 1986, served both as the final nail in the coffin of MBFR and the catalyst for new inter-alliance talks on conventional forces in Europe (CFE). The CFE talks began in March 1989 and cover a wider geographical area, include a greater number of participating states, and tackle a much broader agenda, than MBFR. Other things being equal these extra complications would suggest less prospect of success at CFE than at MBFR. In fact, however, CFE made more progress in its first sixteen months than MBFR made in sixteen years (Sharp, 1990).

Controlling strategic and space weapons: business as usual

Bilateral talks aimed at limiting Soviet and American long range strategic forces (the SALT talks) began in 1969. Two agreements were signed in 1972, one of which expires in 1977, and the other, the ABM treaty, is of unlimited duration. By limiting anti-ballistic missiles, the ABM Treaty codified Soviet and American acceptance of vulnerability to each other's offensive nuclear missiles as the basis of stable deterrence. From 1973 until 1979, the Standing Consultative Commission (SCC), which was established to resolve ambiguities in compliance with the ABM Treaty, served as the bedrock of the US–Soviet arms control regime. Through the Ford and Carter administrations, both the US and the Soviets used the SCC in a co-operative manner to establish common definitions of acceptable behaviour and to ban practices that undercut the ABM treaty provisions. President Jimmy Carter and General Secretary Leonid Brezhnev signed a SALT II treaty in June 1979, but Carter withdrew the treaty from the US Senate ratification process in January 1980 after the Soviet invasion of Afghanistan. Carter's disillusionment with the Soviet Union made bilateral arms control impossible for the rest of his term in the White House.

During the early 1980s, the first Reagan administration adopted a highly confrontational attitude to the Soviet Union in general and to East–West arms control diplomacy in particular. Any ambiguity in treaty compliance was dealt with by confrontational challenge rather than quiet diplomacy; a far cry from the first six years' experience with the SCC. President Reagan resumed bilateral Strategic Arms Reduction Talks (START) in March 1985, but set a higher priority on promoting strategic defences than on limiting offensive strategic weapons. President Reagan sold his Strategic Defense Initiative (SDI) to the American public in March 1983 as a way to eliminate the threat of nuclear missile attack on the continental United States. But defence analysts argued that SDI threatened both the Soviet Union and the NATO allies because it undermined the ten-year understanding, codified in the ABM Treaty, that shared vulnerability was the basis of strategic stability.

The major unresolved issues in the START talks at the end of the Reagan administration were how to limit land mobile intercontinential ballistic missiles (ICBM), whether to limit or ban sea-launched cruise missiles (SLCM), and whether and how to limit space-based defences (Kampelman, 1989). The Soviet Union wanted to retain mobile missiles and to ban SLCMs, the Reagan administration wanted the reverse. The Soviet Union wanted to ban space-based ballistic missile defences, whereas the United States wanted freedom to pursue President Reagan's strategic defence initiative (SDI).

President Bush seemed less committed to SDI than President Reagan, but SDI was a difficult programme for the Bush administration to cut as many Republicans made support for SDI a litmus test of conservative credentials. The US Congress, however, seemed less inclined to appropriate funds for SDI once President Reagan had left the White House. This lack of enthusiasm for SDI in Washington appeared to be one reason why, in September 1989, Foreign Secretary Shevardnadze stopped insisting on a ban on SDI as a precondition to new limits on offensive strategic missiles (USIS, 1989). The Bush administration was not as committed as President Reagan was to the concept of deep cuts in offensive strategic forces, and reversed the Reagan policy to ban mobile missiles, on condition that the Congress appropriate funds for both the new MX missile and the new Midgetman missile (*International Herald Tribune*, 20 September 1989).

The Gorbachev leadership was clearly as anxious during the Bush administration as it was in the Reagan years to cut both sides' strategic forces. One optimistic sign in the summer of 1989 was that the Soviets agreed to the Bush administration's proposals to negotiate a set of verification procedures for START before limitations were actually negotiated. Previously the Soviet Union had always insisted that verification procedures should follow agreed limits. But US delegates argued that a START treaty would be easier to ratify if US senators had already been convinced that verification was adequate. American legislators and scientists had already visited radar and missile sites in the

Soviet Union and cruise missile launchers in the Black Sea to test inspection procedures during 1989 (Vertic, 1989).

Controlling chemical and biological weapons

Multilateral talks on chemical and biological weapons (CBW) have been under way for many years in Geneva. Despite the rhetoric in favour of a complete ban on CBW, however, the Reagan administration's accomplishments in this area were not as impressive as those of preceding administrations. In 1969, President Nixon halted the production of unitary CW (pending the development of binary CW), renounced BW, and destroyed American BW stockpiles. These unilateral actions paved the way for the multilateral Biological Weapons Convention (BWC) in 1972. In 1975 the United States Senate finally ratified the 1925 Geneva Protocol on CBW. No new CW were produced in the United States between 1969 and 1987. It is noteworthy that the moratorium begun by President Nixon was continued by Presidents Ford and Carter, even though President Carter had to resist pressure from the Army Chemical Corps to produce munitions from the binary agents developed during the Nixon and Ford years.

By contrast, the Reagan administration requested funds not only to produce binary CW, but also to research the offensive capabilities of biotechnology. Binaries were rationalized as bargaining chips in the negotiations aimed towards a CW ban, whereas military research and development in biotechnology was deemed necessary to provide an adequate defence against a breakout of the Biological Weapons Convention. The moratorium on production of binaries was kept in effect through the early Reagan years by Congress, but production funds were eventually released in November 1986 when President Reagan signed into law the 1987 Defense Authorization Act (Robinson, 1987).

France also announced plans to produce binary CW in its five-year defence plan in early 1988 and, before the elections in the summer of 1988, insisted on the right to maintain a stockpile of CW even under a CW convention. In a speech to the United Nations on 29 September 1989, however, President Mitterrand reversed the French position on CW stockpiles and further claimed that France did not actually possess CW. This raised eyebrows in the arms control community since earlier French statements had insisted on maintaining a chemical deterrent as long as others possessed one (*Le Monde*, 7 November 1986). It had been widely assumed (and not denied by French authorities) that France maintained several hundred tons of chemical agents for weapons use, having discarded large quantities of old CW stocks in the 1960s (SIPRI, 1987, p. 110). This suggests that the definition of what constitutes a chemical weapon may need to be clarified; for example, whereas a munition filled with chemical agent is manifestly a chemical weapon, some countries might not define chemical agents stored separately from their assigned delivery system as weapons (SIPRI, 1989, p. 107).

A number of other events in the 1980s undermined the prospects for a global ban on CW. Most serious was the fact that, with precious little outcry from the international community, Iraq broke the long-term taboo on chemical warfare, not only against Iran but also against its own Kurdish population. In addition, with assistance from Western chemical companies, several Third World countries appeared to be seeking a chemical weapons capability. The Foreign Trade Law in the FRG was tightened in early 1989 after it became clear that West German firms had helped develop a CW plant in Libya in 1988. But Third World appetites for a chemical deterrent set back prospects for a global CW ban at the Paris CW Conference in January 1989, when several delegates there suggested they could not renounce CW until the nuclear powers renounced their nuclear deterrent.

Soviet and US interest in curbing CW proliferation in the Third World led to more co-operation between Washington and Moscow in pursuit of a chemical warfare convention (CWC). In Wyoming, in September 1989, Secretary of State James A. Baker and Soviet Foreign Secretary Eduard Shevardnadze signed an agreement to conduct pre-treaty inspections of CW production and storage sites in the context of a CWC. On 25 September 1989 at the United Nations President Bush offered to eliminate up to 80 per cent of US CW stocks if the Soviet Union would reduce to equal levels (Bush, 1989). This was a less magnanimous gesture than it first appeared, however, since the US Congress had already mandated the destruction of 90 per cent of old US chemical weapons by 1997 as new binary weapons became available. President Bush did not make any commitment to stop production of binaries although he offered to destroy all US CW when other nations capable of producing CW adhered to a CWC (*Independent* and *Financial Times*, 26 September 1989). Secretary Shevardnadze made a more dramatic offer the following day to destroy all Soviet CW before signing a CWC if the United States would do the same (Shevardnadze, 1989).

Strengthening the Biological Weapons Convention (BWC)

The BWC concluded in 1975 bans the development, manufacture, stockpiling and use of biological weapons and toxins, but allows the research and development of similar systems as prophylactics. The BWC provides for review conferences every five years but (unlike the ABM Treaty) does not provide for a consultative process in the case of ambiguous compliance. Hence when anthrax broke out in the Sverdlosk region of the Soviet Union in 1979 there was no mechanism through which the United States could challenge the Soviet Union to explain what seemed to be a treaty violation. The Sverdlosk incident was clumsily handled by both Soviet and US authorities and in 1982 a UN resolution called on the signatories to the BWC to call a conference to establish effective compliance procedures. The Soviet Union voted against the resolution and the recommended conference was not convened. Between the 1980 and the 1986 review conferences the dispute about Sverdlosk continued to fester. In addition, allegations about the use of 'yellow rain' toxins in South-East Asia and Afghanistan further undermined confidence in the BWC, as did the quantum leap in biotechnology research and development; 500 biotechnology firms registered in 1986 in the United States alone.

Soviet attitudes changed once Gorbachev had taken over the leadership. At the 1986 BWC Review Conference, for example, the Soviet Union reversed its earlier objection to adding a protocol to strengthen the compliance mechanism, and the Final Declaration of the conference provided for more transparency and information exchange about scientific research in the biological area. Twenty-five of the 111 signatories to the BWC exchanged information during 1988 (SIPRI Yearbooks 1987; 1988; 1989). In addition, in 1988, Soviet scientists presented material to the American Academy of Arts and Sciences to demonstrate that the outbreak of anthrax near Sverdlosk in 1979 had been due to natural causes (Meselson,1988).

Imposing limits on nuclear testing

Multilateral talks aimed at a ban on nuclear testing continued through the 1980s without result in the form of an agreement. Nevertheless, consistent with their approach to START and a CWC, in September 1989 the Soviet Union signed an agreement with the United States to allow on-site verification procedures. The most encouraging sign of Soviet interest in a complete test ban, however, was the moratorium on Soviet testing imposed by Mikhail Gorbachev from August 1985 until February 1987. The other nuclear powers did not follow suit, claiming the need to modernize their nuclear arsenals. In November 1986, however, parliamentarians in many of the non-nuclear powers, under the auspices of Parliamentarians for Global Action, invoked Article 11 of the 1963 Limited Test Ban Treaty to convene an Amendment Conference to convert the LTB into a comprehensive ban. By September 1989, fifty-four signatory states had signed the request for such a conference to the UN Secretary General (Hardenburgh, 1989).

Curbing nuclear proliferation

Continued testing by the nuclear powers through the 1980s undermined the Nuclear Non-Proliferation Treaty (NPT), which was up for review in 1990. Nuclear 'threshold' countries grew increasingly impatient with calls from the nuclear powers for others to renounce a weapons capability as they continued to modernize their own arsenals (Simpson, 1989). For their part the nuclear powers grew increasingly alarmed by the number (more than twenty) of developing countries that were acquiring a ballistic missile capability that might serve as delivery vehicles for nuclear or chemical munitions. Seven developed countries (UK, Canada, FRG, France, Italy, Japan and the United States) established a Missile Technology Control Regime in 1987 designed to curb the export of ballistic missile technology (SIPRI, 1989; IISS, 1989). As with the Nuclear Non-Proliferation Treaty regime, however, this was another example of the haves imposing limits on the have-nots and is unlikely to be effective in curbing Third World appetites for the latest weapons technology.

DETERMINANTS OF SUCCESS OR FAILURE

Previous experience shows that a successful arms control agreement has to run the gauntlet of a wide range of political, military and technological impediments. These include the need to overcome doubts not only from sceptics in the military and political leadership in each party to the treaty, but also the anxieties of allies who may feel dependent on the forces being limited. Doubts may arise about the advisability of the limits being imposed, the feasibility of verifying compliance with the agreement, and the need to compensate for loss of capability in one category of force with extra strength elsewhere.

Of the factors that effect the outcome of arms control talks the three most important are: first, the political climate between the main protagonists, including the image each has of the other, the recent history of interaction between them and the personalities of key leaders; second, the distribution of power between the parties, not only military but also economic and political; and third, the political relations within each party, and between each party and its alliance partners.

The political climate

Rarely have arms agreements done more than codify some aspect of the status quo. This has usually meant agreements that set numerically equal ceilings on selected categories of forces. Traditionally arms control and disarmament agreements codified recently achieved stability after conflict or recently achieved parity after arms races. Before the nuclear era, the 1817 Rush–Bagot agreement demilitarized the Great Lakes after the war of 1812; the Treaty of Versailles demilitarized Germany after the First World War; and 1922 Washington Naval Treaty codified American achievement of naval parity with Britain.

Since 1945, nuclear arms control diplomacy has been a means of managing East-West competition rather than a means to reduce arms. SALT I codified the achievement of Soviet–American strategic parity; and the NPT was an attempt by the nuclear weapons club to limit the nuclear powers to those that had tested nuclear weapons by 1967. The 1987 INF agreement was thus outside the normal pattern of agreements in that it created a new balance – of zero – because the side that was superior was willing to level down to parity.

Political attitudes and arms control possibilities

In Eastern and Western governments alike at least three attitudes compete for priority among foreign and defence policy makers: the confrontational, the competitive and the co-operative (Sharp, 1989a).

Those with confrontational attitudes assume long-term continuation of the Cold War, see alliance cohesion in terms of standing firm against the enemy, and view East–West arms control as a dangerous letting down of the guard.

Those with competitive attitudes see the other side as potential security partners as well as potential adversaries. They see NATO and the WTO as the best structures on which to build a stable East-West relationship in Europe and elsewhere. They feel the division of Europe should not be overcome as much as made more tolerable. Arms control is seen primarily as a way to maintain the status quo, to manage the competition and make defence procurement on each side more predictable and less threatening between two different political and socio-economic systems. When states enter into negotiations and adopt confrontational or competitive bargaining tactics, force levels are more likely to rise than fall as each side fears the other gaining an advantage and seeks to level up to parity in all those force categories in which it is behind.

Those with co-operative attitudes tend to be impatient with the traditional pace of arms control diplomacy and to look for unilateral initiatives to accelerate the process of building down the military confrontation, especially in Central Europe. These attitudes reflect a more utopian vision of international relations, in which détente can lead to entente and eventually a healing of the East–West divide. Co-operative leaders in Europe tend to favour moving beyond the current adversarial bloc structure, and to build a new pan-European collective security system based on the thirty-five nation CSCE process.

Gorbachev's co-operative approach to arms control

Through the 1970s and into the early 1980s competitive tactics prevailed in both the United States and the Soviet Union. Negotiations were conducted on a strictly tit-for-tat basis. Each side inched slowly towards the negotiating position of the other to produce a number of status quo nuclear arms control agreements: SALT I, SALT II, PNET and the TTBT.

As we enter the 1990s, what is new and hopeful is that confrontational and competitive attitudes between East and West are beginning to give way to a spirit of co-operation. When Mikhail Gorbachev assumed the leadership of the Soviet Union in early 1985 he was manifestly impatient with the traditional arms control approach. Fired in part by the need to free resources for the domestic economy, Gorbachev adopted a more enlightened view of international relations than his predecessors; this allowed him to reshape the foreign and defence policy agenda for the Soviet Union, and to change Soviet arms control policies in several important ways.

On several occasions Gorbachev and his senior colleagues have criticized the offensive and confrontational policies and military postures of their predecessors as undermining rather than enhancing Soviet security. The deployment of SS-20 missiles, which encouraged the deployment of new American missiles in Western Europe, and the invasion of Afghanistan which undermined East-West détente and the strategic arms control dialogue in the early 1980s, are often cited as mistakes of the Brezhnev period. Moreoever, Soviet historians are beginning to question even earlier policies and to make an attempt to learn from past mistakes (Dashichev, 1988).

Leonid Brezhnev and his colleagues sought arms control agreements primarily as a way of codifying strategic parity with the United States, a way of demonstrating that the correlation of forces was moving in favour of the socialist camp (Aspaturian, 1980; Sharp, 1984). Mikhail Gorbachev, by contrast, eschews the whole notion of the correlation of forces as a guide to policy. He has no desire to codify the status quo. He wants instead to use arms control diplomacy as a vehicle for change. He wants to reorder priorities from military to civilian spending at home and to move from a competitive to a co-operative relationship with former adversaries (Gorbachev, 1988). Thus he has tried to broaden the East–West arms control agenda to include discussions of military doctrine and the conversion of military industry, as well as the more traditional goals of setting limits on deployed forces (Baklanov, 1989; Belousov, 1989; Finegenov, 1989).

Power differential between the parties

The primary motivation to seek an arms control agreement is not to be left in a militarily disadvantageous position. Saving resources and improving international relations may also be important by-products, but these can more easily be achieved by unilateral cuts. States thus usually initiate international negotiations on arms control when they want to curb the military forces of an adversary. This usually occurs when the status quo is about to change for the worse, for example when an adversary is about to develop or deploy new generations of weaponry beyond the budgetary or technological capability of the state initiating the talks.

Between 1945 and 1985, the Soviet pattern was to respond to each new American innovation in weaponry with an arms control proposal before imitating the new technology (Sharp, 1984).

In the United States it was usually anticipation of a Soviet surge to catch up with the USA that prompted an arms control initiative. As early as 1964, for example, Robert McNamara proposed bilateral talks on strategic arms limitation when it became clear that the Soviets could easily overtake the United States strategic forces if developments proceeded unchecked. Under the old thinking of the Brezhnev regime the Soviet leadership waited until they had caught up with the United States intercontinental delivery capability, in the late 1960s, before agreeing to negotiate limits on their strategic forces.

NATO ministers proposed MBFR in June 1968 to stem unilateral NATO reductions or at least seek matching reductions from the WTO. But talks did not begin until 1973. The Soviets were willing to negotiate nuclear arms control in the late 1960s but were not ready to accept limits on their conventional forces. After NATO changed its doctrine to flexible response in 1967 the

Soviets assumed they must prepare for a protracted non-nuclear conflict in Europe. In their judgement this required enhancing and improving, not reducing, their conventional strength (Amirov *et al.*, 1988; MccGwire, 1987).

By the late 1980s, however, Mikhail Gorbachev saw little point in mindlessly matching NATO capability. On the contrary he believed that his predecessors' pursuit of matching every American innovation in weaponry had been an important factor in the crippling of the Soviet economy. His criterion for Soviet military force requirements was thus 'sufficiency' rather than parity (Gorbachev, 1986).

Impact of the sufficiency criterion on arms control

Accepting sufficiency rather than chasing superiority or parity had two important effects on Soviet arms control policy. It produced a less competitive, more co-operative and conciliatory, attitude towards bargaining (two or three tits for a tat, instead of a rigid tit for tat). Secondly, it allowed for unilateral concessions without any consequent loss of security or bargaining strength.

Gorbachev has thus been able to make bolder concessions to Western positions than previous Soviet leaders felt able to do. This was manifest in Soviet movement towards Western, neutral and non-aligned positions at the Stockholm Conference through 1985 and 1986, towards American positions at the INF talks, and in the many concessions made by the Soviet delegates at the CSCE Review Conference in Vienna from 1986 through 1989, especially on human rights issues, on the mandate for the new talks on conventional forces in Europe (CFE), and on adjustments to WTO positions at CFE during 1989 (Sharp 1989b; 1990).

Gorbachev and his senior military officers admitted repeatedly from 1985 that there were major asymmetries in the forces of NATO and the WTO, and that overall levels should be reduced by the side that is ahead coming down. This was the principle underpinning the 1987 INF agreement when the Soviet Union gave up more systems than did the United States to reach an equal global ceiling of zero in intermediate-range land-based missiles.

At the CFE talks, both sides agreed to seek alliance limits on six categories of force: tanks, artillery, armoured personnel carriers, aircraft, helicopters and manpower, in a zone stretching from the

Atlantic to the Urals (ATTU). At the CFE mandate talks in Vienna during 1987 and 1988, the Soviet Union initially argued for the inclusion of naval, chemical and nuclear forces, so the agreements reached during 1989 represent significant concessions to the Western position.

It was clearly more important to the Soviet leadership to conclude an agreement that reduced excess forces than one that required equal sacrifices on both sides. In this Mikhail Gorbachev was in tune with those civilian analysts who have tried to define minimum levels of forces irrespective of the other side (Sagdeyev; Kokoshin *et al.* 1987; Zhurkin, Karaganov and Kortunov, 1987). By contrast the military leadership still continued to nurture the desire to match US developments if arms control failed to do so. Marshall Akhromeyev told the National Press Club in Washington DC in July 1989, for example, that the Soviet Union would have to deploy something equivalent to the new US Stealth bomber, (*New York Times*, 29 July 1989).

Unilateral actions

On several occasions Gorbachev has cut Soviet military capability unilaterally, moves that are never popular with the military. Marshall Sergei Akhromeyev, for example, claimed that the moratorium on Soviet nuclear testing 'damaged Soviet interests' (*Washington Post*, 31 August 1986). After Mikhail Gorbachev lifted the moratorium there was much speculation about the possibility of another unilateral initiative given the lack of any reciprocal gesture from the other nuclear powers, most Western analysts thought that Mikhail Gorbachev would not risk another failure that might endanger his political position at home. In the Soviet Union, military spokesmen, even those enthusiastic about conventional arms reductions, were uniformly against cutting WTO troops unilaterally (Akhromeyev, 1989). Some civilian analysts made the case for unilateral reductions, especially in those force categories where Soviet officials admitted that the WTO was ahead (Zhurkin, Karaganov and Kortunov, 1987). Ironically, both those arguing for and those arguing against unilateralism invoked the cuts made by Nikita Khrushchev in the late 1950s and early 1960s to bolster their case. Those in favour stressed the economic benefits. Those against stressed the weakening of Soviet defences and the likely damage to military career patterns (*Moscow News*, 8 November 1988).

In the event, Mikhail Gorbachev overrode the objections of his senior military advisers and at the United Nations General Assembly in December 1988 announced unilateral cuts in precisely those forces identified by NATO as the most offensive: combat aircraft, artillery, tanks, infantry fighting vehicles and assault and bridging units (Gorbachev, 1988).

At the Paris Conference on chemical weapons in January 1989, Foreign Minister Eduard Shevardnadze announced that Soviet chemical weapons would be destroyed unilaterally, whether or nor a chemical ban was concluded (Shevardnadze, 1989a). And at the concluding session of the CSCE follow-up meeting in Vienna Shevardnadze announced that Soviet troops scheduled to leave Eastern Europe would also be removing their nuclear weapons. When US Secretary of State James Baker visited Moscow in May 1989, Mikhail Gorbachev said that 500 nuclear warheads would be unilaterally withdrawn from Eastern Europe: 284 missiles warheads, 166 air-dropped bombs and 50 nuclear artillery shells. Eduard Shevardnadze repeated this information in Bonn later in the month. (Shevardnadze, 1989b) In early July, in a speech to the Council of Europe in Strasbourg, Gorbachev said that the Soviet Union was willing to withdraw all nuclear charges from the territory of its allies if the United States would do likewise. At the same time Gorbachev acknowledged the need to reconcile NATO's desire for nuclear protection and Moscow's desire for nuclear disarmament. In an attempt to meet Western concerns Gorbachev proposed a meeting of experts to establish optimum levels to achieve minimal deterrence.

Power differentials and the verification problem

In the 1890s, the Tsar's Finance Minister was anxious to hide Russia's military weakness (Tuchman, 1967). At the League of Nations Disarmament Conference in the early 1930s, however, it was the Western powers, especially in the United States and Britain, which objected to inspection by foreign powers and the Soviet delegate Litvinov who advocated international supervision. At the United Nations talks on disarmament in the late 1940s, however, the Soviet delegates reverted to the Tsarist position, and resisted on-site inspections as intrusive espionage. This position was maintained in effect until the Soviets signed the Stockholm Document in 1986.

As long as the Soviet Union was manifestly inferior to the West, Soviet leaders maintained the traditional attitude to secrecy about military data, and resisted any kind of inspection of Soviet territory. Even satellite reconnaissance was opposed in the early 1960s. This policy began to ease somewhat in the later Brezhnev years with verification by satellite (national technical means) and some data being exchanged in connection with the SALT agreements and the MBFR negotiations.

But it was not until the Gorbachev years that the Soviets provided data outside a legal obligation to do so, or signed an international agreement that permitted on-site inspections of Soviet territory. Data was provided in the context of the INF agreement signed in December 1987, as had been the case at the SALT agreements also. But the Soviet Union also produced data on naval and conventional forces as well as on defence spending, beyond the context of treaty obligations. On 18 October 1988 Deputy Foreign Minister Vladimir Petrovsky provided Soviet naval data to the First Disarmament Committee of the UN General Assembly in New York (Petrovsky, 1988). Official WTO data on NATO and WTO forces in the Atlantic to Urals zone was published in late January 1989 (WTO, 1989). Each alliance focused on different force categories, and even defined tanks and artillery in different ways, so that initially the two sets of data seemed contradictory. Once the counting rules had been straightened out, however, the data sets were not difficult to reconcile (Forsberg *et al.*, 1989).

Mikhail Gorbachev first gave details of the Soviet defence budget on 30 May 1989 in a wide-ranging review of foreign and defence policy (*Guardian*, 31 May 1989). Newly elected Soviet deputies were appalled at the enormity of the figures, but others found the figures too low to be credible and called for more detail and more public debate on military appropriations by the thirty-eight member Committee on Questions of Defence and State Security (*Moscow News*, 10 September 1989). In an interview in *Pravda*, Minister of Defence Dimitry Yazov stated that Soviet military spending for FY 1989 totalled 77,300 million roubles or 15.6 per cent of the state budget. Yazov broke the budget down as follows: 32,600 roubles on equipment, 15,300 million roubles on research and development, 20,200 million on the upkeep of the army and navy, 4,600 million on military construction, 2,300 million on retirement benefits to servicemen, and another 2,300 million on miscellaneous items (*Pravda*, 20 June 1989). Despite widespread scepticism in the Western press, some economists judged the release of Soviet budgetary data a sincere effort to provide information, given that the pricing system still has to be perfected (Deger, 1990).

In September 1989 the Soviet Finance Minister announced that the defence budget would be cut back to 70,800 million, and in mid-December 1989 the new budget breakdown was given as follows: total spending 70,976 million roubles, comprising manpower 31,036.5 million, military research and development 13,154 million, armed forces upkeep 19,323 million, military development and construction 3,715.8 million, pensions 2,444 million, other expenses 1,306.2 million (*Pravda*, 16 December 1989). This represented a cut of 8.2 per cent from the previous year so was in line with an earlier promise by Mikhail Gorbachev to cut back by 14 per cent over two years (*Financial Times*, 26 September 1989). Earlier in the year in testimony before the Joint Economic Committee of the US Congress the CIA had estimated that the withdrawal from Afghanistan, the INF Treaty and the unilateral force cuts announced in December 1988 would account for a one-third to half of the 14 per cent cuts and that the rest would be likely to come from cutbacks in military research, development, testing and evaluation (RDT and E). During 1988, Defence Minister Yazov, Deputy Defence Minister Shabanov and Deputy Foreign Minister Bessmertnykh had all criticized earlier allocations to RDT and E (United States Central Intelligence Agency and Defense Intelligence Agency, 1989).

Other examples of increased transparency were the invitations to Western observers to visit several controversial Soviet radar sites, the Shikany chemical weapons facility in the Lower Volga, the Soviet nuclear test sites at Semipalatinsk, and the Black Sea for an experiment in the detection of nuclear armed missiles on surface ships (Goldansky, 1988; Vertic, 1989). There were also invitations to US congressional delegations to observe the withdrawals of Soviet forces from Eastern Europe and the conversion of military enterprises from military to civilian production (Gorbachev,

1988; US Congress, 1989). *Glasnost* was also apparent in the Moscow-based Group for the Public Monitoring of the Reduction of Soviet Armed Forces and Armaments (GON) (*Krasnaya Zvezda*, 16 May 1989). Finally, the increasingly sophisticated analysis on international security issues emerging from the civilian institutes in Moscow in the late 1980s suggested that Gorbachev was encouraging a serious debate on priorities.

The domestic impediments to arms control

Even the simplest kind of bilateral negotiating forum involves at least five separate sets of negotiations, that between the two main protagonists, between each main protagonist and its domestic special interest groups, and between each main protagonist and its allies.

Prudent military planning and arms control ought to be compatible. In the real world, however, those who make their living in the military or in the defence industries tend to see the practice of arms control as against their interests. Leading an inspection team onto foreign territory to verify an arms control agreement is not regarded as proper soldiering in the same way that leading troops into battle used to be and, while tractors may be more profitable than tanks in the long term, persuading enterprises to convert from defence to civilian production will take time. Traditionally, governments have catered for the interests of the military industrial complex by compensating for limits in one category of force with increases elsewhere (Sharp,1982). The result has been that only very strong heads of state could override domestic impediments to conclude any kind of arms control agreement. Even then, the payments to special interests along the way produced arms control agreements that merely codified the status quo and offended no one (Miller, 1984).

Mikhail Gorbachev is clearly impatient with status quo arms control. Some Western defence analysts emphasized that most of the cuts announced by Gorbachev in the late 1980s were consistent with a military desire for a leaner and more efficient fighting force (Donnelly, 1988b; Herspring, 1989). But Gorbachev also seemed manifestly less willing than his predecessors to tailor Soviet negotiating proposals to the wish lists of his military. On the contrary, some of his proposals, such as parity in manpower, tanks and combat aircraft in the ATTU zone, imply highly asymmetric cuts and acceptance of WTO military inferiority overall. These cuts will also require the need to change military training and doctrine (Hall, 1989). Clearly Gorbachev makes arms control policy from the top down, not to please the military.

Plans for nuclear disarmament announced in Moscow in January 1986, ambitious proposals for conventional arms control in Europe offered in East Berlin in April 1986, the summit meeting with Ronald Reagan in Reykjavik in October 1986, and the announcements of unilateral Soviet force cuts in his speech to the General Assembly in December 1988 were cases in point. NATO leaders who must co-ordinate positions among sixteen governments are understandably not enthusiastic about negotiating arms control agreements at summit meetings. They are particularly nervous about bilateral meetings which negotiate agreements over the heads of the smaller powers. Many West European leaders were especially badly shaken by President Reagan's willingness to bargain away all the United States' ballistic missiles at the 1986 Reykjavik summit (Sharp, 1987).

If Reykjavik made some NATO allies nervous about whether and how American presidents might meet West European interests in future summit meetings with Mikhail Gorbachev, they were more comfortable with the replacing of the old guard in the senior echelons of the Soviet military with new men more sympathetic to arms control. In many cases, younger, presumably more flexible, officers were catapulted to promotion over older and more experienced colleagues (Herspring, 1989).

There was much speculation in the West about the opposition of the 'old guard' to the unilateral moratorium on Soviet nuclear testing imposed by Mikhail Gorbachev from August 1985 to February 1987. Many observers suggested that while nuclear cuts hardly affected military careers Gorbachev would not risk offending senior officers in the Soviet ground forces by making unilateral cuts in conventional forces (Phillips and Sands, 1988). Certainly in the Soviet press it was only non-military analysts who espoused unilateral measures, while the military urged reciprocal moves by both East and West and made negative references to the unilateral cuts made by Nikita Khrushchev (*Moscow News*, 1988).

Marshall Akhromeyev resigned as Soviet Chief of Staff on the same day that Gorbachev announced the unilateral cuts at the

UN, and General Kulikov was replaced as Chief of Staff of WTO forces in early February 1989. Some Western analysts saw these changes as evidence of military unhappiness with the Gorbachev initiative. Once the decision to cut WTO forces unilaterally had been made, however, senior military officers like Marshall Sergei Akhromeyev, Colonel General Vladimir Lobov and Major General Yuri Lebedev, who had all previously opposed unilateral cuts, now rallied round to support the policy. In *Pravda* on 19 December General Lobov claimed that the cuts were 'guided by our new political thinking and by the defensive character of the Soviet military doctrine. In other words we are demonstrating in practice the unity of the political and military technical aspects of the military doctrine of the USSR and the other Warsaw Pact nations' (*Pravda*, 19 December 1988). General Lebedev sought to reassure the military officers about to be demobilized: 'All of them shall have work, a place to live etc. . .We have a detailed programme here which calls for a major organizational effort' (*Krasnaya Zvezda*, 16 December 1988). In an interview with Stanislav Kosterin in *Sovetskaya Rossia*, Marshall Akhromeyev said that the 'decision to reduce our armed forces by 500,000 announced by Mikhail Gorbachev at the United Nations on December 7 is absolutely correct and justified both politically and militarily' (*Moscow News*, February 1989). This contrasts sharply with the military responses to Khrushchev's cuts in the 1960s.

Another indication of Gorbachev's determination to reorder priorities in the domestic economy is the seriousness with which he seems to be trying to convert military plants to the manufacture of civilian goods. In his December 1988 speech he invited foreign observers to inspect such conversions in the Soviet Union and in his speech to the Council of Europe in Strasbourg in July 1989 he called for a meeting of experts from East to West to discuss conversion under the auspices of the Economic Commission for Europe (ECE) based in Geneva. Although progress in this area is slow, there have been important organizational changes designed to facilitate a better integration of civilian and military sectors of the economy, especially in the transfer of managers from successful military production plants to take charge of civilian enterprises. For example, a new Machine Building Bureau is now headed by I. S. Silaev, who formerly headed the defence-related Ministry of Aviation Industry, and a new State Committee for Computer

Technology and Information Services has been created, headed by N. V. Gorshkov, transferred from the Ministry of Radio Industry, formerly a defence facility (Larrabee, 1988).

Some Western firms co-operated in the Soviet conversion process. In the United States, Pepsicola bought Soviet tanks for scrap metal. In the FRG, firms helped the Soviet Union to convert INF launchers into mobile cranes, and in Sweden steel companies bought old Soviet tanks to melt down for car parts and metal piping (*Time*, 4 April 1988; *Sovetskaya Rossia*, 10 February, 1989; *Guardian*, 8 July 1989). While happy to help Soviet defence industries convert to civilian production, Western analysts were apprehensive about how a CFE agreement might affect Western defence industries (Taylor, 1989). In particular, during the summer of 1989 West European members of Nato's high level task force took issue with US proposals for production controls in the context of a CFE verification regime. If controls only applied to the ATTU zone the continental United States and Soviet territory east of the Urals would not be covered, thereby putting European industry at a disadvantage *vis-à-vis* both the United States and the Soviet Union (*Guardian*, 13 September 1989).

The alliance security dilemma and arms control

Allies can and do serve as both the sand and the oil in the gears of arms control. This should come as no surprise since alliance cohesion, which rests largely on the need to pool resources against a common threat, is obviously undermined by arms control agreements that portray the adversary as less threatening.

As Glenn Snyder was the first to show, allies are doomed to oscillate between the fear of entrapment in a conflict not of their own choosing, and fear of abandonment in a crisis (Snyder, 1985; Snyder and Diesing, 1977). Thus, when the superpowers are not on speaking terms or when negotiations in process are going badly, fear of entrapment dominates and the alliance partners are the first to urge conciliation and a return to serious bargaining.

But when the United States and the Soviet Union approach agreement, fear of abandonment overtakes allies anxious about their security guarantees. The West European reaction to the Reykjavik summit in 1986 is a case in point (Sharp, 1987). In the late 1980s, Western governments had to cope with publics who found Mikhail Gorbachev's brand of arms control more appealing than that being sold by the senior NATO governments.

Western governments were unresponsive to the Soviet moratorium on nuclear testing and initially lukewarm in their responses to the promised cuts in WTO conventional forces. Nevertheless, public opinion polls in Western Europe showed that President Gorbachev's unilateral initiatives reduced the perception of a Soviet military threat. Initially, the widely held public view in the West of a more conciliatory Soviet Union did not translate into more co-operative bargaining by Western governments. On the contrary, at the CFE talks NATO asked for deeper Soviet cuts after Gorbachev's December 1988 speech than they had been planning to do before. But in the spring of 1989 public impatience with Western procrastination prompted the Bush administration to seize the initiative in time to present more constructive proposals to the NATO summit in late May 1989.

Bush proposed, and NATO ministers agreed, to include aircraft and manpower in the CFE talks and to accelerate the schedule for reaching a first agreement. The President also managed to tone down the intra-alliance dispute about whether to modernize or limit shortrange nuclear forces by proposing SNF negotiations as soon as a CFE had been concluded and implementation begun (NATO, 1989). While NATO publics applauded President Bush's initiatives, some defence and foreign policy experts complained that the United States was trying to pre-empt all the cuts that might accrue to NATO in a CFE agreement, rather than share them throughout the alliance. Hence the argument became one of burden shedding rather than burden sharing. Others argued that the Bush initiatives were in danger of overloading the arms control systems and that it would have been better to negotiate a first-stage agreement based on NATO's initial proposal to set limits on main battle tanks, armoured personnel carriers and artillery.

WTO intra-alliance relations

Just as East–West arms control triggers fear of abandonment in some NATO governments while East–West tensions trigger fear of entrapment in others, so did the communist governments of Eastern Europe suffer security dilemmas as a result of military integration with the Soviet Union. In general, the prospect of

reductions in stationed Soviet forces triggered fear of abandonment in the more orthodox communist party leaderships of East
Germany and Czechoslovakia, because these two regimes could not
be sustained without a Soviet military presence. Other non-Soviet
WTO countries, particularly Poland and Hungary, welcomed the
prospect of East–West arms control and especially the reduction
of stationed Soviet forces.

There is some evidence to suggest that when the Soviets proposed
withdrawals from Eastern Europe at a WTO meeting in mid-1988
Czechoslovakia and East Germany opposed unilateral cuts but all
the others endorsed the idea, Hungary the most enthusiastically.
After a meeting of WTO defence ministers in Sofia on 17 December
Hungary, Poland, Czechoslovakia, Bulgaria and the GDR all
followed suit with announcements of troop and budget cuts of
their own.

In September 1989 the Hungarian Prime Minister, Miklos
Nemeth, invoked a recent WTO decision that accorded more
autonomy to the East European states, to justify a request
for the removal of half of the Soviet nuclear-capable missiles
(Frogs and Scuds) stationed on Hungarian territory. Nemeth
said that removing the missiles would improve relations with
Hungary's neutral neighbours Austria and Yugoslavia (*Guardian*,
9 September 1989). This begs the question, on which Germany
were the remaining Frogs targeted?

One of the questions that remains unanswered at this writing
is what impact a CFE agreement will have on the multilateral
and bilateral relationships in the WTO. Radical reductions in
Soviet forces, and perhaps their removal altogether from Hungary
and Czechoslovakia, would mean that these forces no longer
served under Soviet command. Will a reduced Soviet presence in
Eastern Europe unleash old rivalries in the region, or will there be
some kind of military co-operation among East European states
analagous to the West European Union? How will the WTO
cope with non-communist member states in its midst? Will the
non-communist states want to become militarily neutral as they
develop market economies and plural political systems or will they
let political and economic reforms evolve under the architecture of
the two military alliances? Soviet Academician Oleg Bogomolov
has suggested that a neutral Hungary would not pose a threat
to Soviet security (*Economist*, 18 February 1989). But would

the Soviet leadership be as sanguine about a neutral Poland or Czechoslovakia?

CONCLUSION

Mikhail Gorbachev's diplomacy accelerated the pace of arms control and disarmament in the second half of the 1980s. He startled Western governments by accepting their most radical proposals for a zero INF agreement, for highly asymmetrical cuts at the CFE talks and for on-site inspections of military facilities in the Soviet Union. Moreover, Gorbachev provided data on military forces and budgets, and made unilateral cuts that helped to build trust and confidence in the Soviet Union as a co-operative security partner rather than a threatening adversary. At the same time, however, the impact of Gorbachev's new thinking, and especially his renunciation of the Brezhnev doctrine of military intervention in other socialist states, unleashed radical changes in Eastern Europe, and a flood of refugees from East to West Germany that put German unification back on the agenda of international politics. Together with unrest in the Soviet republics, these changes suggested a period of instability that could complicate arms control efforts.

The Western response to the new Soviet thinking was mixed. On the left of the political spectrum there was enthusiasm for the new opportunities presented by co-operative Soviet behaviour to achieve radical force reductions and move towards less confrontational security arrangements in Europe. In the political centre the approach was cautious at best, and on the right two tendencies emerged to retard a positive response to Gorbachev. On the one hand there was nostalgia for the certainties of the Cold War as opposed to the turbulence of the new détente (Eagleburger, 1989). And on the other was a triumphalism proclaiming that Gorbachev's conciliatory tactics were due primarily to Western strength, hence the need to maintain coercive pressure on Moscow with competitive military strategies (Fukuyama, 1989; Thatcher, 1989). In the United States the Strategic Defence Initiative and the Maritime Strategy were both designed in part to force the Soviets to compete in technological races they could not possibly win.

This aggressive approach unsettled those European leaders who preferred a more conciliatory attitude towards the Soviet Union. On the other hand, during the October 1986 Reykjavik summit European conservatives were alarmed by President Reagan's unilateralism and what they considered unseemly Soviet–American collusion against the tenets of nuclear deterrence. These anxieties were allayed during the first Bush administration and NATO communiqués in the late 1980s stressed the need to maintain a full spectrum of nuclear forces, albeit at lower levels, regardless of the balance in conventional forces. Nevertheless, NATO governments responded to public criticism of Western complacency in the face of Gorbachev's unilateral initiatives with what appeared to be serious efforts to move forward in a number of arms control forums. In particular President Bush expanded the agenda and accelerated the schedule at the CFE talks. Bush also bowed to pressure from West Germany and, despite opposition from Mrs Thatcher, endorsed negotiations to limit shorter range nuclear forces as soon as a CFE agreement had been concluded.

If Mrs Thatcher proved to be the sand in the gears of NATO arms control diplomacy, in the WTO (at least until late 1989) it was the GDR and Czechoslovakia who wanted to retain the architecture of the Cold War and slow the pace of disarmament, while Poland and Hungary supported the more radical disarmament measures espoused by Gorbachev. By early 1990, of course, the GDR and Czechoslovakia favoured more radical disarmament measures. In the GDR, Gregor Gysi, the new communist party leader (albeit not a member of the government) proposed 50 per cent cuts in the armed forces of both German states, and in Czechoslovakia the foreign minister called for the removal of all Soviet troops by the end of the year.

In sum, despite the new thinking that permeated WTO arms control diplomacy since Gorbachev came to power, the dominant thinking in Western capitals remained damage-limiting rather than dynamic. On the other hand the late 1980s witnessed much political progress outside the arcane realm of arms control negotiations. Democracy began to emerge in Eastern Europe, East–West contacts multiplied in all spheres, individual Western enterprises increased their joint ventures with progressive forces and looked for ways to develop international economic competence in the East. Indeed, some arms control practitioners suggested in late 1989 that political events had made traditional arms control negotiations redundant (Adelman, 1989). The danger for the 1990s might be that traditional arms control policies could hold back progress that might otherwise be expected from the new thinking in political, economic and cultural relations (Freedman, 1989). The lesson for the 1990s seems to be not to overload arms control with grandiose expectations but to reserve the process as the means to codify what had been achieved unilaterally, in particular to make unilateral cuts irreversible and to establish co-operative verification and compliance mechanisms that would defuse the remaining confrontational aspects of NATO–WTO relations and build the foundations for a new pan–European security system.

REFERENCES

Adelman, Kenneth L. (1989), 'In Malta the thinking was old', *International Herald Tribune* 6 December.

Akhromeyev, Sergei (1989), 'Arms control and arms reduction: the agenda ahead', *SIPRI Yearbook 1989* (Oxford: Oxford University Press), pp. 461–74.

Amirov, Oleg, Kishilov, Nikolai, Makarevsky, Vadim, and Usachev, Yuri (1988), 'Conventional war: strategic concepts', in Yevgeny Primakov (ed.), *Disarmament and Security 1987 Yearbook* (Moscow: USSR Academy of Sciences, Institute of World Economy and International Relations), pp. 354–69.

Aspaturian, Vernon (1980), 'Soviet global power and the correlation of forces', *Problems of Communism*, vol. 29, no. 3 (May–June).

Baklanov, Oleg (1989), 'Defence in peaceful offensive', *Government Herald*, no. 17 (Moscow), translation from Novosti Press, 31 August.

Belousov, Igor (1989), 'Goods for people on the military conveyor belt', *Sovestskaya Rossia*, 10 February.

Bush, George (1989), Speech to the United Nations General Assembly, 25 September.

Carnesale, Albert, and Haass, Richard (eds) (1986), *Learning From Experience With Arms Control*. Final Report to the Arms Control and Disarmament Agency (Cambridge, Mass.: J. F. Kennedy School of Government).

Dashichev, Vyacheslav (1988), 'East–West: quest for new relation. On the priorities of the Soviet state's foreign policy', *Literaturnaya Gazeta*, 18 May 1988. reprinted in FBIS–SOV–88–098 20 May.

Dean, Jonathan (1988). 'The INF treaty negotiations', *SIPRI Yearbook 1988* (Oxford: Oxford University Press), pp. 375–94

Deger, Saadet (1990), 'World military expenditure', *SIPRI yearbook 1990* (Oxford: Oxford University Press).

Donnelly, Christopher (1988a), *The Red Banner: The Soviet Military System in Peace and War* (London: Jane's).

Donnelly, Christopher (1988b), *Soviet Approaches to Arms Control*, Bulletin No. 41 (London: Council for Arms Control).

Eagleburger, Lawrence, (1989), Speech to Georgetown University, 13 September.

Fieldhouse, Richard W. (1988), 'Calendar of planned notifiable military activities in 1988 and forecast for 1989, as required by the Stockholm Document', *SIPRI Yearbook 1988*, (Oxford: Oxford University Press), pp. 338–46.

Fieldhouse, Richard W., and Krohn, Axel (1989), 'Implementation of the Stockholm Document and calendar of planned notifiable military activities in 1989 and forecast for 1990', *SIPRI Yearbook 1989* (Oxford: Oxford University Press), pp. 403–15.

Finegenov, Pavel (1989) 'Beating swords into ploughshares', *Pravda*, 15 March.

Forsberg, Randall, *et al.* (1989), *Cutting Conventional Forces* (Brookline, Mass.: Institute for Defense and Disarmament).

Freedman, Lawrence (1989), 'The politics of conventional arms control', *Survival*, vol. 31, no. 5, pp. 387–96.

Fukuyama, Francis (1989) 'The end of history', *The National Interest*, no. 16.

Goldansky, Vitaly (1988), 'Verification deterrence and nuclear explosions', *International Affairs* (Moscow), June.

Gorbachev, Mikhail (1986), Political Report of the CPSU Central Committee to the 27th CSPU Congress, Eng. trans. *Novosti*, Moscow.

Gorbachev, Mikhail (1987), *Perestroika: New Thinking for Our Country and the World* (London: Collins).

Gorbachev, Mikhail (1988), Speech to the United Nations General Assembly, 7 December.

Gorbachev, Mikhail (1989), Speech to the Council of Europe, Strasbourg, 6 July.

Griffiths, Stephen Iwan (1990), 'The implementation of the INF treaty', *SIPRI Yearbook 1990* (Oxford: Oxford University Press).

Hall, Robert C. M. (1989), 'Perestroika and the Soviet armed forces' structural and optical/tactical changes', paper presented at the University of Birmingham, 26 September.

Hardenburgh, Chalmers (1989), *The Arms Control Reporter* (Brookline, Mass.: Institute for Defense and Disarmament).

Herspring, Dale R. (1989), 'The Soviet military and change', *Survival*, vol. 31, no. 4 pp. 321–38.

International Institute of Strategic Studies (IISS) (1989), 'Missile proliferation in the Third World', *Strategic Survey 1988–1989*, pp. 14–25.

Kampelman, Max (1989), 'START: completing the task', *Washington Quarterly*, vol. 12, no. 3, pp. 5–16.

Larrabee, F. Stephen (1988), 'Gorbachev and the Soviet military', *Foreign Affairs*, vol. 66, no. 5.

Lundin, S. Johan (1989), 'Chemical and biological warfare: developments in 1988', *SIPRI Yearbook 1989*, pp. 99–128.

Madariaga, Salvador de (1929), *Disarmament* (New York: Coward McGann & Geoghan).

MccGwire, Michael (1987), *Military Objectives in Soviet Foreign Policy* (Washington, DC: Brookings).

Meselson, Mathew S. (1988), 'The biological weapons convention and the Sverdlosk anthrax outbreak of 1979', *Journal of the Federation of American Scientists* (Public Interest Report), vol. 41, no. 7.

Miller, Stephen E. (1984), 'Politics over promise: the domestic impediments to arms control' *International Security*, vol. 8, no. 4, pp. 67–90.

North Atlantic Treaty Organization (1988), *Conventional Forces in Europe: The Facts* (Brussels: NATO Press Service), November.

North Atlantic Treaty Organization (1989), *A Comprehensive Concept of Arms Control and Disarmament* (Brussels: NATO Information Service), 29–30 May.

Petrovsky, V. F. (1988), 'Multilateral Mechanisms and their role in the military sphere of comprehensive security', Statement to the First Committee of the United Nations General Assembly, 18 October.

Phillips, R. H., and Sands, J. I. (1988), 'Reasonable sufficiency and Soviet conventional defense', *International Security*, vol. 13, no. 2, pp. 164–78.

Ponomarev, Boris (1989), 'From arms-bristling economies to disarmament economies: Gorbachev's UN address guides world to action', *Pravda*, 30 January.

Robinson, Julian Perry (1987), 'Chemical and biological warfare: developments in 1986', *SIPRI Yearbook 1987* (Oxford: Oxford University Press), pp. 97–110.

Sagdeyev, Roald, Kokoshin, Andrei, *et al.* (1987), *Strategic Stability Under the Conditions of Radical Nuclear Arms Reductions* (Moscow: Committee of Soviet Scientists for Peace Against the Nuclear Threat).

Sharp, Jane M. O. (1981–2) 'Re-structuring the SALT dialogue', *International Security*, vol. 6, no. 3, pp. 144–76.

Sharp, Jane M.O. (1984), 'Are the Soviets still interested in arms control?', *World Policy Journal*, vol. 1, no. 4, pp. 814–49.

Sharp, Jane M. O. (1987), 'After Reykjavik: arms control and the allies', *International Affairs*, vol. 63, no. 2, pp. 239–57.

Sharp, Jane M. O. (1989a), 'Belief systems and arms control possibilities', in David Carlton and Carlo Schaerf (eds), *Perspectives on the Arms Race* (London: Macmillan), pp. 114–34.

Sharp, Jane M. O. (1989b), 'Conventional arms control in Europe', *SIPRI Yearbook 1989* (Oxford: Oxford University Press), pp. 369–402.

Sharp, Jane M. O. (1990), 'Negotiations on conventional forces in Europe: development in 1989', *SIPRI Yearbook 1990* (Oxford: Oxford University Press).

Shevardnadze, Eduard (1989a), Speech to the Paris Conference on Chemical Arms Control, 8 January.

Shevardnadze, Eduard (1989b), 'Shevardnadze's press conference in Bonn', *Pravda*, 14 May.

Shevardnadze, Eduard (1989c), Speech to the United Nations General Assembly, 26 September.

Simpson, John (1989), *Nuclear Non-Proliferation: 1990, a Crucial Year?*, Bulletin No. 45 (London: Council for Arms Control).

Snyder, Glenn H. (1984), 'The security dilemma in alliance politics', *World Politics*, vol. 36, no. 4, pp. 461–95.

Snyder, Glenn H., and Diesing, Paul, (1977), *Conflict Among Nations: Bargaining, Decision Making and System Structure in International Crises* (Princeton, NJ: Princeton University Press).

Steel, Jonathan (1989), 'Gorbachev comes clean on Soviet defence bill', *Guardian*, 31 May.

Tate, Merze (1942), *The Disarmament Illusion. The Movement for a Limitation of Armaments to 1907* (New York: Macmillan).

Taylor, Trevor (1989), 'Conventional arms control – a threat to arms procurement?', *The World Today*, col. 45, no. 7, pp. 121–4.

Thatcher, Margaret (1989), Speech to the International Democratic Union, Tokyo, 22 September.

Tuchman, Barbara (1967), *The Proud Tower: A Portrait of the World Before the War* (Toronto: Bantam).

United States Central Intelligence Agency and Defense Intelligence Agency (1989), 'The Soviet economy in 1988: Gorbachev changes course', paper presented to the National Security Subcommittee of the Joint Economic Committee, Washington DC, 14 April.

United States Congress, House Armed Services Committee, 101st Congress, 1st Session (1989), *Status of the Soviet Union's Unilateral Force Reduction and Restructuring of its Forces*, Report of the Committee Delegation to West Berlin, East Germany and the Soviet Union, 6–18 August (Washington DC) 16 October.

United States Information Service (1989), *Baker–Shevardnadze Summit, 25 September* (New York: United States Information Service).

Verification Technology Information Centre (Vertic) (1989), *Trust and Verify*, No. 3.

Warsaw Treaty Organization (WTO), Committee of the Ministers of Defence of the Warsaw Treaty Member States (1989), 'On the relative strength of the armed forces and armaments of the Warsaw Treaty Organization and the North Atlantic Treaty Organization in Europe and Adjacent Water Areas', *Pravda*, 30 January.

Zhurkin, Vitaly, Karaganov, Sergei, and Kortunov, Andrei (1987) 'Reasonable sufficiency: or how to break the vicious circle', *New Times*, 12 October, pp. 13–15.

6

Crisis management: from Cuba to Sarajevo

PHIL WILLIAMS

The concept of crisis management has been a source of considerable controversy between those who regard it as a necessary art in the nuclear age and those who dismiss it as a short-term palliative which fails to deal with the underlying causes of conflict. In a sense both sides are right. Crisis management is preoccupied with the short term and rarely addresses the more fundamental, long-term sources of conflict. On the other hand, it is necessary to survive the short term in order to get to the long term – and crisis management is essential to survival. Crisis prevention is obviously preferable to crisis management, but in circumstances where crises prove unavoidable the only alternative to crisis management is crisis mismanagement. Even so, the popularity of crisis management has undergone various shifts. The first section of this chapter examines these shifts, while the second focuses on the nature and techniques of crisis management. The third part considers the relationship between crisis management and crisis prevention and examines ways in which the capacity for crisis management might be enhanced. The final section offers some concluding observations.

CRISIS MANAGEMENT IN VOGUE

After the Cuban missile crisis the concept of crisis management was very much in vogue: the United States had gone to the brink of war, had made the Soviet Union back down, and had done it in a way that left the decision-makers with a sense not only of achievement but of euphoria. Although this euphoria stemmed partly from relief that nuclear war had been avoided, it encouraged a belief in ideas of management and control, and it provided perhaps the ultimate rationale for the strategy of flexible response that had already been enunciated by the Kennedy administration. US decision-making during the crisis of October 1962 was held up as a supreme example of rational problem-solving, of centralized and effective civilian supervision and control of military operations, and of the irrelevance of domestic politics to critical decisions on war and peace in the nuclear age.

These initial and somewhat self-congratulatory assessments of the handling of the Cuban missile crisis were increasingly challenged on several grounds. The first assault on the idea of Cuba as a textbook example of crisis management came from those who contended that the missile crisis significantly increased the danger of war. Added to the enthusiasm for the use of the military option by some members of the United States decision-making group, the danger of inadvertent war increased considerably during the crisis. The straying of a U-2 over Soviet air space, the shooting down of an American U-2 over Cuba, the enthusiasm and zeal with which the US Navy implemented the quarantine (and especially the extensiveness of its anti-submarine warfare activities) were all events which almost led to a crossing of the line between coercive bargaining and overt violence, and which could have precipitated uncontrollable escalation (Sagan, 1985).

A second challenge came from those who believed that the missile crisis had been resolved peacefully only because there were marked asymmetries in terms of the balance of nuclear power, and balance of conventional power in the Caribbean, and the balance of interests (that is, the stakes at issue). It was this unique constellation of structural factors, all working in the same direction, rather than any particular skill in brinkmanship or crisis bargaining which enabled the United States to emerge triumphant. To draw generalized lessons about crisis management from the events of October 1962 and to expect that the United States could invariably force the Soviet Union to back down, therefore, would be to ignore elements of the missile crisis which are unlikely to be repeated.

The third challenge, and for many critics the most compelling, focused specifically on the assumption that United States decision-making had been rational. This critique had several facets. One strand in the critique was that dissent about the implications of the Soviet installation of missiles in Cuba had effectively been stifled and that diplomatic means of dealing with the problem had been ruled out without proper discussion. This is sometimes attributed to what Irving Janis has termed 'groupthink' – a phenomenon in which group members stifle their doubts in order to retain their positions as valued members of the group (Janis, 1972). It is also attributed to the fact that President Kennedy saw the installation of the missiles as a personal challenge, was unwilling to contemplate a weak response, and prematurely cut off debate on this point. A second and, in some respects, closely related element in the critique of rational decision-making suggests that the United States' response to the emplacement of Soviet missiles in Cuba was motivated by political rather than strategic considerations. It is argued that Kennedy saw the Soviet move as something which could make his administration politically vulnerable in the run up to the mid-term congressional elections and, therefore, took a harder line than considerations of security would have warranted. Thomas Halper has even contended, on the basis of Cuba and other cases, that presidents define situations as crises not because they involve threats to national security but because they challenge presidential images of strength and resolve (Halper, 1971). In this perspective crisis decision-making has more to do with political expediency than with rational assessments of security threats.

This focus on the domestic political dimensions of the crisis was part of a broader challenge to the notion of rational decision-making enunciated most fully by Graham Allison (Allison, 1971). The alternative models of decision-making developed by Allison – the governmental-politics and organizational-process models – denied that decisions could be understood as the outcome of rational calculation by a monolithic government focusing on foreign policy problems. The governmental-politics model replaced the value-maximizing statesman of the rational-actor model with the value-maximizing politician or bureaucrat concerned only with advancing his own position or that of his organization. The organizational-process model suggested that there was little rationality in the process, focusing instead on government actions as the output of large, inflexible organizations operating according to standard operating procedures. Both these alternatives to the rational-actor model helped to explain aspects of United States behaviour in the missile crisis that were otherwise inexplicable. More significantly, they also highlighted the dangers inherent in crisis management. Many of these dangers stemmed from the difficulty of maintaining centralized control over the actions of large organizations charged with the responsibility for the implementation of crisis decisions.

The trend away from the rational-actor model was given further impetus by the insights into the psychological bases of decision-making yielded by the work of analysts such as Alexander George (1980), Robert Jervis (1976) and Richard Ned Lebow (1981). These analysts identified psychological problems and biases that could come to the fore in the stress of crises with potentially disastrous results. The severe stress that is an inevitable concomitant of major confrontations – especially if they are prolonged – can impair the attention and perception of the decision-makers, increase cognitive rigidity, lead to narrow perspectives and tunnel vision, and encourage the belief that one's own options are limited while the adversary has considerable freedom of action (Lebow, 1987, pp, 143–4). Nor is this the only problem. Decision-makers may fail to understand the adversary's dilemmas and problems and ignore the possibility that their own actions helped to trigger the crisis. They may all make 'the fundamental attribution error, a cognitive bias that inclines people to see the actions of others as expressions of basic predispositions while they see essentially the same actions on their own part as responses to situational pressures' (Lebow, 1987, p. 140). In these circumstances, miscalculation of the adversary's resolve could occur all too easily. Evidence for such propositions was found in the reappraisal of the Cuban missile crisis. It was revealed that in October 1962 stress had a debilitating impact on the deliberations of the decision-makers, two of whom became so withdrawn that they ceased to play any serious part in the discussions. Apart from this, stress did not prove overwhelming, but there were several points during the crisis – especially with the shooting down of the U-2 over Cuba – when the initial reaction was emotional and only a further period of reflection prevented as escalatory response. Further evidence of the impact of stress was obtained from the growing variety of historical crises that were subjected to re-examination by contemporary analysts.

THE SECOND WAVE: BACK
TO SARAJEVO

Amongst the studies which added a historical richness to the analysis of crisis that had hitherto been lacking, those by Snyder and Diesing (1977) and by Lebow (1981) stand out. The Snyder and Diesing study was a seminal work, examining international crises in relation to the structure of the international system, bargaining strategies and decision-making. Whereas this study was relatively optimistic in terms of the prospects for crisis management, however, the analyses by Lebow were more pessimistic. Having initially considered twenty-six historical cases covering the period from 1897 to the Middle East War of 1967, Lebow subsequently focused more narrowly on what had gone wrong in July 1914 (Lebow, 1987). This both reflected and accentuated an important trend as the Sarajevo crisis became the dominant influence on a second wave of thinking about crisis management. This second wave emphasized the dangers inherent in crises, and suggested that Cuba had not been as far removed from 1914 as had been thought. Organizational and psychological factors had almost pushed events out of control in October 1962 and only good fortune prevented what had initially been hailed as a superbly managed crisis from turning into a badly mismanaged one.

A closely related feature of the second wave of crisis management was that it was less concerned with the techniques of crisis management and rather more concerned with organizations, force structures and doctrines and how these might affect crisis outcomes. There was a far greater sensitivity for example, to command and control requirements. The work of Paul Bracken, in particular, sensitized analysts to the dangers stemming from the fact that the warning and alert systems of the superpowers had become interlocked (Bracken, 1983). The likely result of this was that, in a crisis, any change in the alert status of either superpower would be detected by the adversary and lead to a response in kind. This in turn could provoke a further increase in the alert status of the first superpower, thereby continuing an escalatory spiral in which the precautionary actions of each side were interpreted by the adversary as preparatory for an attack. 'Such a process, stoked by misperceptions, malevolence, human frailty and political turmoil, could produce a level of threat unlike any we have ever seen and ignite an armed conflict between the superpowers' (Gottfried and Blair, 1988, p. 3). It is not inconceivable that, at some point in this process of reciprocal amplification of threat, pre-emption could begin to appear an attractive option to one or both sides.

The emphasis on Sarajevo – which ran through the second wave – was regarded by some analysts as evidence of a new historical awareness that enriched the analysis of crises and by others as a poor use of history in which 1914 was used simply to demonstrate the dangers of nuclear crises. If Cuba had led to unwarranted optimism about crisis management, Sarajevo had the opposite effect, doing much to discredit theories of crisis management. The difficulty with this was that it threw the baby out with the bath water. Warning against overoptimism about crisis management was one thing; dismissing it as a dangerous illusion was quite another. Yet the debate was not fully joined as very few analysts were prepared to defend crisis management. Consequently, the concept became increasingly unfashionable.

In spite of this trend, the importance of crisis management was underlined by analyses based upon quantitative analyses of crises in the twentieth century. Michael Brecher, Jonathan Wilkenfeld and Sheila Moser (1988) produced a handbook of crises that provided data on 278 international crises and 627 foreign policy crises. Although the scope of what was a massive study went way beyond crisis management, the analysis confirmed the view that crisis management had taken on an urgency in the nuclear age that had not been evident before 1945. The authors noted that in the years up to the end of the Second World War violence was the primary instrument of crisis management when two or more of the great powers were highly involved (Brecher, Wilkenfeld and Moser, 1988, p. 71). The less involved the great powers were the more reliance was placed on negotiation and other non-violent techniques of crisis management. This pattern changed markedly after 1945, and the probability of violence was low when the superpowers were directly involved in crises. Furthermore, it was clear from the analysis that for the superpowers the threat of force had become a substitute for its actual use. This confirms arguments which suggest that crisis management, although not a completely new phenomenon, took on a new importance in relation to confrontations between the superpowers in the nuclear age. The nature of crisis management, therefore, must now be explored.

THE NATURE OF CRISIS MANAGEMENT

Although the two waves of interest in crisis management differed very considerably over the effectiveness of crisis management, they differed far less over the nature of crisis management or the techniques it involves. There has also been agreement that crises are situations in which there is a high threat to values, finite time for decision-making, and an increase in the probability of violence. Furthermore, most analysts of crises have recognized the dual nature of the phenomenon – crises are times both of danger and of opportunity and can be understood as involving both bilateral competition and shared danger (Schelling, 1966). The difficulty for policy-makers lies in the attempt to find the appropriate balance between these two elements. On the one hand, they will want to exploit the opportunities as part of the competition, thereby ensuring that the crisis is resolved on a satisfactory basis in which the vital interests of the state are secured and protected; on the other they will want to minimize and contain the dangers and control and regulate the crisis so that it does not get out of hand and lead to war (Williams, 1976). The essence of skilful crisis management lies in the reconciliation of the competing pressures which are inherent in the dual nature of crises. Yet this is easier said than done. Snyder and Diesing summed up the dilemmas at the head of crisis management in the comment that it is necessary to coerce prudently and to accommodate cheaply (Snyder and Diesing, 1977, p. 207). The difficulty is that the more prudent one's actions, the less impact will they have in terms of coercion. Similarly, the cheaper the accommodation, the less incentive there is for the adversary to strike a bargain and to bring the crisis to an end. Crisis management requires that policy-makers not only recognize the inherent dilemmas but that they are willing and able to make the difficult trade-offs that are required.

As part of their response to these dilemmas, decision-makers have developed what appear to be tacit codes of conduct for the management of crises. Such rules are fairly rudimentary and have no status in law. Some critics even suggest that the notion of 'rules' is inappropriate, that it implies a degree of awareness about – and acceptance of – mutual restraint in both Washington and Moscow that may not be present. This argument gains added credence because of the difficulties of obtaining definitive evidence about the calculations made by Soviet decision-makers in crises. Yet in recent meetings of Soviet and American analysts there has been broad agreement that the behaviour of both superpowers has been constrained by certain basic rules of prudence. It also appears that there was considerable agreement between Soviet and Western scholars on the minimum content of these rules (Allison, 1989, p. 12). Furthermore, it is possible to discern patterns and practices of restraint that are both important and enduring. These appear to operate in a wide variety of circumstances and gain added impact because of precedent. The fact that certain forms of behaviour were avoided in the past encourages the belief that they should be – and will be – avoided in the future. 'Repeated practices by intelligent governments are not due to mere habit or case-by-case calculation but reflect a self-imposed guide for conduct' (Allison, 1989, p. 13). These practices also reflect self-consciousness about the need for restraint as well as an expectation of reciprocity. Yet these 'rules of prudence' are more akin to rules of thumb than to rules of science and, in essence, are very simple. Although the prescriptions of crisis management are sometimes regarded as 'over-generalized and over-simplified' (Richardson, 1988, p. 25) this simplicity may be a source of strength rather than weakness as it contributes to the efficacy of the rules or conventions. The rules themselves can be understood under several headings: rules of bargaining, decision-making procedures, and rules of operational control.

Among the bargaining rules is the belief that care should be taken to avoid backing the adversary into a corner where escalation begins to look less unattractive than acquiescence in one's demands. Yet this depends to a great extent on the balance of interests at stake in the crisis. This is partly a matter of the importance of the stakes and partly a matter of the degree of symmetry. The more fundamental the interests that are involved on both sides the less easy it will be for them to achieve a compromise. It is perhaps a fortuitous feature of past superpower crises that they have all been asymmetrical in terms of the balance of interests. There has ultimately been a recognition that the superpower with more at stake will be prepared to bargain more vigorously and take higher risks in order to protect those interests. In the final analysis, the balance of interests in a crisis may be more important than any other single consideration in determining the relative resolve of those involved.

This proposition is sometimes challenged by those who argue that the strategic balance is the most important factor in determining the bargaining process and, by extension, crisis outcomes. Those who were hawks in the Cuban missile crisis generally take this position (Blight and Welch, 1989, p. 202). In effect they are claiming that abstract considerations of victory or defeat in either a rapid or a sustained nuclear exchange have a profound impact on policy-makers' propensity to take risks in crises. There is a more sophisticated variant of this argument which suggests that although the side with the nuclear advantage is unlikely to behave recklessly, the government which regards itself as inferior will be much more cautious in its behaviour and more willing to back down (Betts, 1987). Although the issue is impossible to resolve in a final or definitive manner, these arguments are not persuasive. In past superpower crises, policy-makers on both sides – at least if their behaviour is indicative of their calculations – have been enormously circumspect. What seems to have deterred them from high-risk behaviour and highly coercive bargaining tactics is not the possibility that they might lose a nuclear war but simply the danger of nuclear war. Strategic analysts may offer refined assumptions about possible outcomes in limited nuclear exchanges confined to counter-force targets; policy-makers make gross calculations that are perhaps best summed up in the comment by McGeorge Bundy that 'A decision that would bring even one hydrogen bomb on one city of one's own country would be recognised in advance as a catastrophic blunder, ten bombs on ten cities would be a disaster beyond history and a hundred bombs on a hundred cities are unthinkable' (Bundy, 1969). Obviously it is not entirely impossible that one or other of the superpowers could have an irrational leader who is oblivious to the basic vulnerabilities and fears of the nuclear age. Yet nuclear weapons have so far created what might be described as a symmetry of fear. In circumstances where both sides are afraid of war and reluctant to engage in high-risk behaviour the balance of interest becomes crucial.

Each side has an interest in appearing to have more at stake than is actually the case. Yet, in past Soviet–American crises, neither government has really attempted to manipulate the situation in this way. Because crises have profound elements of shared risk reduction, the bargaining process has generally been an exercise in clarification as much as in coercion. Much of the bargaining has been intended to reveal or accentuate the basic pattern of interests involved in the crisis. This was evident, for example, in the Middle East crisis of October 1973. The threats of Soviet intervention were intended primarily to make clear to the United States that there were limits to Soviet tolerance and that Washington could not remain indifferent to the fate of the Egyptian Third Army. This is not to dismiss Soviet preparations for intervention as a bluff; it is simply to contend that intervention was very much a last resort for Moscow and that its preparations were designed primarily to obviate the need for direct involvement.

The Soviet threat to intervene in the Middle East highlights another striking feature of the bargaining process – the way in which the superpowers ensure that they retain their freedom of action. Soviet threats preceded Soviet actions and there was no attempt by Moscow to impose a *fait accompli* on the United States. Indeed, this concern with maintaining freedom of choice – for both oneself and the adversary – rules out the use of some of the more coercive bargaining moves. While much of the early theoretical literature on crisis bargaining highlighted the advantages that could occur from locking oneself into a particular course of action, in practice this has looked far less attractive to policy-makers. The idea was that an irrevocable commitment would make clear to the adversary that he had to back down if the crisis was to be settled peacefully. One danger was that the adversary might not perceive such a commitment for what it was. Another problem was that if the adversary also became locked in, then collision would be unavoidable. Not surprisingly, therefore, irrevocable commitments have been made only in support of the status quo and as part of an effort to prevent crises through deterrence rather than as part of the bargaining process during confrontations (Young, 1968).

Another, and closely related, feature of the bargaining process is that it has generally involved non-forcible bargaining. Although there have sometimes been arguments in favour of resort to force, ultimately neither the Soviet nor the American government has been willing deliberately to cross the line between coercion and violence and use military force against the troops of the adversary. Although both have been prepared to threaten violence, where there have been non-forcible options these have always been used in the first instance. This pattern was evident in the American airlift to Berlin in 1948 which was deemed preferable to sending a tank convoy to break the Soviet blockade – a restraint that was subsequently reciprocated in the Soviet reluctance to interfere significantly with the airlift. Its importance was further underlined in the Cuban missile crisis when the United States chose to blockade or quarantine Cuba rather than initiate an airstrike to take the missiles out. An air strike and an invasion would almost certainly have involved killing Russians, and although these options were not excluded, they were to be adopted only in the event of lesser and more prudent actions failing to achieve their purpose. In a similar vein, the Soviet Union chose not to challenge the blockade and run the risk of initiating even a localized military clash between Soviet and American forces.

While the record appears to be impressive, the rules can sometimes become rather tenuous. It appears that in the Cuban missile crisis it was far from being a foregone conclusion that neither side would cross the threshold between coercion and violence. Both the American decision to opt for a blockade rather than an airstrike and the Soviet decision not to challenge the blockade were close run things. The main reason that the advocates of the blockade prevailed over those preferring the air strike was that the blockade – in the words of McGeorge Bundy – 'did not begin with sudden death, and it was a first step not a last. If Khrushchev would not remove his missiles merely to lift the blockade – and not many argued that he surely would – further steps could be taken' (Bundy, 1989, p. 398). It appears too that Khrushchev's initial reaction was to challenge the blockade and that it was Soviet First Deputy Premier, Anastas Mikoyan, who either persuaded Khrushchev to order the Soviet ships to stop (Garthoff, 1989, p. 66) just before they reached the quarantine line or himself gave countermanding orders to this effect (Blight and Welch, 1989, p. 306).

On both sides there were hawks and doves, and the doves ultimately prevailed. The implication is that the rules of crisis management are rather more fragile than suggested above. On the other hand, it is significant that there were members of the decision-making groups who were acutely sensitive to the possibility that events might get out of control. As Blight and Welch point out, the difference between the hawks and doves in the Excom was that the former focused on probabilities – and saw the probability of escalation as low because of the United States' strategic advantage – whereas the doves focused on the possibility of an unmitigated disaster, and were much more sensitive to the possibility of inadvertent escalation (Blight and Welch, pp. 201–21).

Such concerns were certainly not groundless. The possibility of miscalculation is inherent in the bargaining process. In order to minimize such a likelihood the superpowers have ensured that they maintain the channels of communication during crises. Yet the problem is not simply one of transmission and reception; it is also one of understanding. The decision-makers must interpret the communications properly. Although this seems a straightforward task the difficulties of assessment are considerable even when the adversary is not attempting either to deceive or to create and exploit ambiguity. Successful communication requires that the adversaries achieve a degree of empathy and mutual understanding. It is particularly important in crises that each side makes efforts to understand how the situation looks to the adversary – and does not simply treat the adversary as operating according to some kind of universal strategic logic. This is all the more important if the crisis is precipitated through misperception, misunderstanding or miscalculation. The difficulty is that cultural stereotypes, ethnocentrism, preconceptions and wishful thinking all hinder the communication process. Resort to such simplifying devices is attractive because they make decision-making easier by offering ways of coping with complexity. The quality of the resulting decision, though, is often much poorer as a result of such attempts to escape from complexity. Communication and empathy are essential, therefore, if the decisions are to be of a high quality.

At the same time, successful bargaining and communication depend upon a reasonable degree of rational decision-making. Yet, as suggested above, the concept of rational decision-making has been challenged by those who emphasize the importance of bureaucratic, political and organizational factors in determining government choices both in crises and under more normal circumstances. But to conclude from this that the notion of rationality is irrelevant to crisis decision-making would be a mistake.

One of the problems with discussions of rationality is that critics attack what is effectively a straw man. They claim that perfect or comprehensive rationality (in which decision-makers have a clear hierarchy of values, explore the universe of possible alternatives, evaluate these alternatives in terms of likely gains and losses and choose the one which maximizes their values) is unattainable. This does not mean that more modest notions of rationality are inappropriate in describing crisis decision-making. Concepts such as 'bounded rationality' or 'limited rationality', in which policy-makers sacrifice rather than maximize, offer more realistic descriptions which reflect the fact that decision-makers are constrained in terms of time, the capacity to process massive amounts of information, and the ability to evaluate options under conditions of extreme uncertainty. The point, though, is that they do make the attempt to consider a range of alternatives and to think through likely outcomes in relation to each of the possible options.

The critique of rationality is on stronger ground in the argument that there is no single or simple hierarchy of values or goals. But the implication of this is not that notions of rational decision-making are inappropriate but that rationality has to take a slightly different form. One of the difficulties faced by policy-makers is that they have values or goals which are not entirely consistent with each other. Consequently, the pursuit of one goal may harm the attainment of another goal that is equally important. The task for policy-makers, therefore, is to find policy options that reconcile the competing values or at least involve acceptable trade-offs. Consequently, they have to decide 'how much of one value is worth sacrificing for some of another value' – and, since alternatives 'combine objectives or values in different ways', they have to weigh up the objectives and alternatives side by side before finally choosing that option which offers the best combination of values (Lindblom, 1973, pp. 124–8). This is particularly relevant to decision-making in crises where policy-makers are concerned with both coercive impact and prudence. Options have to be evaluated against both criteria with the key calculations being made at the margin. Since different options will combine coercion and prudence to different degrees, policy-makers have to ensure a satisfactory if not an optimum mix. The decision of the United States government to 'quarantine' Cuba rather than opting for an airstrike can be understood as an outcome of a process of rational appraisal of this kind. The blockade was important in establishing US credibility and clearly had some coercive impact. Although it was less coercive than an airstrike, and did not solve the problem of removing the missiles, it was more prudent and seemed to offer the best means of reconciling competing demands.

The argument that rationality requires trade-offs amongst competing goals and values rather than the choice of an alternative designed to maximize one particular goal or value does not undercut the notion of rational decision-making. On the contrary, it underlines the point that the process is a highly intellectual one. One of the problems with accounts of United States decision-making during the Cuban missile crisis that emphasize the importance of bureaucratic and political factors is that they give insufficient attention to the fact that those involved were engaged in intellectual problem-solving of a very high order. Decision-making during the crisis was not determined by simple bureaucratic politics. The extent to which members of the decision-making group changed their positions suggests that where different individuals stood cannot simply be explained in terms of where they sat. In this episode few individuals stood still; many of those involved changed from supporting one option to supporting another.

This is not to claim that the decision-making process worked perfectly. There are always imperfections in any decision-making process. Nevertheless, US decision-making in the Cuban missile crisis deserved the description by Irving Janis that it was a case of 'vigilant appraisal' (Janis, 1972). Nor was this atypical of decision-making in international crises. An awareness of the high stakes and the danger of miscalculation places a premium on careful calculation. There is also a premium on maintaining control over events during the crisis. This requires not simply calculated decision-making but an awareness of the importance of the implementation process. The danger is that options will be poorly implemented and result in the use of force, even though this has not been authorized by the political leadership. Such a situation is likely to be worsened by the fact that any use of force will be construed by the adversary as the result of deliberate choice. This is hardly surprising as governments typically regard the behaviour of others as more centralized than it really is.

The issue of control relates to what Alexander George has termed the operational requirements of crisis management. According to George, these requirements 'attempt to integrate the political and military considerations that come into play in a confrontation and often compete, or conflict sharply, in the formulation and implementation of crisis policy' (George, 1984, p. 226). In crises there are major incompatibilities between the political logic of control that is integral to crisis management and the military logic of preparedness in case crisis management fails. The military authorities want to ensure that in the event of hostilities they are in a position to mount successful resistance. The problem is that measures taken to enhance preparedness may either appear provocative to the adversary or lead him to conclude that war is inevitable and that it would be advantageous to strike first rather than wait. In order to prevent such occurrences, it is essential for military autonomy to be restricted. Crises are by nature primarily political interactions, and it is necessary for the political authorities to maintain close control over military actions. Furthermore, these actions must be tailored to political purpose and designed to convey political measures whether of resolve or restraint. They should also be closely integrated with diplomacy and political communication. In order to achieve this, 'the tempo and momentum of military movements may have to be deliberately slowed down and pauses created to provide enough time for the two sides to exchange diplomatic signals and communications, and to give each side adequate time to assess the situation, make decision, respond to proposals, etc' (George, 1984, p. 226). In other words, military actions should be part of an overall effort at crisis management. The difficulty is that the civilian authorities do not always fully understand the implications of the military actions that they may be asked to authorize, while the military do not always appreciate the possible political consequences of actions they want to take. Rules of engagement are of particular relevance here. Although the rules of engagement have to be permissive enough for the state's military forces to defend themselves against tactical surprise, they have to be sufficiently restrictive to prevent provocative or unauthorized actions which in periods of high tension could spark off unwanted escalation. The Stark incident in the Gulf revealed what could happen if the rules are too stringent, while the shooting down of the Iranian airbus by the *Vincennes* highlighted the problems that can arise if they are too permissive. Although in neither case was there superpower confrontation these two episodes reveal the dangers that can arise.

Rules of engagement can be understood as a device to ensure that miliary actions in a crisis are effectively controlled. They are clearly one element in a broader approach to crisis behaviour which places considerable emphasis on the rules of the game. James Richardson has suggested that such rules are useful only if applied 'with discrimination and judgement'. They are stronger in the negative form in that it is dangerous to neglect the rule, but offer no positive assurance that observing the rule will bring success. The danger is that the connotations of 'crisis management' may encourage overconfidence in the general validity of its rules and thus their indiscriminate application (Richardson, 1988, p. 25). Such a comment is a valid warning against overconfidence in the rules of crisis management. Yet far from denying the need for care and flexibility most analysts of crisis management have been explicit about the need for bringing precisely these qualities to the application of rules. Alexander George, for example, has acknowledged that

> the requirements of crisis management provide only general guidelines for policy planners and decision-makers; the challenging and critical task is to devise a version of the strategy of crisis management that is tailored to the special configuration of each crisis situation. Since crises differ substantially in structure and dynamics, in what is at stake, the large diplomatic-military context, the level of risks and opportunities posed, and domestic and international constraints operating on decision-makers, different variants of the strategy need to be improved for each case. (George, 1984, p. 227)

Indeed, some crises will be much easier to manage than others.

The issue of manageability is related in part to the nature of the participants. Crisis management is a concept that has developed primarily in the context of US–Soviet relations and it is far from self-evident that it is equally relevant or applicable in situations where the superpowers are not directly involved. Where war is regarded as a usable instrument of policy, the prospects for the peaceful resolutions of crises diminish considerably, especially if the stakes are high for both sides. Although this is unlikely in a nuclear context, the possibility that crazy states will precipitate confrontations and prove resistant to deterrence cannot be entirely excluded. And where nuclear weapons are not involved governments may regard crises as little more than a period of transition to war in which the key is to start hostilities in the best possible military position. This is especially the case in the Third World where war continues to play an important role as the ultimate arbiter of disputes between states, and where hostilities may be regarded as a means of fulfilling important goals such as domestic consolidation, the restoration of national honour, or ideological or religious vindication. In these circumstances, crisis management is either irrelevant or impossible.

This is particularly disconcerting because of the probability of unrest and instability in the 1990s among Third World states. Towards the end of the 1980s, there appeared to be something of a downturn in conflicts in the Third World. The end of the Iran–Iraq War, the Soviet withdrawal from Afghanistan and negotiations on both Southern Africa and Kampuchea led some commentators to claim that peace was breaking out in the Third World. Yet there were also signs that regional conflict and instability could increase rather than decrease during the 1990s. The spread of ballistic-missile technology, the rise of indigenous Third World arms suppliers and the potential for the proliferation of both nuclear and chemical capabilities mean that existing political disputes are likely to be exacerbated by a new technological overlay which will increase regional security dilemmas and encourage pre-emptive instabilities during crises. Even if the incentives for crisis management increase, therefore, the opportunities may well decline.

It is somewhat ironical that although the second wave of crisis-management analysis was much more pessimistic than the first, the focus was still very much on the superpowers. Despite the historical richness of many of the studies, the lessons that were drawn from past crises were considered almost exclusively in relation to Soviet–American crises. Yet even here, there could be a move towards greater complexity. Although the superpowers have attempted to avoid major confrontation since the Cuban missile crisis – and were successful in defusing the Middle East crisis of October 1973 – the brief flare-up during the October war illustrated the dangers of what have been termed bipolycentric crises (Shoemaker and Spanier, 1984). The key point about such crises is that they are not totally under the control of the two superpowers. In the Middle East War of 1973 both Israel and Egypt proved highly resistant to superpower domination and both took actions which dragged Moscow and Washington into a confrontation (brief as it was) that both would have preferred to avoid. The possibility that this could occur once again and that during the 1990s the superpowers will be drawn into regional conflicts on opposing sides cannot be excluded. Nevertheless, it is noteworthy that the superpowers have attempted to move from a relationship based on intermittent co-operation to manage crises when they occur to more extensive and ambitious forms of co-operation to prevent or avoid crises.

FROM CRISIS MANAGEMENT TO CRISIS PREVENTION

Even during the Cold War the superpowers developed certain 'norms of competition' which ensured that crises between them, if not prevented altogether, were at least kept to a minimum. The development of spheres of influence, for example, can be understood as a device for avoiding miscalculation and confrontation. The norm of asymmetric intervention outside the blocs supplemented the tacit agreement on spheres of influence and ensured that when one superpower was involved in regional conflict the adversary stayed on the sidelines. In the early 1970s, as part of the US–Soviet détente, an attempt was made to extend this process through an agreement on the basic principles to guide superpower relations. The Basic Principles Agreement of 1972 and the Prevention of Nuclear War Agreement of 1973 made explicit the fundamental desire of both superpowers to avoid direct confrontation – and apart from the brief confrontation over the Middle East during the war of October 1973, there has not been a US–Soviet crisis since October 1962. Yet in other ways the global codes of conduct enunciated in the early 1970s were seriously deficient. The demands that both sides always observe restraint were simultaneously too vague and too stringent and the accords suffered from the lack of any procedural mechanism whereby the superpowers could consult over allegations that the norms were being violated. By creating expectations that were overoptimistic, the codes of conduct contributed to subsequent allegations that the Soviet Union had broken the rules of détente. The final result, therefore, was less to facilitate crisis prevention than to magnify the distrust which led to the demise of the détente of the 1970s.

If the first attempt by the superpowers to establish a semi-formal crisis-prevention regime failed, there is still an interest in moving in this direction, as was apparent in the late 1980s both in Europe and in the Third World. As part of the moves towards a new détente from the mid-1980s onwards, the superpowers placed considerable emphasis on discussion of regional problems. This time, however, the issues were discussed on a case-by-case basis – an approach that appeared to be yielding results as the superpowers gradually moved towards strategic disengagement in the Third World. To some extent this was simply a reflection of the underlying realities. Both Washington (in Vietnam) and Moscow (in Afghanistan) had discovered that the Third World is resistant to superpower domination. The increased awareness of this basic reality had a dual impact. On the one side, it made both reluctant to get involved militarily in conflicts that were difficult to win; on the other, it made each superpower much more relaxed about the adversary, secure in the knowledge that any gains it made were likely to be equally tenuous. Although this shift was obscured to some extent by the Reagan doctrine, with its support for wars of national liberation fought against Marxist-Leninist regimes, the implementation of this policy was far less vigorous than the rhetoric. Furthermore, the limits of the interventionist impulse were underlined by Secretary of Defence Caspar Weinberger in a speech in November 1984 outlining the preconditions which had to be met before the United States should intervene militarily in the Third World.

The implication is that in the 1990s both superpowers will prove very reluctant to be drawn into regional conflicts on opposing sides. Although elements of competition will remain in the superpower relationship, it is not inconceivable that in the 1990s Moscow and Washington will attempt to collaborate in imposing short-term restraints if not long-term solutions on regional conflicts in the Third World. The task will not be an easy one as small states are able to exercise 'reverse influence' on their patrons. Nevertheless, the common interest of the superpowers in insulating their relationship from regional disruptions ensures that the effort will be made.

The other area where crisis-prevention considerations appear to be more significant than ever before is Europe. Partly because of Gorbachev's 'new thinking' about security, and partly because of the economic constraints on defence spending, both military blocs in Europe are attempting to reduce their force levels. There has also been a recognition that particular kinds of force structure can contribute to crisis stability. One of the most important developments of the late 1980s was the Soviet recognition that military forces, equipped, trained and deployed in ways which provided a capacity for a surprise attack, were invariably regarded as threatening by others. More important than reductions in force levels, therefore, are moves that are being made – and will almost certainly continue – to restructure forces towards a more defensive posture. Although this is particularly important on the Warsaw Pact side, there is also a recognition by NATO that certain elements in its force posture could be construed as threatening. The ultimate result of the talks on Conventional Forces in Europe (CFE), therefore, could be to achieve greater stability at lower levels of forces.

This is all the more likely to the extent that the force reduction and restructuring are accompanied by confidence-building measures or, as they are sometimes described, measures of military *glasnost*. By increasing transparency of military activities in Europe, it might be possible to minimize the prospects for mistakes and miscalculations in a crisis. The irony is that greater military stability will coincide with a decrease in political stability. Consequently, it would seem both necessary and appropriate to supplement the changes in force postures of NATO and the Warsaw Pact with some kind of political mechanism whereby the two sides can exchange views on disturbing political trends, can identify potential flashpoints and initiate joint measures to prevent instability from spilling over into an East–West crisis.

The idea of a joint crisis-prevention and management centre in Geneva to deal specifically with European security problems is one that has considerable merit. It would provide an early-warning mechanism of potential difficulties, it could act as a directorate for inspection and verification activities, and it could monitor any disturbing military movements. Furthermore, in the event that NATO and the Warsaw Treaty Organization did find themselves in a confrontation, such a centre could facilitate communications, encourage restraint and de-escalation and provide a monitoring service to ensure that the relaxation of alert measures is done in a symmetrical fashion and that dangerous vulnerabilities are thereby avoided. Although there might be some objections to such a centre on the grounds that there is insufficient trust between NATO and the Soviet bloc, that it would be used for espionage, or that it would be remote from the centres of decision, none of these arguments is compelling. In many respects it would simply be a formalization of the exchanges between the military forces of the two sides that began to be developed in the late 1980s. Furthermore, the arguments about espionage are greatly exaggerated given that a large part of the purpose of such a centre would be to facilitate communication and information exchange – at least on specific issues. The objection about the irrelevance of the centre in a crisis is more serious, given that the key decisions would be made in Washington and Moscow (and perhaps Bonn). Nevertheless, the centre would be available as an additional mechanism for crisis management should the two sides decide to use it. It would not be a substitute for existing channels of communication, but the services of a centre in which the staff had developed relevant expertise and common understandings about the significance of certain actions could prove of considerable importance. Perhaps equally important, such a centre would stand as a symbol of both the change in East–West relations and the desire to move towards a more explicit and systematic effort to prevent crises.

Yet without accompanying changes, the creation of a centre would provide only a partial response to the need for more effective crisis prevention and crisis management. Perhaps the most important single change that needs to occur is one of attitudes. There has been a tendency in the past to assess force postures, strategic deployments, and even arms control agreements in terms of their contribution to deterrence, defence and, on occasion, arms race stability. An important criterion that is insufficiently used in such assessments is the impact on crisis stability. Would new deployments, changes in posture, reductions through formal agreements or unilateral initiatives enhance or detract from crisis stability? Should a crisis occur would they add incentives for pre-emption, intensify security dilemmas, and erode political control over the military? If the answer to any of these questions is yes, then it is necessary to assess whether the gains in deterrence from proceeding are worth the potential loss in terms of crisis management and control.

Even if greater emphasis is placed on considerations of management and control in determining force postures, this does not mean that crises will prove manageable. It is worth reiterating that crisis management is a highly problematic undertaking, the success of which cannot be readily guaranteed. The only alternatives to crisis management, however, are successful crisis prevention or crisis mismanagement. The improvement in US–Soviet relations in the latter half of the 1980s provides at least some grounds for hoping that in the 1990s the emphasis will be on crisis prevention.

REFERENCES

Allison, G. T. (1971), *Essence of Decision: Explaining the Cuban Missile Crisis* (Boston, Mass.: Little, Brown).

Allison, G. T. (1989), 'Primitive rules of prudence', in G. T. Allison and W. L. Ury (eds), *Windows of Opportunity* (Cambridge, Mass.: Ballinger).

Betts, R. (1987), *Nuclear Blackmail and Nuclear Balance* (Washington: Brookings).

Blight, J. G., and Welch, D. A. (1989), *On The Brink* (New York: Hill & Wang).

Bracken, P. (1983), *The Command and Control of Nuclear Forces* (New Haven: Yale University Press).

Brecher, Michael, Wilkenfeld, Jonathan, and Moser, Sheila (1988), *Crises in the Twentieth Century*, vol. 2 (Oxford: Pergamon).

Bundy, McGeorge (1969), 'To cap the volcano', *Foreign Affairs*, vol. 48 (1), pp. 1–20.

Bundy, McGeorge (1989), *Danger and Survival: Choices about the Bomb in the First Fifty Years* (New York: Random House).

Garthoff, R. L. (1989), *Reflections on the Cuban Missile Crisis* (Washington, D.C.: Brookings).

George, A. L. (1980), *Presidential Decision-Making in Foreign Policy* (Boulder, Colo: Westview).

162   *Strategy and international security*

George, A. L. (1984), 'Crisis management: the interaction of political and military considerations', *Survival*, vol. 26, no. 5, pp. 223–4.

Gottfried, K., and Blair, B. (eds) (1988), *Crisis Stability and Nuclear War* (New York: Oxford University Press).

Halper, T. (1971), *Foreign Policy Crises: Appearance and Reality in Decision-Making* (Columbus, Ohio: Merrill).

Janis, I. (1972), *Victims of Groupthink* (Boston, Mass.: Houghton Mifflin).

Jervis, R. (1976), *Perception and Misperception in International Politics* (Princeton, NJ: Princeton University Press).

Lebow, R. N. (1981), *Between Peace and War: The Nature of International Crisis* (Baltimore; Md: Johns Hopkins University Press).

Lebow, R. N. (1987), *Nuclear Crisis Management: A Dangerous Illusion* (Ithaca; NY: Cornell University Press).

Lindblom, C. E. (1973), 'The science of muddling through', in F. Kramer (ed.), *Perspectives on Public Bureaucracy* (Cambridge, Mass.: Winthrop).

Richardson, J. L. (1988), 'Crisis management: a critical appraisal', in G. Winham (ed.), *New Issues in International Crisis Management* (Boulder; Colo: Westview).

Sagan, S. 1985), 'Nuclear alerts and crisis management', *International Security*, vol. 9 (no. 4), pp. 99–139.

Schelling, T. C. (1966), *Arms and Influence* (New Haven; Conn.: Yale University Press).

Shoemaker, C. S., and Spanier, J. (1984), *Patron–Client State Relations* (New York: Praeger).

Snyder, G., and Diesing, P. (1977), *Conflict Among Nations* (Princeton, NJ: Princeton University Press).

Williams, P. (1976), *Crisis Management* (London: Martin Robertson).

Young, O. (1968), *The Politics of Force* (Princeton, NJ: Princeton University Press).

PART THREE

The rise of
conventional strategy

7

NATO strategy and conventional defence

COLIN McINNES

The conventional forces of NATO and the WTO stationed either side of the inner German border present an awesome accumulation of military power. The scale, sophistication and sheer destructive power of these forces is unprecedented in peacetime. The cost is similarly enormous. Yet for NATO these forces have occupied a somewhat uncertain place in alliance strategy. The common (though not unchallenged) perception of overwhelming Soviet/Warsaw Pact conventional strength, when coupled to an emphasis on deterring war, has led to a strategy based on nuclear reliance. The conventional defence of NATO territory may be a formally agreed principle in the Alliance, but the cost of providing the forces to do this, and the awful consequences of even a conventional war in Europe, have tended to erode that principle in favour of an emphasis on deterring war by the threat of nuclear escalation.

But this is changing. Dissatisfaction with a strategy based upon early nuclear use has been apparent throughout the 1980s, not only in the peace movement but amongst 'mainstream' academic and military analysts (Bundy *et al.*, 1982). Ideas for the better use of conventional forces, and doctrines for winning the first conventional battles, have been developed. Of particular note are the development of an operational level of war, extended/deep battle concepts, the emphasis on seizing the initiative, the development of ideas for tactical and operational offensives when on the strategic defensive and for a more manoeuvre-oriented defence, and finally the movement away from a systems approach to war to one where human factors are acknowledged as being significant to the outcome of battle. When coupled to improvements in equipment and morale (particularly in the British and American armies), this new military thinking in NATO has helped to produce greater confidence amongst military commanders in the conventional component of NATO strategy.

CONVENTIONAL DEFENCE IN NATO STRATEGY

NATO strategy rests upon the principles of defence and deterrence. The balance between these principles, and consequently the role of conventional forces, has been the subject of debate in the 1980s, identifiable in four main approaches to NATO strategy.

(1) Flexible response – inflexible escalation

The NATO strategy of flexible response is sufficiently vague and general to allow a number of interpretations. One such interpretation, which has been termed 'inflexible escalation', rests on the premiss that what deters war in Europe is the threat of nuclear escalation. Thus it is argued that it is *nuclear* deterrence which has kept the peace for forty years, and the strategy of flexible response ensures the credibility of nuclear use. The expectation is that limitation will prove impossible once nuclear weapons are used, and that this risk of uncontrolled escalation deters war (Bracken, 1983; Freedman, 1986, pp. 130–1).

In this approach conventional forces have a limited capability to defend against 'smash and grab' raids, but their main function is to create a sufficient obstacle that, if the Soviets were to attack, that attack would have to be massive and unambiguous. This, coupled to the loss of substantial numbers of service personnel (especially Americans) would make nuclear use credible. NATO's conventional forces would therefore act as a tripwire for the use of nuclear weapons, which once used would escalate (or threaten to escalate) beyond control. Security is guaranteed not by the ability to defend NATO territory, but by the surety of nuclear escalation.

This approach is not far removed from NATO's position in the 1970s. Conventional forces suffered from poor morale and equipment failings, military doctrine was pessimistic, negative, even defeatist, equipment stockpiles were low, and early nuclear use appeared inescapable (ESECS, 1983, pp. 10 and 141). This position posed a number of serious problems. First, security was based upon a threat of nuclear use which, if enacted, would in all probability prompt a Soviet nuclear reply against NATO territory. Moreover, given the short range of some NATO nuclear systems, radioactive fallout and even blast would affect NATO territory. NATO would thus be inflicting, directly and indirectly, nuclear devastation upon its own territory (Bundy *et al.*, 1982, pp. 756–7).

Secondly, the credibility of nuclear use was questioned. In an age of nuclear parity, would the United States permit the use of its nuclear weapons to defend Europe? In addition American nuclear strategy appeared to have moved decisively away from a retaliatory strategy to one based on warfighting. Such a strategy raised the spectre (at least in European eyes) of a nuclear war limited to Europe. The surety of escalation to the strategic level, the central component of the inflexible escalation approach, was therefore under threat: if nuclear war could not be controlled, there was little incentive for the US to use nuclear weapons since ultimately its own homeland was at risk; but if it could be controlled (implicit in the warfighting approach), given parity at the strategic level there was no incentive for the US to escalate the war beyond the battlefield (Pierre, 1986, pp. 10–11). Nuclear use began to appear irrational and incredible. But since conventional forces were unable to contain a conventional attack, security policy based on inflexible escalation was bankrupt.

(2) Raising the nuclear threshold

Dissatisfaction with this inflexible escalation approach has led a number of analysts, military and academic, to argue in favour of raising the nuclear threshold (Beach, 1986; ESECS, 1983; Pierre, 1986). This approach advocates postponing nuclear use until a later time in the conflict (perhaps up to a month after the commencement of war, based on NATO's target of thirty days of war stocks). Thus attention has been paid to improving conventional capabilities as the means by which nuclear use may be delayed. For this to have any meaning conventional forces have to acquire the role not merely of a slow fuse to nuclear release but as defenders of NATO territory. However, this approach argues, such a defence could not succeed indefinitely against Warsaw Pact conventional superiority. Although the extent of Pact superiority has been the subject of a lively debate in the 1980s which has revealed many areas of comparative NATO advantage (Biddle, 1988; Chalmers and Unterseher, 1988; Cohen, 1988; Epstein, 1988; Holmes, 1988; Mearsheimer, 1988; NATO, 1988; Posen, 1988), advocates of raising the nuclear threshold tend to assume that NATO would be hard pressed to defend successfully, using conventional weapons alone over a protracted period of time (Beach, 1986, p. 155). Moreover, deterrence would still rest upon the threat of nuclear use. Raising the nuclear threshold would not change the security paradigm based upon nuclear threats, but rather would create an opportunity for a diplomatic solution to a conflict before nuclear weapons were used.

Exploiting this opportunity may not be easy, however. If the Soviets were sufficiently motivated to launch a large-scale attack against NATO (a venture not to be undertaken lightly), it seems unlikely that they would stop merely because NATO *threatened* to use nuclear weapons. That threat would have existed while the Soviets were contemplating aggression and failed to deter then. Nor does it seem likely that, having launched an invasion, Soviet leaders would suddenly 'come to their senses' and withdraw. Rather something would have to be done to change the minds of Soviet leaders. Since that something cannot, by definition, be a nuclear response – not even a 'demonstration shot' to indicate resolve – then it must be some event at the conventional level. By increasing the emphasis on conventional forces, advocates of raising the nuclear threshold hope to *deny* the Soviets a quick victory (one won within a few days by forces stationed in Eastern Europe). But again the question must be asked: why would the Soviets stop and negotiate at this stage? Having committed themselves to an invasion, having incurred substantial costs, having weakened NATO perhaps critically, and with second echelon forces about to be committed to the attack, would the Soviets stop and talk?

It is of course possible that, having been denied a quick victory, the Soviet Union would realize that it had miscalculated and would therefore sue for peace. But this would seem to rely on two further factors. First, that NATO demonstrates a *continuing* ability to defend conventionally, removing any perception that NATO's defensive lines would crumble if the war was continued. And second, that the Soviet leadership is sufficiently shocked into stopping and reversing the momentum of war. Merely slowing a Soviet advance would seem unlikely to provide the sort of shock necessary to reverse the momentum of war.

Thus although the opportunity might exist for a diplomatic solution, it is unclear why the Soviets might stop and talk. Nor does raising the nuclear threshold address the central problems of nuclear reliance identified above, namely of the credibility and consequences of nuclear escalation. Security is still inextricably linked to a threatened nuclear response, and whether this response comes early or late, these same fundamental problems are encountered.

(3) Minimum deterrence

Whereas the two previous approaches view nuclear deterrence as the ultimate guarantor of security, and consequently place escalation at the centre of NATO strategy, the minimum-deterrent approach views nuclear weapons as useful only in deterring *nuclear* threats and as weapons of the last resort. Any other use would be incredible, irrational, or at the very least unwise. Conventional forces must therefore defend NATO territory and deter conventional attack. These two roles of defence and deterrence are inextricably linked since a powerful defensive capability would act as a deterrent to attack. Although this approach is most clearly identified with the advocates of a nuclear no-first-use policy (Bundy *et al.*, 1982), no-first-use is not necessary to the minimum-deterrent approach since a willingness to escalate may be envisaged as a last resort (Baylis, 1988, pp. 49–50).

The minimum-deterrent approach rests on two key foundations. First is the belief that it is in no one's interest to go nuclear. Hence minimum-deterrent arsenals are thought sufficient to deter conventional war from escalating. A nuclear warfighting capability is not required, and may even be dangerously counterproductive in encouraging notions that limitation is possible and that escalating to the nuclear level might therefore be somehow 'safe'. Second, conventional deterrence is created through the demonstrable ability to deny a quick victory to the Warsaw Pact. It is widely assumed that if the Soviets ever launched a large-scale attack they would not want to become bogged down in a prolonged war of attrition. The offensive component in their doctrine therefore emphasizes a quick, *blitzkrieg*-style victory (Donnelly, 1985, pp. 23 and 27; Vigor, 1983, pp. 2–9). This would be secured largely by in-place forces – the first strategic echelon, stationed in East Germany, Poland and Czechoslovakia. If NATO has the ability to hold or, even better, to defeat this force, denying the Soviets a quick victory, then attack may be deterred by conventional means.

For minimum deterrence, therefore, much more is required of conventional forces. Their role is not merely to provide a tripwire for nuclear forces, but to demonstrate an ability to defend NATO territory successfully, and even threaten to win at the operational level. This poses a number of problems, the two most significant being whether the mechanics of conventional deterrence are sufficiently well understood, and whether a successful conventional defence is possible within NATO resource constraints.

The focus of most deterrence theorizing has been in the nuclear field. Interest in conventional deterrence, and particularly in how NATO conventional forces might deter a Soviet attack, is more recent and has received much less attention (Lebow, 1987; Mearsheimer, 1983; Orme, 1987). The requirements for conventional deterrence are consequently somewhat less well understood than nuclear deterrence. The deterrence paradigm is traditionally based upon either threat of unacceptable punishment (that is, damage to the state), or the ability to deny aggression the gains it seeks (Snyder, 1961). As conventional weapons do not threaten the same scale of damage as nuclear forces, they have limited use as weapons of punishment; hence conventional deterrence concentrates on the ability to defend successfully and so deny victory. The problem here is how to ensure that a potential aggressor does not perceive the chance of victory as worth taking a risk for.

The second problem is whether NATO can defeat the WTO's first operational echelon, let alone the first strategic echelon. This is a complex and highly judgemental question. A number of recent analyses of the conventional balance have (implicitly or explicitly) suggested that conventional defence may be possible (Epstein, 1987, pp. 36–45; 1988; Mearsheimer, 1982; 1988; Posen, 1984; 1988). But the question of the feasibility of conventional defence cannot be reduced to an analysis of the conventional balance, no matter how sophisticated that analysis. Not only is the likely outcome of a conventional conflict highly scenario-sensitive, but it is also a question of military doctrine – of how the forces on both sides are used. Military doctrine would play a critical role not merely in determining the shape of battle, but in the outcome as well. Here new doctrines such as Follow-on Forces Attack (FOFA), AirLand Battle and Bagnall's Northern Army Group (NORTHAG) concept have boosted NATO's confidence in its ability to defeat the first operational echelon, though doubts remain over subsequent echelons. Conventional defeat does not now seem likely in the first few days of war, but cannot be postponed indefinitely. Moreover, although NATO commanders can make judgements over what they believe their conventional capability to be, whether this judgement is shared by their WTO counterparts is less certain. And it is the WTO who must judge whether NATO's conventional capabilities are sufficient to deter attack.

(4) Common security/non-provocative defence

The three approaches to NATO strategy outlined above are all marked by the centrality of deterrence. Moreover, security is achieved by essentially unilateral means, through the possession of forces deemed sufficient to deter attack. The common security approach in contrast adopts a much wider view, seeing security as a function of a political relationship. Military factors play an important part in this relationship, but are not the only determinants. In particular this approach rejects the notion that long-term security is attainable through unilateral means. It stresses the 'security dilemma' inherent in the traditional approach (Jervis, 1978), and instead sees security as a problem which has to be approached through co-operative rather than confrontational means, and by the promotion of the common good rather than old-style national security.

Thus a common security framework emphasizes non-provocative military postures. The conventional forces of both sides would be organized and equipped for demonstrably defensive roles, and offensive capabilities would be eroded. Both the 'natural' advantages of the defence (cover, familiarity with terrain, preparation of obstacles, and so forth) and modern high technology (such as smart mines and electronic barriers) could be exploited in area defence concepts as part of a movement towards 'defensive defence'. Conventional forces would therefore be capable of a strong and effective defence. Offensive actions would be made more difficult not merely by this defensive capability but by the bilateral reduction in offensive capabilities. Thus attack would be deterred by the poor prospects of success, while the adoption of a non-provocative defence would reduce tension and promote common security. The nuclear threshold would be progressively raised, and dependency on nuclear weapons eventually removed as far as possible from the security framework.

The common security approach proposes a radically different alternative to existing NATO strategy. It would involve major changes to the organization, equipment and doctrine of conventional forces. Aside from the broader political issues involved in this approach, critics have noted that the area defence concepts proposed as part of the 'defensive' orientation of conventional forces would create a number of problems, particularly: how would lost territory be recovered? Could forces be organized to be sufficiently flexible to deal with a variety of threats and possible scenarios? Could comparatively static forces cope with the physical and psychological effects of modern artillery attack? And how would the defensive plan avoid being identified well in advance, posing a set problem which can be planned against (Gates, 1987, pp. 301–7)? Although these points have been addressed by some non-offensive defence thinkers (Unterseher, 1989) the radical nature of the proposals has led to a wary reaction in NATO defence ministries (*Statement on the Defence Estimates*, 1987, p. 2).

Conclusion

While there appears to be considerable disaffection with the concept of inflexible escalation, a critical mass of support has yet to be formed in favour of common security. But what the 1980s saw is a growing interest in the use of conventional forces, either to raise the nuclear threshold or to provide a deterrent against conventional attack. The argument pursued above suggests that for both minimum deterrence and raising the nuclear threshold it is insufficient for NATO merely to delay a Pact victory. Rather NATO must either demonstrate an ability to win the first battles and, by denying the Soviets a quick victory, deter aggression, or it must shock the Warsaw Pact sufficiently in a war as to force them to stop and sue for peace. Thus if NATO is to raise the nuclear threshold or move to a posture of minimum deterrence, it must threaten to inflict a significant defeat upon the Soviet Union and its allies in the event of war. It is in this context that the developments in NATO's conventional military doctrine in the 1980s must be judged.

MILITARY DOCTRINE

The 1980s saw a number of major developments in military doctrine, most notably the US Army's AirLand Battle doctrine, NATO's FOFA mission concept, the British Corps Concept and subsequent NORTHAG concept of operations, and in the German field manual HDv 100–100 and *Bundeswehr 2000*. Some of these developments have been directly and explicitly linked to concerns over NATO strategy, but at other times they have evolved under their own momentum or under pressure from technology or Soviet military doctrine. Regardless of whether these developments were explicitly linked to NATO strategy or not, the thrust of this doctrinal debate has been in broadly the same direction as that over NATO strategy: how to provide a more effective conventional defence.

AirLand Battle was developed between 1977 and 1981 under General Donn A. Starry at the US Army's Training and Doctrine Command (TRADOC), and was adopted as official US doctrine with the publication in 1982 of a new edition of the Army's 'how to fight' manual, FM 100–5 *Operations*. The doctrine was subsequently refined with a new edition of FM 100–5 appearing in 1986. Although not formally sanctioned by NATO, the expectation is that FM 100–5 will guide American commanders in Europe. AirLand Battle was more of a reaction firstly to Soviet operational and technological developments and secondly to perceived deficiencies in existing doctrine than an explicit attempt to raise the nuclear threshold (FM 100–5, 1982; 1986; Hanne 1983; Richardson 1986;

Romjue, 1984; Starry, 1983). In contrast NATO's FOFA mission concept was explicitly linked to the nuclear question (Office of Technology Assessment (OTA), 1987, p. 3). Drawing upon some of the deep-attack ideas emerging from TRADOC, planners at SHAPE technical centre produced a study on attacking WTO second-echelon forces (follow-on forces). With strong backing from the then Supreme Allied Commander Europe (SACEUR), General Bernard Rogers, the plan was approved as NATO policy by the Defence Planning Committee in November 1984, and passed on to NATO's international staff for refinement. During this process FOFA progressed from a general concept of the destruction, disruption and delay of follow-on forces at a variety of distances from the forward line of enemy troops, to a set of specific tasks linked to new and emerging weapons (OTA, 1987, pp. 50–2).

Like FOFA, the British Corps Concept was conceived in the early 1980s with the intention of raising the nuclear threshold. Largely the product of 1 (BR) Corps' commander, General Sir Nigel Bagnall, with Bagnall's appointment as commander of NORTHAG in 1983 the concept was introduced into the broader framework of army group operations (Bagnall, 1984).

The most sensitive area of development, however, has been in West German military doctrine, since any conventional conflict would be fought primarily on German territory. The Bundeswehr's doctrine is still governed by the two overriding requirements of deterrence and forward defence. But the German field manual HDv 100–100 and German acceptance of Bagnall's ideas in NORTHAG have both displayed acceptance of elements of the new thinking.

NATO's new military thinking incorporates a number of key elements which, although not necessarily universally accepted, are sufficiently widespread as to be considered trends. The first of these is the development of an operational level of war.

(1) The operational level of war

Although the Soviets have long identified a level of warfare between strategic and tactical, for NATO this distinction was a major innovation in the 1980s. It involves the use of field armies, army groups or other major commands in a single operational plan or concept. Divisions and commands below the divisional level are considered as fighting at the tactical level, while corps act as the link able to fight at the tactical and operational level.

Creating an operational level was important for a number of reasons. Given the importance of air support to modern land warfare, not just in the close support but in the deep interdiction role, the operational level provided a framework for co-ordinating air and land operations and for assigning priorities. Secondly the operational level allowed commanders to concentrate substantial forces at the decisive point in battle, creating the necessary mass and firepower to seize the initiative. This would be particularly important if the Soviets attempted to break through in strength along only a few key axes of advance. In such a situation the penny-packet forces available at the tactical level would be unable to concentrate sufficiently. A corps or army group, however, would be better placed to amass, co-ordinate and control such forces. Finally, commanders at the operational level could raise their eyes from the immediate battle to project future developments and plan accordingly. The battle could thus be extended in time and space, with commanders looking deep into enemy territory to monitor and attack forces behind the front line.

(2) The extended battlefield

This latter point marked a second important development in military thinking, namely the concept of the extended battlefield. A central feature of Soviet military doctrine, developed from their experiences in the Second World War, is the echeloning of forces at all levels into successive waves to maintain momentum and exploit the advantages of mass (see Figure 7.1). Unlike Western-style reserves which would be used on an *ad hoc* basis as battle developed, these second-echelon forces would be assigned targets in advance of war as part of an overall plan. In the late 1970s studies at TRADOC identified these follow-on forces as a major threat, but also as presenting opportunities for NATO given their relatively predictable pattern of organization and deployment. Starry in particular began to encourage staff at TRADOC to 'look deep' at these second-echelon forces before they were committed to battle. As TRADOC looked deep so they began to see potential targets, and hence developed the idea of striking deep. Thus battle was extended in depth by hitting forces deep in enemy territory,

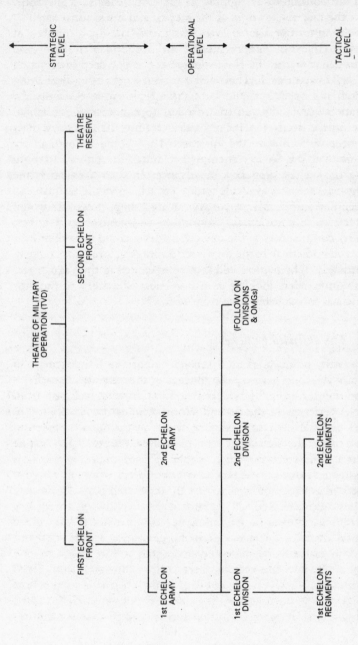

Figure 7.1 Schematic illustration of Soviet/Warsaw Pact concept of echeloning
Source: Office of Technology Assessment, 1987, p. 63

in time by monitoring developing threats, projecting trends and attacking enemy forces before they were committed to battle, and in command by placing greater emphasis upon the higher command levels and the operational art (Hanne, 1983, p. 3; Romjue, 1984, pp. 25–7). As this extended-battle concept became a central feature of AirLand Battle, so the deep-strike element was picked up by staff at NATO's military headquarters, SHAPE. Under the direction of SACEUR General Bernard Rogers, SHAPE technical centre began a series of studies in 1979 on reducing the numbers of WTO troops which could reach the front line. Initial studies focused on air interdiction against the second operational echelon, but as the threat from operational manoeuvre groups began to assume greater significance in SHAPE's thinking, so plans developed for attacking all echelons using a variety of (largely new) conventional weapons (Flanagan, 1988, p. 87). Thus FOFA progressed from a plan to disrupt and delay the arrival of the second operational echelon to a set of specific tasks against identifiable echelons using a range of emerging technologies (ETs: see Figure 7.2).

Attacking enemy forces behind the line of battle was hardly a novel idea, and an interdiction mission already existed for NATO aircraft and nuclear-armed missiles. What was new was the idea that ETs enabled conventional weapons to attack targets previously assigned to nuclear weapons (thus raising the nuclear threshold), and the direct coupling of interdiction strikes to Soviet echeloning. Deep strike could exploit echeloning in a number of ways. By metering the arrival of Soviet follow-on forces it could prevent NATO conventional defences from being overwhelmed. Moreover, by attacking these forces before they reached the forward edge of the battle area (FEBA) it could reduce their capabilities and fighting effectiveness. Thus deep strike could help compensate for Soviet numerical advantages, while the new technologies offered the potential of a new generation of force multipliers. Studies at TRADOC and elsewhere produced strong indications that an emphasis on fighting the close battle alone would lead NATO to being ground down by successive waves, but that deep strike could have a major impact by attacking these forces. Extending the battlefield would also allow NATO commanders to create 'windows' in time and space where they could seize and use the initiative (see below). Finally new weapons and sensors

CATEGORY	RANGE (km)	TARGET ECHELON	DESIRED EFFECT	OPERATIONS
1	5–30	2nd echelon regiments of engaged divisions	Destruction	Attacks vs. regiment columns by air, artillery and missile forces
2	30–80	2nd Tac echelon (2nd echelon divisions of 1st echelon armies)	Destruction	Air and missile attacks vs. divisional columns; air and missile attacks vs. regiment assembly areas
3	80–150	2nd Tac echelon	Disrupt	Air and missile attack of divisional columns and assembly areas; air attack of chokepoints and halted units; air and missile attack of command posts
4	150–350	2nd Operational echelon (2nd echelon armies of 1st echelon fronts)	Disrupt/ Delay	Air and cruise missile attack of units on roads
5	350–800	2nd Strategic echelon (2nd echelon fronts)	Delay	Cruise missile attack vs. bridges and rail network and vs. units on rails

Figure 7.2 Categories of FOFA operations
Source: Office of Technology Assessment, 1987, pp. 78–9, 203–8

would enable corps to provide long-range fire support to bolster other corps under heavy pressure (OTA, 1987, p. 4; Romjue, 1984, pp. 36 and 46).

As the deep-strike concepts were fleshed out so it became apparent that several different approaches were emerging, in particular over whether the aim was destruction or delay, how deep to strike, the priorities to be accorded to attacking the different echelons and the emphasis to be given to airfield destruction (OTA, 1987, p. 7; Romjue, 1984, p. 56). Critics moreover questioned whether the new technologies could accomplish the demanding tasks asked of them, especially in the light of possible Soviet counter-measures (Canby, 1985). Doubts emerged over the funding of FOFA given NATO's failure to realize the 4–7 per cent annual increase identified by Rogers as being necessary to finance the mission (Greenwood, 1985; Rogers, 1982), while questions were raised whether FOFA's explicit emphasis on high technology might not spur on a qualitative arms race, whether the use of near identical platforms for nuclear and conventional missions might blur rather than emphasize the nuclear divide, whether the new technologies might be destabilizing given the advantages conferred on the side which struck first, whether deep strike might act as a Trojan Horse to persuade the European members of NATO to buy new American systems, and whether the Soviets might simply overcome deep strike by placing greater emphasis on the first echelons and front loading their forces (Bellany and Huxley, 1987; OTA, 1987).

(3) Offensive actions and seizing the initiative

A final concern expressed over FOFA reflected a more general concern that NATO doctrine, including naval doctrine (Friedman, 1988; Watkins, 1986), was becoming increasingly offensive in character. AirLand Battle explicitly identified an offensive spirit as an essential prerequisite for battlefield success. Reacting to criticism that the 1976 edition of FM 100–5 had been too defensively oriented (Lind, 1977, pp. 57–61; Romjue, 1984, pp. 14–15), AirLand Battle developed the idea of engaging in offensive operations at the tactical and operational level when on the strategic defensive. Similar ideas emerged in the Bagnall reforms of 1 (BR) Corps and NORTHAG, particularly in the planned use of the counter-stroke as a deliberate offensive manoeuvre against the flank of an advancing enemy force

(Bagnall, 1984; Farndale, 1985). The emphasis of both AirLand Battle and Bagnall's reforms, however, was on offensive actions at the tactical and operational not strategic level (Richardson, 1986, p. 8).

This requirement for offensive action rather than a purely defensive battle was based upon a particular conception of the balance between mobile and positional elements in modern warfare, and a belief in the importance of seizing the initiative. AirLand Battle was

> based on securing or retaining the initiative and exercising it aggressively to accomplish the mission. The object of all operations is to impose our will upon the enemy – to achieve our purposes. To do this we must throw the enemy off balance with a powerful blow from an unexpected direction, follow up rapidly to prevent his recovery and continue operations aggressively to achieve the higher commander's goal. (FM 100-5, 1986, p. 14)

Similarly Bagnall stated that

> there is no alternative to us attempting to seize the initiative ourselves at an early stage. Unless we achieve this we will only be reacting to Soviet moves and, as a greatly inferior force, would inevitably be ground down in a battle of attrition. (Bagnall, 1984, p. 60)

The initiative would be secured by surprise attacks against invading forces which, if successful, would be rapidly exploited. Advancing WTO forces would be thrown off balance and forced into a position of having to react to NATO military moves rather than imposing their will on the Atlantic Alliance (Hanne, 1983, p. 7). Unable to exploit their numerical advantage, and unable to conduct battle on their own terms, Pact forces would hopefully be thrown into confusion, their momentum broken up and force effectiveness reduced.

(4) Mobility and manoeuvre

For American and NATO commanders, seizing the initiative became the key to battlefield success. The initiative was something best achieved by surprise (counter-)offensive actions. This in turn reinforced the movement in the 1980s towards a manoeuvre-oriented doctrine, emphasizing mobile rather than positional elements.

There is a danger in caricaturing 1970s doctrine as being dominated by firepower and positional battles compared to the fast-moving, mobile operations advocated in the 1980s. Doctrine in the 1970s as in the 1980s emphasized the importance of mobility. The difference lay in the *way* in which mobility was to be used rather than in mobility *per se*. Both the British concept of 'killing zones' and American 'active defense' advocated mobility in the positioning of forces along enemy axes of advance, where they would engage in a series of battles emphasizing firepower rather than manoeuvre. New anti-tank missiles in particular seemed to offer substantial advantages to concealed defensive forces. Mobility would also be used at the tactical level to improve survivability, but counter-attacks would be small-scale operations organized at the divisional level with limited aims (Karber, 1976, pp. 28–9; Starry, 1978; Romjue, 1984, pp. 8–9 and 18–19; TRADOC, 1976, p. 27). In contrast AirLand Battle was a much more manoeuvre-oriented doctrine, summed up in the key word 'agility':

> Agility – the ability of friendly forces to act faster than the enemy – is the first prerequisite for seizing and holding the initiative . . . [It] permits the *rapid concentration of friendly strength against enemy vulnerabilities.* This must be done repeatedly so that by the time the enemy reacts to one action, another has already taken place, disrupting his plans and leading to late, uncoordinated, and piecemeal enemy responses. It is this *process of successive concentration against locally weaker or unprepared enemy forces* which enables smaller forces to disorient, fragment and eventually defeat much larger enemy formations. (FM 100-5, 1986, p. 16, emphasis added)

AirLand Battle thus advanced the idea of a succession of powerful blows from unexpected directions conducted against enemy *weak points* to throw the enemy off balance, rather than against the decisive point of an enemy breakthrough (FM 100-5, 1986, p. 16). This was not the classic manoeuvre strategy of envelopment, but one whereby battle would be sought on favourable terms and the maximum use made of surprise. Similarly both Bagnall and Farndale promoted the use of the counter-stroke, an offensive flanking action against enemy forces either on the march or who had yet to take up defensive positions, which if successful would allow a numerically inferior force to destroy a larger enemy force and seize the initiative (Farndale, 1985; 'Halberdier', 1983).

As the British and Americans began to advocate manoeuvre-oriented doctrines, so the West Germans were increasingly placed in a dilemma. On the one hand, unless NATO doctrine was to become hopelessly confused, there was a requirement for the Bundeswehr at the very least to take account of the new thinking; on the other hand, given the substantial proportion of West German population and industry near the inner German border (IGB), and the lack of operational depth in West Germany, there was an understandable fear that a manoeuvre doctrine would place large sections of West Germany at risk. In addition German officers argued that the terrain close to the IGB offered many of the best defensive positions in West Germany. Thus a compromise emerged in the Bundeswehr reflecting this distinctively German predicament. A cohesive forward defence was to be maintained as close to the IGB as terrain would allow. In addition the doctrinal manual HDv 100-100 emphasized both the importance of holding defensive positions, and that such positions were only to be abandoned if ordered by higher commanders. But Bundeswehr doctrine also shifted to acknowledge the importance of gaining the initiative, of avoiding set-piece attritional battles, and of using sophisticated barriers (such as mines) to block an advance and allow reserves to manoeuvre, attack and destroy enemy forces. In particular the West Germans agreed with Bagnall that forward defence must not lead to a static linear deployment of forces, but rather that strong reserve forces must be used aggressively to wrest the initiative off the enemy.

It would be a mistake to view the West Germans as clinging to positional elements for purely political reasons as other NATO countries moved to a fully mobile concept of operations. NATO's new military thinking does not advocate a totally mobile style of warfare. Indeed the ground on the Central Front is littered with sufficient obstacles as to make fluid battles with no positional elements appear impractical (Faringdon, 1986). Rather in certain circumstances positional warfare should be used. The NORTHAG

Concept for example talked of holding 'vital areas', which if captured were to be retaken (Bellamy, 1987, p. 147). Similarly AirLand Battle considered a range of defensive options from manoeuvre to positional battles, emphasizing that commanders must be flexible in their approach and use the best means relevant to each situation (Romjue, 1984, p. 71). It is important to note, however, that both Bagnall and AirLand Battle viewed positional defensive operations as precursors to manoeuvre, wearing the enemy down and allowing friendly forces to concentrate elsewhere.

(5) The human dimension

A final important development in the 1980s was a new emphasis on human factors in war: 'The most essential element of combat power is *competent* and *confident leadership* . . . agility is as much a mental as a physical quality' (FM 100-5, 1986, pp. 13 and 16, emphasis in original). Whereas military doctrine in the 1970s was strongly influenced (particularly in the United States) by the 'calculus of battle' and a systems approach to war, the 1980s was marked by a re-emergence of the moral dimension of warfare. The view which emerged was that the outcome of battle was determined not merely by physical factors such as numbers, rates of fire, lethality, speed and distance, but by the more human qualities of morale, leadership, training and the will to win (Richardson, 1986, p. 6). For Farndale, the successful outcome of a counter-stroke was dependent upon the skill of commanders in applying the operational art, of troops being well trained and 'imbued with aggressive spirit', and of bold and imaginative leadership from the front (Farndale, 1985, pp. 6–8). Some US Army commanders even began to talk, in terms not far removed from Ardant du Picq and the generals of the First World War, of battle being a clash of wills, and of the result of battle being dependent upon the psychological ability to endure and prevail (Romjue, 1984, pp. 53–5). Technology was not important. Indeed deep-strike concepts in particular were explicitly linked with the development of new technologies. But battle was fought by soldiers *using* weapon systems, and the capabilities and will of the soldier were at least as important as the system in determining the outcome of battle.

CONCLUSION

The 1980s saw a number of developments in NATO military
doctrine which, when coupled to improvements in equipment,
produced a greater confidence in NATO's conventional capabilities. These developments paralleled the debate over NATO
strategy in reducing nuclear reliance. But is this confidence well-
placed, and does NATO's military doctrine remain compatible
with political developments in the changing strategic environment
of the early 1990s?

Doubts over the effectiveness of deep strike have been raised
above. Doubts can also be expressed over other aspects of NATO's
new military thinking. The emphasis on manoeuvre requires mobile
forces using speed and surprise for effect and survival. Mobility
however is hindered not merely by geographic constraints in West
Germany (the lack of strategic depth, increased urbanization, rivers
and canals, forests, and so forth) but by technological developments.
New battlefield surveillance aids may reduce the possibility of
surprise and render mobile forces vulnerable to attack; hi-tech
and low-tech barriers (from smart mines to anti-tank ditches)
can now be rapidly constructed to limit manoeuvrability; and
WTO forward air assets, particularly anti-armour helicopters,
could prove devastatingly effective against forces moving in the
open. Similarly morale factors may be important in avoiding an
early collapse, but they do not contribute decisively to battlefield
success. The French may have lost in 1940 because of poor
morale (amongst other factors); but they did not win in 1914
despite an emphasis on offensive spirit and the will to win.
Moreover, as resource constraints (financial and manpower) begin
to bite in the early 1990s morale, as well as equipment levels,
may suffer.

No military strategy is risk-free, and current doctrine is no
different in being vulnerable to military, technological and resource
developments. What is different is that NATO's new military doctrine has increased the element of risk in the hope that, if everything
works, the payoff will be worth the gamble. Manoeuvre doctrines
are difficult to implement successfully and can fail dramatically. But
if they are successful they can reap disproportionate returns. FOFA
is reliant on a variety of new technologies working synergistically.
If one part of the system fails, the knock-on effects could be

considerable; but if the whole system works the benefits could be decisive.

Perhaps the greatest single problem, however, is the changing strategic environment. The defence agenda of the early 1980s was governed by a perception of a Soviet threat, demonstrated by the invasion of Afghanistan and the deployment of the SS-20, and centring on massive Soviet conventional superiority in Europe and nuclear parity or even US inferiority (Committee on the Present Danger, 1978; 1982). As the Soviet threat receded in the late 1980s, and as the Gorbachev-inspired new military thinking is translated into arms reductions by the Soviet Union, so the defence agenda is changing to one of reciprocal security dominated by arms control and confidence building. NATO's military doctrine and force structure, emphasizing manoeuvre by large armoured formations, offensive actions, seizing the initiative and deep strike, appear ill-suited to this changing agenda. The 1980s saw developments in military doctrine and the debate over NATO strategy running in roughly the same direction. As the strategic environment begins to change there is a danger that NATO's doctrine and force structure may hinder or fall foul of such changes. Non-offensive defence and common security do not dominate the defence agenda at present, but the indications are that the future of existing doctrines and force structures are numbered.

REFERENCES

Bagnall, General Sir Nigel (1984), 'Concepts of land/air operations in the central region I', *RUSI Journal*, vol. 129, no. 3, pp. 59–62.
Baylis, J. (1988), 'NATO strategy: the case for a new strategic concept', *International Affairs*, vol. 64, no. 1, pp. 43–59.
Beach, General Sir Hugh (1986), 'On improving NATO strategy', in A. Pierre (ed.), *The Conventional Defense of Europe: New Technologies and New Strategies* (New York: Council on Foreign Relations).
Bellamy, C. (1987), *The Future of Land Warfare* (London: Croom Helm).
Bellany, I., and Huxley, T. (eds) (1987), *New Conventional Weapons and Western Defence* (London: Cass).
Biddle, S. (1988), 'The European conventional balance: a reinterpretation of the debate', *Survival*, vol. 30, no. 2, pp. 99–121.
Bracken, P. (1983), *The Command and Control of Nuclear Forces* (New Haven, Conn.: Yale University Press).

Bundy, M., Kennan, G., McNamara, R., and Smith G. (1982), 'Nuclear weapons and the Atlantic Alliance', *Foreign Affairs*, vol. 60, no. 4, pp. 753–66.

Canby, S. (1985), 'New conventional force technology and the NATO–Warsaw Pact balance: part I', in *New Technology and Western Security Policy: Part II*, Adelphi Paper No.198 (London: IISS), pp. 7–20.

Chalmers, C., and Unterseher, L. (1988), 'Is there a tank gap? Comparing NATO and Warsaw Pact tank fleets', *International Security*, vol. 13, no. 1, pp. 5–49.

Cohen, E. (1988), 'Toward better net assessment: rethinking the European conventional balance', *International Security*, vol. 13, no. 1, pp. 50–89.

Committee on the Present Danger (1978), *Is America Becoming Number Two? Current Trends in the US–Soviet Military Balance* (Washington, DC: Committee on the Present Danger).

Committee on the Present Danger (1982), *Has America Become Number Two? The US–Soviet Military Balance and American Defense Policies and Programs* (Washington, DC: Committee on the Present Danger).

Donnelly, C. (1985), *Heirs of Clausewitz: Change and Continuity in the Soviet War Machine* (London: IEDSS).

Epstein, J. (1987), *The 1988 Defense Budget* (Washington, DC: Brookings).

Epstein, J. (1988), 'Dynamic analysis and the conventional balance in Europe', *International Security*, vol. 12, no. 4, pp. 154–65.

ESECS (1983), *Strengthening Conventional Deterrence in Europe: Proposals for the 1980s* (London: Macmillan).

Faringdon, H. (1986), *Confrontation: The Strategic Geography of NATO and the Warsaw Pact* (London: Routledge & Kegan Paul).

Farndale, General Sir Martin (1985), 'Counter stroke: future requirements', *RUSI Journal*, vol. 130, no. 4, pp. 6–9.

Flanagan, S. (1988), *NATO's Conventional Forces: Options for the Central Region* (London: Macmillan).

FM 100-5 (1982), *Operations* (Washington, DC: HQ US Army).

FM 100-5 (1986), *Operations* (Washington, DC: HQ US Army).

Freedman, L. (1986), *The Price of Peace: Living with the Nuclear Dilemma* (London: Firethorn).

Friedman, N. (1988), *The US Maritime Strategy* (London: Jane's).

Gates, D. (1987), 'Area defence concepts: the West German debate', *Survival*, vol. 29, no. 4, pp. 301–17.

Greenwood, D. (1985), 'Economic implications: finding the resources for an effective conventional defence', in S. Windass (ed.), *Avoiding Nuclear War: Common Security as a Strategy for the Defence of the West* (London: Brassey), pp. 77–86.

'Halberdier' (1983), 'Counterstroke: an option for the defence', *British Army Review*, no. 73, pp. 30–2.

Hanne, W. (1983), *AirLand Battle and the Operational Maneuver Group* (Carlisle Barracks, Pa: Strategic Studies Institute, US Army War College).

Holmes, K. (1988), 'Measuring the conventional balance in Europe', *International Security*, vol. 12, no. 4, pp. 166–73.

Jervis, R. (1978), 'Cooperation under the security dilemma', *World Politics*, vol. 30, no. 2, pp. 167–214.

Karber, P. (1976), 'Dynamic doctrine for dynamic defense', *Armed Forces Journal International*, October, pp. 28–9.

Lebow, R. (1987), 'Deterrence failure revisited', *International Security*, vol. 12, no. 1, pp. 197–213.

Mearsheimer, J. (1982), 'Why the Soviets can't win quickly in central Europe', *International Security*, vol. 7, no. 1, pp. 3–39.

Mearsheimer, J. (1983), *Conventional Deterrence* (Ithaca, NY: Cornell University Press).

Mearsheimer, J. (1988), 'Numbers, strategy and the European balance', *International Security*, vol. 12, no. 4, pp. 174–85.

NATO (1988), *Conventional Forces in Europe: the Facts* (Brussels: NATO Press Service).

Office of Technology Assessment (1987), *New Technology for NATO: Implementing Follow-On Forces Attack* (Washington, DC: US GPO).

Orme, J. (1987), 'Deterrence failures: a second look', *International Security*, vol. 11, no. 3, pp. 3–40.

Pay, J. (1988), 'The battlefield since 1945', in C. McInnes and G. Sheffield (eds), *Warfare in the Twentieth Century: Theory and Practice* (London: Unwin Hyman), pp. 213–35.

Pierre, A. (1986), 'Enhancing conventional defence: a question of priorities', in A. Pierre (ed.), *The Conventional Defense of Europe: New Technologies and New Strategies* (New York: Council on Foreign Relations), pp. 9–39.

Posen, B. (1984), 'Measuring the European conventional balance: coping with complexity in threat assessment', *International Security*, vol. 9, no. 3, pp. 47–88.

Posen, B. (1988), 'Is NATO decisively outnumbered?', *International Security*, vol. 12, no. 4, pp. 186–202.

Richardson, General W. (1986), 'FM 100-5: the AirLand Battle in 1986', *Military Review*, March, pp. 4–11.

Rogers, General B. (1982), 'The Atlantic Alliance: prescriptions for a difficult decade ahead', *Foreign Affairs*, vol. 60, no. 5, pp. 1,145–56.

Romjue, J. (1984), *From Active Defense to AirLand Battle: The Development of Army Doctrine 1973–82*, TRADOC Historical Monographs Series (Washington, DC: US GPO).

Snyder, G. (1961), *Deterrence and Defense* (Princeton, NJ: Princeton University Press).

Starry, General D. (1978), 'A tactical evolution – FM 100-5', *Military Review*, August, pp. 2–11.

Starry, General D. (1983), 'To change an army', *Military Review*, March, pp. 20–7.

Statement on the Defence Estimates 1987 (London: HMSO).

TRADOC (1976), 'TRADOC's reply', *Armed Forced Journal International*, October, p. 27.

Unterseher, L. (1989), *The Spider and the Web: The Case for a Pragmatic Defence Alternative* (Bonn: SAS).

Watkins, Admiral James D. (1986), 'The maritime strategy', *US Naval Institute Proceedings*, special issue, January, pp. 2–17.
Vigor, P. (1983), *Soviet Blitzkrieg Theory* (London: Macmillan).

8

Alternative defence:
the new reality

MICHAEL CLARKE

Since the early 1980s the concept of 'alternative defence' has been synonymous with radical critiques of existing defence policies. It has normally been regarded as being at the opposite end of the spectrum of argument from the more traditional views that support official defence policies in major Western governments. The alternative school of thought is 'alternative' in that it is concerned to devise an acceptable non-nuclear defence policy for Western countries. The school is usually distinguished by the belief that a 'non-provocative', conventional, defence for Western Europe is militarily feasible. As such it would also be politically preferable since it would provide a more secure basis for the pursuit of détente and co-operation between East and West (Alternative Defence Commission, 1983; 1985; 1987). Establishment arguments, by contrast, have maintained that defence policies must be based on the concept of nuclear deterrence. There was very little in common between them.

In a world where the realities behind defence policies have changed with remarkable rapidity at the turn of the decade, it would be unfair to both establishment and alternative arguments to continue to portray them as defining the ends of a rather broad spectrum. We are witnessing a certain amount of uneven convergence between many of the premisses of each.

The present state of the Western defence debate can be stated starkly. Where establishment and alternative arguments encounter each other in a discussion of the best future for NATO, some on both sides regard their opposite numbers as unable to appreciate the real problem and simply continue to disagree. Some alternative thinkers are concerned to redefine the nature of international security itself and will have no truck with NATO or the politics that support it, particularly in a Europe in which the Berlin Wall has come down: some establishment writers believe that nuclear deterrence is simply a fact of life and that the best security guarantee remains the Atlantic Alliance as presently organized. A growing number of both establishment and alternative analysts, however, take more pragmatic positions than these and are interested in the way the present changes taking place in Europe might affect their view of future security. Such analysts, from both sides of the conceptual fence, find that they agree on a surprising number of details and on some of the assumptions behind them. On the other hand, where they do not agree, the difference between them is fundamental. The purpose of this chapter, therefore, is to analyse their discussion in order to reveal the extent of convergence that has occurred and the nature of the deeper disagreements that remain.

THE AREAS OF AGREEMENT

The methodology of the military balance

There is a growing consensus among defence analysts on the need to interpret figures of the military balance in Europe more carefully. The best analyses have always been careful to build in the appropriate caveats to their figures (International Institute for Strategic Studies, 1988, pp. 233–41; Kelly, 1984), but in the past they have not been used so sensitively. Official figures from Washington, Moscow, London and Brussels have almost always been used to prove a particular point and have never provided an uncontroversial view of the balance (Department of Defense, 1988, pp. 106–18; NATO, 1988; *Statement on the Defence Estimates*, 1988, pp. 60–4; USSR Military Academy, 1982).

A major outcome of the last decade of defence debates has been to make analyses of the conventional balance of forces more sensitive. Even official publications have become noticeably more anxious to point out the difficulties of definition and of arriving at a single clear picture. In general, there is an acceptance that numbers of troops and equipment are only meaningful when they are expressed as parts of usable combat units. Thus, the calculation of broad troop numbers tells us very little, since differing levels of training and combat readiness, different roles and the ambiguity over what constitutes 'a soldier', do not allow for genuine comparisons. Equally, the measurement of divisions is hardly definitive since divisions are differently structured, manned and equipped between the two alliances. Total numbers of tanks are not in themselves very helpful if they do not discriminate between modern front-line tanks and stockpiles of retired models, and so on (Biddle, 1987).

In view of these problems there is a reasonable measure of agreement that a meaningful static balance of ground forces can be arrived at if a common unit of counting is adopted – such as the 'armoured division equivalent' – and assessed in the light of a realistic expectation of reinforcement over a certain period (Mako, 1983). Equally, there is reasonable agreement among academics, if not between official statements, that air-power resources are uniquely difficult to assess. The flexibility, mobility and importance of technological innovation to the success of air power make its calculation highly subject to speculative assumptions. Nevertheless, it is possible to specify static comparisons of air power by including available front-line reinforcement numbers, both home- and carrier-based, by breaking 'combat aircraft' down into interceptor and attack roles, by measuring deliverable tonnages of ordinance, and by trying to calculate a sortie rate based on aircraft numbers measured against some estimate of the survivability of operating bases over a given period (Epstein, 1984).

Naval power, because of its flexibility, presents similar problems. Again, there is some agreement that the critical calculation is in the degree of difficulty of the roles that naval power would be required to perform in a period of hostility. The relationship of naval assets to geographical starting positions also has to be assessed: the United States is a long way from Europe; but the Black Sea and the Baltic can easily be bottled up, and so on. In this way a tentative analysis can be made of the balance of relevant naval power as it applies to the European theatre (Kaufmann, 1983).

The calculation of the military balance

On the basis of the above, it is possible to specify with more certainty than many would have thought possible a few years ago what the static balance looks like in Europe. Indeed, the opening of the Conventional Forces in Europe (CFE) talks in March 1989 revealed that both NATO and the WTO were generally agreed on the outlines of the military balance in Europe, after more than a decade of fruitless talks in which they had disagreed. Whatever result the CFE talks might reach, it is clear that they began from a reasonably agreed basis, and this is reflected in the greater consensus within Western debates on the nature of the balance.

In terms of ground forces the Warsaw Treaty Organization (WTO) at the beginning of the CFE talks in 1989 had a meaningful advantage on the Central Front of the order of eighty-nine armoured division equivalents, after about fourteen days of operations, as against about sixty-four that NATO could be expected to field. NATO is in a more vulnerable position on its flanks. In the north relatively small WTO forces could win significant territory to use as bases, and in the south a major conflict could be fought by large numbers of comparatively unsophisticated WTO forces. There is no disagreement that NATO is outmanned on the ground in Europe.

Nor is there much disagreement that NATO's naval forces are actually in a far better position to carry out their roles than are the navies of the WTO. If NATO is unable to keep its sea-lines of communication open it will almost certainly owe more to its own inefficiencies than the power of the Soviet navy. Indeed, as Griggs points out (1988, pp. 55–65), it would be quite feasible for NATO's navies to intervene directly on the Central Front through the use of conventional cruise missiles for deep interdiction.

There is less unanimity over the balance of forces in the air, chiefly because it seems increasingly to represent a decisive military advantage for NATO and the establishment is reluctant to admit that the West might hold such a trump card. The WTO fields some 8,000 fixed-wing combat aircraft, but NATO's total of around 5,000 excludes some 1,750 normally based in the US and Canada. And if missions are examined then it emerges that NATO aircraft can deliver higher tonnages of ordinance – between three and seven times the deliverable tonnages of the WTO – particularly at longer ranges (Kelly, 1986).

Qualitative assessments are, by general consent, matters of even more delicate judgement, but the weight of the most careful analyses clearly gives NATO a continuing advantage in quality and reliability. As the military hardware of the WTO catches up with NATO, so it finds itself a whole generation behind in software, and probably more than a generation behind in the integration of complex battlefield systems.

The overall consensus that emerges from both sides of the debate is that NATO and the WTO are not sufficiently alike to allow for a threat assessment to be decided by bean-counting. Equally, it is generally agreed that it is almost inconceivable that commanders on either side would feel particularly confident that they would be able to succeed in their military missions. A future war in Europe would be a desperately uncertain business for both sides. NATO is not facing an efficient steamroller; nor is the WTO facing a rock-solid defence (Meacham, 1986).

Asymmetrical strategic requirements

There is a general consensus that the military balance has to be seen in the context of the strategic tasks that both alliances would have to perform in time of conflict. It is no longer plausible for the establishment to argue that the Soviet threat might consist of a 'bolt from the blue' attack to win Western Europe for the communist world, or that a Soviet 'land grab' for Western Germany might take place. These, and similar versions of the threat, are seldom heard and now lack all credibility after the events of 1988 and 1989. If the establishment analysts now reject unrealistic scenarios of the Soviet threat, most of the alternative defence school would accept that the concept of a threat – indeed a Soviet threat – is not invalid, and that in an uncertain world it would be imprudent to live defenceless next to a military giant. Both schools also generally agree that a threat of war still exists, if not in the politics of 1990 then at least implicitly in the existence of two alliances with opposing warplans. If leaders felt that a war in Europe had become likely, then it is very credible to believe that Soviet, and perhaps Western, leaders would pre-empt it, since to go second would impose enormous costs to their military planning.

If it is accepted that an East-West war is still theoretically possible, then the mission that Soviet forces have to perform is, by general agreement, a daunting one. They have to do no less than completely destroy the NATO alliance while limiting damage to the Soviet homeland, eject the United States from the European continent, establish control over a minimum of twelve more countries and then look for a stable peace settlement. If this is an exceedingly tall order, it is nevertheless the case that nothing else makes military sense. To attack NATO and not finish it off, to leave the United States in Europe, or even to leave a possible bridgehead for some future US use, would be a military victory that left the Soviet Union in a position of inherent insecurity for the indefinite future (MccGwire, 1987).

Of course, the tallness of the order does not mean that it may not be attempted by the Soviet Union as a lesser evil in very dire circumstances. Nor does it mean that Soviet leaders might not initiate a dangerous adventure without fully understanding the military picture, or merely hope for the best in a fluid situation. Nevertheless, there is little disagreement about the essential nature of the Soviet strategic task in any future conflict and its enormity is not lost on contemporary Soviet leaders who claim to have redefined their military requirements towards a position of 'defensive sufficiency' (MccGwire, 1988).

In the short term, NATO's obvious disadvantage is a lack of space on the Central Front to absorb an attack. In the longer term, however, its advantage is that there is a great deal of space – increasingly urbanized – that the WTO would have to control in order to achieve its mission. If NATO holds well enough on the Central Front, then it would be difficult for the WTO to utilize any advantage it may have gained on the flanks. In particular, the entry of Spain into NATO and the reorientation of Portuguese defence policy which has thereby been stimulated has given NATO an enormous geographical benefit. For since 1982 Soviet planners have had to contemplate the prospect of crossing the Pyrenees and opening up two large pincers to conquer Spain and Portugal. Anything less leaves territory and bases open to the United States at some time in the future.

NATO's military deficiencies

Along with a recognition of the general outlines of the overall conventional picture, there is a very close measure of agreement between establishment and alternative arguments about the nature of NATO's real deficiencies. Indeed, the list of specific military measures that many alternative analysts draw up as a means of implementing their alternative strategies are often highly coincidental with the list of reforms that the establishment is trying to make in order to implement the present strategy better (Center for Strategic and International Studies, 1987; Unterseher, 1987). Most are reminiscent of the measures that were on the agenda of NATO's Long Term Defence Plan of the 1970s and the Conventional Defence Initiative of the 1980s.

Desirable reforms include the need to make greater use of reserves; to build up stocks of ammunition and spares to approach the thirty-day requirement; to provide for greater dispersal of logistical centres; to provide more, and dispersed, prepositioned equipment; to improve and integrate reinforcement plans; to make better use of landscaping to create barriers as force multipliers; to address the persistent problem of the malpositioning of NATO forces; and to take measures to increase the general interoperability of NATO national forces. Any alliance which operates no less than six different battlefield communication systems, none of which are capable of speaking to another, whose overall ammunition stocks can be numbered in days rather than weeks, and whose prepositioned material for US reinforcements is held in a small number of well-known and absolutely vulnerable sites, seems to have a good deal of room for improvement.

NATO's command deficiencies

Underlying almost all known deficiencies within NATO is the problem of command, control, communication and intelligence (C3I). On the problems and prospects of C3I, at least in the conventional field, there is again a good measure of agreement. This is less the case in the business of nuclear release procedures, since what appears to the alternative analyst to be dangerous chaos is justified by the establishment as a calculated uncertainty.

In the conventional field, nevertheless, it is generally agreed that NATO's C3I is absolutely crucial to a robust defence but presently less good than it would need to be. There is also agreement that NATO could have a crucial advantage over the WTO if it were able to integrate C³I resources to create an accurate and simultaneous picture of the battlefield. Computerized C³I, in effect, offers NATO the prospect of a startling picture that could penetrate the fog of war that would exist at the local level.

Emerging technology

Some alternative defence analysts put a great deal of faith in the prospects for new technology, on the assumption that the general trend in the technology of the battlefield is moving against the tank and other instruments of heavy armour. This may be true in a very general sense, but most alternative thinkers share the wary attitude of the establishment that emerging technologies (ET) may not necessarily represent advances in cost-effectiveness.

Though the promises of ET are as yet unrealized, more options are opening for anyone who would redesign, or reform, a military strategy for NATO (Mason and McInnes, 1988). There are two respects in which ET seems capable of having an evolutionary effect on future battle plans, whoever shapes them. In the first place, ET almost certainly puts greater lethality into smaller packets. At the every least, we can expect to see greater mobility in comparatively heavy weapon systems in the foreseeable future. Secondly, ET offers the prospects of better passive and active defensive operations than ever before, through the use of sensors, simultaneous communication, remotely piloted vehicles, slurry mines, smart mines, and so on. These two developments, of course, can assist offensive as well as defensive operations and choices will be made as ET appears on the battlefield.

New battle plans

Since 1982 NATO has seen the implementation of a series of new national battle plans which all point broadly in the same direction. The adoption of the AirLand Battle concept by the US army has served as the focus for a series of reforms, particularly within the British and West German forces, which have emphasized speed, flexibility and manoeuvre (Clarke, 1987; 1989). In the case of AirLand Battle, US planners seem to have rediscovered the virtues

of soldiering after the traumas of Vietnam. In Britain, the impact
of such developments coincided with a growing realization that
the British Army on the Rhine had become a good defensive force
that was slow to go onto the offensive and make the most of
local opportunities. In the Federal Republic the political necessity
to affirm the principle of forward defence had overridden any real
thinking about extensive mobility, but the shift in US thinking
proved to be a key that unlocked a series of military imperatives
for the Bundeswehr.

The trend towards new military doctrines of speed and mobility
has, however, rather split the alternative defence camp. Some see it
as an example of potential NATO aggression that can only work in
an escalatory way and which explicitly integrates the use of nuclear
and conventional forces in a warfighting plan. On the other hand
a number of alternative analysts have seen in these developments
one of the essential characteristics of successful defence; the ability
to win back what has been lost (Booth and Baylis, 1989, pp. 122–3).
In this view, a wholly static defence for Western Europe is unlikely
to be militarily effective. While static elements are important to any
alternative defence, since the circumstances of Western Europe they
promise to be unusually effective, it is generally regarded as vital
that the defender should have available some powerful mobility.
On this interpretation, AirLand Battle and the doctrines associated
with it represent some movement in the right direction. As time
goes on, so it is likely that such plans will be seen not as a
trend towards a greater nuclear threat but rather as a desire to
institutionalize better soldiering throughout the allied forces.

Short-range nuclear weapons

Whatever views analysts take about the matter of nuclear deterrence, there is little disagreement that the Intermediate Nuclear
Force Agreement of 1987 began by removing the wrong rung
on the nuclear ladder. And with INF weapons removed, the
political symbolism of short-range weapons has taken on much
greater significance: so much so that the ability to modernize the
short-range stockpile has become for some leaders yet another
test of NATO's deterrent resolve, when only five years ago it
was difficult to find any significant support, outside Bonn, for
the continuance of short-range weapons.

Political views and deterrent logic aside, it is extraordinarily difficult for any analyst to make a military case for short-range nuclear weapons. All of their fundamental problems, analysed in the early 1980s, apply with equal force even to a modernized and streamlined stockpile. Concentrations of enemy forces are best 'held at risk' by weapons of longer ranges; short-range nuclear devices would be very difficult and dangerous to use in a discriminating way once hostilities had broken out; their C^3I requirements are unrealistically high since they have to be used early and/or close; they are the most urgent targets for an enemy toying with the idea of pre-emption; they require that dedicated weapons systems be kept out of the action at exactly the time when they will be needed for conventional roles; and far from spreading the 'nuclear risk' equally among the allies, they are just as likely to spread immobility among policy-makers as their implications become obvious. There is little serious dispute that from a strictly military perspective the disappearance of short-range systems would add to the flexibility that NATO would have both in a crisis and in a conflict. Their importance in 1990 is entirely political; they are a symbol in the argument that NATO is being propelled with imprudent haste towards effective denuclearization.

Greater weapons co-ordination within NATO

The alternative and the establishment analyst have both arrived, by different routes, at a rough agreement on the necessity for greater co-ordination of weapons production. Alternative thinking has always maintained that greater weapons co-ordination is necessary to iron out one of the most egregious types of NATO inefficiency. This is important for the alternative camp, not only because it suggests that NATO will ultimately obtain better value for money, but also because it reduces one of the prime motives for weapons 'gold-plating' which has been seen as the enemy of efficient defence. Where national production runs of a weapon system are necessarily limited and the unit costs of production are high, it is inevitable that more roles and accessories are heaped upon a small number of weapons platforms. More collaborative weapons programmes, however, need not be subject to the same pressures.

Some alternative thinkers have castigated the 'gold-plating' of weapons as a symptom of the general problem of what Mary Kaldor (1981) has called the 'Baroque Arsenal'. For them the alternative to gold-plating is a series of low-technology weapons produced in very high numbers. But most alternative writers do not take this view. Technology does make a difference and a high-technology, multi-role system is not necessarily gold-plated. Collaborative weapons systems may indeed be charged with the performance of multiple roles. But a long production run and common servicing allow for a more sensible adaptation of the system to varying needs.

On the other side of the argument, the establishment has come more warily to the idea of increased collaboration. It has been pointed out for years that collaborative projects tend to cost more than comparable national projects, take longer to develop and are prone to inefficiencies. Even in the early 1980s there was little enthusiasm for them outside academic and some party political circles. The establishment has recognized, however, that the situation has changed a good deal.

It is now the case that virtually no major weapons systems can be produced nationally. The French arms industry retains more independence than most and there is still, just about, a pattern of national tank production in NATO. But the trends are all moving in the collaborative direction. The choice that defence planners are increasingly facing is to develop a collaborative, more expensive weapons system, or else develop no weapons system. This is the harsh reality of high-technology research and development costs (*Statement on the Defence Estimates*, 1988, pp. 39–42). Establishment analysts have also recognized, moreover, that the experience of collaboration in the 1970s has served as a learning process and that the 1990s represents a second stage in collaboration.

A European pillar within NATO

Directly related to the issue of collaboration is the broader question of whether there will be a more distinctive 'European pillar' within the alliance. Both alternative and establishment writers are interested in this problem, and although they have different expectations of a strengthened European pillar, their interest in it has a common root. For discussion over a European pillar

– perhaps through the European Community or the Western European Union – is a discussion about the future structure of the Atlantic Alliance. On this issue there are conservatives and progressives in both camps. Conservatives, either alternative or establishment, see the development of a European pillar as a way of preventing major structural change within the Atlantic Alliance: it is a device to keep the United States committed by improving European efficiency. On the other hand, progressives on both sides see it rather as an evolutionary development within the structure of the alliance. It will provide an orderly framework for the sort of changes that are bound to occur in the future.

There is no easy reconciliation between these views, but it is significant that essentially the same argument is taking place within both alternative and establishment schools of thought. Both schools want NATO to remain in being for the foreseeable future and do not relish the prospects of a political crisis within the alliance that could result from persistent neglect of major transatlantic issues. The problem for both is how best to preserve NATO unity, increase its military efficiency, and maintain a public commitment to it at a time when so much else is changing.

The need for a new Harmel formula

Agreement on the need to pursue détente and arms control has always existed in both camps. The difference now is that for the first time they both mean it. In the past both camps had been sceptical of the prospects of political dialogue; in the case of the establishment because it really did not trust the East; in the case of the alternative writers because they did not trust the West. Both, however, recognized in the late 1980s that in the era of Soviet *perestroika*, where Gorbachev was determined to restructure completely the Soviet armed forces and hence was determined to curse the West by granting all its arms control wishes, NATO simply could not avoid a more overtly political approach to the East. There was need for a new Harmel formula, to replace the 1967 decision to create the military conditions for détente. And by 1990, when the future of East European political life was in the balance, 'Harmel' and even 'détente' seemed hardly adequate to the task that history was posing for the West.

Thus, somewhat to everyone's surprise, real conventional arms control is now seriously on the political agenda and in a way that looks set to avoid the sterile outcome of the conventional force talks of the 1970s. It is impossible to argue that the Soviet Union is not serious about arms control: its unilateral arms cuts have been well in excess of those which would be needed for a propaganda victory. If Mr Gorbachev is bluffing then the bluff is so reckless as to be irresistible for the West to call. This is not to say that arms control in Europe is heading for inevitable success, but Gorbachev has, at the very least, promoted a spirit of 'new thinking' in arms control circles (Karber, 1989).

A new approach to arms control, 'confidence-building' as a major part of stability and a 'European common security regime' are all now realistic possibilities. There is, of course, no shortage of suspicion as to Soviet motives and scepticism at the arms control prospects (Sherr, 1988). That, however, is not really the point. For, whether sceptical or not, all analysts agree that NATO's military policy must be genuinely integrated with its political approach to the East and that we have to be clearer about the objectives of arms control negotiations (Freedman, 1986).

AN ASSESSMENT OF CONVERGENCE AND DIVERGENCE

None of the above should be taken to mean that alternative and establishment defence analysts see eye to eye on all these issues. Very often they arrive at complementary conclusions for very different reasons. The importance of this part of the analysis is to point out that there is, nevertheless, a degree of convergent thinking on such practical matters. There are certain steps that NATO ought to take, and processes already under way that it should build upon, to remedy some of its conventional inefficiencies; there are some long-standing problems in the matter of weapons procurement which NATO can no longer fail to come to grips with; and there is a rapidly changing political context which has raised more searching questions about the future of the alliance than anything else over the last forty years.

Such convergent thinking can only go so far because both schools of thought still make different assumptions about the nature of

East–West relations. For the alternative analyst a solution to NATO's practical problems is a way of constructing a non–nuclear alternative to the present flexible response doctrine. Alternative writers can see NATO moving in a series of directions that *could* facilitate the development of a very robust conventional defence. They feel they have proved that military alternatives do exist for the alliance, indeed have to be addressed, and that NATO itself is beginning to recognize this logic.

For the establishment, in contrast, solutions to such problems are not a way of looking for alternatives but rather of bolstering flexible response and adapting it to some radically new circumstances. On this argument NATO has always been an evolutionary alliance, and though the pace of evolution may have gone into a higher gear in recent years, there is nothing particularly surprising in anything that is now under discussion.

The limits of their convergence brings us to the real nature of the divergence between the two schools of thought. It can be characterized as disagreement over three central assumptions.

(1)   The assumption that security is an end product more than a process

Establishment analysts have tended to assume that Europe has stumbled on a secure status quo since 1945. On this basis such analysts argue that an alternative strategy would create a crisis within NATO that might become highly damaging, even disintegrative. Nuclear weapons perform an important symbolic function that helps keep the alliance united. This assumption underlies arguments about the financial cost of alternatives – that NATO could not afford to compensate for the loss of nuclear capacities. And it underlies arguments that conventional alternatives would simply raise the visibility of armed forces in European politics and create a 'new militarism', if not a new arms race.

The challenge is not to rebutt such arguments, though all of them can be convincingly rebutted, but rather to explore the assumption itself. All the establishment arguments that we have characterized in this discussion would accept that security is a dynamic commodity and that the circumstances surrounding an alliance never stand still. Nevertheless, when they consider European security this insight is often ignored. NATO is assumed to 'work' and the present arrangement is well understood. If the strategy is a muddle, this in itself may be good for deterrence and in any case it is a familiar muddle. There are good political reasons going back over many years, say the defenders of the present situation, to account for the type of muddle we have. The alternative defence lobby, they say, would dismantle – and the telling verb 'dismantle' occurs with significant frequency – some key features of the present arrangement without sufficiently clear ideas as to what will replace them (Booth and Baylis, 1989, pp. 245–6; *Statement on the Defence Estimates*, 1987, p. 2); the alternativists fail to appreciate the delicate balance of political compromises behind the present strategy and are asking NATO to take a leap into the dark. On this basis, the establishment is able to construct a series of bleak scenarios and 'what ifs' that make alternative writers seem reckless. And if NATO overreacts to the changes in Eastern Europe and is pushed along on a tide of political euphoria, it risks throwing out the baby with the bath water.

Alternative writers, however, do not accept that the present situation is essentially stable. They do not accept that NATO or the WTO are in control of the processes they claim to police and see the continuation of present military policies as more of a leap in the dark than the alternatives they propose. Alternative writers see security more as a continuing process rather a political status quo. As such, they are concerned to exert some clear political control over the dynamic processes of change, where at least, they claim, the alternatives would be worked out by a process of analysis rather than political incrementalism (Generals for Peace and Disarmament, 1984, pp. 58–104; Windass, 1985, pp. 1–61).

(2) The assumption that the Soviet threat is synonymous with the structural threat

Many pages of argument have been devoted to the establishment proposition that any raising of the nuclear threshold in Europe, and certainly its removal, would make conventional war more likely. Alternative defence, it is often said, would make Europe safe for conventional war, and from a German point of view the chemistry of the explosives detonated on their territory would be of purely academic interest. Equally, a non-nuclear defence policy would leave Western Europe open to nuclear blackmail, certainly by the Soviet Union and ultimately by other powers as well. Such arguments derive from an assumption that there is no fundamental difference between the threat that the Soviet Union poses and that which is posed by the structure of East-West alliances and their battle plans.

The establishment is still sceptical whether the Soviet threat is in real decline and claim to require evidence of long-term nature for the proposition. It argues that even if the Soviet Union has no aggressive intentions at present, it would be very foolish for NATO to assume that such intentions may not be reversed some time in the future (*Statement on the Defence Estimates*, 1989, p. 1); so the Soviet Union is still a potential threat because its interests remain antagonistic to outs, and like all great powers it would be prepared to blackmail the West if it thought it could get away with it.

The establishment, however, also integrates a different type of threat into this analysis. Crisis in Europe or elsewhere may lead Soviet leaders to miscalculate or misjudge their behaviour, and this may lead to the switch in intentions that is generally feared. The system of East-West relations may malfunction and we might face an aggressive WTO that has manoeuvred itself into a political corner. In other words, we face both a 1939 scenario (the aggressor deliberately starts a war) and a 1914 scenario (a crisis creates an aggressor who accidentally starts a war). In the arguments of the establishment, the second type of threat reinforces the first (Booth and Baylis, 1989, pp. 269–70).

For the alternative school there is a clear and important distinction between these two sorts of threat. Alternative writers may grudgingly agree that the Soviet Union should, for the time being at least, be considered a credible threat on grounds of its capabilities and historical antagonism to the West. More importantly they see the second threat – the structural problem – not only as more dangerous, but also as a key to the first: reduce the second threat and you have a real chance to eliminate the first by building on the political foundations which are thereby laid. The Soviet threat has been as much 'reactive' as 'assertive', and now that the assertive threat appears to be in steep decline, we have the opportunity to encourage a political transformation by addressing the reactive elements of it (Shenfield, 1985; 1987).

For the alternative defence writer the structural issue is crucial. The prospects of war in Europe are, in themselves, very low. But nuclear strategies make the prospect of war more likely by creating military structures that are built on offensive nuclear strikes and hence are prone to pre-emptive action. This is where the alternativists construct their own gloomy scenarios: they argue that military tension has been institutionalized and that in a crisis our political options are limited. For the alternative writer, nuclear weapons have not kept the peace in Europe so much as Europe has been extraordinarily lucky since the early 1960s not to have experienced a major crisis where modern nuclear strategies have been tested.

(3) The assumption that retaliation is necessary

Most basic of all is the assumption that the West cannot safely dispense with the capacity to retaliate. Some very diverse arguments are derived from this, such as the need to retain *all* military options in order to maintain maximum uncertainty in the calculations of the opposition. Another variation is that NATO must retain the ability to make deep strikes into WTO territory in order to relieve military pressures at the front. For similar reasons, NATO cannot make any no-first-use declarations or establish nuclear-free zones, since this will merely succeed in reducing the options of NATO commanders without exerting equal constraints on WTO commanders.

In reality all these arguments derive from a sensible military instinct that offensive capabilities should not be eschewed even in defensive warfare. The alternativist might argue about the type and amount of offensive capacity necessary for successful defence but in most alternative formulations the principle that limited counter-thrusts are part of a successful defence is not contested.

The real arguments derive from more fundamental premisses about retaliation proper. If the establishment sees the Soviet threat as more dangerous than the systemic threat then there is something to be deterred: the Soviet Union will be tempted to use, or threaten, its nuclear weapons if it feels it can derive an advantage from them. Only effective retaliation can deal with this (MccGwire, 1986).

For the alternative writer, the threat of nuclear retaliation has become (even if it was not always) the essence of the real, systemic threat. The West does not need a retaliatory strategy against the

Soviet Union, since alternatives exist, and is simply making the real threat worse by clinging to it.

In effect, the alternativist and the defender of the establishment survey their common concerns and agree about many of the details. The alternative writer is able to maintain that a robust conventional strategy for NATO is within its grasp. That does not mean that it will happen, but both see that it is achievable. Both have reappraised NATO's standard wisdom of many years that the WTO would 'be at the Channel in five days were it not for the nuclear deterrent', and so on. And both have a realistic appreciation of NATO's, and Gorbachev's, current problems. 'So', says the alternativist, 'you agree that it is feasible that NATO could successfully defend itself by conventional forces alone?' 'Yes', says the traditionalist, 'but successful defence will not be enough. Without a retaliatory capacity, I cannot feel secure.' At this point both ought to be aware that they make different assumptions about the nature of European security, the real nature of the threat and the nature of the political processes by which security is achieved.

THE LEVELS OF SECURITY ANALYSIS

A recognition of divergent assumptions does not mean that the analysis cannot go any further. The assumptions can be examined more carefully, if we acknowledge that what we call 'the strategic debate' is really a series of very different debates about any number of diverse and overlapping issues. The debate under discussion takes place at different levels of analysis and the prospects for change in its fundamental assumptions are correspondingly different at each level.

The operational level

The operational level of security analysis is that which covers the military establishments and NATO's political and military secretariats. It is the level where the military professionals have to perform their given roles in the light of their specific problems. At this level security debates are surprisingly flexible. For though the military may be regarded as essentially conservative in their attitude, they are only conservative within whatever paradigm of security thinking exists at a particular time. Debates at the operational level are more agnostic on nuclear issues than is normally assumed, or else very ambiguous, since the military is normally called upon to perform miraculous feats with inadequate resources.

The military have plans and procedures to use nuclear weapons in Europe, and as loyal troops they would put them into operation if called upon to do so. Thus, it is claimed, the strategy is not a muddle; the military knows what it would do and regularly rehearses the procedures. And many in the military are prepared to make a strong case for the possession of any weapons system that might provide them with another military option.

Clear operational plans, however, do not in themselves produce a coherent strategy and calls for maximum military options are less compelling to the military professional than a concern that existing options should be exercisable. Professionals at the operational level are only too aware of NATO's conventional inefficiencies, and planning is driven by a tendency to worst-case analyses, as indeed it should be at this level. The result is that arguments over alternatives focus on a narrow range of issues.

Whether or not deterrence is necessary, whether or not we are dealing with the Soviet threat wisely, and so on, are not questions to be addressed at the operational level. At this level the problem is much simpler. Faced by so many operational inefficiencies which create a wastage of resources (as opposed to the WTO which is relatively rich in military resources), is a remedy highly unlikely or even impossible? Furthermore, will the CFE talks, if they are successful, still leave NATO at a disadvantage on the ground in Central Europe? If so, then NATO's nuclear weapons may be thought to compensate for the wastage, or the disadvantage, though they do not remedy them.

If, on the basis of this argument, the operational planner accepts that nuclear weapons are necessary, then the next question becomes whether nuclear weapons are genuinely usable at the operational level. Many military professionals would agree that NATO's nuclear weapons could not be employed with any flexibility and assume that they would not, in reality, use any nuclear devices in a conflict. More than that, it is highly questionable whether even selective nuclear use in Europe could avoid such widespread chaos and destruction as to render any conventional battle plans inoperable. In other words, if a credible *operational* nuclear scenario is not possible for NATO then nuclear use can only be argued at the political level, since it can only be seen as a deterrent.

The political level

Security arguments at the political level are inevitably dominated more by the heart than the head and are an amalgam of several other good (and bad) arguments. Nevertheless, arguments about alternative defence at this level focus on a wide, but relatively coherent, range of issues.

To begin with, the justification for deterrence is a gut political judgement backed up by the general weight of public opinion which perceives a threat. Alternative defence arguments have generally tried to go with this political grain and thus centre around the question of whether the deterrent has to be nuclear, and hence retaliatory, in character. There is a real distinction between retaliation and defence, and the logical argument between the establishment and the alternativist, as we have seen, turns on it. But at the political level the alternative argument seeks to command political support by offering leaders something of a hybrid formula – 'defensive deterrence' – that retains the political weight of the deterrent concept while moving away from its nuclear retaliatory element. For the alternative writer, the 'deterrent' is that the West will fight, effectively, in a general war that the Soviet Union cannot hope to win in any meaningful sense. Catastrophic and mutual destruction does not have to be part of it: an unsuccessful conventional war will be catastrophic enough and more than adequate punishment.

Secondly, political arguments turn upon the symbolic value that nuclear weapons have traditionally had within NATO. The alternative writer is anxious to point out to the NATO politician that unity through nuclear symbolism has become a two-edged sword with Western publics, and that conventional defence, if properly handled, can provide equally potent and less dangerous symbols of political unity. Symbols, in any case, are a matter of human perception and will change over time. Establishment thinking, on the other hand, sees nuclear symbolism as uniquely, and continually, appropriate in the world of practical politics: nuclear weapons are simple, obvious and very dangerous, and nothing else can command such attention.

Ultimately the argument about symbolism will be determined not so much by the willingness of politicians to be convinced, but by the way in which transatlantic change is handled in the next few years. In a situation of great political turbulence in Europe, which may well serve to heighten differences of interests across the Atlantic, mechanisms to handle change and solve any differences may assume great importance as symbols of continuing unity. On the other hand, if the transatlantic problems of the 1980s are left to drift in the new circumstances of the 1990s then it is entirely possible that in an atmosphere of frustration and anger the United States, or the Federal Republic, might regard loyalty to NATO's nuclear strategy as an acid test of unity and elevate its symbolic role even further.

The level of strategic theory

One can sympathize with the position of the operational military planner or the practical politician more readily than with the academics, observers, journalists and specialists who have populated the world of 'strategic theory' for the last forty years. For at this level there has been a great deal of new information but precious little new thinking for a long time.

Nuclear strategists have done a great service by articulating the nature of deterrence and its myriad implications. It is a central concept in contemporary strategic studies, and the strategists, it is generally agreed, have put their collective finger on an important aspect of human relations and have developed the insight to an impressive extent.

The problem, say the alternative school, is that the concept of deterrence has been elevated, though not always by strategists, to become a general law of East–West relations, out of touch with the political realities it is assumed to underpin. Thus, until the 1980s, deterrence in Europe was not generally analysed in terms of the politics of the Soviet Union or trends in Soviet thinking. Rather, it was analysed in terms of a mirror image of the West to which the Soviet Union was assumed, on the logic of deterrence, to conform. 'The threat' was assumed to exist in something of a political vacuum.

This construction is now visibly changing, however, under the impact of Gorbachev's policies, the collapse of East European communist governments, the vehemence of strategic debates within the West, and the general decline in the strength of superpower bipolarity. Neither Soviet nor Western politics can now be ignored by strategists and there seems to be a greater recognition that the concept of deterrence has to establish its relevance in a way that is specific to a particular political context.

This is the nub of the argument between establishment and alternative analysts in their guise as strategic thinkers. Is the political context of European security becoming significantly distinct from the broader context of 'East–West security' (or what we might term 'superpower security') such that different security arrangements have become feasible? Deterrence has a timeless quality about it, and for the establishment analyst even radical changes in the political context do not diminish its essential relevance (Freedman, 1989). That is to say, deterrence exists existentially in that leaders cannot avoid being aware of a conceivable deterrent relationship in the politics between them. But for the alternative writer the relevance of deterrence is decided by the context. The existential quality of deterrence can be rendered irrelevant (as indeed it is between the United States and Britain, for example) by security arrangements which grow out of, and are appropriate for, the politics of the situation. Leaders are not bound to play at deterrence just because the game is there to be played.

REFERENCES

Alternative Defence Commission (1983), *Defence Without the Bomb* (London: Taylor & Francis).

Alternative Defence Commission (1985), *Without the Bomb: Non-Nuclear Defence Policies for Britain* (London: Paladin).

Alternative Defence Commission (1987), *The Politics of Alternative Defence* (London: Paladin).

Biddle, S. D. (1987), 'The European conventional balance debate: a reinterpretation', in W. T. Wander (ed.), *Nuclear and Conventional Forces in Europe* (Washington, DC: American Association for the Advancement of Science), pp. 25–58.

Booth, K., and Baylis, J. (1989), *Britain, NATO and Nuclear Weapons* (London: Macmillan).
Center for Strategic and International Studies (1987), *NATO: Meeting the Coming Challenge* (Washington, DC: CSIS).
Clarke, M. (1987), 'AirLand Battle and the application of new technology', in I. Bellany and T. Huxley (eds), *New Conventional Weapons and Western Defence* (London: Cass), pp. 151–62.
Clarke, M. (1989), 'Conventional defence: reappraisals and new approaches', in B. George (ed.), *Jane's NATO Yearbook 1989–90* (London: Jane's)
Department of Defense (1988), *Soviet Military Power* (Washington, DC: US Department of Defense).
Epstein, J. (1984), *Measuring Military Power: The Soviet Air Threat to Europe* (Princeton, NJ: Princeton University Press).
Freedman, L. (1986), *Arms Control: Management or Reform?* (London: Routledge & Kegan Paul).
Freedman, L. (1989), 'The evolution and future of extended nuclear deterrence', in *The Changing Strategic Landscape*, Adelphi Paper No. 236 (London: International Institute for Strategic Studies), pp. 18–31.
Generals for Peace and Disarmament (1984), *The Arms Race to Armageddon* (Leamington Spa: Berg).
Griggs, R. A. (1988), 'Maritime strategy on NATO's Central Front', *Military Review*, vol. 63, no. 4, pp. 55–65.
International Institute for Strategic Studies (1988), *The Military Balance 1988–89* (London: IISS).
Kaldor, M. (1981), *The Baroque Arsenal* (New York: Hill & Wang).
Karber, P. A. (1989), 'The military impact of the Gorbachev reductions', *Armed Forces Journal International*, January, pp. 54–64.
Kaufmann, W. (1983), 'Non-nuclear deterrence', in J. D. Steinbrunner and L. Sigal (eds), *Alliance Security: NATO and the No-First-Use Question* (Washington, DC: Brookings), pp. 43–90.
Kelly, A. (1984), *Not By Numbers Alone*, Peace Study Papers No. 11 (Bradford: University of Bradford School of Peace Studies).
Kelly, A. (1986), 'The conventional balance of forces', M. Phil. thesis, University of Bradford.
MccGwire, M. (1986), 'Deterrence: the problem – not the solution', *International Affairs*, vol. 62, no. 1, pp. 55–70.
MccGwire, M. (1987), *Military Objectives in Soviet Foreign Policy* (Washington, DC: Brookings).
MccGwire, M. (1988), 'A mutual security regime for Europe?', *International Affairs*, vol. 64, no. 3, pp. 361–80.
Mako, W. (1983), *US Ground Forces and the Defense of Central Europe* (Washington, DC: Brookings).
Mason, Sir R. and McInnes, C. (1988), *New Technology and Western Security*, International Research Paper No. 1 (Aberystwyth: Department of International Politics).
Meacham, J. (1986), 'NATO's Central Front', *Economist*, 30 August.
NATO (1988), *Conventional Forces in Europe: The Facts* (Brussels: NATO).

Shenfield, S. (1985), 'Assertive and reactive threats', in S. Windass (ed.), *Avoiding Nuclear War* (London: Brassey), pp. 63–76.

Shenfield, S. (1987), *The Nuclear Predicament: Explorations in Soviet Ideology* (London: Routledge & Kegan Paul).

Sherr, J. (1988), 'Advance through retreat", *The Times*, 19 February, p. 12.

Statement on the Defence Estimates 1987 I, CM 101-1 (London: HMSO).

Statement on the Defence Estimates 1988 I, CM 344-1 (London: HMSO).

Statement on the Defence Estimates 1989 I, CM 675-1 (London: HMSO).

Unterseher, L. (1987), *Conventional Land Forces for Central Europe*, Bradford Peace Research Report No. 15 (Bradford: University of Bradford).

USSR Military Academy (1982), *Whence the Threat to Peace?* (Moscow: USSR Military Academy).

Windass, S. (ed.) (1985), *Avoiding Nuclear War* (London: Brassey).

PART FOUR

Regional Perspectives

9

New thinking about defence in the Soviet Union

ROY ALLISON

Official Soviet military doctrine under Gorbachev is in a period of transition which may fundamentally alter the content of Soviet defence policy. A broad debate on defence issues is under way among Soviet academic and military specialists, stimulated by the more innovative members of the Soviet elite. This reflects a more sophisticated view of military power as an ingredient of Soviet national security and challenges the orthodoxies of the Brezhnev era on defence. For the Soviet Party leadership, the new content of Soviet military doctrine appears to be intended as a contribution to a broad political strategy aimed at the more effective management of Soviet foreign relations at a reduced cost in the 1990s.

THE NEW CONTEXT TO SOVIET DEFENCE DECISION-MAKING

The interaction between different aspects of Gorbachev's reform agenda allows for the possibility that Soviet 'new thinking' on international security will capture and subsequently transform the Soviet defence agenda only for the latter to fall victim to the eventual collapse of Gorbachev's political/economic programme in other areas. We should also remain aware that in Soviet thinking a specific military doctrine, regardless of its characteristics at any given time, only defines the short- to medium-term Soviet outlook. The doctrine may be modified or supplanted if the strategic context in which it was originally formulated changes. But changes in Soviet defence decision-making under Gorbachev may be intended to provide the foundations for a long-term Soviet commitment to new principles in defence policy.

Since the Twenty-Seventh Party Congress in February 1986 the Party under Gorbachev has downgraded the position of military representatives in the ruling coalition and sought to ensure the primacy of the Party in determining the character and evolution of military doctrine. Although Gorbachev has shown no intention of trying to supplant the expertise and institutional functions of the Soviet Ministry of Defence, he may be seeking some institutional alternative to the General Staff to act as a consultative and planning body on defence issues. After his resignation as Chief of the General Staff in December 1988, Marshal Akhromeyev became a special adviser to Gorbachev. Gorbachev has also established new centres of expertise on military security issues attached to the International Department of the Central Committee and the Foreign Ministry. These now compete with established specialist centres governed by the Soviet professional military. A Scientific Co-ordination Committee linked to the Foreign Ministry has been assigned the task of integrating Soviet academic opinion into the policy-making process.

More significant still is Gorbachev's proposal to introduce a legislative procedure whereby all departments engaged in military and military industrial activity would be under the control of the new Soviet Parliament (the Supreme Soviet). In principle this should lead to greater accountability for decisions involving the use of military forces beyond Soviet borders and the planning of defence construction (see Shevardnadze, 1988c). Following the March 1989 multi-candidate elections held in the USSR the Soviet General Staff officer Major-General Lebedev was hopeful that even 'decisions of war and peace' would soon be made only in the Supreme Soviet (Lebedev, 1989). The idea has been raised of creating a group of deputies in the Supreme Soviet 'with special, deeper [military] information, who are not "bound" by department interests', like the US Congressional Armed Services Committees (Kondrashov, 1989). Most promising, in June 1989 a new Defence and State Security Committee of the Supreme

Soviet was established to oversee the Soviet 'military-industrial complex' and the KGB (*Guardian*, 28 June 1989).

Certain Soviet military representatives have openly called for 'democratization' in defence decision-making, for a mechanism to enable the correction of foreign and defence policy and bring to it alternative ideas and recommendations (Kirshin, 1988, pp. 35–8). Greater 'democratization' in Soviet defence decision-making would mean that changes in Soviet military strategy and key military decisions could not be undertaken so easily in the future on narrow technocratic grounds. A process in this direction is supported by the gradual extension of *glasnost* in the military sphere, expressed most notably in the Soviet commitment to intrusive verification procedures, in the publication of data in January 1989 on the Warsaw Pact armed forces in Europe, and in Gorbachev's public estimate in May 1989 of aggregate Soviet military expenditures – £77.3 billion (see Gareev, 1988a; Shevardnadze, 1988b; *Statement by Warsaw Treaty*, 1989).

Although the institutional strongholds of the Soviet military elite may be weakened under Gorbachev, it is evident that the support of Soviet military leaders is required to sustain any radical shift in military doctrine or force requirements. Gorbachev has sought to maintain such support by linking the more defensive non-provocative orientation of this doctrine with at least the medium-term economic imperatives of Soviet power and the Soviet state. A consensus has been broadly reached between the Party and the military that the technological modernization of the armed forces, especially investment in basic research, will only be possible within the broader framework of the economic rehabilitation of the USSR. One military specialist underlined that 'the technological re-equipment of industry has a very great significance for the output of military technology, raising its effectiveness, reliability, simplifying maintenance'. He argued that the future of Soviet military technology depended on a powerful economy (Lukava, 1986, pp. 12–13).

For Gorbachev a reduction in defence expenditures, linked to an amelioration of East–West confrontation, forms a precondition of such economic recovery and is made possible, he argues, by the new Soviet approach to military security and defence. Colonel-General Gareev, Deputy Chief of the General Staff, has argued similarly that 'The need for the Soviet Union and the other socialist countries to have a defensive military doctrine is determined not only by the interests of international security but also because of their internal tasks'. The achievement of *perestroika* in his opinion would only be possible 'in circumstances of peace and reliably guaranteed security' (Gareev, 1988b, p. 4). The counterpart to this logic, however, is that the credibility of the new Soviet military doctrine remains at least partly hostage to the fortunes of the Soviet domestic programme for economic reform.

NEW THINKING ON INTERNATIONAL SECURITY AND THE CONCEPT OF REASONABLE SUFFICIENCY

The current Soviet debate on military defence should initially be set in the broader framework of change in the Soviet conception of security under Gorbachev. This shift has been an evolutionary process, and many principles officially adopted by the Gorbachev leadership had been in circulation earlier in the 1980s in specialist debates in Soviet civilian institutes. Traditional Soviet assumptions about security derived from the correlation of forces concept had been challenged by the growing interdependence of states (a well-developed theme in Soviet specialist writings before Gorbachev assumed power) and by the evident reduction in Soviet security in the early 1980s despite massive military commitments in the late Brezhnev years. By the mid-1980s different responses to the dilemma of Soviet security had coalesced in the Soviet political elite (Shenfield, 1987). Gorbachev began to associate himself with a group of significant ideas which confronted the Brezhnevite orthodoxy and were officially sanctioned by Party meetings in the period 1985–7.

Most fundamental is the new Soviet commitment to mutual security and appreciation of the internecine quality of the security dilemma, which in the past was fuelled by adversary imagery and a tendency to pursue military responses to essentially political problems. Soviet spokesmen now characterize mutual security as the natural objective for states mutually vulnerable to potential nuclear war and to the wholesale devastation inherent in such war. For Soviet leaders, doctrinally conditioned to a zero-sum view of systemic conflict between East and West, this recognition of the mutual basis of security forms a radical departure from the autarkist approach to security which characterized Soviet policy in the Brezhnev period.

The gradual Soviet redefinition of nuclear war as nuclear catastrophe has encouraged the Soviet leadership to elevate war prevention to a formal position in Soviet military doctrine. Whereas Soviet military doctrine was previously defined as a system of views on the preparation for war and for waging it, under Gorbachev war prevention has been proclaimed as 'the highest objective and the core of military doctrine'. Significantly, however, this formulation does not simply encompass nuclear war. Soviet military officials now maintain that it is difficult 'to have any hope of achieving political objectives even in conventional war' on account of the destructiveness of modern conventional arms, especially in Europe (see Chernyshev, 1988). As a result this doctrinal revision may undermine traditional arguments by the Soviet military hierarchy to justify resource allocation and force levels.

The Soviet General Staff has sought to argue that war prevention is reflected in Soviet defence activities and requires constant analysis of the current state of the military balance and assessment of prospective developments 'in order reliably to restrain possible aggression' – a traditional requirement (Gareev, 1988b, pp. 4–5). The Soviet military-political leadership appears to be agreed, however, that the notion of war prevention should be defined primarily as a political task. Consequently the role of political-military considerations (such as strategic stability) is raised, and political-diplomatic efforts, such as arms control and measures to reduce regional and international tensions, are put on an equal footing with military technical efforts. Indeed, the formal insertion of war prevention into Soviet military doctrine gives Gorbachev a legitimate doctrinal basis for trading off current forces and future increments of military power (which could be useful in the event of war) for additional military-political stability (which could reduce the probability of war) (Meyer, 1988, p. 134).

The concept of 'reasonable sufficiency' has been used by a growing number of Soviet civilian specialists to describe just such a process, although 'sufficiency' has assumed a variety of hues in recent Soviet discourse. The notion of 'sufficiency' can be traced back in Soviet thinking to the early 1980s when Brezhnev sought to deflect pressure for substantial increases in Soviet defence investments. When Gorbachev originally called for 'limiting military potentials to reasonable sufficiency' at the Twenty-Seventh Party Congress he appeared to be calling for joint efforts by East and West to reverse the arms race and achieve far lower force levels. The element of reciprocity was evident in Gorbachev's claim that the level of sufficiency should be linked to the positions and actions of the Western states. A Warsaw Treaty Organization (WTO) meeting in Berlin in May 1987, which formally adopted the new defensive Soviet military doctrine, stated cautiously that the USSR only sought armed forces and armaments which would 'strictly comply with the limits of sufficiency for defence'.

This formulation left Soviet military officials free initially to interpret the sufficiency criterion as an expression of the need to maintain the current military balance (or 'overall approximate parity') and thereby to uphold the requirements of 'reliable defence'. The military was disinclined to view the principle of 'defence sufficiency' as a constraint independent of 'the nature and intensity of imperialist military preparations' (see Kostev, 1987, p. 13; Yazov 1987a; 1988). In other words the WTO should carefully assess Western military capabilities and ensure that Soviet force levels preclude Western superiority. Such a view of 'defence sufficiency' implied a lower limit to optimal force levels.

For Marshal Kulikov, the commander-in-chief of WTO forces, the concepts of reasonable sufficiency and military-strategic parity both applied to a relative balance of the military forces and potentials of the opposing sides, and only differed in as much as 'reasonable sufficiency presumes a lower threshold of the military opposition, while military-strategic parity many be on various levels' (Kulikov, 1988, pp. 81–2). He interpreted reasonable sufficiency, therefore, as a fixed lower level of parity. This was a reasonable goal for strategic arms control. However, since Soviet military leaders maintained that an approximate overall parity also pertained between NATO and WTO conventional forces, Kulikov's views had conservative implications for conventional arms control.

In the period 1987–9 a number of Soviet civilian specialists arrived at a radically different interpretation of reasonable sufficiency. One of their premises was that Soviet force procurement levels had hitherto simply been reactive to Western military deployments, and that this action–reaction process had been employed by the West as a deliberate strategic device to exhaust the Soviet Union economically through an arms race. In their view the USSR should in the future determine its own force levels according to its own criteria and priorities. Viewed from this perspective the criterion of reasonable sufficiency could permit asymmetrical responses to Western military measures, or even unilateral Soviet force reductions (see Zhurkin, Karaganov and Kortunov, 1987a, pp. 13–14; 1987b, p. 3).

The civilian definition of reasonable sufficiency also reflected the view that the essential dilemma of Soviet military security derives from the geostrategy of the contemporary military confrontation, which involves the Soviet Union on many fronts. The Soviet Union, it was observed, had taken part in a simultaneous confrontation with 'all the other major world powers situated near or far from Soviet borders, and in the entire range of armed forces and armaments'. As a result, Soviet concern with security over the past decade had heightened constantly despite an unprecedented commitment of resources to defence (Arbatov, 1988, pp. 80–1). To escape this dilemma the Soviet analysts Zhurkin, Karaganov and Kortunov maintained that the principle of reasonable sufficiency should envisage 'rejection of autonomous regional force levels, i.e. of the creation of forces tasked to achieve victory in several independent theatres of military operations' (Zhurkin, Karaganov and Kortunov, 1987c, pp. 19–20; 1987a, p. 15). This followed an assertion by Gorbachev himself, at a meeting of the Ministry of Foreign Affairs in May 1986, that the idea 'rooted in the minds and deeds of some strategists that the Soviet Union can be as strong as any possible coalition of opposing states is absolutely untenable' (noted in Shevardnadze, 1988c).

The civilian case for a low threshold for sufficiency was supported by a forcible assertion, published in the Party's theoretical journal, that the possibility of war in Europe, be it nuclear or conventional, is virtually nil. The authors admitted that 'invasion from the West' remained the main threat scenario in the 'mass consciousness' of the Soviet people, but denied, with minor qualifications, that such a threat still exists. The implication of their argument was that new criteria were necessary to determine the Soviet forces' posture in the European theatre (Zhurkin, Karaganov and Kortunov, 1988, pp. 42–50). Another specialist argued that, even if war were to break out between NATO and the Warsaw Pact in Europe or the Far East, the high likelihood of escalation into a wide-scale nuclear exchange meant that the requirements for tactical nuclear munitions and the quantitative levels of conventional armed forces in Europe could be substantially reduced (Arbatov, 1988, p. 82). One analyst went further to castigate the Soviet 'tank mentality', a legacy of wartime tank losses, which was outmoded in the 1980s (Shlykov, 1988, p. 116).

The tenor of such civilian views was clearly at odds with the outlook of the Soviet military establishment. Marshal Akhromeyev argued that defence sufficiency could not be viewed onesidedly in light of 'the constant military threat posed by the active military preparations of imperialism'. His successor as Chief of the General Staff, Colonel-General Moiseyev, warned early in 1989 that 'the aggressive orientation of imperialist policy has been maintained'. He criticized Soviet publications which underestimated the seriousness of the threat (Akhromeyev, 1987, p. 26; Moiseyev, 1989a).

The Soviet political leadership appeared to side with civilian views that sufficiency was a political concept which called for a reordering of Soviet (and Western) threat perceptions as much as an adjustment of military hardware levels. Foreign Minister Shevardnadze argued before the United Nations in June 1988 that 'Sufficiency is not just a certain level of armaments, but above all a certain frame of mind, a psychological and political disposition towards ever smaller arsenals – sufficient for defence but not for attack'. He portrayed sufficiency as a means of ensuring security by non-nuclear means, as a concept of security 'deriving from the collective actions of states', and suggested that the United Nations, the Security Council and the Military Staff Committee be reinvigorated for this purpose (Shevardnadze, 1988a).

At a less elevated level, the newly proclaimed WTO military doctrine linked the sufficiency concept with the requirement to reduce armed forces and armaments in Europe 'down to a level at which neither side, while ensuring its defence, would have the means for making a surprise attack on the other side or for starting offensive operations in general'. Thus reasonable sufficiency from the outset was an idea inextricably tied to the gathering debate on 'defensive defence' in the Soviet Union (as analysed in detail below), which in turn was understood to require the restructuring of the military-strategic conceptions underlying the military doctrines of both sides (see Zhurkin, Karaganov and

Kortunov, 1987a, pp. 18–20). The implementation of the concept of reasonable sufficiency, in the words of one analyst, would require 'a defensive character for the armed forces' structure and disposition, a defensive orientation of military doctrine, of combat and operational training and exercises' (Semeiko, 1988, p. 53).

All this is in turn linked to the character of and potential for strategic stability at the conventional level. Soviet specialists are aware that parity or equilibrium at this level by no means denotes stability or rules out large-scale offensive operations (ibid.). They argue in addition that in practice it would be impossible to realize at this level a material threat analagous to that of unacceptable retaliatory damage at the strategic nuclear level. Andrei Kokoshin has argued cogently that strategic stability at the level of conventional arms and armed forces should, therefore, be based on a complex of conditions in which it would be evident to both sides that the 'the defensive capabilities of the WTO substantially exceed the capability of NATO to undertake offensive operations' and, equally, that the defensive potential of NATO outweighs WTO offensive capabilities (Kokoshin, 1988a, p. 29; 1988b, p. 8). The tension between such new Soviet thinking on defence and traditional military patterns of thought forms the main part of this chapter. Before addressing this debate, however, we should consider how new thinking on security has influenced Soviet views on nuclear deterrence.

NEW THINKING ON NUCLEAR DETERRENCE

Authoritative Soviet statements early in the 1980s indicated a growing belief within the Soviet military elite that nuclear escalation could be avoided during East–West hostilities and a future war could be confined to the conventional level. By the mid-1980s the Soviet General Staff was openly critical of previous Soviet military theory, which had been premissed on the inevitability of escalation from such conflict to large-scale nuclear use and had originally regarded nuclear weapons simply as a means of sharply increasing firepower in combat. The build-up of nuclear arms, it was observed, had resulted in a situation in which their mass use would be futile and mutually catastrophic. This reality, and the revolution in conventional military technology, led to 'a break with the view that it is possible to wage war using nuclear weapons at all' (Ogarkov, 1985, p. 51) and to a growing belief in 'the possibility of a comparatively long war with the use of conventional weapons' (Gareev, 1985a, p. 240). Soviet military spokesmen supported such a possibility with the claim that NATO's strategy of flexible response covers preparations for both a prolonged conventional war and a nuclear war (Kostev, 1987, p. 9). At the same time the Soviet military command has been forceful in its assessment of the risks attached to nuclear use at any level and has continued to reject in principle the notion of 'limited' nuclear war or the possibility of intra-war bargaining above the nuclear threshold.

Soviet military and civilian analysts have been in dispute, however, over the implications of these views. The General Staff has continued to support the need to provide for a reliable and credible deterrent on all basic levels of a potential conflict. Correspondingly Soviet military publications in the first years of Gorbachev's rule continued to assess the role that nuclear weapons play in general purpose forces, how they may be used not only on a strategic, but also on an operational and tactical scale (see, for example, Kir'yan, 1986, p. 407–8, 412–16). In other words, in considering Soviet deterrence requirements Soviet military leaders still assumed the need for a war-waging capability. By 1987, however, this rationale was under criticism from civilian 'new thinkers' and certain military theorists on several grounds.

In the first place, the very idea of nuclear war began to be redefined as a 'nuclear catastrophe', and 'nuclear winter' research only reinforced this perception. Preparations for a nuclear war, albeit for purposes of deterrence, had a certain logic, but preparations for the contingency of 'catastrophe' could not be similarly justified. Reasonable sufficiency, civilian specialists argued, would permit a lower level of deterrence than that necessary for credible 'warfighting', and the goal of 'war prevention' anyway highlighted the need for nuclear disarmament.

The prominent commentator Alexandr Bovin has even claimed that second nuclear use, a nuclear retaliatory strike, would be unjustified. In arguing that 'nuclear pacifism' in relation to nuclear war was the only politically justified position, Bovin found himself at odds with the Soviet military establishment and struck at the heart of the deterrent philosophy (*Izvestiya*, 5 February 1988). Gorbachev himself has argued against the efficacy of nuclear deterrence as a long-term policy and called for comprehensive global denuclearization. In reality, however, it is unlikely that this objective (as opposed to theatre denuclearization) is shared by the larger part of the Soviet political leadership, which probably regards a substantially lower level of strategic deterrence based on a stable configuration of nuclear forces as the desirable end product of nuclear arms control.

Under Gorbachev all Soviet spokesmen, including military leaders, are agreed that strategic parity in itself cannot exclude the potential danger of war, and that a continuation of the arms race could raise the danger of war 'to the point at which even the military-strategic parity will cease to be a factor of deterrence' (see Akhromeyev, 1987, p. 43; Kulikov, 1988, pp. 44–5). Civilian intellectuals around Gorbachev have proceeded to criticize nuclear counterforce concepts as inherently destabilizing and some, such as Bovin, have even raised military hackles with the assertion that parity is not essential for nuclear deterrence.

In recent years Soviet defence analysts have given particular emphasis to the likelihood of the inadvertent outbreak of nuclear war and have reinforced the dangers of escalation to the nuclear level from any intersystemic military engagement (for elaboration of the latter see Kirshin, Popov and Savushkin, 1987, pp. 146, 222, 262). Defence Minister Yazov has indicated that Soviet political control over the employment of nuclear weapons has been progressively tightened (*Pravda*, 27 July 1987). Indeed, tightening controls to preclude the unsanctioned use of nuclear arms is claimed to be part of the Soviet non-offensive strategy.

Despite this, Soviet military specialists have argued that the general threat of the accidental initiation of nuclear war has increased as the result of deficiencies in the system of control of nuclear arms and the methods of forward basing (Kirshin, 1988, pp. 42, 44). Such technological determinism, coupled with assertions which downgrade the threat of deliberate attack, serves to establish the ideological and doctrinal context for reducing the role of military power in Soviet foreign policy in general, and for carrying out major strategic force reductions in particular (Meyer, 1988, pp. 136–7).

MILITARY VIEWS ON FUTURE
STRATEGIC OPERATIONS:
OFFENCE AND DEFENCE

At the time Gorbachev came to power in 1985 the Soviet General Staff was evaluating the impact of new military-technological trends on the theatre offensive strategy which had been developed under Brezhnev in the 1960s and 1970s. In an interview in May 1984 Marshal Ogarkov described a 'qualitative leap in the development of conventional means of destruction [which] will inevitably entail a change in the nature of the preparation and conduct of operations'. He argued that 'automated search and destroy complexes, long-range high-accuracy terminally guided combat systems. . .and qualitatively new electronic control systems' made it possible 'immediately to extend active combat operations not just to the border regions, but to the whole country's territory, which was not possible in past wars'. All this greatly enhanced 'the initial period of war and its first operations' (Ogarkov, 1984).

The Chief of the Military Science Directorate (and subsequently Deputy Chief) of the General Staff identified similar trends, and stressed that the introduction of new high-precision arms in particular gave rise to the need fundamentally to rethink operational-strategic issues of the defence of the USSR (Gareev, 1985b, pp. 28–9). It was evident that deep-strike, precision-guided weapons meant that the defender's strikes would no longer be confined to the tactical zone, but could be conducted across the depth of the enemy's deployment. Furthermore, the new military technologies gave the defender the chance to seize the initiative from the attacker. Consequently Soviet military planners appeared convinced that they had entered a transitional phase towards a revolutionary shift in military affairs. In their view, technological breakthroughs would inescapably transform the conventional battlefield (see Hall, 1988; Petersen and Trulock, 1988, pp. 6–11, 20–2).

One element of this reappraisal, confirmed by Soviet military spokesmen under Gorbachev, was particularly significant. In the initial period of contemporary war, it was predicted, 'military operations over a short time period will spread on an unprecedented scale, will cover land, sea and airspace', and 'in such conditions the distinction between the front and the rear in practice disappears' (Lukava, 1986, pp. 28–9). The author of a 1987 work on the evolution of military science confirmed this view: 'At the contemporary stage there clearly appears a firm trend of the broadening of the predicted bounds of military conflict, according to the quantity of forces taking part and the means, according to the depth and breadth of the fronts of military operations' (Gayvoronskogo, 1987, p. 232). He conceived of the possibility of 'the simultaneous defeat of the enemy throughout the strategic depth' and predicted 'the conduct of active military operations also in the rear of the enemy'. This assessment followed the lead of Gareev, who had concluded in 1985 that 'today the tendency of the further convergence [*sblizheniya*] of the methods of action of troops on the offence and in the defence is increasingly evident' (Gareev, 1985a, p. 245). A senior Soviet military theoretician had already argued at the beginning of the 1980s that the distinction between offensive and defensive operations was becoming less clear, since both attacker and defender would seek to fulfil their mission by 'active offensive methods' (Vorob'yev, 1980).

Soviet evaluations of this new scenario of military operations have expressed particular concern over innovations in Western strategic theory which would enable NATO to exploit the potential of the new and emergent conventional arms technologies. The Soviet military command has dwelt on the role assigned to the 'operational-strategic conceptions' of Air-Land Battle and 'combat with second echelons' (see, for example, Akhromeyev, 1987, p. 24; Kulikov, 1988, p. 66). Soviet specialist military publications have continued to argue that the latter NATO concept, which was officially endorsed as 'follow-on-forces-attack', requires 'the massive use of precision-guided conventional weapons of various purposes and radii of action against troops and objects of the Warsaw Pact, which are located not only in the zone of immediate combat actions, but deep in the rear'. This in turn would increase the opportunities for NATO's armed forces 'to rout enemy forward groupings and conduct offensive combat actions for the achievement of political and military-strategic goals' (Perov, 1988, pp. 9–10; and see Chernyshev, 1988). Related Soviet claims that NATO has sought to create a first-strike potential using only conventional weaponry reflect an underlying concern that changes in Western strategy would enable a counter-attack to disrupt critically the integrity of any broad Soviet strategic offensive operation.

It is apparent, therefore, that compulsions have arisen for Soviet military planners to undertake a wholesale reappraisal of the offence–defence relationship to suit the new operational requirements of the future battlefield (see Covington, 1987). In particular, it is understood that military realities require greater attention to be paid to strategic defence. This growing interest in strategic defence on military-technological grounds may be encouraged by a lack of confidence within the current Soviet General Staff that the Defence Council under the Gorbachev leadership would be ready to authorize a pre-emptive conventional offensive in a major East–West crisis leading to war in Central Europe. Hesitancy in taking the necessary political decision could lose the Warsaw Pact the initiative and force it onto the strategic defence in the face of a large-scale NATO attack (Warner, 1989, p. 26).

There is no question, however, that Soviet strategists would be as poorly prepared for such defence as they were at the time of Hitler's attack in June 1941. Soviet military planners have now prepared a strategic defensive operation as well as a strategic offensive operation for each theatre of military action in Europe. Studies on defensive operations were established under the guidance of the General Staff in the early 1980s and a series of high-level conferences were held to examine the potentialities of defensive operations. This work was well under way by the time Gorbachev assumed office. More recently the need to enlist Soviet military historians into the reappraisal of military art was implied at a top-level meeting which criticized the lack of attention in Soviet studies given to the initial (defensive) period of the Great Patriotic War (*KZ*, 5 July 1987).

In 1988 certain Soviet military writers still chose to interpret defensive operations in their traditional Soviet rendering purely as the means to create favourable conditions to pass over to the offensive (Ionin, 1988, pp, 19–20, for example). Despite a growing Soviet appreciation that new technological trends were undercutting the dominance of tank forces on the contemporary battlefield, a strong defence of the utility of massed tank forces to achieve the goals of strategic offensive operations of a group of fronts was published in the same year (Anan'ev, 1988, pp. 122–3, 450). Most military officers differentiated between actions on the strategic, operational and tactical levels. They noted that during the Second World War strategic defence encompassed local offensive operations, and the retention of defensive zones was combined with counter-attacks. Highly mobile forces were tasked to strengthen Soviet troops on the most dangerous axes, while artificial obstacles played a major role in achieving stability (see, for example, Kunitskiy, 1988, pp. 8–9; Marashev, 1986, pp. 9–16).

The Soviet military leadership maintained by 1987 that a defensive orientation would extend to the military-technical side of Soviet military doctrine. Yet at this time Marshal Akhromeyev interpreted this new approach only to mean that 'the delivery of preventive, pre-emptive strikes' was excluded and that Soviet forces were bound to look to 'retaliatory defence operations'. In response to an aggression Soviet forces would inflict 'crushing retaliatory blows at the enemy and will act with utmost resolve and vigour' (Akhromeyev, 1987, pp. 26–7). Defence Minister Yazov in turn described Soviet defence as designed 'to halt the attack of the opponent, to render it lifeless, not to permit the loss of territory, to achieve the destruction of the invading enemy forces'. But the last objective, in his view, could not be managed only by defence. It necessitated a transition to a decisive 'counteroffensive' (Yazov, 1987b, pp. 32–3). Marshal Kulikov echoed this line early in 1988 (Kulikov, 1988, pp. 77–9; see also Postnikov, 1988, p. 18).

These views indicate that in the initial years of Gorbachev's rule the Soviet military command had little interest in a form of 'defensive defence' that would preclude large-scale counter-offensive action (a concept of operations which generated capabilities similar to those required for large-scale offensive action). If the Soviet Union were to be caught unprepared then long-range 'defensive' strikes across the depth of the NATO deployment could yield valuable time for the completion of the mobilization of the Warsaw Pact forces and an effective transition to offensive operations. In the worst case NATO could be fought along key defensive axes on Warsaw Pact territory, but only with the intention of encircling NATO forces and shifting offensive operations onto NATO territory.

Such a concept of operations, however, did not harmonize with the criteria of 'non-offensive defence' which began to be elaborated in the USSR, principally by civilian analysts, following the official proclamation of the new Soviet 'defensive' military doctrine in 1987.

NEW THINKING ON NON-OFFENSIVE
DEFENCE

Soviet civilian defence specialists described the key element of defensive defence in 1987 as the requirement for each nation to lower the pre-emption potential of its armed forces by structurally denying them the means to invade enemy territory (or strike rear-area targets with aircraft and missiles). Such a reconfiguration would also require a pledge against the first use of nuclear weapons. The goal was deterrence by defensive strength alone. They viewed non-provocative defence in turn as requiring the removal of offensive weapons from the arsenals of the opposing states and military groupings. The defences of each side, it was argued, would need to be conceived by the other as non-offensive and non-threatening if they were indeed to be non-provocative (*Disarmament and Security Yearbook*, 1987).

These definitions were drawn from alternative Western defence thinking, especially from views espoused by Western social democrats, but were welcomed as compatible with new Eastern proposals and appear to have strongly influenced recent specialist discussions on defence and military strategy in the USSR. This reliance on innovative thinking in Western defence debates apparently extended to the Soviet leadership. In March 1988 Central Committee Secretary Anatoly Dobrynin revealed that 'we have followed with growing interest the concept being elaborated in the West of "non-offensive, non-provocative defence" as an alternative to one based on nuclear deterrence'. He described this idea and the Soviet concept of reasonable sufficiency as have a common premiss: 'preserving only defensive functions for the armed forces' (Dobrynin, 1988, p. 21; and see Dobrynin, 1987). The first tentative descriptions of the idea of non-provocative defence in the Soviet military press similarly described the idea as the brainchild of Western scholars and opposition parties (Makarevsky, 1989).

Within the Soviet political context, however, the ideas of non-offensive or non-provocative defence had to be validated on the basis of indigenous Soviet military experience and supported by arguments applied to the defence environment in which the Soviet Union currently found itself. Consequently, as a number of Soviet civilian analysts have acquired more expertise in conventional defence and theatre strategy they have built on the growing interest in the notion of strategic defence by Soviet military leaders to pursue an anti-offensive defence orientation which in effect challenges central postulates of traditional Soviet military thinking.

Andrei Kokoshin has argued that the Soviet strategic offensives in the second half of 1943 and in 1944–5 only became possible after the USSR had managed to deprive Germany of the strategic initiative. He has tried to revive interest in the 'defensive' school of Soviet military and military-political thought associated above all with the strategist Alexander Svechin, which had been 'crushed under the guise of criticism' at the end of the 1920s. He has also stressed that since the Second World War states have produced means of defence at an increased tempo, including anti-tank artillery, anti-tank mines and various kinds of missile complexes, and has cited the conclusion of Marshal Ogarkov that at a certain stage their skilled use has balanced the means of offence by the means of defence (Kokoshin, 1988a, pp. 23–7; 1988c).

In a pioneering article with Major-General V. Larionov (who represents a small but apparently growing innovative current within the Soviet military establishment) Kokoshin used the Second World War battle of Kursk to indicate the possibilities of skilfully opposing an attack in conditions where 'diverse and sufficient forces and means of non-provocative defences' are present. For the authors an examination of this seminal battle refutes doubts over whether a 'well-grounded pre-positioned defence' is capable of resisting a powerful onslaught by offensive forces. They admit that at Kursk defence was formed in the course of war and therefore should not be regarded as an analogy for 'the non-offensive structure of armed forces and their strategies which are based on mutual confidence in peacetime'. Yet they argued that the new Warsaw Pact military doctrine would require Soviet military professionals 'to reconsider a number of broadly held postulates of military theory and practice', in particular 'the conviction that only "an all-out offensive leads to victory"' (Kokoshin and Larionov, 1987, pp. 32–3, 39–41).

A central premiss of the Soviet new thinking on defence is that the mutual fear of surprise attack could be removed if both sides were to agree on structural limitations to their offensive capabilities. But it is understood that any process in this direction is likely to be frustrated unless political means are used to halt destabilizing trends in military technology. Therefore, while Kokoshin agrees with Soviet military officials that the appearance of long-range high-precision weaponry 'is capable of overturning the traditional propositions of military art', he is adamant that this change would be by no means 'in the direction required by the new thinking in. . .international security' since it would result in a new and costly high-technology arms race. In his view this mandates a ban on 'the creation of non-nuclear armaments based on new and traditional physical principles which, in their destructive capabilities, would approach nuclear or other means of mass destruction' (Kokoshin, 1988a, pp. 28–9; 1988b, p. 8). Overall, while Soviet military officials may accept a revision in the offence–defence ratio out of military necessity, civilian specialists appear opposed to offensive capabilities as a matter of political principle.

As previously observed, Kokoshin argued that strategic stability at the conventional level could only be secured through creating a complex of conditions in which it would be evident to both sides that 'the defensive capabilities of the Warsaw Pact [strategic, operational and tactical] substantially exceed the capabilities of NATO to undertake offensive operations and vice versa: NATO's defence clearly exceeds the capabilities for the offensive of the Warsaw Pact forces'. He suggested that the experience of small, neutral European states could be taken into account in forming new strategic and operational concepts, since these states possess a significant potential for effective defence but in practice are not capable of carrying out any kind of large offensive operations. Kokoshin has concluded that the whole structure of forces and means of NATO and the Warsaw Pact, their systems of control and communication, should be such that if armed conflict were to break out the political leadership and military command of the sides could control it, 'with the intention of terminating it at the earliest possible stage' (Kokoshin, 1988a, pp. 29, 32; 1988b, p. 8; Kokoshin and Larionov, 1987, p. 11).

It is understood at the same time by such civilian specialists that any modern offensive force contains elements that are intended for defence, just as any modern defensive force has units and formations intended for counter-attacks and counter-strikes. Equally, they are aware that at the tactical and operational levels the strategy of defence includes not only purely defensive, but also clearly offensive operations and combat actions. Tanks, artillery, missile systems and aircraft alike may be used both in offence and defence; the strategic and tactical missions assigned to the forces determine whether particular weapon systems are used offensively or defensively. In so far as such distinctions are possible, however, Soviet defence intellectuals favour restructuring the military potentials of both alliances primarily by way of reducing their offensive elements, not building up their defensive elements (see Kokoshin and Larionov, 1989, p. 21).

In this context Kokoshin and Larionov have constructed a framework of four analytical variants or scenarios to assess the means to strengthen strategic stability in Europe. The essence of the first variant is that each party is oriented in the event of war to conducting decisive strategic offensive operations and to carrying military operations as rapidly as possible to the territory and air space of the enemy. This scenario 'corresponds to deeply rooted traditions of military thought'. In the second variant each side orients its strategy and operational art so that at the initial stage of a conflict they refrain in a premeditated way from attack and only conduct defensive actions. This would require well-developed positional defence. The attack would be repulsed in the course of a defensive battle, which would permit a retreat and giving up some territory, before reserves drawn from the interior would be used for a transition to a decisive counter-offensive (on operational and strategic scales) leading to the full destruction of the enemy on its territory. This is the scenario which was considered loosely analagous to the Kursk battle. Variant three presupposes that each of the sides only retains the capacity to destroy enemy groupings which have invaded its own territory. The essence of such defence is that military operations are not carried over the territory of the side which began the war; they only restore the *status quo ante*. The notion of victory is attainable only on the operational and tactical scale but excluded on the strategic scale. Finally, the fourth variant presupposes that each side, on the basis of agreement or mutual example, chooses a deeply defensive variant of operations on the strategic and operational levels which excludes the material possibility of undertaking offensive or counter-offensive operations. High mobility would be mutually agreed only for tactical-level troop formations, which could be used for carrying out counter-attacks. This fullest version of non-provocative defence would exclude strike aviation, strike complexes and great mobile and strike power (tanks and air assault divisions) from the arsenals of the sides. Victory would only be attainable on the tactical scale, but be excluded on the strategic and operational levels.

Kokoshin and Larionov argued that the fourth variant would best correspond to the idea of strengthening strategic stability and the reduction of the military potentials of the sides to the limits of sufficiency, dictated only by the needs of defence. In their opinion it would also correspond to a large extent to the need or task of localizing armed conflict (Kokoshin and Larionov, 1988, pp. 24–30). Kokoshin subsequently revealed that among General Larionov's colleagues at the General Staff Academy 'there is apparently a consensus. . .that our four-model scheme provides a good framework within which to consider the issues'. He told an interviewer in November 1988 that 'Things are moving very quickly here. There is now the real possibility that the USSR will adopt the third model as its goal. We shall see what are the results of the current major review of military strategy' (*Rethinking Victory*, p. 18). This claim, if taken at face value, implies that Soviet new thinking on defensive defence may capture the defence agenda in the near future. In conclusion, therefore, we will consider how far recent evidence supports the view that a process of material change in official Soviet thinking on military strategy is under way at the highest levels.

THE OFFICIAL SYNTHESIS: NON-OFFENSIVE DEFENCE AND MILITARY STRATEGY

The new military doctrine proclaimed by the Warsaw Pact states in May 1987 provided at best imperfect evidence that the Soviet leadership was seeking a more defensive concept of military strategy. The bloc states called for a reduction of armed forces and conventional armaments in Europe down to a level 'at which neither side, while ensuring its defence, would have the means for making a surprise attack on the other side or for starting offensive operations in general' (a political aspiration). Yet they claimed that they already complied strictly 'with the limits of sufficiency for defence, for repelling possible aggression' (which implied no real departure from traditional military strategy) (*Documents of the Warsaw Treaty*, 1987, pp. 18–20).

Over the following year new thinking in the Party leadership and military interpretations of 'defence sufficiency' appeared to be at odds. Foreign Minister Shevardnadze expressed the former in appealing before the United Nations for nations to adopt a 'defensive strategy' and accordingly to reorient their military structures 'exclusively to the objectives of non-offensive defence'. In his view this presupposed 'a radical overhaul of armaments structures and distribution and changes in the very nature of military activities and in the development of armed forces' (Shevardnadze, 1988a). But these sentiments conflicted with the unrelenting commitment of the Soviet military leadership throughout 1987 to the capabilities necessary to inflict a 'crushing counteroffensive'.

The first signs of a shift in this maximalist position within the Soviet General Staff began to appear in 1988. At the seventieth anniversary of the Soviet army and navy in February, Marshal Akhromeyev overturned standard Soviet operational art in declaring that 'in the event of aggression, the main type of military operations by our armed forces will be defensive operations' (Akhromeyev, 1988a; see also Gareev, 1987). He described this defence as 'active', but implied significantly that military activity would be limited, controlled and non-escalatory in character: 'If the aggression is stepped up and widened, retaliatory strikes will be made in the light of the developing situation' (Akhromeyev, 1988a). Colonel-General Gareev similarly asserted that defence was becoming the main type of combat action at 'the outset of a war'. He claimed that 'the thrust of the operational and combat training' of the Warsaw Pact troops and forces had changed to conform with this, and promised that the new defensive orientation would be reflected in the operational planning and development of the Soviet armed forces (Gareev, 1988a; 1988b, p. 6). These statements implied that of the four scenarios for defence elaborated by Kokoshin and Larionov the Soviet military command, under prompting from the political leadership, may at least have accepted the broad outlines of the second variant and was possibly considering the third variant as the basis for future policy.

In autumn 1988, however, Soviet General Staff had not yet achieved a clear definition of non-offensive defence for its own purposes. One senior political official revealed that the General Staff and Ministry of Defence were currently working 'on the problem of defining what non-offensive defence is, what the criteria are for the structure of the armed forces, the deployment of the armed forces, the character of the armed forces' (Zagladin, 1988). Gareev was prepared to speculate on defence of a local nature 'based on holding major key areas and positions and making widespread use of various obstacles'. Reinforced areas could be formed on some axes, and he argued that a reduction in forces allocated to defence would increase the importance of creating 'highly-mobile reserves for rapid manoeuvring towards threatened axes' (Gareev, 1988b, p. 9).

Although Soviet military strategy may still be in a period of revision at the highest levels, certain notable steps have already been proposed, promised or adopted. In September 1988 Akhromeyev suggested that the Soviet armed forces would adopt specific changes towards a non-offensive structure: limitations would be imposed on strike weapon systems; force groupings would be altered, and such groupings would be deployed with defensive missions in mind; and steps would be taken to change the configuration of Soviet forces in Europe to decrease the concern of Western countries (Akhromeyev, 1988b, p. 13; see also Moiseyev, 1989b).

This speech prefigured the substantial changes announced by Gorbachev at the United Nations in December, which will heavily reduce forward-deployed Soviet tank forces, result in the withdrawal of specific forces designed to facilitate offensive operations, and restructure the remaining Soviet armoured divisions in Eastern Europe to enhance their defensive content. Offensive operational concepts such as that of operational manoeuvre groups may also be discarded. According to one Soviet military specialist four of the six Soviet divisions earmarked for withdrawal from Eastern Europe are parts of operational manoeuvre groups in northern East Germany (Larionov in Fialka, 1989, p. A18). Gorbachev promised also that Soviet forces along the border with China would also be reduced and configured in a more defensive mode.

Gorbachev's New York initiative has had the effect of undercutting the Soviet capacity to undertake a standing-start attack in Europe in the absence of a reinforcement of the forces remaining in place. The Soviet military described the reductions as 'the first step towards restructuring our armed forces in a way that excludes the possibility of deploying them in sudden large-scale offensive operations' (Chernyshev, 1989). It is this structural process which, if indeed under way, is most significant. Soviet military specialists admit that the necessary superiority of strength can be created for offensive operations on some narrow sector of the front by weakening other sectors. But their argument has been that the withdrawal of offensive forces would require any attempt at an offensive thrust to be preceded by a regrouping and concentration of forces which would be detected by the other side, and surprise attack would thereby be eliminated (see, for example, Milshteyn, 1987; Simonyan, 1988, p. 53).

Gorbachev's New York initiative may provide evidence of a substantive shift in official Soviet military strategy. According to one report (Nitze, 1988) the Soviet military now expects that following an outbreak of East–West hostilities (which they claim would be inadvertent or initiated by NATO) the USSR would remain on the defensive for perhaps twenty or thirty days before counter-attacking. This extended defensive phase would help to discourage rapid expansion in the scale of the conflict and would provide a better chance to achieve an early political termination of hostilities (see also Karpov, 1989). The Soviet withdrawal of tank forces and equipment announced in December 1988 would fit this scenario of operations, since the built-in time delay before Soviet leaders would launch an offensive in earnest would enable the USSR to redeploy forces and means forward to the front line.

Marshal Akhromeyev reportedly claimed that a major WTO exercise held in March 1988 used the following scenario: a defensive Pact response to a NATO invasion of Eastern Europe, followed by a limited counter-offensive over a three-week period that halted after expelling NATO forces from Pact territory. Only failing a political termination of the war in this period would the USSR have been ready to resume its offensive thrust westwards to defeat NATO forces (Warner, 1989, p. 25). Another WTO exercise in April 1989 required WTO defending forces to aim only at restoring their original positions and not to push deep into enemy territory. A senior Soviet officer stated on this occasion that, to conform to the new military doctrine, he would not permit a WTO 'counter-attack' in war to cross over into NATO territory, but would restore 'existing boundaries' (*Newsnight*, 20 April 1989; see also Lebedev, 1989).

The two military exercises outlined above approximate respectively to variants two and three of the strategic framework drawn up by Kokoshin and Larionov. The official adoption of model two by the Soviet leadership would in itself constitute a notable change in Soviet military strategy. The adoption of model three (which may be difficult without some reciprocal Western steps) would restrict Soviet strategic objectives beyond WTO borders in warfare in Europe and clearly switch the emphasis to successes and failures at the operational and tactical level. Both scenarios imply the creation of a defensive buffer zone in Eastern Europe, which would permit Soviet WTO allies to implement a more nationally oriented defence policy and encourage very significant reductions in Soviet forces in Europe *vis-à-vis* those of NATO (see Hall, 1988, pp. 35–6). This is consistent with Soviet acceptance of the principle of equal lower ceilings for NATO and WTO conventional forces in Europe at the CFE negotiations. Indeed, populist appeals in Eastern Europe for the removal of Soviet forces – as vocally expressed, for example, in Czechoslovakia in February 1990 – may compel Soviet leaders to withdraw most of their forces back to Soviet territory even in advance of the timetables agreed in CFE treaties. The progressive breakdown in the cohesion of the Warsaw Pact military command structure following the emergence of new popular governments and democratic movements in the non-Soviet Warsaw Pact states in 1989–90 means that earlier Soviet military planning premised on unified 'coalitional warfare' by the WTO is no longer realistic. New bilateral security arrangements are likely to emerge between the USSR and East European states based to an increasing extent on the national defence interests of the latter states.

CONCLUSION

By spring 1987 the new Soviet outlook on international security adopted by the Gorbachev leadership began publicly to challenge core principles and threat assessments of traditional Soviet defence thinking. This effort, which probably followed protracted discussions in the Defence Council, could be understood both as a more sophisticated response to the immediate security/defence needs of the USSR and as a measure of the commitment of Soviet reformers to extract the Soviet state from the danger of imminent economic collapse. Formidable obstacles to the new thinking on defence could, however, be anticipated.

In the first place the resistance of professional Soviet officers to the most challenging element of new thinking on defence – the notion of non-offensive defence – is only natural, since official adoption of this concept would overturn a commitment to offensive operations which is deeply ingrained in Soviet strategic culture. To achieve such a transformation the outlook of the General Staff and the Soviet military elite would need to change wholesale. Although General Staff plans are allegedly being revised in the light of the defensive military doctrine it was admitted in this context at the end of 1988 that 'deep-rooted stereotypes of the mass consciousness shaped in previous years cannot be overcome overnight or within a short period' (*KZ*, 28 December 1988). The Party elite will have to wage a protracted political campaign over many years in the armed forces if it is to maintain its objective of reconstituting the traditional offence-dominant strategic culture of the Soviet military hierarchy.

Second, Gorbachev will need to convince the Soviet military command that the maintenance of 'reliable defence' is consistent with any reconfiguration of Soviet forces envisaged by new principles in defence thinking. An announcement by Gorbachev early in 1989 of a 20 per cent cut in the output of Soviet military production conforms to the principle of shifting from quantitative to qualitative indices in defence production, which was approved at the Nineteenth Party Congress, with the apparent support of Soviet military leaders. The Chief of Soviet General Staff has even claimed that 'in military science and design bureaus many long-term technical development projects linked with the utilisation of offensive arms systems have been dropped from plans' to conform to the new Soviet military doctrine (Moiseyev, 1989b). But it will remain a core Soviet security interest to maintain basic R&D in advanced new military technologies (offensive and defensive) to offset qualitative advances in Western arms even if levels of Soviet forces are substantially reduced and reconstituted and Soviet military strategy revised.

Third, to ingrain new defence thinking in the Soviet political fabric it is in Gorbachev's interest to further civilianize defence policy-making and to extend military *glasnost*. Again this demands a fundamental recasting of Soviet political and strategic culture and is likely to confront vested institutional interests. The pace of political reform now apparent in Moscow raises the possibility, however, that a new institutional setting may emerge to encourage such a change in attitudes. Traditional threat assessments based on crude correlation of forces thinking and fuelled by over-ambitious strategic plans are likely to be further undercut and more difficult to revive if significant elements of Soviet defence policy are subject to scrutiny in the new Supreme Soviet and made accountable in some degree to this body. In this way the new thinking on defence may be assisted by the developing political process of democratization in the USSR.

If the internal Soviet programme of *perestroika* fails to measure up to expectations in the 1990s and if radicals in the current leadership are displaced it is possible that the political will necessary for a shift towards a truly defensive Soviet defence posture (in association with changes in Western defence efforts) will be dissipated. In this case it is likely that a more balanced mix of offensive and defensive Soviet capabilities determined by military-technological criteria will develop. But whatever the complexion of the Soviet leadership it will remain a fundamental Soviet interest to secure a more equitable balance between political/economic and military means in safeguarding national security. Consequently a reversion to the militarist excesses of the 'old thinking' is unlikely so long as favourable relations with Western states offer a firmer prospect of economic revitalization than would a policy of autarky. Much will depend ultimately on Western responses to Soviet initiatives in this vulnerable period of transition.

REFERENCE

Abbreviations:
KZ   *Krasnaya Zvezda*
MEMO   *Mirovaya ekonomika i mezhdunarodnye otnosheniya*
SShA   *SShA: Ekonomika, Politika, Ideologiya*
SU   *BBC Summary of World Broadcasts. Soviet Union*

Akhromeyev, Marshal S. (1987), 'Doktrina predotvrashcheniya voyny zashchity mira i sotsializma', *Problemy mira i sotsializma*, no. 12, pp. 23–8.
Akhromeyev, S. (1988a), article in *Trud*, 21 February.
Akhromeyev, S. (1988b), 'The Olof Palme Memorial Lecture', Stockholm International Peace Research Institute, 29 September.
Akhromeyev, S. (1988c), article in *Rabotnichesko Delo* (Sofia), 6 December; cited in SU 0331 A1/3.

Anan'ev, I. (1988), *Tankovye armii v nastuplenii* (Moscow: Voenizdat).

Arbatov, A. (1988), 'Parity and reasonable sufficiency', *International Affairs* (Moscow), no. 10, pp. 75–87.

Chernyshev, V., Col. (1988), 'Obychnaya voyna v Yevrope?', *KZ*, 29 March.

Chernyshev, V. (1989), Moscow home service 6 January, in SU/0354 A1/7.

Covington, S. (1987), *The Role of the Defence in Soviet Military Thinking* (Sandhurst: Soviet Studies Research Centre, Royal Military Academy).

Disarmament and Security Yearbook (1987) (Moscow: IMEMO).

Dobrynin, A. (1987), *Pravda*, 5 May.

Dobrynin, A. (1988), 'Soviet foreign policy: basic principles and new thinking', *World Marxist Review*, vol. 31, no. 3.

Documents of the Meeting of the Political Consultative Committee of the Warsaw Treaty Member States, Berlin, May 23–29, 1987 (1987) (Moscow: Novosti).

Fialka, J. (1989), 'Russia's troop cuts in Europe reflect broad military shift', *Wall Street Journal*, 25 April.

Gareev, M. (1985a), *M. V. Frunze – Voenny teoretnik* (Moscow: Voenizdat).

Gareev, M. (1985b), 'Tvorcheskiy kharakter sovetskoy voennoy nauki v velikoy otechestvennoy voyne', *Voenno-istorichestkiy-zhurnal*, no. 7, pp. 22–30.

Gareev, M. (1987), statement at Soviet Foreign Ministry press conference, in *KZ*, 23 June.

Gareev, M. (1988a), interview in *Argumenty i Fakty*, no. 39, cited in SU/0267 B1-2.

Gareev, M. (1988b), address at the Royal United Services Institute, 19 October.

Gayvoronskogo, Colonel-General F. (ed.) (1987), *Evolyutsiva voennogo iskusstva: etapy, tendentsii, prinstipy* (Moscow: Voenizdat).

Hall, Major R. (1988), 'Command and control of the future battlefield: the Soviet view', defence fellowship thesis, Ministry of Defence.

Hines, J., Petersen, P., and Trulock III, N. (1986), 'Soviet military theory from 1945–2000: implications for NATO', *Washington Quarterly*, Fall, pp. 117–37.

Ionin, G. (1988), 'Osnovy sovremennogo oboronitel'nogo boya', *Voenny Vestnik, no. 3, pp. 18–21.*

Karpov, Deputy Foreign Minister V. (1989), statement at press conference 31 January, *Vestnik Ministerstva Inostrannykh Del SSSR*, vol. 4, no. 38 (1 March), p. 42.

Kirshin, Major-General Yu. (1988) (Deputy Chief of the Institute of History of the USSR Ministry of Defence), 'Politika i voennaya strategiya v yadernyy vek', *MEMO*, no. 11, pp. 34–45.

Kirshin, Yu., Popov, V., and Savushkin, R.(1987), *Politicheskoe soderzhanie sovremennykh voin* (Moscow: Voenizdat).

Kir'yan, M. (1986), head of author's collective, *Istoriva voennogo iskusstva* (Moscow: Voenizdat).

Kokoshin, A. (1988a), 'Razvitie voennogo dela i sokrashchenie vooruzhennykh sil i obychnykh vooruzheniy', *MEMO*, no. 1.

Kokoshin, A. (1988b), 'Sokrashchenie yadernykh vooruzheniy i strategicheskiya stabil'nost', *SShA*, no. 2, pp. 3–12.

Kokoshin, A. (1988c), 'Alexander Svechin: on war and politics', *International Affairs* (Moscow), no. 11, pp. 118–26.

Kokoshin, A., and Kortunov, A. (1987), 'Stabil'nost i peremeny v mezhdunarodynkh otnosheniyakh', *SShA*, no. 7, pp. 3–12.

Kokoshin, A., and Larionov, V., Major-General (1987), 'Kurskaya bitva v svete sovremennoy oboronitel'noy doktriny', *MEMO*, no. 8, pp. 32–40.

Kokoshin, A., and Larionov, V. (1988), 'Protivostoyanie sil obshchego naznacheniya v kontekste obespecheniya strategicheskoy stabil'nosti', *MEMO*, no. 6, pp. 23–31.

Kokoshin, A., and Larionov, V. (1989), 'Shifting the emphasis to defence', *New Times* (Moscow), no. 10.

Kondrashov, S. (1989), *Izvestiya*, 4 February.

Kostev, Rear-Admiral G. (1987), 'Nasha voennaya doktrina v svete novogo politicheskogo myshleniya', *Kommunist vooruzhennykh sil*, no. 17, pp. 9–15.

Kulikov, Marshal V. (1988), *Doktrina zashchity mira i sotsializma* (Moscow: Voenizdat).

Kunitskiy, Major-General P. (1988), 'Esli oborona prorvana. . .', *Voennoistoricheskiy zhurnal*, no. 12, pp. 3–10.

Lebedev, Major-General Y. (1989), speech on 17 April in New York, in 'Meeting Report of Institute of East–West Security Studies'.

Lukava, Colonel G. (1986), 'Faktor vnezaposti v agressivnoy politike imperializma', *Kommunist vooruzhennykh sil*, no. 11, pp. 23–9.

McConnell, J. (1985), 'Shifts in Soviet views on the proper focus of military development', *World Politics*, vol. 37, no. 3.

Makarevsky, Major-General V. (1989), 'Neprovokatsionnaya oborona', *KZ*, 31 March.

Marashev, Major-General A. (1986), 'Nekotorye voprosy strategicheskoy oborony v Velikoy Otechestvennoy voyne', *Voenno-istoricheskoy zhurnal*, no. 6.

Meyer, S. (1988), 'The sources and prospects of Gorbachev's new political thinking on security', *International Security*, vol. 13, no. 2, Fall, pp. 124–63.

Milshteyn, Lt-General M. (1987), *New Times* (Moscow), July, cited in SU/8621 A1/7.

Moiseyev, Colonel General M. (1989a), election meeting address in *KZ*, 10 February.

Moiseyev, M. (1989b), article in *Pravda*, 13 March 1989.

Newsnight (1989), interview on BBC 2, 20 April 1989.

Nitze, Ambassador P. (1988), interview on 12 December 1988 with European reporters via WorldNet, the satellite television system of the US Information Agency.

Ogarkov, Marshal N. (1984), *KZ*, 8 May 1984.

Ogarkov, N. (1985), *Istoriya uchit bditel'nosti* (Moscow: Voenizdat).

Perov, Lt-General I. (1988), 'The aggressive essence of new US and NATO concepts', *Zarubezhnoe voennoe obozrenie*, no. 2, pp. 7–17.

Petersen, P. and Trulock III, N. (1988), *A 'New' Soviet Military Doctrine: Origins and Implications* (Sandhurst: Soviet Studies Research Centre, Royal Military Academy).

Postnikov, General S. (1988), 'Razvitie sovetskogo voennogo iskusstva v Kurskoy bitve', *Voenno-istoricheskiyzhurnal*, no. 7, pp. 10–18.

'Rethinking victory – an interview with Andrei Kokoshin' (1988), *Détente*, no. 13, pp. 17–18.

Semeiko, Lt-Colonel (1988), 'From realistic positions', *Soviet Military Review*, no. 1, pp. 51–4.

Shenfield, S. (1987), *The Nuclear Predicament: Explorations in Soviet Ideology*, Chatham House Papers No. 37 (London: RIIA/Routledge & Kegan Paul).

Shevardnadze, E. (1988a), statement at UN third special session on disarmament, Tass 8 June, in SU/0174 A1/2–3.

Shevardnadze, E. (1988b); letter to the UN Secretary General on *glasnost* in the military field, Tass 10 June, in SU/0176 A1/3.

Shevardnadze, E. (1988c), speech on foreign policy reform, *Argumenty i Fakty*, no. 37, 10–16 September, cited in SU/0254 A1/3.

Shlykov, V. (1988), 'On the history of tank asymmetry in Europe', *International Affairs* (Moscow), no. 10, pp. 105–16.

Simonyan, Major-General R. (1988), 'From realistic positions', *Soviet Military Review*, no. 1.

Statement by the Committee of the Ministers of Defence of the Warsaw Treaty Member States (1989) (Berlin).

Vorob'yev, Major-General I. (1980), 'The relationship and reciprocal effects between offence and defence'. *Voennaya Mysl'*, no. 4. As translated in *Tap Chi Quan Doi Nhan Dan* (Hanoi), 1982, no. 1, DIA trans. LN-893-86; cited in Peterson and Trulock (1988).

Warner, E. III (1989), 'New thinking and old realities in Soviet defence policy', *Survival*, vol. 31, no. 1, pp. 13–33.

Yazov, General D. (1987a), *Pravda*, 27 July 1987.

Yazov, D. (1987b), *Na strazhe sotsializma i mira* (Moscow: Voenizdat).

Yazov, D. (1988), *KZ*, 23 February 1988.

Zagladin, V. (1988), Secretary of the Foreign Affairs Commission of the Supreme Soviet, on Soviet television 30 October, cited in SU/0304 A1/3.

Zhurkin, V., Karaganov, S., and Kortunov, A. (1987a), 'Reasonable sufficiency – or how to break the vicious circle', *New Times*, no. 12, pp. 13–15.

Zhurkin, V., Karaganov, S. and Kortunov, A. (1987b), 'Reasonable means sufficient', *Twentieth Century and Peace*, no. 12, pp. 2–9.

Zhurkin, V., Karaganov, S. and Kortunov, A. (1987c), 'O razumnoy dostatochnosti', *SShA*, no. 12, pp. 11–12.

Zhurkin, V., Karaganov, S. and Kortunov, A. (1988), 'Vyzovy bezopasnosti – starye i novye', *Kommunist*, no. 1, pp. 42–50.

10

New directions in European security

ADRIAN G. V. HYDE-PRICE

JOHN ROPER

From Lisbon to Leningrad, the air is electric with the expectation of change. In Western Europe '1992' symbolizes a renewed commitment to the process of closer economic and political integration, while in Eastern Europe and the Soviet Union *glasnost* and *perestroika* promise the most extensive and significant changes in the communist world since Stalin's 'revolution from above' in 1929–33. These developments take on an even greater significance given the relative decline in the power and authority of the two superpowers, and the continuing problems associated with deploying the weapons required for nuclear deterrence in Europe. The implications of these trends and developments extend far beyond the boundaries of either Western or Eastern Europe, but are likely to have a major impact on political and economic relations in Europe. It is clear therefore that the assumptions underpinning the postwar European security system can no longer be taken for granted. Indeed, François Heisbourg has gone so far as to argue that Western Europe has in fact entered its most unstable political and strategic situation in its postwar history, given the conjuncture of major change in the USSR and renewed tensions in the Atlantic Alliance.[1] The sense that we are at an historical moment of change in Europe was made clear when a noted conservative and hard-headed *Realpolitiker* like the late

Franz Joseph Strauss could declare at a press conference in Moscow in December 1987 that 'The post-war period has now ended. A new chapter has opened up' (*Süddeutsche Zeitung*, 31 December 1988).

Despite its inauspicious and turbulent origins, the European security system has proved a remarkably stable structure, which has contributed to the maintenance of peace on the continent for nearly forty years. However, it has been a stability based on the division of Europe. For those who are more optimistic, the changes in the air at the moment seem to hold out the prospect of unfreezing the two blocs and overcoming the division of the continent. Those who remain more sceptical, however, foresee crisis and instability, and warn of the perils of raised expectations and utopian illusions. It is thus apparent that we are in a period pregnant with both opportunities and risks, and that the prospect of change is unsettling to many, because of the uncertainties it involves.

Our concern in this chapter is to consider what is changing or likely to change in the next decade; what the direction of these changes is likely to be; and whether these developments can be directed into a process of dynamic change, which maintains the stability of the European system without precluding social, economic and political changes in both parts of Europe. To begin with, it is necessary to outline the key features of the European security system.

THE KEY FEATURES OF THE EUROPEAN SECURITY SYSTEM

By the European security system we mean the military, political, social and economic system which emerged as a result of the postwar settlement and the breakdown of the wartime alliance of the 'Big Three', and which was finally stabilized as a result of the response of the leading protagonists on both sides to the twin dramas of the Cuban missile crisis and the building of the Berlin Wall. This security system was predicated on the division of Europe, a state of affairs which was tacitly accepted by all the key players involved almost from the outset. The European security system itself is characterized by three specific features, described below, which radically distinguish it from the previous European balance of power arrangements.

(1) Superpower dominance

Europe's heyday, in terms of world influence, was the nineteenth century; since the turn of the century the relative power of the European states has been in decline. The Great War was a milestone in this process, but the watershed was the Second World War. As stillness descended over the battlefields of Europe in May 1945, vast tracts of the continent lay in ruins, its political and social structures smashed by the years of war and occupation, or, in the the case of Britain, its economic power sapped by its mobilization for total war. Into this power vacuum stepped the two military and political superpowers, the USA and the USSR. Of the two, only the USA was a truly global power with an economic potential to match its military might, but the Soviet Union nonetheless commanded the largest conventional forces on the continent and was the ideological and political leader of a large and influential international movement.

Very soon, traditional historical, ideological and political differences reasserted themselves, and the wartime 'Grand Alliance' gave way to the Cold War. The two superpowers emerged as the leaders of hostile military and political alliances in Europe, seeking to rally their supporters behind their leadership, and disciplining, where necessary, recalcitrant members. The two alliances, however, were highly asymmetrical. On the one hand, the USSR was a European power, whereas the USA was not. On the other, the USA was generally welcomed to Europe by most of the governments and publics of Western Europe, whereas the military presence and political influence of the Soviet Union was not so universally welcomed by the populations of Eastern Europe. Superpower pre-eminence declined somewhat as postwar European recovery proceeded apace, a process which was evident first in the West, and only later in the East. However, both alliances experienced their 'difficult' members, namely France and Romania, in the 1960s.

Nevertheless, the superpowers have continued to play a decisive role in the European security system, as the inability to isolate European détente from the general health of the superpower relationship over the last two decades makes clear.

(2) The division of Germany

Since the 1648 Treaty of Westphalia, Germany has been the axis on which the European balance of power has revolved. With the unification of the former statelets and principalities of the Holy Roman Empire into the Bismarckian Reich, and the subsequent industrial expansion of Wilhelmine Germany at the turn of the century, Germany emerged as a major threat to the stability of Europe. Europe was faced with the difficulties of seeking to absorb the energies and ambitions of imperial Germany, an industrial and military giant situated in the heart of the continent. Twice in the first half of this century, this problem has engulfed Europe in the devastation of total war.

The postwar division of Germany into the Federal Republic of Germany (FRG) and the German Democratic Republic (GDR) has in some ways provided a workable solution to the perennial problem of German power. As Richard Vine has powerfully argued,

> The division of Germany has provided reassurance in Eastern and Western Europe; it has provided stability in large measure by removing the specter of a security threat to the Soviet Union or to other European countries. There are few determined rooters for a politically reunited Germany, not even in the two Germanies. A divided Germany, with one part 'hostage' in the Eastern security system, may be an indispensable condition to continued system stability for the foreseeable future. (Vine, 1987, p. 33)

Both German states have emerged as the most important European economic and military powers of the respective alliances. As a single unified state, their power and influence would be immense. This would be perceived as potentially threatening by Germany's neighbours, and the prospect of reunification itself makes many Europeans reluctant to consider radical changes to the present security system.

(3) Nuclear deterrence

The advent of the nuclear age, with the success of the Manhattan Project and the atomic destruction of Hiroshima and Nagasaki, fundamentally changed the rules of the game of the international system. Nuclear weapons have negated Clausewitz's central precept of war as a continuation of politics by other means, and have imposed a new and powerful discipline on both superpowers and their European allies. The pre-Second World War balance of power system has been consigned to the dustbin of history by nuclear deterrence.

WHAT IS IN FLUX?

It is of course self-evident that since its emergence the postwar European security system has experienced a number of evolutionary changes and transformations, even though its essential structures have remained intact. Today, however, a number of trends are in evidence in both sides of Europe, as well as in transatlantic relations, which together might entail qualitative changes in Europe. These are as follows.

1992 and the development of a West European security identity

As the 1980s unfolded, *Eurosclerosis* gave way to *Europhoria*. The single European Act of 1986 commits the twelve to build a unified internal market by 1992. Political co-operation has been deepened through the European Political Co-operation (EPC). Closer economic and financial integration poses the issue of a single Euro-currency and a central European bank, and Jacques Delors in July 1988 said that 80 per cent of economic and social decision-making would soon pass from national capitals to the European Community (EC). Whatever cold water might be poured on these and other more ambitious visions of a united Europe by neo-Gaullists like Margaret Thatcher, it is evident that closer West European integration will be a feature of the 1990s.

Whereas the establishment and growth of the European Economic Community (EEC) was initially a matter of the six, then the nine, and then the twelve, today the implications of 1992 go far beyond the structures of the EC, and now affect the whole architecture of Europe. Deepening integration in the Community will exert a magnetic pull on other European states, both in the

European Free Trade Association (EFTA) and in the Council of Mutual Economic Assistance (CMEA), and will give Western Europe a greater collective weight in the global economy and in other international forums.

Integration in the EC is to some extent complemented and accompanied by closer West European security co-operation, which takes place through a variety of institutional forums. EPC is limited by the Single European Act to the economic and social aspects of security. 1992 could have important implications for arms procurement, while projects like Eureka[2] also have significant spillover effects for defence industries. The Western European Union (WEU) was reactivated in 1984,[3] and bilateral defence co-operation, notably between France and the FRG, has been another important development. Whatever the varied motivation and concerns of the major actors in this process, namely France, the FRG, the UK and Italy, a strong impetus to it has come from the changing nature of transatlantic relationships in the Reagan period. This takes us on to our second point.

US–West European relations

The 1980s were a troubled decade for transatlantic relations. Although there have been plenty of disputes and differences between the USA and its European NATO allies since 1949, it can be argued that the disputes of the 1980s were qualitatively different. The initial policy of the Reagan administration, with its military build-up and belligerent stance towards the 'Evil Empire', led to growing US–West European differences over such issues as economic sanctions, SDI, Grenada, the bombing of Libya and Ostpolitik. Underlying these specific issues are two long-term trends: firstly, the continuing relative decline of US power and, second, the growing economic weight of Western Europe within the Atlantic Alliance. With the Bush administration, serious problems still plague transatlantic relations. The twin US economic problems, the budget deficit and the trade deficit, will sharpen the burden-sharing debate, and raise the threat of 'bringing the boys back home'. Changes in US global interests, both as result of increased economic priority to the Pacific rim and as a consequence of an increasing perception of growing stability in Europe, will stimulate the debate over the desirability of a reassessment of

US strategic interests and the deployment of US military power. Finally, Reagan's wish to make nuclear weapons 'impotent and obsolete' reflected in his SDI policy, and his apparent adoption of the goal of a denuclearized world at Reykjavik, are symptoms of a more general view in the United States, where many see nuclear weapons as having a primary role in deterring a nuclear attack on the USA itself, whereas many West Europeans see them as deterring all war. These and the associated dilemmas of extended deterrence have intensified over the last decade. Although there is no reason to believe that a precipitate US military and political withdrawal from Europe is likely at the moment, it is likely that the nature of the political relationship and the form of its institutional structures will undergo significant changes in the years ahead.

Soviet perestroika and the 'new political thinking'

After years of Brezhnevite stagnation, the Soviet Union has embarked on a farreaching and comprehensive reform programme, which promises a fundamental transformation of Soviet society and of its relations with the outside world. The impetus behind this came from the growing realization amongst key sections of the Soviet elite that the crisis of performance of Soviet 'developed socialism' was assuming the proportions and the character of a systemic crisis (this was apparent from the debate on contradictions in socialism – for an exposition and analysis of these debates see Kux, 1984). As Gorbachev made clear as early as 1984,[4] if the Soviet Union was to enter the twenty-first century as a superpower, then fundamental economic, political and social reform was imperative. As a consequence of the leadership and generational change since 1985, therefore, the Soviet state and society have been dragged into the trauma, excitement and upheaval of *perestroika* and *glasnost*.

What makes this reform process of particular importance for European security is the emphasis given by the new Soviet leadership to the interrelationship between domestic and foreign policy reform. The Soviets now stress the overwhelming importance of interdependence, and the aim of the current reforms is to further the integration of the USSR into the world system (both in terms of the global economy and the international 'community of nations'). Gorbachev, as a latterday reincarnation of Peter the Great, insists that the Soviet Union can only be an economic and political superpower (rather than 'Upper Volta with missiles') if it opens itself up to the outside world. Domestic *perestroika, glasnost* and *demokratizatsiya* are therefore both a complement to, and are complemented by, the 'new political thinking'.

At the heart of the 'new political thinking' is a reassessment of the relationship between class interests and all-human concerns. Growing global interdependence has given added weight to general human interests and to common global problems such as the arms race, environmental pollution and Third World poverty. A bipolar, class concept of the international system has been rejected in favour of a new, developing concept of a complex, multipolar world in which international relations cannot be reduced to class interests and class struggle. This means that détente is no longer seen as a specific form of class struggle, and that 'imperialism' is no longer seen as intrinsically and irredeemably militaristic and aggressive.

At the same time, the 'new political thinking' has important implications for Soviet security policy. With the Gorbachev-Schevadnadze team firmly in command, common security has emerged as a central theme. In the nuclear age, the Soviets now emphasize, Clausewitz's oft-quoted dictum is no longer apposite, and security can no longer be achieved militarily in opposition to the other side, but only on the basis of mutual understanding and trust. Closely linked to this new emphasis on common security is a rethinking of military doctrine and a new approach to regional security issues. Gorbachev has consequently advocated the principle of *necessary sufficiency*, recognized the existence of asymmetries in certain weapon systems, made substantial concessions on arms control and confidence- and security-building measures (CSBMs), called for a defensive military doctrine for the WTO (including its technical-operational aspects), announced significant unilateral arms cuts and reduced the Soviet defence budget.

It should not be forgotten that many aspects of the 'new political thinking' have not yet been completely accepted or assimilated by key groups in the foreign and security policy establishment in the Soviet Union, and that a reversal of the more compromise-oriented policies of Gorbachev cannot be excluded. However, if the 'new political thinking' does come to govern the operational aspects of Soviet foreign and defence policy, then the significance of the Soviet domestic and foreign policy reforms for European security is potentially enormous. First, a more tolerant and pluralistic Soviet political system would undermine popular Western perceptions of a 'Soviet threat'. Second, successful economic reform and market-oriented decentralization would facilitate East–West trade and economic co-operation. Third, if the USSR were to join the international division of labour and the global economy, it would signal its final transformation from the bastion of the world revolution into a status quo power. Fourth, if changes in Soviet military doctrine and force deployments in Europe removed the Soviet Army's capability to launch a large-scale short-warning armoured offensive against NATO, the pre-eminent security threat to Western Europe would be removed. Fifth, if the Soviet Union is serious about international co-operation to solve common global problems, then the West has a ready partner with which to co-operate in tackling some of the causes of instability in the international system. Finally, Soviet talk of a multipolar world and of a 'common European home' might be indicative of a growing Soviet recognition of the need to develop a specific regional policy for Europe substantially insulated from the vagaries of the superpower relationship.

Soviet–East European relations

One of the central features of European security has been Soviet domination of Eastern Europe since liberation by the Red Army in 1944–5. Helmut Sonnenfeldt argued fifteen years ago that East–West détente could never be placed on a sound footing until Soviet–East European relations assumed a more 'organic' character (US Congress, 1976). More recently, Timothy Garton Ash has argued that 'the question of a new security order in all of Europe is inextricably intertwined with the question of a new political order in Eastern Europe' (*Independent*, 9 December 1988). Change in the countries of East Central Europe is therefore closely bound up with change in the broader European security system, and in this light it is significant to see that farreaching changes are under way in some of the countries of East Central Europe at the present.

On his election to the post of General Secretary, Mikhail Gorbachev declared that his 'first commandment' would be to improve relations with the USSR's East European allies (*Pravda*, 12 March 1985). Since then, three themes have been repeatedly stressed:

First, an emphasis on the desirability of bloc-wide integration through the CMEA combined with economic modernization and *perestroika*; second, more consultative methods of alliance management and a greater use of multilateral forums; and third, greater tolerance of national diversity and experimentation. If, as J. F. Brown has argued, 'Since Stalin the main general aim of Soviet policy towards Eastern Europe has been to find the right balance between *cohesion* [of the "socialist community"] and *viability*' [of the existing socialist regimes] (1988, p. 42), then it is clear that Gorbachev is primarily concerned with the latter. The Soviets now aspire to create economically viable and politically legitimate socialist allies in Eastern Europe, and recognize that there are no universally valid solutions to the problems that socialist countries face. They are therefore willing to give their CMEA allies greater leeway to experiment with economic and political reforms reflecting specific national conditions and traditions. Only on this basis, Gorbachev seems to believe, can the socialist community advance towards a more durable and organic 'unity in diversity'.

The process of reform in Eastern Europe is fraught with dif-ficulties and dangers. To begin with, it should not be forgotten that disturbances in the region have historically tended to follow leadership changes in the Soviet Union (Larrabee, 1988, p. 43). Second, the reform process in Hungary and Poland takes place against the backdrop of chronic economic decline and deepening social problems. Third, *perestroika* in Eastern Europe has also inten-sified the trend towards diversity and differentiation, both between Eastern Europe and the Soviet Union, and between individual East European states. Finally, as the *Pax Sovietica* in Eastern Europe disintegrates, traditional national and ethnic rivalries are reasserting themselves (most notably in the Hungarian–Romanian dispute over Transylvania). The mixture of *glasnost* and communism is proving a potentially volatile mixture, and, as Charles Gati has suggested, the attempt to combine the leading role of the communist party with 'market socialism' and 'socialist pluralism' could 'unravel in Warsaw, Budapest or Prague', creating a conservative backlash of old-style communists against Gorbachev (1987, p. 975).

Eastern Europe is therefore potentially the location for the most significant changes in the European security system. The fault-line in the Europe of the Yalta settlement runs through the countries of East Central Europe, and today these countries are caught between the conflicting pressures of 1992 in Western Europe and *perestroika* in the USSR. As Alex Pravda has written, 'Political and economic weaknesses and growing heterogeneity in the Eastern bloc at a time of increasing contact with a prosperous and fast-integrating Western Europe pose serious problems for Moscow' (*International Herald Tribune*, 25 August 1988). Although the West has an interest in supporting and encouraging reform and systemic change in Eastern Europe, it has no wish to see a major crisis erupt in the region which would destabilize the East–West security balance (Vine, 1987, p. 36). If the process of dynamic change in Eastern Europe degenerates into mass popular unrest and political upheaval, the implications for European security are ominous. In this respect, Christoph Bertram's remarks are particularly apposite; 'It is, after all, the nightmare of all of those who are worried that the real European security problem is not the threat of Russians marching to the Rhine but of domestic unrest in Eastern Europe sliding inexorably into a European war. That is the way in which many a European war has begun' (1988, p. 136).

The situation in Eastern Europe is therefore becoming increasingly ambiguous. One possible scenario is the 'Yugoslavization' of Eastern Europe: in other words, if countries like Hungary achieve their aim of eventually becoming *de facto* neutral states, they will not be like Austria or Sweden (who enjoy a tacit Western security guarantee), but like Yugoslavia (which does not). In this respect, the political and security map of Europe is likely to become increasingly more complex and differentiated. The key issue in Soviet–East European relations today is what the limits are to Soviet tolerance of change and diversity in the socialist countries of East Central Europe. It does seem as if the 'Brezhnev doctrine' (the Soviet doctrine of the limited sovereignty for members of the 'socialist community') in its traditional form no longer governs Soviet–East European relations, although it is clear that the USSR continues to have important security and political interests in Eastern Europe. At what point the Soviets would decide that these interests were threatened by the reform process in individual socialist states is in many ways the six-thousand-dollar question: the answer to this question is central to the future development of the European security system.

THE CHANGING EAST–WEST RELATIONSHIP

The changes currently under way in both parts of the divided continent have stimulated and facilitated important developments in East–West relations in Europe. Since the mid-1980s there has been a substantial thaw in the climate of US–Soviet relations, with an inexorable trend away from cold war belligerency and bellicosity towards a new period of improved political relations. The euphoria of détente has given new hope to those seeking to move beyond the Europe of the settlements of Yalta and Potsdam. However, the experience of détente in the 1970s provides a sobering warning against overoptimistic expectations about the irreversibility of détente and the possibility of overcoming the two blocs. Nevertheless, there is good reason for believing that the current period of growing East–West understanding is no brief interlude in a perennial Cold War, and that the prospects for a more positive and co-operative long-term development in East–West relations in Europe are more favourable than in the 1970s. The most important factors involved in this assessment are as follows.

The changing nature of détente

The new period of détente, which has been gathering pace since 1986–7, is different in its character and assumptions from that of the 1970s, and the nature of its leading protagonists has also changed. First, the Soviet Union today is very different from the Soviet Union of Brezhnev – given the change in assumptions and perspectives arising from the generational change which has accompanied Gorbachev's accession to power. The USSR today recognizes its economic and political weaknesses, and is ideologically on the defensive. Its changed approach to 'peaceful coexistence' is evidenced by the fact that it no longer characterizes détente as a 'special form of class struggle'. Second, following eight years of the Reagan presidency, America is no longer suffering the traumas of the post-Vietnam syndrome, but is enjoying a renewed sense of confidence and self-assurance. At the same time the Bush administration is likely to be more pragmatic and technocratic than the early Reagan administration, seeking to accommodate US power to the realities of an increasingly multipolar world.

Third, the Europeans have a much richer experience of détente than they did in the early 1970s, and are therefore better equipped to be able to manage the East–West détente process than they were in the past. They also demonstrated in the early 1980s that they wished to see more durable East–West co-operation in Europe, partially insulated from the changing superpower relationship (this is particularly apparent in the case of the two German states) (Kiep, 1984–5).

The 'CSCE process'

The various follow-up meetings and specialist conferences of the thirty-five-nation Conference on Security and Cooperation in Europe (held in Helsinki in 1975) have provided a useful forum for pan-European discussions on security, political, cultural and humanitarian issues in the continent. The CSCE process has contributed to the development of a more stable security system in Europe in a number of ways. First, the Helsinki conference itself acted in some respects as a *de facto* peace treaty, and helped to take some of the heat out of territorial and boundary disputes resulting from the postwar settlement. Second, CSCE has remained a symbol of commitment of all participating states to the goal of lowering tension and promoting co-operation across the ideological and political divide. It has therefore helped the European members of NATO and the WTO press on their respective alliance leaders the need for restraint and moderation, and provided opportunities for maintaining intra-European dialogue at times of East–West confrontation. Third, it has given the small and medium-sized states (especially in Eastern Europe) a larger voice in the discussion on European security, and has allowed them to articulate their own specific national interests. Fourth, it has helped reinforce a sense of a common European identity, especially in East Central and South–Eastern Europe, despite obvious cultural, social and political differences. Fifth, it has given the neutral and non-aligned states in Europe a more prominent and constructive role to play in the European security system, as mediators between the two military alliances. And finally, it has contributed to the development of a growing body of international law and agreements governing East–West relations in Europe, including human rights. The Vienna Final Document of January 1989 was an important agreement in this respect, in that it included more specific pledges on human rights than were in the Helsinki Final Act, and established more operational criteria for evaluating the performance of individual states in this sphere. It is in this sense that the Soviets talk of *Europa prava* (a Europe whose interstate relations are regulated by international law and agreements), and see the CSCE process as providing the 'scaffolding' or 'house rules' for the 'common European house'.

Arms control issues

The current phase of détente has begun with two successful arms control and confidence-building agreements – the Stockholm CSBM Agreement of September 1986 and the Washington INF Treaty of December 1987. In the conventional sphere, the prospects for the CFE (the 'Conventional Forces in Europe' talks) look much better than MBFR because of a whole range of factors, including the Soviet acknowledgement of 'asymmetries' and the area covered by the talks. At the same time the WTO is now committed to 'reasonable sufficiency' and a defensive military doctrine (in its technical and operational aspects too), whilst in the West there is a growing concern to lower the reliance on nuclear weapons and a perception of a declining 'Soviet threat'. On both sides of the military divide, the idea of 'common security' is gaining adherents. Thus the prospects for improving the military balance in Europe and achieving stability at lower levels of armaments look much better than in the 1970s.

Economic co-operation

Economic, technical and scientific co-operation was the subject of the second basket of the Helsinki Final Act, but it has remained the least developed of the three baskets. However, there are a number of new factors which might facilitate the deepening of this aspect of the East-West relationship. Firstly, mutual recognition of the EC and the CMEA on 25 June 1988 and the establishment of official relations between the two bodies has cleared the way for separate agreements between individual CMEA states and the EC. Secondly, Western Europe has recovered from the 1973 oil price rise shock, and is enjoying a new period of economic growth and financial confidence (despite the upset of

'Black Monday' on 19 October 1987). Thirdly, *perestroika* in the Soviet Union and some other CMEA states could potentially facilitate economic co-operation by creating more favourable trading structures and more compatible industrial and economic practices (joint ventures and the gradual opening of the socialist economies to the global economy). The Soviets and East Europeans are also increasingly interested in participating in research projects like Eureka, and have expressed an interest in the establishment of a European-wide energy grid system, a common industrial development fund and a European school of management. The UN Economic Commission for Europe (ECE) could also play a more central role in encouraging pan-European economic co-operation if its functions and remit were expanded. Nevertheless, there are a number of outstanding problems (including shortcomings in existing joint venture legislation, incompatibilities in pricing and industrial structures, CoCom lists,[5] the lack of any Western co-ordination in loan monitoring to Eastern Europe, and the implications of 1992) which continue to plague East–West relations in the economic and technological spheres, and although the prospects for intra-European economic co-operation look brighter than at any time since the early 1970s, this remains an area whose potential has yet to be significantly tapped.

Political relations

Political relations between East and West in Europe are today much better than in the 1970s. Both sides have gained experience since the early days of détente, and mutual trust and understanding has begun to develop. This was most apparent in the relations between the two Germanies, both of whom demonstrated a considerable commitment to intra-European co-operation and understanding, even when the chill winds of the 'Second Cold War' threatened to create a new ice-age in inner-German relations. It is also significant that political tensions now no longer coincide with the East–West divide: for example, relations between the 'two fraternal socialist allies', Hungary and Romania, are now amongst the worst in Europe, whilst Austro-Hungarian relations are a model of good-neighbourliness and mutual co-operation.

Societal trends

Although in some respects rather nebulous and difficult to quantify, social trends constitute an important determinant of the long-term development of East–West relations. In both parts of Europe a phase of societal development associated with the spread of manufacturing industry and mass production (known as 'Fordism') has passed – smokestack industries are giving way to the rise of the service sector, new high-tech industries and the growth of the white-collar middle classes. Throughout Europe, the more traditional class-based social structure based on a large urban working class is becoming both more stratified and, at the same time, more diversified and complex. This process, patchy and uneven though it is, has advanced furthest in the north and west of Europe, but it is also apparent in other parts of the continent: in Eastern Europe, the move away from state socialism and central planning towards 'socialist pluralism' and 'market socialism' arises in part from the decline in the size and influence of the urban proletariat and the rise of the intelligentsia. The increase in tourism and travel, the development of communications and new information technology, the rising levels of education and training, the development of a cosmopolitan youth culture, the diffusion of 'post-industrial' values (concerned, for example, with ecology, environment, peace, feminism) into East Central Europe, and the levelling impact of mass society in an age of European television satellite broadcasting, videos and so on, have gradually been eroding the socio-cultural features of the East–West divide. Despite significant differences in social and political structures, the trends towards at least a limited form of 'convergence' are increasingly perceptible, largely as a result of changes in Eastern Europe and the Soviet Union. Whereas in the 1960s the talk was of *Wandel durch Annäherung* ('Change through rapprochement'), in the 1990s the causal relationship implied here might be reversed, so that we see *Annäherung durch Wandel*.

WHITHER EUROPE? PROSPECTS FOR CHANGE IN THE EUROPEAN SECURITY SYSTEM

What then, are the prospects for the future of the European security system? Given the changes at work in both East and

West, and the new dynamics of East–West relations in Europe, what are the prospects for overcoming the division of Europe and ending the military confrontation between NATO and the WTO?

To begin with, it should be noted that grand designs and bold visions for the future of the continent in the postwar period are nothing new. Over the last four and a half decades, a wide variety of different and competing conceptions of a radically transformed Europe have been articulated. The struggle against Nazi Germany and fascism in Europe itself engendered a broad but diffuse anti-fascist alliance which aspired to a new European federal arrangement, democratic and socialist, which would transcend narrow nationalist interests. In the 1960s, President de Gaulle championed the idea of Europe 'From the Atlantic to the Urals', free from superpower domination (and, of course, with a leading role for France on continental Europe). At the same time, the West Germans began articulating their hopes for a future *europäische Friedensordnung* (a 'European peace order'), which would provide the context for a peaceful solution to the division of Europe and the division of Germany. In the 1980s, the leftwing West German security expert Peter Bender (amongst others) called for the 'Europeanization of Europe', involving the 'decoupling' of Europeans (East and West) from Moscow and Washington, and a 'third way' between the two superpowers. On the other hand, Zbigniew Brzezinski, President Carter's somewhat conservative National Security advisor, has advocated a unilateral withdrawal of US ground forces from Europe over a ten-year period, as a way of defusing the military confrontation with the Soviets in Central Europe and encouraging the West Europeans to overcome their 'cultural hedonism and political complacency' and spend more on their own defence. In this way, he believes, a momentum will be generated behind the 'organic growth' of a free and united Europe (1984–5, p. 300).

Such grand designs and bold visions have run aground on the rocks of vested interests, established practices and the inertia generated by a functioning status quo. The postwar division of Europe has created a logic that it is hard to escape from. As early as 1948, George Kennan expressed his reservations about the division of Germany and the establishment of two rival military blocs in Europe and warned that 'from such a trend of developments,. it would be hard . . . to find "the road back" to a united and free Europe' (quoted in Dawisha, 1988, p. 195). He also counselled that it would be up to the Europeans themselves 'to discover the paths of escape' from the division of the continent into hostile blocs (see Steel, 1988, p. 147). The European security system which emerged from the postwar settlement, based as it has been primarily on nuclear deterrence and the superpower alliances, has enforced a discipline on the quarrelsome Europeans which as brought peace to the continent for one of the longest periods in its bloody history. The two military alliances themselves have played an important role in intra-alliance management, and have provided useful mechanisms for regulating and ameliorating intra-European conflicts. As Richard Vine has argued, 'Conflict *between* the two systems tends to center on the nature and values of the systems themselves, on the assumption of a security equilibrium. Conflict among countries *within* each system has either disappeared or has been diverted into other outlets' (1987, p. 10).

One could therefore argue that proposals which entail a fundamental change in the structures of the European security system, involving the dismantling of the two alliances and the withdrawal of the two superpowers from Europe (whatever this means in the case of the Soviet Union), pose serious problems for the overall stability of Europe. There is no reason for assuming (as, for example, Zbigniew Brzezinski seems to) that if the constraints of Yalta (and, one might add, of nuclear weapons) were removed, Europe would reach a pacific and humane equilibrium, and embark on a process of peaceful historical development. Europe for much of its history has been a continent racked by bitter national, political, class, religious and ethnic rivalries. The decline of the two superpowers, therefore, raises a series of potentially difficult questions for the Europeans, East and West. Lawrence Freedman has argued that the attempts of the West Europeans to act in unison have in practice been 'modest in ambition and partial in success', and that consequently the decline in American power 'contains the risk of a revival of internal European competition and rivalry'. Furthermore, he argues that

If the Soviet hold over Eastern Europe does loosen up and the division of the continent becomes blurred, then another possibility is that traditional patterns of European politics, which managed to produce two world wars this century, will reassert themselves and take over from the straightforward alliance confrontation. The question of German reunification – producing a pre-eminent power in central Europe – will have to be addressed and mechanisms will have to be developed for handling disputes between European states that had hitherto been managed through the alliance system. (Segal *et al.*, 1988, p. 123)

One can argue that Professor Freedman both underestimates the significance of West European integration and gives too much weight to the 'German question'. Nonetheless, there is an important grain of truth to the central thrust of his argument, which is that it would be a mistake to ignore the destabilizing potential of traditional historical and national rivalries in Europe, and to assume that superpower disengagement from, and denuclearization of, the European continent would tend to lead to the emergence of a harmonious and stable security regime in the region.

Nevertheless, although a fundamental change in the structures of the European security system (defined as either the break-up of the blocs or the denuclearization of Europe) is neither currently on the immediate East–West agenda nor necessarily desirable, this does not mean that nothing of significance is changing or will change. It is likely that in the coming decade the Europeans may have to adjust to a situation in which the leadership role and the military commitment of two superpowers to Europe could be significantly reduced – their national and collective autonomy would therefore expand. Second, the disagreements associated with extended deterrence and nuclear weapons in Europe are likely to intensify, as the controversy over NATO's shortrange modernization plans indicates. Third, as a number of leading Western politicians have suggested, the Cold War seems to be over, and East–West relations are tentatively improving; this has reduced Western perceptions of a 'Soviet threat', and is facilitating the gradual blurring of the systemic divide in Europe (most notably in the cases of Austria and Hungary). Finally, Europe is undergoing parallel but opposite processes of change, consisting of growing integration in the West and growing fragmentation in the East. The implications of these two contradictory processes, and their possible interaction, cannot as yet be gauged with any accuracy, although one should not exclude the prospect of their leading to substantial changes in the economic, political and security arrangements of Europe.

Therefore, although the formal structures of European security are likely to remain in place, their content and context are gradually being transformed by a series of endogenous and often barely visible processes. There are deep currents at work in Europe which are beginning to erode some of the basic assumptions of the postwar European security system, although until relatively recently they have only been perceptible as ripples on the apparently calm surface of European politics. Given the changes currently under way in the Soviet Union and in Eastern Europe, and the growing self-confidence and economic achievements of Western Europe, the prospects for expanding pan-European co-operation look better than at any time since the Second World War. However, seeking the immediate removal of the blocs as a first step in this process could be counter-productive. Europe is stable today because since the early 1960s (if not before), the policy of both sides has been to ameliorate the consequences of the military, economic and political division of Europe, rather than to remove that division. Stability within the two blocs has come to be a necessary precondition for improving relations between the two blocs. Internal bloc cohesion therefore seems to be a prerequisite for a reduction of East–West tensions. Giving precedence to the demand for the dissolution of the two alliance systems would therefore be politically inept, and 'would be placing an enormous obstacle across important positive steps towards a more stable coexistence . . . What matters most is not the existence of the "blocs" but their character' (Booth, 1988, p. 8). Similarly, the dismantling of the Berlin Wall, that great symbol of the East–West divide, would not necessarily contribute to the stability of Europe.

Furthermore, if a new political and security arrangement in Europe is to be achieved – one that is both durable and stable – then it is necessary to go beyond détente as a form of conflict management and crisis management, and to develop, through a form of pan-European co-operation and interdependence, a basis for a relationship which would represent not merely the absence of war but a positive peace. This would incorporate many of the objectives and aspirations which are embodied in the West German notion of an *europäische Friedensordnung*, as well as in Gorbachev's idea of a 'common European home'. The security dimension of this would seem to require the adoption of some of the proposals for non-provocative defence (which have been developed around the 'common security' theme), as well as a minimal nuclear deterrent (see Buzan, 1987). It would also seems to require a firm rejection of any form of 'fortress Europe' for Western Europe (*vis-à-vis* the East Europeans) after 1992, and implies the continuation of trends towards growing liberalization and greater national autonomy in Eastern Europe.

At the same time, however, the two socio-economic and political systems in Europe are likely to retain certain distinctive and essential characteristics for the foreseeable future which will not be eradicated by the current reform process in either part of Europe. These characteristics are likely to include a greater emphasis on the collective provision of public goods and services in the East, as well as a continuing central role for the communist parties within the political systems of the socialist countries, despite the development of a form of 'socialist pluralism'. The continuation of a form of 'competitive coexistence' will therefore require the development of what has been called (by the West German Social Democratic Party, the SDP, and the East German ruling Communist Party, the SED) a 'culture of political strife' (as opposed to a culture of military confrontation – 'jaw, jaw', rather than 'war, war'), which will provide for a peaceful resolution of political disputes between the two rival (but increasingly interdependent) systems. In this respect, the CSCE process can make a major contribution towards the negotiation of and agreement on a set of rules of the game for regulating relations between European states, which will provide a commonly accepted set of assumptions and procedures governing the conduct of intra-state relations in Europe. Maintaining and reinforcing the existing stability of the European security system, therefore, while managing its internal transformation and structural readjustment, will thus constitute the great task of the 1990s.

NOTES

1   See his article in *The Times*, 11 December 1987. François Heisbourg also developed this point in a talk on 'The Alliance after an INF

agreement' which he presented at the Royal Institute of International Affairs on 3 December 1987.

2 The EUREKA ('European Research Coordination Agency') Programme involves research into high technologies similar to the US Strategic Defence Initiative although it is directed towards non-military use; it dates formally from 17 July 1985. It involves the then ten member states of the European Community, as well as Austria, Norway, Portugal, Spain, Sweden and Switzerland, along with the European Commission itself.

3 The Western European Union in its present form was established by the Modified Brussels Treaty of 1954. Its role then was to monitor German rearmament and to provide an arrangement for the stationing of British forces in West Germany. It was revived to meet regularly at ministerial level in 1984 to provide the institutional basis for a 'European pillar' in NATO, and its original membership of Britain, France, the FRG, Italy and the Benelux countries was enlarged to include Spain and Portugal in 1988. Its most significant achievements since 1984 are the 1987 Platform document and the co-ordination of naval deployments in the Gulf at the time of the Iran–Iraq war.

4 Three months prior to his election to the post of CPSU General Secretary, Gorbachev warned that 'Only an intensive economy developing on the foundation of the newest science and technology can serve as a reliable basis for raising the wellbeing of the workers, and can assure the strengthening of the country's position in the world arena; only an intensive economy will permit it to enter the new millennium with dignity as a prosperous major power' (*Izvestiya*, 12 December 1984). The significance of this speech is analysed in the European Strategy Group Report (1988, p. 56).

5 CoCom, or the Coordinating Committee for Multilateral Export Controls, dates from 1950, and is an informal arrangement between the NATO countries less Iceland but plus Japan and Australia. The purpose of the CoCom lists is to establish strategic export controls on the sale of militarily useful technology to the Soviet Union and its allies. For a discussion of this and other East–West trade issues see Hanson (1988).

REFERENCES

Bertram, C. (1988), 'Change in Moscow – continuity in Europe?', *The World Today*, vol. 44, nos 8–9, pp. 137–9.

Booth, K. (1988), *Steps Towards Stable Peace in Europe: A Theory and Practice of Coexistence* International Politics Research Paper No. 4 (Aberystwyth: University College of Wales).

Brown, J. F. (1988), *Eastern Europe and Communist Rule* (Durham, N.C.: Duke University Press).

Brzezinski, Z. (1984–5), 'The future of Yalta', *Foreign Affairs*, vol. 63, no. 2, pp. 279–302.

Buzan, B. (1987), 'Common security, non-provocative defence, and the future of Western security', *Review of International Studies*, no. 13, pp. 265–79.

Dawisha, K. (1988), *Eastern Europe, Gorbachev and Reform. The Great Challenge* (Cambridge: Cambridge University Press).

European Security Group (1988), *The Gorbachev Challenge and European Security* (Baden Baden: Nomos Verlagsgesellschaft).

Gati, C. (1987), 'Gorbachev and Eastern Europe', *Foreign Affairs*, vol. 65, no. 5, pp. 958–75.

Hanson, P. (1988), *Western Economic Statecraft in East–West Relations. Embargoes, Sanctions, Linkage, Economic Warfare, and Détente* (London: Routledge & Kegan Paul).

Kiep, W. (1984–5), 'The new Deutschlandpolitik', *Foreign Affairs*, vol. 63, no. 2, pp. 316–29.

Kux, E. (1984), 'Contradictions in Soviet socialism', *Problems of Communism*, vol. 33, no. 6, pp. 1–27.

Larrabee, S. (1988), 'Eastern Europe: a generational change', *Foreign Policy*, no. 70, pp, 42–64.

Segal, G., Moreton, E., Freedman, L., and Baylis, J. (1988), *Nuclear War and Nuclear Peace*, 2nd edn (London: Macmillan).

Steel, R. (1988), 'Europe's superpower problem', *SAIS Review*, vol. 8, no. 2, pp. 137–49.

US Congress (1976), *United States National Security Policy vis-à-vis Eastern Europe: The Sonnenfeldt Doctrine*, hearings before the Subcommittee on International Security and Scientific Affairs, House of Representatives, Ninety-Fourth Congress, Second Session (Washington, DC: US GPO).

Vine, R. (ed.) (1987), *Soviet–East European Relations as a Problem for the West* (London: Croom Helm).

11

New directions in thinking about security in the Third World

CAROLINE THOMAS

The traditional approach to security in the Third World, based on the Realist conception of international relations, fails to identify and address the most pressing current security concerns of the poorer states. This state-centric, geopolitical approach identifies physical threats outside the territorial boundary of the state, and sees the build-up of military power as the appropriate response to the perceived external challenge. It will be argued below that the primary physical threats to the security of the overwhelming number of Third World states are internal, not external; they result from the granting of international legitimacy to states which lack domestic legitimacy. In addition, it will be argued that non-military threats of international proportions, especially debt and the ecological crisis, threaten not only Third World states but also the security of peoples and states across the whole world. Thus development and international co-operation are vital components of any strategy aimed at greater security in the Third World or globally. A positive response from the northern indus-trialized states will be crucial, but the evidence so far is not encouraging.

THE STATE AND INSECURITY IN THE THIRD WORLD

An analysis of security in the Third World which attempts to deal with over a hundred diverse states as a single grouping is inherently suspect. As Robert Rothstein states, 'there is no such thing as "the" security problem in the Third World: differentiation within the Third World itself is growing' (1986, p. 14). Nevertheless, the great majority of these states share a fundamental security problem: while enjoying international legitimacy, they lack internal legitimacy. This has resulted in a crisis for many Third World states which has profound implications for security domestically, regionally and globally.

Most conflicts within the Third World are intrastate rather than interstate. Despite popular belief to the contrary, internal challenges to political authority are a more frequent cause of military conflict in the Third World than border disputes. Even where interstate conflict has occurred, it has rarely resulted in a change in territorial boundaries. The creation of Bangladesh is a noteworthy exception. This situation exists because of the way in which statehood has been achieved in the post-Second World War era and because of the norms governing international relations today, notably sovereignty and non-intervention.

Two major studies undertaken by the Hungarian scholar Istvan Kende provide thorough data on the occurrence of war from 1945 to 1976. For the period 1973–86, this chapter relies on information compiled by Kidron and Segal (1987) in *The New State of the World Atlas*. Kende defines war as any armed conflict in which the following criteria obtain: regular armed forces of the government in power must be involved; there must be a certain degree of organized fighting on both sides; there must be a certain continuity between the armed clashes (1971, p. 6). He divides wars into the following categories: internal anti-regime, with or without foreign participation; internal tribal and other conflicts, with or without foreign participation; and border wars. The main type of war has been the anti-regime category, mainly with foreign participation. Kende explains the contrast between the border wars which predominated in the pre-1945 history of the international state system and the current situation thus:

[this is an] unequivocal consequence of the current political situation. The simultaneous existence of countries belonging to two different social systems; the fact that they represent more or less a balance of power; that antagonistic social and political groups, classes, and tendencies often are present within a country; and that the contrast between the national and colonial (or neo-colonial) forces has intensified in the process of disintegration of the colonial system – have all led to conflicts in which power itself is at stake. (1978, p. 232)

Kende identifies 120 wars in the period 1945–76, of which seventy-three were internal anti-regime wars, twenty-nine were internal tribal or similar, and only eighteen were border wars. For the period 1973–86, Kidron and Segal identify sixty-six anti-regime or internal wars, and thirty border wars (1987). Both analyses omit many domestic conflicts where the fear of anti-regime activity prompts the government to use its armed forces and police for organized and systematic repression of civilians – for example, in Chile, Argentina and Guatemala.

The preponderance of internal war is seen not only in the number of wars but also in the number of years spent at war and the percentage of total time at war (Kende, 1978, p. 232). One interesting feature of such wars since the wave of independence in the early 1960s has been the increasing foreign involvement of Third World states, many of which have developed imperialist tendencies. Another has been the increasing import of arms from the northern states, especially the Western powers, but also latterly from certain Third World arms exporters, (Brzoska and Ohlson, 1986). All these facets deserve attention, yet constraints of space determine that only the element fundamental to all the others is explored in this section, namely state formation and its implications for security.

State formation in comparative perspective

The coincidence of nation and state in Europe is generally regarded as providing the model for statehood, since it assumes bounded territories, social homogeneity and the monopolization of violence by a single centre (Tilly, 1975). The European pattern developed over several centuries in a conflictual and competitive international environment. The process was slow, and the vast majority of states disappeared. The hostile nature of that geopolitical environment meant that arms and men were necessary to defend or extend a ruler's territory. These had to be financed by ever-increasing taxation (Mann, 1986). Rulers realized that the promotion of development was vital to their survival (Hall, 1985). This can be summarized by saying that the bureaucratic power of the ruler to reach the inhabitants of a territory became highly developed (Weber): European states, to use Mann's distinction (1985), became powerful infrastructurally as well as despotically.

The realization of statehood throughout most of the Third World over the past forty years stands in great contrast to the European experience. International law established that on decolonization the inherited colonial boundaries would be the legitimate boundaries of the newly independent states. The contemporary international system, by legitimizing these former colonies as sovereign states, froze into place artificial political constructs in which domestic political consensus was lacking. State and nation simply did not coincide in the way they had come to do in Europe. Moreover, whereas in Europe the hostility of the international environment had been a motor for integration and development, for the Third World states today the benign nature of the international environment – that is, the protection given by the norm of sovereignty – provides no such imperative. As Mullins remarks, 'The result has been a separation between the struggle for national existence and the drive for development' (1987, p. 2). In other words, the relative lack of geopolitical pressure has meant that many states have not been forced to interact with their societies. This is seen particularly clearly in their limited capacity to extract taxation and to mobilize their people (Migdal, 1988). In addition, the superpower competition has meant that even desperately poor states like Somalia have been able to acquire vast arsenals of weaponry through client status. The possibility of external patronage on such a scale was absent during the development of the European system of states. Thus the incentive for survival which propelled the extension of the power, authority and infrastructure of the European state, and which was so vital for nation-building, is absent in contemporary new states. Present governments can take comfort in the fact that the norms of the international community militate against the territorial disintegration of states. States which contravene the principle of non-intervention suffer international obliquy. Thus we have seen occupying armies retreat, such as in Vietnam, Afghanistan, Uganda and Kampuchea, and we have seen attempts at secession squashed, as in Nigeria and the Congo. This has had a crucial effect on the security of Third World states and their governments and populations. They exist as states juridically, but not as 'social facts'. (Jackson and Rosberg, 1982; 1986).

Few security analysts have investigated the problem of state formation in comparative perspective. Mohammed Ayoob's contribution (1984) is important. He maintains that the differences in state-formation between West and South are primarily relative and time-based. In other words, given more time, the states in the South will make the same progress in nation-building as the states of Western Europe. Yet it is argued here that while time is certainly a significant factor, the nature of the international system is even more crucial. Irrespective of the time-scale involved, a benign international environment will have a different effect compared with a hostile one. The imperative for nation-state-building will not be as strong in the former as in the latter. Thus the implications for local, regional and global security will follow a different pattern. The survival of states in their present geographical form is, theoretically, guaranteed by the relatively benign international system, yet the latter provides no mechanism for promoting peaceful change within those states or indeed for recognizing the legitimacy of social change. Clearly without peaceful change, both those states themselves and the international system will continue to be beset by great instability (Damadoran, 1984, p. 298).

Implications for security

Since nations and states do not coincide in most of the Third World, we cannot talk of national security as we do in the developed world. Indeed continual reference to the ideal of 'national security' in the Third World is usually without empirical foundation and inappropriate. The concept of national security lends an air of legitimacy to policies of repression and patterns of expenditures that serve an extremely narrow sectional interest in these states (Thomas, 1989). It is therefore dangerous to the very people whose security is being considered. Even so, many of the new thinkers persist with this usage, and in making this concession to the old approach undermine their own position (Al-Mashat, 1985; Azar and Moon, 1988). In reality, we can often recognize only regime security. Where there is no societal consensus, security policies are formulated by an elite with the express intention of satisfying those sections of the population whose support is needed to maintain itself in power. It is the conferring of international legitimacy on the post-colonial state that allows the situation to continue. The state exists by legal right rather than by social fact and domestic legitimacy. The opposite was true in the case of the development of the states of Western Europe. Thus today there exists a host of internally fragmented states where the development of nation-statehood has not got under way. The situation invites secession, irredentism and external intervention (Gavshon, 1981; Mayall, 1978; 1983; Williams, 1989), and places huge obstacles in the way of economic development and distributive justice within the poorer states. Without these, the security of the state and people, rather than just of the regime, cannot be achieved.

Unlike the term national security, state security has unpleasant connotations in Western analyses. Several Third World states have undergone some kind of social and/or political revolution, and these are generally seen to be pursuing an unjust state security policy. Vietnam, Iran, Nicaragua, Cuba, Ethiopia and Mozambique are examples (Gellner, 1964; Hall, 1985; Moore, 1967). Yet many such states have achieved more in terms of consensus-building and thus nation-state-building in the post-revolutionary phase than they did in the earlier period of their independent history. Of course, there are glaring exceptions, such as Cambodia under the Khmer Rouge. Yet while certain groups in particular states have been displaced, such as the Bahai in Iran, the general trend in most post-revolutionary states is still towards greater social and economic mobilization and political inclusion. Some such states strive for the eradication of gross disparities in the income and wellbeing of their citizens in the short term. Yet these are the very ones criticized by the West for the pursuit of illegitimate state security: Cuba, Nicaragua, Vietnam and China formerly. Jeane Kirkpatrick's controversial differentiation (1982) between totalitarian and authoritarian regimes exemplifies the point: the former are states perceived by Western leaders as hostile to the West, while the latter are seen as being friendly to the West. The former pursue state security, the latter, national security. Empirically, we can reverse this analysis: the post-revolutionary states often approximate the

European model of nation-state to a far greater degree than the so-called authoritarian states of Latin America or Africa. They do not practise Westminster-style democracy, but then neither do the authoritarian states. They are concerned with distribution, and aim to satisfy the basic needs of the majority of their people, and China, Cuba and Nicaragua have had some astonishing successes in this regard. Authoritarian governments, however, leave welfare to the magic of the market. In sum, if we persist in using the term national security in the Third World context, then we must apply it to those states where it has meaning – often, the post-revolutionary states. It is a further irony that the very hostility of the West has helped forge a stronger domestic consensus in these states.

Hitherto, the overarching geopolitical structure of the East–West divide has resulted in efforts at social change in the South being interpreted generally by the major Western powers – and some in the Third World – in the imported language of bipolar ideological competition. Similarly, the Soviet Union has often seen changes in government personnel as reflecting a Third World state's position *vis-à-vis* the East–West divide. Thus the room for manoeuvre of Third World states in terms of indigenous development and political choices, and thus in security policy, has been severely limited. Non-alignment is therefore a privileged policy which few have been able to follow. As a result, most observers of the Third World believe that a way must be found for dealing with social, economic and political change in a manner which respects the sovereign right of all states to choose their own path without interference from outside. Change in the Third World invariably results not from East–West antagonisms but from indigenous factors and it should not automatically be seen as a threat to the security of the superpowers.

Weapons cannot take the place of negotiation and co-operation in the search for a strategy for a more secure Third World and global system, but of course they play a deterrent role and in some cases have even become a major Third World export (Brzoska and Ohlson, 1986). While the question of whether weapons are systems or causes of conflicts is a perennially difficult one, there is no doubt that their acquisition can create as many problems as they potentially solve. Acquisition can stimulate arms races and contribute to regional conflict (Rose, 1988; Smith, 1985). This can be seen for example in the Gulf War, the Horn of Africa and the Western

Sahara. The consumer is usually vulnerable to the supplier, with Iran's position in the Gulf War providing an excellent example. Occasionally, the consumer can try to manipulate the supplier, as happened between Egypt and the USSR. The acquisition of weapons fails to secure a state against domestic threats and drains the coffers, reducing the resources available for development.

There are a few signs of potential negotiated settlements leading to peaceful change, such as in Namibia and possibly in the Western Sahara, but both examples have arisen only after protracted military conflict. Moreover, there are far more examples where the activities of external powers have been directed towards sustaining the military conflict or bringing it to an end through military victory by their arms sales policies, thereby foreclosing the possibility of peaceful change – Central America and the Gulf War spring to mind. In the former case, regional powers have been working for a negotiated settlement, but their efforts have been hindered by the attitude of the hegemonic power. In the latter case, arms sales policies of developed states, coupled by the unClausewitzian approach to war of the leaders, especially of Iran, led to protracted conflict and 'peace through exhaustion'.

A DEVELOPMENT STRATEGY FOR THIRD WORLD SECURITY

During the 1980s there emerged a growing body of literature about Third World security which challenges the dominant Realist paradigm of Western international relations and security analysis. Although it covers a wide spectrum of opinion, the general theme is an advocacy of the primacy of a socio-economic development strategy for security; military strategy is seen as being necessary but not sufficient for security. As such, it addresses many of the security issues emanating from the process of state formation outlined above.

The relationship between the physical quality of life (PQLI) and the level of security in a state has been an interesting source of investigation (Al-Mashat, 1985). From a detailed study of over forty states, Al-Mashat found that improvements in the PQLI correlated negatively with the level of security unless the government had responded to the psychological needs of the population via an increase in distributive justice and democratization of the political system. In other words, in countries where improvements in basic needs were not accompanied by greater political participation, an increase in instability was the result. Developments in South Korea and China in the latter half of the 1980s lend weight to his findings. This is an important lesson for Third World states.

The non-military components of security, such as economic vulnerability, ecological factors, ethnic fragmentation and domestic coping mechanisms have also attracted attention (Azar and Moon, 1984, pp. 103–35; 1988). Azar and Moon devised an analytical framework based on the 'hardware' and 'software' elements of security. Hardware refers to physical capabilities such as military and economic power, and policy infrastructure such as choice of weapons, strategic doctrine and intelligence. In contrast to conventional security analysts Azar and Moon have concentrated instead on the software side, since they see it as the social base of national security, and thus of fundamental importance. Its major components are legitimacy, integration and 'policy capacity'. Legitimacy shapes the political context of security management; integration shapes the social and cultural base; policy capacity determines the scope and range of behaviour and thus gives direction to the management of security.

Security in the context of Third World states refers not simply to the military dimension, but to the whole range of dimensions of a state's existence which are already taken care of in the more developed states, especially those of the West (Thomas, 1987, p. 1). The massive vulnerability of Third World states to factors like the weather, commodity price fluctuations, and a fickle oil cartel, on top of the physical security issues, means – much more so than for developed states – that their search for security must try to decrease their vulnerability on several different fronts. An appropriate security policy for states devastated like Bangladesh by floods, or Jamaica by hurricanes, or Ethiopia by drought cannot be perceived in predominantly military terms. Of course, it is possible, even likely, that the ruling elite of a particular state may choose to adopt an expensive military approach to obtain the hardware to sustain itself in power. Looking to the medium and long term, a vital element of a security strategy would include measures to enhance economic security for states. In terms of new thinking about strategy and international security, it is necessary to discuss paths in addition to the military one which might lead to greater security for states, regimes and people in the Third World in the longer term.

Provision of food is a vital element in the security of Third World states. If they are dependent on international charity or tied aid for this most basic commodity then all the weapons in the world cannot make these states secure. India found this to her cost in the 1960s when reliance on the United States for grain was perceived as a grave violation of her sovereign independence and security. Paarlberg's detailed study (1985) shows that the price for grain included reform of India's agricultural policies, a more vigorous family planning policy, devaluation of the rupee by 36.5 per cent, and changes in India's foreign policy, including less vocal criticism of US policies in Vietnam and more cordial relations with Pakistan. Provision of clean water is fundamental, rarely achieved, and rarely a media item or political issue, yet the health dimension of a state's security is dependent on this. Disease can critically affect the ability of a state to defend itself. We have only just begun to see the devastating impact of AIDS, and without a doubt certain armies in Africa, and possibly elsewhere, are likely to be ravaged by this (Panos Dossier, 1988). This in itself will affect the military dimension of security, just as the widespread development of the disease in the civilian population will affect other elements in the security equation.

In the economic sphere Third World states must function in the international capitalist economy, and to date the workings of that system have militated against development for the poorer states (Amin, 1977; Cardoso, 1979; Frank, 1967; 1978; Wallerstein, 1975; 1979). They suffer from an acute lack of control over the international economic environment. The market which determines the price of primary products can be highly unstable, and development plans can be dashed overnight. These states are vulnerable to the dictates of the IMF, where they exercise no real decision-making power (Cornia, Jolly and Stewart, 1987; Ferguson, 1988; Smith, 1988; Thomas, 1987). They are also seriously insecure because domestic policy decisions of the leading capitalist power, the United States, can have extremely detrimental repercussions on them. A rise in US interest rates adds millions of dollars to debtor states' repayments, and has been particularly harmful to the Latin American states (*Central American Monitor*, 3 April 1989; *South*,

January 1989). Increasing protectionism by the US exacerbates the debt problem for those states, since their opportunities to earn foreign exchange through trade are diminished (*South*, February, April and June 1989). They are vulnerable to the sometimes fickle policies of multinationals, which in pursuit of greater profit can move operations to other countries, as happened in the case of the bauxite industry in Jamaica in the 1970s (Stephens and Stephens, 1986; Thomas, 1987). In addition to these exogenous factors, their economies are at the mercy of the weather. Drought has severely affected the Sahel and the Horn of Africa for several years. Floods in Bangladesh appear to be increasing in severity from year to year, and are wrecking development efforts. A hurricane devastated the local staples of rice, beans and vegetables, as well as the coffee export crop in Nicaragua in 1988 (*Nicaragua Today*, no. 33, Winter 1988, pp. 7–9).

To deal with these uncertainties, Third World governments try to minimize their vulnerability. Thus they have attempted to change the international regimes in which they operate, particularly those of money and trade. In 1974 they called for the New International Economic Order and the Charter of Rights and Duties of States (*Yearbook of the UN*, 1974). The former set out their goals, while the latter put forward suggestions for their achievement. The charter would have resulted in a tremendous increase in the economic security of those states through more secure trade: indexation, cartelization, nationalization and stabilization. All the measures were opposed by the main Western governments; a few Scandinavian countries were an exception from time to time.

The West has traditionally seen the relation of trade and security in terms of the security of its supply of, and access to, raw materials, rather than in terms of the security of price. This attitude continues to hamper the development of a secure long-term trading system between North and South. Any regime which is perceived as unjust by a large number of participants cannot be regarded as stable at its core; indeed the OPEC action of quadrupling prices in the early 1970s showed this to be the case. The outlook for secure trade is bleak given the increasing protectionism of Western states, and the US vote at the UN against the right to development (*UN Chronicle*, February 1987), which underpins the idea of a more secure trading order (Alston, 1988; Tomasevski, 1989). As the single most important economic power, the unwillingness, of the

US to see development in the context of social and economic human rights makes it difficult for Third World states to present a case for change based on a principle of equity. The relative economic weakness of the USSR means that it has little ability to effect trade security for developing countries (Cassen,1985).

NEW PROBLEMS CALL FOR NEW SOLUTIONS

While certain elements of the problem of security remain fairly constant over time, others do not. Today, Third World states are having to cope with two new and potentially disastrous assaults on their security. These stem from the debt crisis and the environmental crisis. The two are sometimes linked, with the former exacerbating the latter, as seen in the cutting down of the Amazon rain forest. Furthermore, both threaten the security of the industrialized world as well as the Third World. These new threats logically require a global strategy if the security of all states is to be improved.

The debt crisis and security

We are witnessing an amazing and threatening transfer of finance at present, with billions of dollars moving out of the Third World each year to the West. In 1988, an estimated $30 billion went along this route (Fidler, *Financial Times*, 15 March 1989). This threatens the internal stability of Third World states, since their populations are carrying an unbearable burden. This then threatens international security because instability in the South sometimes invites Northern military intervention. The debt crisis in turn threatens the developed world because a collapse of the international financial system would bring with it untold misery just as the Depression did in the 1920s and 1930s. The dangers of instability in Latin America are particularly significant, since the United States considers that continent to be part of its backyard. Similarly, the debt problems of Eastern Europe, by creating domestic instability there, could result in greater Soviet involvement. The debt crisis is not simply a crisis for the Third World; it is a global crisis.

In August 1982 the Mexican government announced that it could not repay its foreign debt; the state was bankrupt. The international financial system appeared to be on the verge of collapse, and there was panic among Western governments. The basic cause of the problem was that private banks, encouraged by the US government, had lent large amounts of money (petrodollars) to Third World states in the 1970s at floating rates of interest. US macro-economic policies raised US inflation in the 1970s and caused negative real interest rates and soaring commodity prices, both of which encouraged the Latin American states to borrow more than was prudent. (McKenzie and Thomas, 1984; Feldstein, *Wall Street Journal*, Europe, 16 March 1989). The second oil shock of 1979 was met by contractionary policies by the US government. There was recession in the West, and thus markets closed for Southern imports, and interest rates rose enormously. Many Third World states found that they could not pay the interest on their loans. The US government, the IMF, the Bank for International Settlements, private international banks and the leaders of Western governments took part in a series of negotiations with each other and with the Mexican government and this resulted in an *ad hoc* package, the so-called Mexican Rescue. That package set the tone for the negotiations on rescheduling and new money which have since taken place for a host of Third World borrowers who have been unable to pay. A piecemeal approach has been adopted by the creditors, dealing on a case-by-case basis with the crisis in each country as it arises. The packages have hinged on the implementation of austerity measures aimed at fostering open economies with minimum state intervention (Mann, *Financial Times*, 23 March 1989). The IMF has played a major role in devising the packages, cajoling the parties into toeing the line, and monitoring results. Yet to date these IMF cures have had little success.

In February 1989 Venezuela was ravaged by riots. That this could happen in Latin America's most stable democracy is evidence that the burden of debt threatens the political stability of the whole continent. The democratic transitions which we have seen in that part of the world are being jeopardized by the adjustments needed to gain more new money via IMF-sponsored package deals. Moreover, the people have been forced to make massive sacrifices in terms of social welfare, and for no immediate reward. The banks are still increasing profits, but the people of Latin America, including the middle classes, believe their sacrifices were made in vain since Western protectionist barriers prevent them from exporting those items in which they are internationally competitive, for example Brazilian steel. Moreover, Third World states are still at the mercy of fluctuating interest rates. In the twelve months up to March 1989, the London interbank rate, to which most Latin American loans are pegged, rose from 7 to 10.5 per cent, adding over $3 billion in annual interest costs just to Mexico's debt service (Truell, *Wall Street Journal*, Europe, 22 March 1989).

While the Latin American states are the biggest debtors, the African states are also crippled. One indirect result of the £120 billion sterling owed by Africa to the industrialized world is the death of millions by hunger and disease through diversion of potential funds away from basic needs (Dowden, *Independent*, 18 March 1989). Ironically, the amount they owe is of little significance to the creditors; even so, Western governments have argued that aid is a disincentive to reform, and have urged the taking of IMF medicine. Thus currencies in many African countries have been devalued, government spending has been cut and subsidies have been removed. The effect on the majority of people has been devastating. In some states, notably Morocco and Sudan, there have been food riots popularly linked to IMF austerity measures.

The shock of the Venezuelan riots and their continental implications, coupled with the prospect of an indigenous Latin Plan for debt emanating from the Group of Eight Latin American states, has finally woken up the US government to the debt threat to US national security (Riddell, *Financial Times*, 13 March 1989). Accordingly, the US Treasury Secretary, Nicholas Brady, has put forward proposals for dealing with the debt crisis which will supersede the ineffective plan of his predecessor James Baker. Brady has introduced the idea of voluntary debt reduction by the banks, aimed at reducing the debt owed by thirty-nine debtor states by 20.5 per cent in three years, or $70 billion out of $340 billion owed. This amounts to a policy of partial debt forgiveness, though that term is not used as it is too politically sensitive for the US public. It has been suggested that the IMF and World Bank should come up with $12 billion over three years, and this should be used to guarantee the remaining debt.

The Brady Plan has raised various problems. First, bringing the responsibility for debt guarantees into the public policy domain will cause problems in the domestic political debates of the industrialized states, since their taxpayers will not willingly pick up the tabs and carry the burden of risk. There have already been signs of discontent in West Germany and Britain in this regard (Lord and Morris, *The Times*, 3 April 1989). Nigel Lawson, then Chancellor of the Exchequer in the UK, reminded fellow members of the Group of Seven of their commitment in September 1988 not to transfer further risk from the private to the public sector. Second, the need for large-scale Japanese financial support in the Brady strategy is clear, thus highlighting the increasingly interdependent nature of the financial system and the erosion of US hegemony. In return for their financial support, the Japanese want to take Britain's place as second largest quota holder at the IMF. This would give them the second biggest say in international financial decisions after the US. Britain, of course, is resisting this. To date the US has resisted an increased role for Japan, but the latter now hold the trump card – the power of the purse.

The Brady Plan, with its new perspective, has opened the door for negotiations but it lacks detail and has raised as many problems as it has addressed. The spectre of debt reduction removes the incentive for new money to be lent, yet without this growth cannot occur in the debtor states. In addition, some banks fear that the plan, which assumes that debtors cannot pay, is an invitation to default. The reactions of the debtor states themselves have been mixed. Many feel that debt reduction has not gone far enough; the latest Mexican study of the conditions for resumed growth suggests that debt servicing needed to be cut by two-thirds, and Mexico is seeking a 50 per cent reduction in repayments this year from $14 billion to $7 billion (Harris, *Financial Times*, 13 March 1989; Truell, *Wall Street Journal*, Europe, 22 March 1989); Venezuela is also looking for a 50 per cent reduction. As a result of such problems, together with the disarray within contending groups – Western governments, Southern governments and banks – the plan seems doomed to failure. In the long term either international security will be enhanced, or we will all lose. At the moment, on the debt question, the latter seems more likely. If large amounts of debt – or all in some cases – are not written off, political stability in Third World states will be eroded further and chaos in the international financial system may well result. Writing off Third World debt is unlikely to bring down democratic political structures in the Western world. Anthony Harris has written that if the Brady Plan results in an effective scheme to meet the global debt crisis, then Brady will 'get credit for Machiavellian skill in political management' (Harris, *Financial Times*, 13 March 1989). We await the outcome in trepidation; the odds are against this accolade being earned.

Ecology and security

The ecological dimension of security is taking on a growing significance: on top of the global threat of nuclear holocaust several states are threatened with extinction through the rising sea level. If current rises continue, we can expect to lose many Third World island states, such as the Maldives, Kiribati and Tuvalu. Also under threat is one low-lying developed state, the Netherlands. Moreover, a large number of coastal cities throughout the world will be flooded, including some capital cities. The ecological dimension of security does not end there: climatic changes can be expected to result in droughts and floods, on the lines of those witnessed recently, and these in turn will result both directly and indirectly in more soil erosion and deforestation; the latter will itself have climatic repercussions. Thus a vicious circle will be established leading to an attack on the ecological security of billions of people, as well as states, and the possibility of widespread death and destruction. The ecological dimension of security is therefore intimately related to the development debate, and both are crucially influenced by the debt issue. In such circumstances, competition for scarce resources is likely to become more severe both between people and states. The development of security cannot be separated from the security of development (Oberg, 1989). The need for co-operation of all states to tackle the root of the problem is clear: states cannot tend to their individual security in these circumstances. Agreeing on solutions and distributing the burden of implementing those solutions, however, will be a politically inflammatory task in both Northern and Southern states.

Many governments are awakening to the security threat posed by damage to the environment. On 16 September 1987, for example, the Montreal Protocol was signed as an adjunct to the 1985 Vienna Convention for the protection of the ozone layer. The latter represented the first-ever agreement to regulate an environmental problem at a global rather than a regional level (*Keesings Contemporary Archives*, 1988, p. 35 678). The protocol provided for the

halving of consumption of chlorofluorocarbons (CFCs) and a freeze
on the consumption of halons by the end of the century. These are
believed to be the major cause of the depletion of the ozone layer.
The latter results in greater ultraviolet damage to people and plants,
and so attacks food and health security by causing crop damage
and cancers. While the convention is concerned primarily with
the ozone layer, it makes an important contribution to tackling
the greenhouse effect.

The greenhouse effect refers to the warming of the oceans and
atmosphere; this results from certain gases in the atmosphere
allowing the sun's rays to reach the earth, but trapping the heat
which would otherwise radiate back into space (Friends of the
Earth, 1989). CFCs are one of the greenhouse gases; they are used
in aerosols, foam plastics, refrigerators and in air conditioners.
However, carbon dioxide produced by burning coal and oil is the
major culprit, and industry, agriculture, power stations, cars and
aircraft all contribute to the problem. Recently, the burning of the
tropical rain forest has been both a major source of carbon dioxide
production, and at the same time a destroyer of the trees that help
take it from the air. The effect of global warming will be to create
increasingly extreme weather conditions. These include drought,
floods, devastating gales and hurricanes, and rising sea levels, all
of which will have a detrimental impact on food production and
development generally. Already the sea has risen 10–15 cms since
1900, and it could rise 1.5 metres over the next century if global
warming continues. A rise of 1 metre would threaten London.

If these disasters are to be prevented, the amount of carbon
dioxide released into the atmosphere must be curbed drastically,
as must the amount of CFCs. No state can achieve this task
alone: co-operation is the only way to manage this threat to
the security of many states. But it will not be easy. Critical
domestic political issues are at stake, especially in the Third
World, for industrialization and the mechanization of agriculture will release these gases as a by-product. Development is
unlikely to be willingly forfeited on the altar of environmental
protection, especially since the developing states rightly perceive
the industrialized states of the North as having been the earliest culprits. The issue of equity must be addressed for any
proposal to be acceptable to the developing states. This was
evident at the three-day Saving the Ozone Layer conference in

London, in March 1989, when China set terms for joining the CFC ban.

The Chinese government insisted that the developed states which have released most CFCs into the atmosphere must make the greatest cuts in production before the developing countries join a global ban on the ozone-depleting gases (Ardill, *Guardian*, 7 March 1988). Dr Liu Ming Pu, leading the Chinese delegation, said that the protocol should allow developing countries to base their level of CFC production and consumption on their economic development, special economic needs and progress in finding safe substitutes. He stressed that most of the environmental needs of the developing world were due to poverty. China's annual CFC production is 20,000 tonnes per annum, compared with the US total of 300,000 tonnes and the Soviet total of 130,000 tonnes. Dr Pu made the point that China, with its 1.1 billion people, probably suffered most from the effects of ozone depletion, although it produced only 2 per cent of the world's CFCs and related gases, whereas the developed world accounted for 80 per cent. He argued that the developed states should do the most in terms of the funding and provision of technology. The Chinese were not alone in their belief that the developed countries should foot most of the bill. President Daniel arap Moi of Kenya, who as host to the UN Environment Programme in Nairobi gave the opening address, hinted at the same message: the polluters must pay. This was adopted also by Mr Ziul Rahman Ansari, Indian Minister of the Environment and Forests. Without the support of key Third World states that are potentially massive consumers, such as China, India and Brazil, the Montreal agreement will have little effect.

As ever, self-interest and international interest seem to be in conflict. To date, the Western states have persisted in telling Third World states not to increase production or consumption of CFCs, but they have offered no material inducement. The Soviet Union, for its part, has argued that the complete phasing out of CFCs would lead to the economic impoverishment of the Third World, and that the West would carry responsibility for this. Its opposition to a radical cut is related to the fact that it wants to continue using CFCs in its own domestic market. The USSR produces for home consumption, not export, and is keen that halons should not be banned totally since they are used widely at home, particularly in the fire-control systems of its nuclear power stations (Wright, *The Times*, 7 March 1989).

Strategies for dealing with the ozone problem and the greenhouse effect must be based on the principle of equity if they are to win the support of the developing states. Without their support, any strategy will be inadequate. President Moi has called for international trade agreements that 'reward equitably' all nations that ratify and implement the Vienna Convention and the Montreal Protocol (Jones, *Independent*, 6 March 1989). Dr Mostafa Tolba, director of the UN Environment Programme, at the close of the London conference urged the setting up of international mechanisms to compensate states who forgo the use of CFCs in the interest of international safety. He urged the UK, as the first state to have burned coal extensively in the Industrial Revolution, to take a lead in action on global warming (Radford, *Guardian*, 8 March 1989). Mrs Thatcher received this proposal very coolly. Yet she was vigorous in her condemnation of Brazil for cutting down the rain forest, and she stated her support for the idea of environmental restrictions on World Bank loans and bilateral deals (McCarthy, *The Times*, 8 March 1989). Such restrictions were regarded by many Third World states as illegitimate interference in another state's internal affairs, undiplomatic, and hypocritical. Yet it seems likely that the bank itself will continue to push the management of the natural environment as an integral part of national economic planning packages, even though this is regarded as environmental imperialism by many developing states (Aufderheide and Rich, 1988; Milne, 1987).

By the end of the conference, in addition to the thirty states which had already signed the Montreal Protocol, thirty-four others had announced their intention either to sign or to give serious consideration to signing. (Importantly, the latter group included India and China.) Their accession will mean that 92 per cent of CFC production is covered, compared with 82 per cent previously. It is hoped that the 50 per cent reduction in production required by the Montreal Protocol will widen the scope and shorten the timescale involved on CFC limits and halons.

The momentum to tackle threats to the security of the environment will be continued in 1990 with the holding of a conference to formulate a plan of action to combat global warming. This is being sponsored by the UN Environment Programme and the

World Meteorological Organization. The negotiations will not be easy. As Hill and Wright have noted, 'The in-fighting is likely to make arms reduction negotiations between the superpowers look like child's play. . .action against the greenhouse effect. . .is as important as the INF Treaty as a safeguard for man's future' (*The Times*, 1 March 1989). The developing states will argue with justification that an equal sacrifice by parties who are unequal to begin with is unfair. A principle of equity would have to allow for the developed states to cut their energy production while allowing the less developed to increase theirs. At present, the developing states are responsible for producing only one-eighth of the greenhouse gases. Friends of the Earth have called for the adoption of 'carbon budgeting', setting agreed limits on each state's output of global warming gases. Whether the governments and publics in the developed states are likely to accept this is another matter. Despite the green rhetoric of the Thatcher government, it decided in 1989 to make drastic cuts in its grants to the Energy Efficiency Office, even though it is generally agreed that a more efficient use of energy is the most important way forward (Hill and Wright, *The Times*, 1 March 1989). It seems likely that short-term national interest will be pursued by those states who are most crucial in the international drive for a more secure global environment.

CONCLUSION

The security challenges which we face require international co-operation on an unprecedented scale. Many of these problems are interconnected. Debt exacerbates the problem of poverty, and gives a huge impetus to ecologically inappropriate land use. Coupled with Northern protectionism it stimulates the production of Third World arms for Third World markets as foreign exchange earning exports. It undermines the political and economic legitimacy of the contemporary international order, and makes for a more confrontational international environment. The fragile nature of the artificial Third World states is compounded by IMF-sponsored adjustment packages which ignore the social and economic context. Indeed, internal legitimacy is eroded further, and the opportunity for outside powers to intervene militarily or through transfers of arms, logistical support and finance increases in tandem. Yet a positive result could emanate from the interconnectedness of all these problems: the situation creates opportunities for bargaining and conflict resolution. For example, there are already growing numbers of deals emanating from both governmental and non-governmental agencies in the North to trade debt for protection of the natural environment. As yet, however, these have been very limited and have met with a mixed response, the governments of certain developing states such as Brazil seeing this as ecological imperialism. However, bargaining power may be changing, as debt and the environment are two issues on which the Third World could increase its international political clout. All the resources of traditional diplomacy, international institutions, pressure groups and conferences are needed for consciousness-raising and co-operation if a survival strategy for the people of the Third World (not simply the governments and other entrenched interests or even states) is to be found. The security problems of North and South are more interdependent today than ever before. A realistic strategy for the security of Third World states must be seen in the context of a holistic strategy for the security of the entire international system. Co-operation within the industrialized world will be necessary, and then between it and the Third World. Despite rhetoric to the contrary, the evidence suggests that the leaders of the industrialized world have not yet recognized this and will resist accepting the major share of responsibility for a more secure world.

REFERENCES

Al-Mashat, A. M. (1985), *National Security in the Third World* (Boulder, Col.: Westview).

Alston, P. (1988), 'Making space for new human rights: the case of the right to development', *Human Rights Yearbook*, Vol. 1, pp. 3–40.

Amin, S. (1977), *Imperialism and Unequal Development* (Sussex: Harvester).

Aufderheide, P., and Rich, B. (1988), 'Environmental reform and the multilateral banks', *World Policy Journal*, vol. 5, pt 2, pp. 301–21.

Ayoob, M. (1984), 'Security in the Third World: the worm about to turn?', *International Affairs*, vol. 60, no. 1, pp. 41–51.

Azar, E., and Chung-in Moon, (1984), 'Third World national security: towards a new conceptual framework', *International Interactions*, vol. 11, no. 2, pp. 103–35.

Azar, E., and Chung-in Moon, (eds) (1988), *National Security in the Third World: The Management of Internal and External Threats* (Aldershot: Edward Elgar).

Brzoska, M., and Ohlson, T. (1986), *Arms Production in the Third World* (London: Taylor & Francis/SIPRI).

Cardoso, F. H., and Faletto, E. (1979), *Dependency and Development in Latin America* (Berkeley, Calif.: University of California Press).

Cassen, R. (ed.) (1985), *Soviet Interests in the Third World* (London: Sage).

Cornia, G., Jolly, R., and Stewart, F. (1987), *Adjustment with a Human Face* (Oxford: Oxford University Press).

Damadoran, A. K. (1984), 'Common security: a Third World approach', *IDSA Journal*, vol. 16, no. 4, pp. 287–99.

Ferguson, T. (1988), *The Third World and Decision Making in the International Monetary Fund* (London: Frances Pinter).

Frank, A. G. (1967), *Capitalism and Underdevelopment in Latin America* (New York: Monthly Review Press).

Frank, A. G. (1978), *Dependent Accumulation and Underdevelopment* (London: Macmillan).

Friends of the Earth (1989), *The Greenhouse Effect Pamphlet* (London: Friends of the Earth).

Gavshon, A. (1981), *Crisis in Africa: Battleground of East and West* (Harmondsworth: Penguin).

Gellner, E. (1964), *Thought and Change* (London: Weidenfeld & Nicolson).

Hall, J. A. (1985), *Powers and Liberties: The Causes and Consequences of the Rise of the West* (Oxford: Blackwell).

Jackson, R. H., and Rosberg, C. G. (1982), 'Why Africa's weak states persist: the empirical and the juridical in statehood', *World Politics*, vol. 35, no. 1, pp. 1–24.

Jackson, R. H., and Rosberg, C. G. (1986), 'Sovereignty and underdevelopment: juridical statehood in the African crisis', *Journal of Modern African Studies*, vol. 24, no. 1, pp. 1–31.

Kende, I. (1971), 'Twenty-five years of local wars', *Journal of Peace Research*, vol. 8, no. 8, pp. 5–22.

Kende, I. (1978), 'Wars of ten years', *Journal of Peace Research*, vol. 15, no. 3, pp. 227–41.

Kidron, M., and Segal, R. (1987), *The New State of the World Atlas* (London and Sydney: Pan).

Kirkpatrick, J. (1982), *Dictatorship and Double Standards: Rationality and Reason in Politics* (New York: American Enterprise Institute/Simon & Schuster).

Mann, M. (1984), 'The autonomous power of the state: its origins, mechanisms and results', *Archives Européennes de Sociologie*, vol. 25, no. 2.

Mann, M. (1986), *The Sources of Social Power: From the Beginning to AD 1700* (Cambridge: Cambridge University Press).

McKenzie, G., and Thomas, S. (1984), 'The economics of the international banking crisis', *Economic Review*, vol. 1, no. 4.

Mayall, J. (1978), 'The battle for the Horn, Somali irredentism and international diplomacy', *The World Today*, vol. 34, pp. 336–45.

Mayall, J. (1983), 'The national question in the Horn of Africa', *The World Today*, vol. 39, pp. 336–43.

Migdal, J. (1989), *Strong Societies and Weak States* (Princeton, NJ: Princeton University Press).

Milne, R. (1987), 'World Bank reforms its "green" policies', *New Scientist*, 9 April.

Moore, B. (1967), *Social Origins of Dictatorship and Democracy* (Harmondsworth: Penguin).

Mullins, A. F. (1987), *Born Arming: Development and Military Power in New States* (Stanford, Calif.: Stanford University Press).

Oberg, J. (1989), 'Note', BISA/ISA Conference, London.

Panos Dossier (1988), *AIDS and the Third World* (London: Panos).

Paarlberg (1985), *Food Trade and Foreign Policy: India, the Soviet Union and the US* (Ithaca, NY: Cornell University Press).

Rosh, R. (1988), 'Third World militarization', *Journal of Conflict Resolution*, vol. 32, no. 4, pp. 671–93.

Rothstein, R. (1986), 'The "security dilemma" and the "poverty trap" in the Third World', *Jerusalem Journal of International Relations*, vol. 8, no. 4, pp. 1–38.

Smith, C. (1985), 'Militarisation and conflict in the Third World', in A. Gauhar (ed.), *Third World Affairs* (London: Third World Foundation), pp. 179–202.

Smith, L. (1988), 'Africa's crisis', *Journal of Development Studies*, vol. 24, no. 2, pp. 250–7.

Stephens, E., and Stephens, J. (1988), *Democratic Socialism in Jamaica: The Political Movement and Social Transformation in Dependent Capitalism* (London: Macmillan).

Thomas, C. (1987), *In Search of Security: The Third World in International Relations* (Brighton: Wheatsheaf).

Thomas, C. (1989), 'Third World instability, security and Western concepts: on an unhappy marriage and the need for a divorce', in C. Thomas and P. Saravanamuttu (eds), *The State and Instability in the Third World* (London: Macmillan), pp. 174–91.

Tilly, C. (ed.) (1975), *The Formation of National States in Western Europe* (Princeton, NJ: Princeton University Press).

Tomasevski, K. (1989), *Development Aid and Human Rights* (London: Frances Pinter).

Wallerstein, E. (1979), *The World Capitalist Economy* (Cambridge: Cambridge University Press).

Wallerstein, E. (ed.) (1975), *World Inequality: Origins and Perspectives on the World System* (Montreal: Black Rose Books).

Williams, P. (1989), 'Intervention in the developing world: a northern perspective', in C. Thomas and P. Saravanamuttu (eds), *Conflict and Consensus in South/North Security* (Cambridge: Cambridge University Press), pp. 144–56.

PART FIVE

Domestic Contexts

12

New visions, new voices, old power structures

HUGH MIALL

Today's nuclear arsenals accumulated by nuclear powers threaten to destroy entire human civilization, to obliterate life systems on earth, and to fatally damage the sacred celestial eco-sphere which sustains all lives to flourish on earth. This apocalyptic omen is the collective creation by those nations whose narrow, self-centred, security conceptions are deeply locked into mistrust, fear and rivalry. Ironically, however, those nuclear giants proved to be obsolete, since everyone including two superpower leaders agreed that nuclear war can never be won, therefore must never be fought. Those security conceptions must be wrong and lacking sound comprehension of the reality of the world.

(Ven. Junsei Terasawa, India, 27 October 1986)

'New thinking' offers a new departure in thinking about international security. Previous policies were designed for nations; 'new thinking' is a policy for the world. It is a response to a world challenge: how can people threatened by common dangers be secure, at a time when self-extinction has become a real possibility? Its answer implies a world perspective: we can only be secure through international co-operation. The interests of all peoples need to be taken into account, but they are interdependent. Countries can be secure only if others are too. Despite our political and social and cultural divisions, common interests override separate interests. Above all, there is the common interest in avoiding a nuclear war.

This is a new vision because it transcends the traditional national-security perspective, which asks only how particular states can be made secure. It is also a timely vision. The nation-state is in decline. A world society is emerging. We have seen the world from space, and it has no borders.

If it is to fulfil its promise, 'new thinking' will need to be taken up across the world. It is already making a wide appeal, and President Gorbachev's advocacy has created a real opportunity to put the arms race into reverse. But to date 'new thinking' has not won over those who occupy the power structures of the West – in particular, the politicians, officials, military officers, scientists and industrialists who control the development, procurement and deployment of new nuclear weapons. They remain committed to the doctrine that nuclear deterrence is the surest guarantee of peace for the indefinite future. This chapter aims to illuminate the clash between these two systems of thought by comparing 'new thinking' with the thinking of nuclear decision-makers in Britain.

CHANGING CONCEPTIONS OF SECURITY

First, it is helpful to distinguish between the conception of security in the pre-nuclear international society, and that characteristic of deterrence theorists and strategists of the postwar world.

In the Europe of 1914, security meant national power, ultimately expressed in the use of military force. The Great Powers were heavily armed, mistrustful of one another's intentions, and jealous of their sovereign interests. To resort to war was considered grave and perilous, but in some circumstances it could be a rational, necessary and statesmanlike decision.

This conclusion was reinforced in the 1930s and 1940s by the rise of fascism in Germany and Italy, militarism in Japan and Stalin's totalitarian communism in the Soviet Union. This was the formative period for the generation that shaped postwar defence policies in the West. The lesson they drew was that the 'free world' must retain a capacity to defend itself at all times against attack by ideologically hostile foes.

The coming of nuclear weapons forced a change in at least some of this thinking. It became difficult to see any circumstances in which it could be rational to resort to war between nuclear powers, if that meant a mutual exchange of nuclear weapons. The security of the state was therefore vested in the dissuasive effects in peacetime of weapons of 'virtually infinite destructive force', instead of in the traditional use of military power to throw back an attack or impose a solution by force after a war had begun.

Deterrence thinking emerged out of pre-nuclear thinking with what seemed, at the time, some startling concepts. Bernard Brodie announced that henceforth the principal role of military forces would be to deter, not to fight wars. Clausewitz had been turned on his head. War could no longer be a continuation of politics by other means. International politics had become devoted to creating an uncrossable barrier between the routine business of politics and the unthinkable prospect of war. It was not so much the front line in Europe but the 'nuclear threshold' on which everything now turned.

THE THINKING OF BRITISH NUCLEAR DECISION-MAKERS

In 1987 the Oxford Research Group carried out a study of the ideas of a number of senior nuclear decision-makers in Britain (Hamwee, Miall and Elworthy, 1989). These interviews gave a fascinating insight into the world view of deterrence thinking, as it exists in defence circles in Britain. Of course, there would be differences in emphasis in the United States, and in the Soviet Union the notion of deterrence was never accepted as it was in the West (Erickson, 1985; Holloway, 1983). Nevertheless the British views make a good case study of deterrence thinking in one country.

Of the thirteen people interviewed, nine had been involved with nuclear weapons policy at high levels, and five had been intimately involved in the Trident and Trident II decision. They included a politician, senior civil servants, a senior military officer, a defence scientist, and a defence contractor. Some of the interviews were given on a non-attributable basis, and so the identity of the interviewees will not be revealed.

The method used was as follows. After interviewing the decision-makers at length, the major beliefs and assertions that were stated were isolated. Diagrams of the connections between the beliefs which had been revealed by the decision-makers were then drawn, using a technique called 'cognitive mapping' (Axelrod, 1976; Eden, Jones and Sims, 1979). The individual diagrams were then merged into a single diagram which represents the core of shared beliefs. This is shown in Figure 12.1.

The diagram uses a simple notation to indicate the links between propositions. If there is a positive arrow from A to B, then an increase in A tends to be associated with an increase in B, or A leads to B; if there is a negative arrow then an increase in A tends to be associated with a decrease in B, or A inhibits B.

The use of cognitive mapping has several advantages over straightforward textual analysis. First, it provides a method by which the most important concepts can be extracted from a mass of material, and the relationships between them presented in a graspable form. Statements on the same subject scattered throughout a long transcript can be readily brought together. Second, the method shows which concepts are most central, and which seem unrelated. It indicates which concepts appear to be premises and which are unsupported. Third, the diagram suggests how ideas are related together in a dynamic structure: it shows how the decision-maker thinks the world works. Fourth, in this case, the method exposed several missing relationships, and helped to identify some of the implicit assumptions in official thinking.

As the diagram shows, the central concept is stable nuclear deterrence, which is believed to prevent the risk of any attack. Three chains of thinking buttress this concept. First, both sides have nuclear weapons, in approximate balance, and this creates a military stand-off which neither dares to break. Second, the existence of stable borders between the military blocs creates a clear line, which both sides know they must not transgress. Third, decision-makers on both sides perceive that the costs of any attack would outweigh the possible gains. This is partly because decision-makers on both sides are rational, or at least sufficiently rational to weigh the risks of launching an attack, and partly because, from NATO's point of view, its nuclear deterrent policies are backed by keeping open the option of first use and by regular modernization of nuclear weapons to make the policy credible.

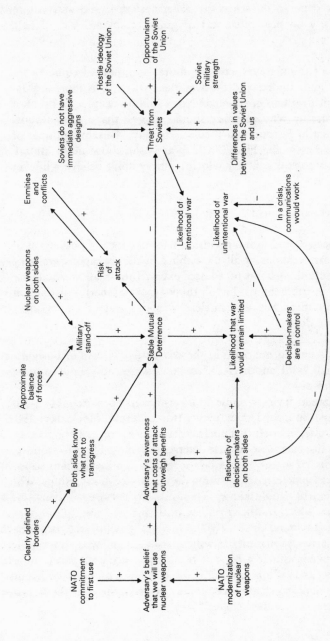

Figure 12.1 A cognitive map of British nuclear decision-makers

Figure 12.1 includes no mention of ethical considerations. These do not seem to influence the belief system significantly; it rests essentially on prudential and pragmatic thinking. One decision-maker said:

> I don't think I ever saw the moral argument. I could never ever quite understand the argument why it was more amoral to kill a million people than half a million people. . . I cannot understand why anybody should suggest that a conventional conflict in Europe which could kill, say, the same number of people as in the First World War is somehow more 'moral' than a nuclear conflict, which I simply don't believe will ever happen.

Another said he had

> no deep-seated moral revulsion from the idea of possession of nuclear weapons at all. . . I think nuclear weapons are very horrible things and to a lesser extent I think all weapons are very horrible things. I don't think I make as sharp a distinction in my mind between nuclear weapons and others as some people do.

Moral issues do not arise in the day-to-day course of business in Whitehall, said another. Discussions were 'not about morality, that's for sure'.

Despite such views, some decision-makers do take ethics seriously and have published their views (for example, Hockaday, 1982). They argue, in brief, that nuclear deterrence is morally preferable to nuclear disarmament because deterrence is more likely to stop wars, while disarmament would be more likely to make them happen, and because deterrence prevents the victory of dictatorships, which disarmament would allow. This rests on a consequentialist view of ethics which has been widely criticized by moral philosophers (Finnis, Boyle and Grisez, 1988). On moral grounds, the critics argue that deterrence must entail a willingness to use nuclear weapons, and that this constitutes a present readiness to commit indiscriminate slaughter and kill innocents (Kenny, 1985). Strategists have disputed that dismantling deterrence would necessarily lead to the negative consequences claimed (Nye, 1986).

Despite the growing criticisms of nuclear deterrence in the 1980s, the decision-makers showed a very high confidence that the system of mutual deterrence is stable: 'I believe we are in a very stable condition now; we can probably make it more stable, 99.95 can become 99.97.' The system of deterrence is 'as stable a system within security parameters as one can possibly devise'. The decision-makers expect the situation of mutual deterrence to last a long time. One said, 'I would expect in 100 years the Russians and the Americans still to have nuclear weapons with the power to destroy each other'. Another said, 'We've got to try and make this work for the rest of human history'.

Because deterrence is stable, the decision-makers are highly confident that war between the major powers cannot occur. 'War is simply not on', said one.

> They know that we know exactly where the Kremlin would go in the event of a crisis . . . and they know we can destroy it. That's why we have peace. I actually do believe that's why we have peace, because they know that we can destroy the command and control structure of the Soviet Union in the event of war.

Even if war began, it would not lead to a nuclear exchange: 'I don't see escalation as being inevitable, I think it's inconceivable to me.' Another said, 'At every stage [of an armed conflict] there is a moment when sanity could be restored'.

Underlying such views are two central assumptions. One is that wars are intentional; when one state launches an attack on another it is a calculated and rational act. The second is that the decision-makers are in control. It is for this reason that the possibility of accidental nuclear war is ruled out: 'The leaders on both sides would be sufficiently aware of the consequences, that. . .I think they would keep the situation under control.'

The main threat which the decision-makers perceive is not an accidental breakdown but the Soviet threat. Even so, the interviews revealed a surprisingly relaxed and long-term view of this threat. The fear assumed in public opinion is of a conventional Soviet attack in Europe, 'the old threat that within a week they could be at the Channel ports'. But the decision-makers expressed a contrary view: 'We're not under any immediate threat . . . It's probably the case that the Soviet Union has no particular expansionist designs at the moment. . . I don't see them as people who have immediate designs against the integrity of this country.'

Another said, 'I'm quite clear that my answer, even pre-Gorbachev, to "are the Russians likely to want to attack the West in your lifetime?" is "no"'. Another said that Soviet military might was insufficient to occupy Western Europe, and another commented that it was ironic that the West had chosen to insure itself against the one move that the Soviet Union almost certainly never intended to make.

One saw the threat in rather different terms: 'I see the danger coming about as the result of internal problems in the Soviet Union. . . Eventually the Soviet Empire will collapse, as all empires do, and that is the moment of peril.'

For most, the real source of threat was hostile ideology.

> The threat, I think, is simply that there are people whose views differ widely enough from ours for there to be a risk over time, and I'm talking about a long time. . . that if bashing us over the head became an easily available option for dealing with the things they disagree with us about we couldn't be sure they wouldn't.

Given the absence of immediate threat, decision-makers tend to see deterrence in terms of an 'insurance policy'.

> I think our basic defence policy is more in the matter of an insurance policy. When you take out insurance on a house you don't do it because you think there is any sort of imminent threat that your house is going to be burned down, but you don't know what is going to happen, anything may happen and you take out insurance on your house.

This analogy is used in a government document: 'Exceptional readiness in the strategic nuclear forces is the most effective and least costly form of insurance against massive surprise attack' (Ministry of Defence, 1980, para. 15).

Insurance sounds desirable, but the image of an insurance policy for a house is unduly benign: domestic insurance policies do not usually threaten the neighbours. But when the risk begins to diminish, the insurer wants a lower premium; and the nuclear deterrers have a public relations problem if the threat begins to disappear. At the least, a period of low threat might suggest an opportunity for seeking disarmament and mutual accommodation. But nuclear disarmament is ruled out by the decision-makers, because it would break the condition of military standoff, undo stable deterrence and thereby remove the bulwark against war.

This points to an interesting relationship made clear by Figure 12.1: there is no feedback from threat to deterrence. The need for deterrence is not related to the level of threat. Consequently deterrence must be retained even when the Soviet Union appears to be co-operative and accommodating. Threat seems to be an existential assumption rather than a variable which affects the system.

The decision-makers believe that NATO's nuclear weapons reduce the threat, but that a reduction in threat does not obviate a continuing need for new nuclear weapons. High levels of armaments on both sides are considered redundant, but not dangerous. It is at low levels of arms that the danger lies. Perhaps for this reason the decision-makers do not appear to see a threat to NATO arising from Soviet responses to NATO's own modernization programmes.

Another omission from Figure 12.1 suggests one of the most important assumptions of all: that there is no effective alternative to deterrence as a means to prevent war. The problem is framed in terms to which there is no other answer. Assuming the worst intentions, what use or threat of force can prevent the risk of attack? The possibility of exploring co-operative measures to achieve the same result, in the context of real intentions, is not considered.

It is not surprising that decision-makers take a unilateral view of these matters; after all, they work in the Ministry of Defence whose *raison d'être* is the security of one country. Moreover, they have to work in the context of an institutional consensus which has built up over years. As Michael MccGwire puts it, 'those who are engaged in the pragmatic policy process of incremental decision-making and implementation are inevitably encased in a perceptual tunnel, where the theoretical analyses determining direction and depth have to be accepted as valid, and assumptions (to the extent that they are recognised) are taken as given' (MccGwire, 1984). Indeed, one of the decision-makers told us that defence decision-making 'is precisely designed not to challenge the underlying assumptions, to take them as almost the air that you're breathing'. It is only when the decision-makers come out of the 'perceptual tunnel' and look around with fresh eyes that they have a chance to challenge the assumptions. And then a significant number change their minds.

DOUBTS AMONG THE DECISION-MAKERS

In recent years, a bevy of senior former officials and military men have spoken out against current NATO plans. The most notable has been Robert McNamara. As US Secretary of Defense he presided over a huge increase in the US arsenal, but he has now become a forceful critic of US and NATO policy. He is urging NATO to renounce its policy of first use, withdraw battlefield nuclear weapons and take other measures to raise the nuclear threshold. In 1982, McNamara, Bundy and Kennan, all once closely involved with US nuclear policies, argued that the use of nuclear weapons could not be expected to remain limited. Admiral Noel Gaylor, a former deputy director of the Joint Strategic Target Planning Staff, and Commander-in-Chief of US forces in the Pacific, also spoke against first use, saying that the danger of escalation following an initial use of nuclear weapons is extremely high (Gaylor, 1984). Admiral Carroll, former second in command of Nuclear Plans and Policies at the Pentagon, wrote that the dangers of nuclear weapons outweigh their limited political utility (Carroll, 1984). In Britain Lord Carver, former Chief of Defence Staff, spoke out against British deterrence policy and the decision to buy Trident. These former insiders do not necessarily endorse the vision of a nuclear-free world, but they are trenchant critics of current policies.

The phenomenon of 'conversion on retirement' may indicate less consensus within the defence establishments than the monolithic public images sometimes suggest. Perhaps the point of official secrecy (like the Great Wall of China) is to keep the dissenters in as much as to keep outsiders out.

The interviews revealed an undercurrent of doubt about some aspects of deterrence policy even among some of the senior decision-makers. One decision-maker, a politician, denied that defence decision-making is rational, and said that he had doubts about the Trident decision before he came into office. A former senior civil servant with nuclear responsibilities doubted the theory of extended deterrence. An official who had been closely involved with Trident doubted whether 'flexible response' would work if put to the test. A former senior military officer was sceptical about whether it is nuclear weapons that have kept the peace for the past forty years. It may be that, in some quarters, the old thinking is showing signs of cracks. At the same time, a new way is beginning to emerge.

NEW THINKING

The 'new thinking' which is developing, in the East and the West, promises a fresh approach to these problems. It is beginning to appeal to and win the support of a wide body of international public opinion, outside the circles of those who make up the strategic defence community.

The first premise of new thinking is that nuclear war is the greatest threat to international security. The top priority for security is therefore to prevent a nuclear war. This shared common interest overrides all sectional interests and conflicts of interest, including ideological conflict; henceforth this must be conducted by peaceful political and economic competition. (The decision-makers would agree that nuclear war would be the greatest disaster, but see the main threat to security as militarized totalitarian state power (Ramsbotham, 1988). They regard stable deterrence as the means to ward off this threat.)

The second premiss is that nuclear war can happen, and that the accumulation of nuclear weapons on both sides makes it more likely. Accidental or unintentional war is a real danger. The continuation of the arms race is one of the greatest threats to mankind. (Decision-makers reject this completely. For them, nuclear war cannot happen so long as both sides modernize their forces and retain a credible deterrent.)

The first premiss leads to the proposition that security is mutual and indivisible. Because all nations have an overriding common interest in preventing nuclear war, their security is interdependent. As the Palme Commission pointed out: 'All nations would be united in destruction if nuclear war were to occur. Recognition of this interdependence means that nations must begin to organize their security policies in co-operation with one another' (Palme, 1982). It is no longer meaningful for one state to pursue its security at the expense of another. Either all are secure, or none are secure. (Defence decision-makers have traditionally not taken mutual security into account because they are concerned with unilateral security. To take an American example, it is now recognized that the decision to 'MIRV' US missiles ended up damaging US security, but nevertheless the US is pursuing many current programmes, such as ASAT, SDI and ASW, which are subject to the same risks. Similarly the Soviet deployment of SS-20s ended up damaging their security.)

The Palme Commission defines security as 'a secure existence free from physical and psychological threats to life and limb'. This is plainly incompatible with mutual deterrence. In contrast, decision-makers identified security with the security and autonomy of the nation.

Common security occupies a similar central position in 'new thinking' to mutual deterrence in deterrence thinking. But it strikes at the heart of traditional views about power and threat. In pre-nuclear times, the greatness of a power was seen to depend on its military, technological and economic strength, relative to its adversaries (Kennedy, 1988). There are many in the Western states and no doubt many in the East who have not relinquished this idea. But 'new thinking' decisively rejects military power as the basis of security, and insists that security can only be found in mutual political accommodation.

Weapons, according to new thinking, are no longer usable in relations between great powers. Even a conventional war in Europe would be devastating, given modern weapons, the density of population, and the spread of nuclear reactors and chemical plants. The threat of nuclear weapons is unacceptably dangerous, because if executed it would lead to mutual suicide and, while maintained, the risk of use can never be excluded. As the Palme Commission stated:

> There is always the danger that the fragile stability of an international system based on armaments will suddenly crumble, and that nuclear confrontation will take its place. A more effective way to ensure security is to create positive processes that can lead to peace and disarmament.

The implications are far-reaching. The notion of common security suggests, first, that national security is obsolete. A nation can no longer obtain security by unilateral means. It can enhance its own security only by enhancing the security of other countries. If it acts to increase the insecurity of other countries, it ends up increasing its own insecurity.

Since nuclear war threatens the survival of all peoples, its prevention must be the overriding security interest of all. It follows that the non-nuclear countries have a legitimate right to participate in disarmament negotiations, and that conflicts· or policy decisions in any part of the world which make nuclear war more likely are a legitimate concern of every country.

The most obvious way in which nations can enhance their own security through enhancing the security of others is by disarmament. In the short term, the logic of this is to proceed with multilateral disarmament where possible and unilateral steps where not, and to take interim measures which build confidence and reduce the risk of war, such as implementing non-provocative force structures, removing the most dangerous categories of weapons, and adopting a posture of no first use. Withdrawing weapons can be a lengthy process, however, and it would be faster, and may be feasible, to modify the systems which control the authorization of firing of nuclear weapons, to mutually shut them off even before the weapon systems have been physically dismantled.

Stringent verification procedures are necessary to ensure compliance and prevent covert rebuilding. As the cuts bite deeper, verification will have to become more and more intrusive and international in scope. The international community will need to be assured that rebuilding can be detected and controlled. This suggests that states will need to submit to an international verification and security regime.

At the same time a kind of international political accommodation will be required, which will place more emphasis on international organization. One important aspect will be a new approach to conflict resolution, since the international community has a strong shared interest in preventing the violent settlement of disputes.

Some of these political changes may seem farreaching, but they are not unrealistic: indeed they are forced by the realities of the age.

Already exchanges of military information and visits by chiefs of staff are taking place that would have been astonishing a few years ago. The changes need not necessarily come all at once, and it is possible to imagine some ꞇtates forming such an order while others remain outside.

Some of these implications suggest that states may have to cede some of their sovereignty to live in a common security regime, but it is worth noting that both the Palme Commission and Gorbachev in *Perestroika* resist this conclusion:

> Renewed renunciation of force as an instrument of national policy is an important element in a policy of common security. Nevertheless, all states must retain the right to use force in their own defence and, in accord with the conditions and procedures specified in the Charter of the United Nations, in collective defence of victims of aggression. (Palme, 1982)

Gorbachev repeatedly insists on the need for mutual recognition by states of one another's sovereignty, and the principle of non-interference in one another's affairs (Gorbachev, 1987).

Figure 12.2 presents a view of 'new thinking', based on the same conventions as Figure 1. Unlike Figure 12.1, it is not based on interviews, and it should be regarded as tentative, since 'new thinking' is still evolving. At the centre is common security, which replaces mutual deterrence as the protection against war. It is reinforced by interdependence and the recognition of common interests, by a process of disarmament and trust-building based on the shared interest in avoiding nuclear war, and by the development of new procedures for resolving conflicts. There is also a domestic aspect – the reduction of militarism through political mobilization. The final part of this chapter returns to this theme.

OLD POWER STRUCTURES

New thinking about security has already begun to have an impact on the old power structures. It is striking that 'new thinking' came to the surface in the unlikely quarters of the Politburo of

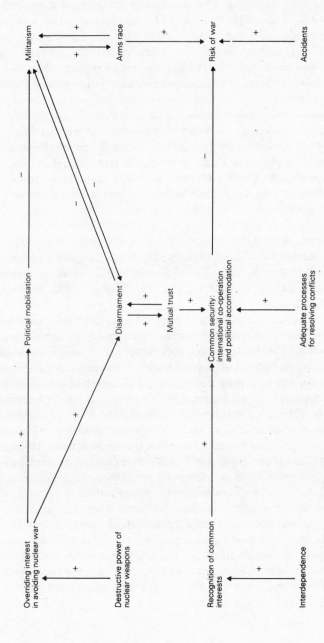

Figure 12.2 New thinking

the Soviet Communist Party – not perhaps where one might have expected it to take hold. This is certainly an old power structure – thirty-two years older than NATO – and one not always noted for innovation.

In the West, so far, the defence establishments have set their face against 'new thinking'. NATO has made it clear that it intends to retain nuclear weapons even if asymmetries in conventional forces are removed:

> Although conventional parity would bring important benefits for stability, only the nuclear element can confront a potential aggressor with an unacceptable risk. Therefore, for the foreseeable future, deterrence will continue to require an adequate mix of nuclear as well as conventional forces. (NATO, 1988)

There are, nevertheless, signs of unease and disunity. Some of the smaller members such as Denmark, Norway, Belgium and Spain are failing to toe the line. The old consensus is breaking down. Opposition parties are turning to 'new thinking' with interest, notably in Germany.

Even so, the institutional and physical infrastructure which has been built up to maintain deterrence has enormous weight and momentum. The factories, reactors, laboratories and bases used to develop, maintain and deploy nuclear weapons have a global distribution and constitute a major sector of industrial and military activity (Arkin and Fieldhouse, 1985); they will not stop working overnight. Besides the physical facilities, there is an immense labyrinth of nuclear decision-making organizations, most of which have access to resources and power at the highest levels (Burke, 1988; McLean, 1986; Miall, 1987). Like all organizations, they have a strong vested interest in continuing what they are doing. In the Soviet Union, the military industrial sector still takes priority, in access to skilled people, materials and funds, over civilian sectors. In the United States the military industrial complex retains a strangehold on the political system. One should not expect, even in a country as centralized as the Soviet Union, that 'new thinking' will have an immediate effect on this infrastructure (MccGwire, 1988); and in the West it will take time and determined political effort to bring it under control.

NEW THINKING:
THE DOMESTIC ASPECTS

Hitherto, the emphasis has been on the international aspects of 'new thinking'. An international response is certainly needed, because one source of the arms race is the mutual fear, hostility and armament between the blocs. However the arms race has another source, in domestic politics and economic structures. There needs to be a response at this level too.

It is found in the 'new thinking' going on in a more sophisticated peace movement, among women thinkers on defence and disarmament, among the green parties and in radical political circles.

For these thinkers, there is a shift in concern from the security of the state to the security of the 'people'. Sometimes there may be a clash between the security of the people and the policies of their own government, and then a policy for security can entail a struggle against the state.

According to this view, real security will come from 'détente from below' – from people reaching out to co-operate with one another across political divides, and resisting the encroachments of their respective military establishments. The military blocs are, in fact, symbiotic with each other and parasitic on their peoples. Neither contributes to real security. The Western military establishment needs the threat of the Warsaw Pact to maintain support for the military industrial complex; the Eastern establishment needs the threat of NATO to preserve the privileged position of the military industrial sector and to maintain its domination over the 'buffer' states of Eastern Europe. Political struggle in both blocs is necessary to challenge these entrenched militarized interests.

In part this struggle depends on a change of identity, for it will not succeed while the people cling to old-fashioned nationalism – hence the effort to develop a dialogue which crosses both national and East–West borders. In part it is a struggle for a renewed form of democracy, to make the agencies of national security accountable and subject to political control (Elworthy, 1987).

These thinkers adopt a broad view of the meaning of 'security'. 'Real security' or 'citizen's security' includes physical and economic wellbeing, civil and political liberties, a sustainable environment and social justice. Correspondingly, a broader view of the threats to security is taken. These are seen to include the large environmental threats, the unjust and unequal relationships between the rich and poor countries, poverty and starvation, oppression of minorities, and so on. It makes no sense to conduct a debate about defence without considering what is being defended; and if the system being defended is oppressive and militaristic, then the prior task is to change it. Here domestic politics has a role to play that is missing altogether in deterrence thinking. Nuclear weapons are meant to protect against dictators who attack from outside; but they offer no defence against and arguably create favourable conditions for the rise of dictators within countries which already possess them.

This kind of new thinking calls for an enlargement of perspective. We need to see ourselves first as human beings, and act in ways which recognize our common human predicament. In this sense a tree-planting project in Ethiopia, a centre for renewable energy technology in Wales and a peace pagoda in Japan are all contributions to 'real security'.

To come full circle, new thinking of this kind connects to ancient thinking. According to a Buddhist perspective, our security depends on others' security not only because we are interdependent, but for the more profound reason that we 'interare' (Thich Nhat Hanh, 1988). The search for security, through wealth, power, defence and similar means, is ultimately self-defeating, because it sets up barriers against each other and ourselves. Only if we recognize our common nature, and treat each other with mutual affection and respect, will there be a basis for real security.

CONCLUSION

New thinking suggests a way out of the trap that unilateral conceptions of security have got us into. Its significance lies not in the details of any particular programme for disarmament. As Gorbachev refreshingly admitted, the minutiae of arms control are 'all Greek' to him. Nor does it lie in any particular proposals for new international arrangements. These remain to be developed in practice. Its significance is that it points to a new direction, down a different path from the one the nuclear deterrers march. It is a path which offers hope.

REFERENCES

Arkin, W., and Fieldhouse, R. (1985), *Nuclear Battlefields* (Cambridge, Mass.: Ballinger).

Axelrod, R. (ed.) (1976), *The Structure of Decision* (Princeton, NJ: Princeton University Press).

Burke, P. (ed.) (1988), *The Nuclear Weapons World* (London: Frances Pinter).

Carroll, E. (1984), 'Nuclear weapons and deterrence', in G. Prins (ed.), *The Choice: Nuclear Weapons Versus Security* (London: Chatto & Windus), pp. 3–14.

Eden, C., Jones, S., and Sims, D. (1979), *Thinking in Organisations* (London: Macmillan).

Elworthy, S. (1987), *Telling the Truth: Women and Decisions on Nuclear Weapons* (Oxford: Oxford Research Group).

Erickson, J. (1985), 'The Soviet view of deterrence: a general survey', in J. Alford (ed.), *The Soviet Union: Security Policies and Constraints* (London: Gower/ISSS).

Finnis, J., Boyle, J., and Grisez, G. (1988), *Nuclear Deterrence, Morality and Realism* (Oxford: Oxford University Press).

Gaylor, N. (1984), 'A commander-in-chief's perspective on nuclear weapons', in G. Prins (ed.), *The Choice: Nuclear Weapons Versus Security* (London: Chatto & Windus), pp. 234–43.

Hamwee, J., Miall, H., and Elworthy, S. (1989), *Assumptions of British Nuclear Weapons Decision-makers* (Oxford: Oxford Research Group).

Hockaday, A. (1982), 'In defence of deterrence', in G. Goodwin (ed.), *Ethics and Nuclear Deterrence* (London: Croom Helm).

Holloway, D. (1983), *The Soviet Union and the Arms Race* (New Haven, Conn.: Yale University Press).

Gorbachev, M. (1987), *Perestroika: New Thinking for Our Country and the World* (London: Collins).

Kennedy, P. (1988), *The Rise and Fall of the Great Powers* (London: Unwin Hyman).

Kennedy, A. (1985), *The Logic of Deterrence* (London: Firethorn).

MccGwire, M. (1984), 'The dilemmas and delusions of deterrence' in G. Prins (ed.), *The Choice: Nuclear Weapons Versus Security* (London: Chatto & Windus), pp. 75–97.

MccGwire, M. (1988), 'A mutual security regime for Europe?', *International Affairs*, vol. 64, no. 3, pp. 361–79.

McLean, S. (ed.) (1986), *How Nuclear Weapons Decisions Are Made* (London: Macmillan/Oxford Research Group).

Miall, H. (1987), *Nuclear Weapons: Who's in Charge?* (London: Macmillan).

Ministry of Defence (1980), *The Future United Kingdom Strategic Nuclear Deterrent Force*, Defence Open Government Document 80/23 (London: HMSO).

NATO (1988), *Conventional Arms Control: The Way Ahead* (Communique, March 2).

Nye, J. S. Jr (1986), *Nuclear Ethics* (New York: Free Press).

Palme, O. (1982), *Common Security: A Programme for Disarmament*, Report of the Independent Commission on Disarmament and Security Issues (London: Pan).

Ramsbotham, O. (1988), 'Deterrence and international justice in the nuclear age', in Council for Christian Approaches to Defence and Disarmament, *Just Deterrence* (London: Pembroke Group).

Thich Nhat Hanh (1988), *Being Peace* (Berkeley, Calif.: Parallax).

13
Rethinking Cold War History

MARY KALDOR

'New Thinking' has hardly penetrated Western policy-making. Indeed, a disturbing feature of the current situation is the way in which 'new thinking' in the Soviet Union seems to have induced a kind of complacency among Western elites. 'We have won the Cold War' is the phrase to be found in the pages of establishment journals like *Foreign Affairs* (Hyland, 1987). The changes taking place in the Soviet Union and in other socialist countries – the new-found enthusiasm for democracy and for markets and the unilateral cuts in military budgets, manpower and armaments – seem like a confirmation of the Western interpretation of the Cold War. The changes are attributed, according to this point of view, to the fact that NATO has stood firm and maintained its military readiness; toughness has paid off. In particular, it is argued that because NATO insisted on deploying cruise and Pershing missiles, the Soviet Union dismantled all its SS-20 missiles. The implication is that NATO should persist in its winning policies; there should be no substantial reductions in Western armaments, no slowing down in the process of continual 'improvement' and 'modernization', and no significant concessions in the arms control talks. That is the way to press the Soviet Union to make further military cuts and to continue economic and political reform.

The complacency among Western elites is both wrong and dangerous. 'New thinking' in the Soviet Union came about not because the West was tough but for internal reasons. If there was any influence from the West, it came from Western 'new thinking' in peace movements or alternative defence circles. The changes in the Soviet Union and Eastern Europe are neither inevitable nor irreversible. (The events in China in 1989 tragically demonstrated the possibility of reversal.) They are uneven and precarious. Astonishing developments have taken place in Eastern Europe, but all the countries in the region face economic, environmental and ethnic problems of gargantuan proportions.

What happens in the Eastern countries depends primarily on internal struggles now taking place between old and new thinkers. NATO's toughness will not help the new thinkers, those who favour democracy and markets. Rather, as shortages, workers' discontent and nationalist passions mount, NATO's toughness will provide an argument for the old thinkers, a rationale for dealing harshly with the opposition. No doubt if the old thinkers do return to power, the case for NATO's toughness will seem to have been confirmed: it was good to stand firm because changes in the Soviet Union are only temporary. Hey presto, opposite arguments are used to support the same policies. NATO has to be tough to encourage change; NATO has to be tough in case change fails.

Western complacency is not just dangerous for the future of the Eastern countries, for the hopes and aspirations of millions of people who suffered from Stalinism. It is also dangerous for the West. Forty years of Cold War has had a corrosive effect on Western society. We have lived in a state of ongoing anxiety, suppressed or open, about war and particularly nuclear war. Roughly a quarter of our scientific and technological resources have been spent on armaments. Military technology has come to epitomize our notions of what is 'advanced', displacing earlier notions of progress, according to which an 'advanced' technology displaces human energy or fulfils some previously unmet need. This conflation of military technology with progress underlies, at least in part, the growing disillusion with science and technology in general. Large parts of the state apparatus have been shielded from public accountability; 'national security' has provided a rationale for interrupting the normal democratic processes. Short of mobilizing a mass movement, it has been difficult to participate in public debates about security.

What is needed now is new thinking in the West as well as in the East. This must involve a critical appraisal of the role of military force, and nuclear weapons in particular, in determining our notions of security. Equally important, it requires a reinterpretation of the history of the Cold War and of the role of the West. New thinking in the West has to be indigenous and distinct in character from new thinking in the East, even if it is influenced by new thinking in the East. But we should learn from the Soviet proponents of new thinking the importance of studying our own history.

The debate between old and new thinkers in the West tends to correspond to the debate about international relations versus peace studies. By and large, international relations has been closely tied to foreign-policy-making especially in the United States. The Realist perspective, which has dominated international relations in the postwar period, with its emphasis on state power, largely defined in terms of military capabilities, provided a legitimizing philosophy for Western foreign policy. In contrast, peace studies, which tended to encompass idealist and/or Marxist perspectives on international relations, emerged from the left and from the peace movement, as a way of articulating and elaborating an opposition to the arms race and the Cold War.

RETHINKING POSTWAR HISTORY

The orthodox Western view of the origins of the Cold War holds that the formation of NATO and the Western military build-up was an inevitable response to the Soviet occupation of Eastern Europe in the early 1940s and the communist takeovers in the late 1940s. NATO was formed in order to stop the spread of communism to Western Europe. Although it now seems clear that Western leaders were primarily concerned about the domestic threat of communism in Western Europe, the orthodox story emphasizes the threat of Soviet invasion and points to the large number of Soviet troops that remained in Eastern Europe after the war. An analogy is drawn with the prewar period and the failure of the League of Nations to react forcefully to Hitler's occupation of the Rhineland and Italy's invasion of Abyssinia. The term 'collective security' which was developed in the League years is applied to the formation of NATO.

Interestingly enough, the orthodox pre-Gorbachev Soviet view has certain similarities. The Soviet military build-up and the creation of the Warsaw Pact is viewed as a response to the establishment of NATO and the creation of a West German state – that is, an external threat from the West. The lesson of the German invasion of 1941 is constantly cited as a reason for military preparedness.

Both these views rest on a Realist understanding of international relations, which presupposes a system composed of states, as unitary actors, who wish to maximize their power. Any state with substantial military capabilities is, therefore, assumed to be expansionist, and hence the necessity for 'balance' in the international system arises.

A particular problem that characterizes Realism in the postwar period is the measurement of 'balance'. In the eighteenth century, a balance of power was measured in Europe through war, even though war also represented a breakdown of the balance of power. In practice, no single European power had sufficient military capabilities to dominate the continent. In the postwar period, the stated objective of the balance of power is not to determine power relations but to avoid war. The problem is that in the absence of war the measurement of military capabilities is a matter of opinion, or 'perception', to use a fashionable term. War games, exercises, scenarios are all used to help the planners solve this problem. However, in practice, politicians have resorted to rather crude numerical calculations of the balance. Those who have absorbed the implications of nuclear weapons and the growing destructiveness of conventional weapons argue (and this argument is now accepted by the Soviet new thinkers) that these numerical comparisons bear very little relation to what is likely to happen in a real war.

It is worth noting that Realism does not mean realistic. When E. H. Carr wrote his classic book on Realism, *The Twenty Years Crisis*, he contrasted Realism with Idealism, chiding the utopianism of the Idealists' schemes of collective security, associated with the enthusiasm for the League of Nations. It was a probably conscious echo of the Marxist distinction between utopian and scientific socialism. International relations had to take into account the realities of power; they had to involve a dialectical intellectual process in which our aspirations for peace

were clearly situated within a real international context characterized by violence, militarism and war. At that time, the realities
of power did indeed mean the expansionist ambitions of Nazi
Germany. But it is not realistic to assume that all great powers
are likely to behave like Nazi Germany. Nor is it realistic to
assume that military preparedness is necessary to guard against
the possibility of expansionist ambitions. What would we do
if faced with Hitler today? Would he be deterred by nuclear
weapons? Or might the threat of unleashing war be too dangerous an approach to security problems? How do we deal with
China today? Does anyone believe that military threats can halt
executions or discourage a takeover of Hong Kong? Nowadays
we have to seek complex, difficult, non-military ways of managing
conflicts, and, in practice, that is what governments do, not always
successfully.

The reality is surely that the world of deterrence, with its
obscure concepts like 'compellence' or 'escalation dominance' or
'countervalue and counterforce' with its, probably unworkable,
technological marvels like the star wars programme or the MX
race track, is rather fantastical and quite remote from the every-
day economic and political realities of power. 'I worry', says
Richard Perle,

> less about what would happen in an actual nuclear exchange
> than the effect the nuclear balance has on our willingness to
> take risks in local situations. It is not that I am worried
> about the Soviets attacking the United States with nuclear
> weapons confident that they will win that nuclear war. It
> is that I worry about an American President feeling that
> he cannot afford to take action in a crisis because Soviet
> nuclear forces are such that, if escalation took place, they are
> better poised than we are to move up the escalation ladder.
> (Scheer, 1983).

Is this a realistic worry?

It is sweeping to claim that all orthodox versions of cold war
history are based on a Realist approach to international relations.
Orthodox Western versions of the Cold War also draw on and are
clothed in Idealist thinking. Again, it is important to distinguish
between Idealist and idealistic thinking. Idealist approaches to

international relations derive from philosophical writings about the links between peace and democracy (Archibugi, 1988). In the eighteenth and nineteenth centuries there was, in Europe, considerable optimism about the prospects for peace based on the spread of democracy within West European countries. If it is practical to eliminate or minimize violence within a domestic context, to develop political and legal methods to settle conflicts in place of trials of physical strength, could not similar methods be developed for settling international conflicts?

Implicit in the Idealist connection between peace and democracy is a rejection of the Realist assumption of states as unitary actors who are either characterized by inherent aggressive tendencies or who are unable to conceive of security except in national/military terms. (Indeed the neo-Realist model of competing states in an anarchic system rather resembles the utopian prototype of free trade so criticized by E.H. Carr.) For the Idealist, there are different types of states and how states behave depends on how they are constructed. There is a presumption that democratic states are less likely to behave aggressively, and there is something in this proposition (even though it is as well to recall that Hitler was democratically elected). Democratic states do come up against domestic constraints on aggression and war as the US did in Vietnam and Nicaragua. Of course, it can be argued that whipping up a war fever, as in the Falklands/Malvinas war for example, or blaming current ills on an external enemy, is also a characteristic of modern democracies – a necessary way of obtaining votes. But this, in turn, raises rather interesting additional questions about the meaning of democracy, the role played by mass political parties, the role of the media, the educational system and so on.

From an Idealist perspective, the Soviet Union is aggressive or potentially aggressive because it is, or was, a totalitarian system. Whereas the Realist views the Cold War as a great power conflict, the Idealist views the Cold War as a conflict of political systems, democracy versus totalitarianism (although both Raymond Aron and Alastair Buchan treated the Cold War as a conflict of political systems, even though they are generally classified as Realists; see Aron 1958; Buchan 1966). This is the version of the Cold War that tends to characterize the thinking of opposition circles in Eastern Europe. This version of the Cold War does not necessarily imply, however, that the only way to contain totalitarianism is through Western military strength. The implication of the Idealist version is that no resolution of the East–West conflict is possible without democratization in the East. But can democratization be achieved through 'rollback'? Are the prospects for democratization weakened or strengthened by a strong Western military presence? Among Eastern opposition thinkers, there are considerable differences of opinion on this point (see Michnik, 1989, and Sabata, 1989, respectively).

If Western orthodox versions of cold war history are influenced by Idealism, the 'old thinkers' in the Soviet Union presented their arguments as Marxist. One of the problems in discussing a Marxist perspective on the Cold War is that it is difficult to speak of a Marxist approach to international relations. This is because there is no Marxist theory of the state, as such, even though Marxists have developed theories of the state. The old thinkers seem to have adhered to a somewhat functionalist view of the state in which the state is a neutral entity, an instrument of society. In capitalist countries, the state is controlled by the ruling classes, and in socialist countries by the working classes. Capitalism is inherently expansionist; hence the capitalist state is aggressive.

A more sophisticated variant of the Marxist argument underpins revisionist histories of the Cold War. The revisionist interpretation of the origins of the Cold War was largely the product of a radical critique of American foreign policy that emerged during the 1960s especially in the Vietnam years (see especially Alperowitz, 1985; Kolko and Kolko, 1972). Essentially, two related arguments were used by the revisionists. The first had to do with the difficulty faced by American capitalism after 1945 in avoiding a return to prewar levels of unemployment without high levels of military spending. The Cold War, by sustaining high levels of military spending and economic assistance both at home and abroad, provided a mechanism for expanding markets. The second argument was more political. The Western left had grown enormously in strength before and during the Second World War. Anti-communism provided an ideological tool for marginalizing and dividing the left; the Western labour movement, for example, was split on cold war lines.

Not all revisionists would necessarily describe themselves as Marxist; but their work could be said to have been underpinned by a Marxist perspective because they saw the Cold War as the outcome of a socio-economic conflict, arising out of the tensions generated by capitalism. Within this general rubric, there were, of course, considerable differences of view. These differences had to do with the inevitability of the Cold War and the characterization of socialist countries. (Marxists like Paul Baran and Paul Sweezy argued that high military spending was a necessary feature of advanced capitalism and only the overthrow of capitalism could engender peace. Other writers, like Galbraith for example, argued that there were other ways of sustaining full employment.)

As with the Idealist version, this interpretation of the Cold War as a socio-economic conflict did not necessarily imply the militarization of the conflict. Evidently this interpretation requires some kind of modification of capitalism for the resolution of the East–West conflict. But is this likely to come about through Soviet military strength? Whether or not the Soviet Union should be regarded as in some sense representing the interests of the working class (as old thinkers would have it) or whether Soviet military capabilities were a necessary response to the militarization of the West is a matter of dispute.

What all these various versions of cold war history share is the notion of a deep-seated East–West conflict. The differences are about the nature of the conflict, whether it is a great power conflict, a conflict of political systems or a socio-economic conflict. There is another interpretation of cold war history which has become more prominent as a result of the dialogue between the Western peace movement and opposition groups in Eastern Europe. This is the notion that there is no East–West conflict as such. There are deep rooted socio-economic and political conflicts within both East and West and the Cold War is a mechanism, for managing those conflicts (Konrad, 1984; Thompson; 1982).

The next section will elaborate this approach towards understanding the Cold War in Europe. However, there is one point worth noting. If indeed one discounts the notion of an interstate or inter-bloc conflict in Europe, this opens up a different interpretation of 'deterrence' or 'balance'. For if the counterfactual that there would have been a war in Europe had it not been for deterrence is likely to be false, then the purpose of a military balance is not war avoidance. It follows that the military balance has to be explained either in terms of domestic pressures, say, the arms economy, or in terms of maintaining the hierarchy of power within the blocs.

AN ALTERNATIVE APPROACH TOWARDS UNDERSTANDING THE COLD WAR

An alternative approach towards postwar history might view deterrence not merely as a war avoidance concept but rather as a world order concept, akin perhaps to the Concert of Europe. In practice, world order includes both the notion of war avoidance *and* the notion of maintaining a stable set of international arrangements within a given political hierarchy. Hence, the Concert of Europe established by the Great Powers (Britain, Austria, Prussia, Russia and France) after 1815 was designed both to avoid war and to contain revolution. These aims were not always consistent and the revolutionary period which began in 1848 marked the demise of the Concert's effectiveness in avoiding war.

I use the term 'imaginary war' to describe the East–West conflict (Kaldor, 1990). By this, I mean that in the postwar period, we have experienced not peace but a perpetual state of imaginary war. We have behaved as though there were a war between East and West, acted out through war games, exercises, military plans, hostile rhetoric, espionage and counter-espionage. It has involved real resources – workers, soldiers, armaments, money. And it has had a profound influence on the way we organize society in both East and West.

Benedict Anderson uses the term 'imagined communities' to describe the coalescing of nationhood (Anderson, 1987). The 'imaginary war' has provided a concept around which groups of nations could coalesce in the postwar period. Precisely because of the way the history of the Cold War was told, East and West were defined in terms of belonging not to a race or an ethnic group but to an idea – democracy or socialism. And because these ideas were abstract, drawing on intellectual categories of thought, Idealism and Marxism, which had deeply influenced political struggles in the modern period, blocism seemed somehow more sophisticated and legitimate than earlier nationalisms.

The imaginary war defined bloc identity and also determined political status. How a war might be fought between East and

West determined who was strong and who was weak. Perceptions of political power were militarized, measured in terms of invented scenarios in which Soviet tanks were pitted against American nuclear weapons or whatever. In his book on nuclear strategy, Freedman ponders whether there is such a thing as strategy in the nuclear age. Strategy means the employment of military force for political ends. But nuclear weapons cannot be used. So what is strategy? (Freedman, 1981).

The riddle is solved if we add the word 'imaginary' to the definition of strategy in a nuclear age. Hence, in the nuclear age, strategy means the *imaginary* use of military force for political ends. No one gets killed in the exercises and war games played out in Europe, except by accident. But certain political propositions are established; the Soviet tank preponderance in Central Europe, Western Europe's dependence on American nuclear weapons, and so on. And these propositions serve to maintain a hierarchical order of nations, dominated by the United States and the Soviet Union, and a consensus (or psychological coercion) around which the blocs can coalesce.

The imaginary war imposes a kind of symmetry on East and West. The Soviet Union is raised to the status of superpower, the West European countries are reduced to client status. Yet seen through an economic prism the status of these countries looks very different. The Eastern countries are much poorer, less populous and less influential than the Western countries. Parts of the Soviet Union are as poor as any Third World country. The West European countries together constitute the richest and largest trading bloc in the world. Likewise, a political definition of power would result in yet another world picture. Soviet rule was brutally imposed on the countries of East Central Europe; these states were, for many years, little more than Russian colonies. Although Western Europe was financially dependent on the United States, the Atlantic Alliance was formed on the basis of consent and even encouragement, from democratically elected governments, at least in the northern part of the region.

To claim that deterrence is a world order, that is, a mechanism, for organizing relations between states, and that the imaginary war does not reflect an East–West conflict, is not a statement about the origins of the Cold War. Rather it is about what happened in practice. However, this approach towards understanding the

Cold War casts a certain light on the various versions of cold war history described above.

The symmetry of the imaginary war stems, it can be argued, from the shared experience of the United States and the Soviet Union in the Second World War. The imaginary war reproduced that experience which, in quite different ways, had resolved problems faced by both societies. Orthodox versions of the origins of the Cold War are probably correct when they insist that there was nothing much the West could have done, short of threatening war, to prevent Stalinist takeovers in Eastern Europe. In retrospect, it is possible to conceive wistfully of the Finlandization option for Eastern Europe: the notion that Soviet security might have been better assured through democratically elected politically stable governments on the Soviet Union's borders. But the East European countries were not like Finland (or even Austria). They were mostly poor and underdeveloped; they had suffered proportionately much more war damage than the West European countries; and anti-Russian sentiments had been inflamed by the behaviour of the Red Army. Perhaps an alternative could have developed in Czechoslovakia where the communists won the popular vote in 1946; but this might have resulted in a different sort of problem, the Yugoslav problem, the problem of an alternative model of socialism which could undermine the (almost mystical) legitimacy of Stalinism during that period. Perhaps also an agreement could have been reached about the two Germanies and perhaps Stalinism might have been less bad had the West been prepared to offer Marshall Aid unconditionally.

Whatever might have been, the onset of the Cold War in the East – the creation of the Cominform in 1947, the two-camp doctrine, the 'salami tactics' of the communist parties in East Central Europe, the show trials and the purges, the emphasis on heavy industry and armaments – were all deeply influenced by the experience of the Second World War.

Stalinism is a totalitarian system in which the state controls (almost) every aspect of social life and in which central planning, based on vertically administered directives, is the mechanism for regulating the economy. In circumstances in which neither consumers nor workers nor factory managers can participate in decision-making about planning, the success or failure of the system depends on the purposes of the plan and the rationality of the planners. But planners can never be perfectly rational. However clever and well-informed, they can never know enough to avoid mistakes and to fulfil the objectives of the plan. In the 1930s, the aim of central planning was rapid industrialization and preparation for war; everything else was subordinated to this aim – agriculture, education, culture and so on. Yet when the Germans invaded in 1941, the Soviet Union was unprepared. Mistakes had been made; factories were located in the wrong places, the wrong sort of armaments had been produced. Within a miraculously short time, factories were moved eastwards and new types of armaments were developed. The Soviet war effort was comparable to the American war effort in terms of the scale of production and, despite the undoubted contribution of lendlease, it was largely an indigenous effort. The war defined the objective of central planning and it was an objective capable of commanding popular support, despite the lack of participation. The experience of fighting provided a way of testing the effectiveness with which the objective was being pursued.

The Cold War reproduced the Second World War experience. Stalinism was imposed on Eastern Europe perhaps for the obvious reasons; the system had been shown to work. It was the known way to achieve rapid reconstruction in East Central Europe and to finance reconstruction in the Soviet Union. (The Soviet Union is estimated to have extracted in the form of reparations, joint companies, unfair terms of trade and so forth, during the years 1948–1952, an amount equivalent to the Marshall Aid provided by the US to Western Europe.) Alternatives were much more risky.

Where the orthodox version is wrong is in the assumption that the formation of NATO can be explained in terms of Stalinism. At that time, no one in Western policy-making circles seems to have believed that the Soviet Union was likely to invade Western Europe. Later, in the 1950s, there were concerns that, after reconstruction, the Soviet Union might build up a sufficient military capability to attack the West. But the interesting question is why perceptions of the Soviet threat changed and why policy-makers became more ready to believe alarmist perceptions. In 1946, the US Joint Chiefs of Staff estimated that the Soviet Union would need sixty-six divisions for occupation duties in Eastern Europe; they expected the Soviet Union to retain some 3.2 million men in ground forces and they calculated this this was 'nearly commensurate with occupation and security requirements'. In 1948, the Joint Chiefs of Staff estimated that the Soviet Union had 2.5 million men in ground forces and thirty-one divisions in Eastern Europe. Even though the Soviet forces in Eastern Europe were fully engaged in occupation duties – deactivating land mines, rebuilding bridges, railways and industrial facilities, organizing prison camps and so forth the JCS estimated that twenty-five divisions might be available to attack Western Europe (Evangelista, 1982–3). There were also, of course, concerns about the strength of communist parties in Italy and France and about the civil war in Greece. But it is difficult to see why the formation of an externally directed military alliance was required to deal with these domestic threats.

Some authors point to forms of political pressure that can be exerted through military capabilities. But this argument is two-edged. During the Second World War, Allied bombing of Germany was supposed to weaken German resolve; it seems to have had an opposite effect, weakening domestic resistance to Hitler and strengthening support for the Nazi war effort. Likewise, in the late 1940s, the formation of a Western military alliance and the creation of a West German state seems to have substantiated the two-camp doctrine and legitimized the imposition of Stalinism.

So why was NATO formed? The revisionist historians, I would argue, offer the most useful clues. The explanation has to be sought in terms of the problems of managing capitalism in the postwar period. The advent of a new pattern of capitalist development, often known as Fordism, in the United States in the 1920s and 1930s had resulted in an enormous increase in productivity in new sectors like automobiles and consumer durables. A corresponding increase in demand could only be achieved through global and domestic distribution. This was achieved during the Second World War when lendlease created new foreign markets and big increases in government spending created new domestic markets.

The Cold War reproduced that spending mechanism. It was by no means the only possible solution. But it had been tried and it had the added political advantage of generating a consensus within the United States (between the old New Dealers and the anti-communist right) and between a rightwards moving United States and a leftward moving Europe (Wolfe, 1987). What came into being in the West in the postwar period was what could be described as an altogether new social system, which we could term Atlanticism. Atlanticism was a commitment to managed capitalism, a mixture of Fordism and Fabianism, that is, a paternalistic social concern shared by New Dealers and Social Democrats within a framework of economic interdependence. The Cold War defined the contours of Atlanticism; to the left lay a socialism which could be dubbed as the enemy and to the right lay nationalism.

Thus, an orthodox/Idealist history of the Stalinist takeovers in East Central Europe can be combined with a revisionist/Marxist version of the formation of NATO, if we leave out the Realist assumption of external military threats. This version of cold war history sees the explanation for the Cold War in terms of socio-economic and political conflicts within each bloc. Far from contradicting each other, Atlanticism and Stalinism were mutually reinforcing, each providing a legitimation for the other. The two systems were locked together in an imaginary struggle of epic dimensions; each depended on the existence of the other.

IMPLICATIONS FOR THE PRESENT

We need to understand this history if we are to interpret the present in a way that can take us beyond the Cold War and the arms race. What is happening today is not just the disintegration of parts of the Stalinist system; Atlanticism as a social system has also, for some years now, been undergoing a slow process of transformation.

During the 1970s and 1980s a new pattern of industrial development has come into existence, gradually displacing the predominance of Fordism, with its emphasis on automobiles and consumer durables, mass production and the intensive use of oil. This new pattern of development is variously called the 'information revolution', 'flexible specialization', or 'fujitsuism', largely, but not exclusively, pioneered in Japan, and involves the use of micro-electronics and new forms of sensing to improve data processing and communications. Improved information has led to big increases in productivity through reducing waste and allowing for a more co-operative, less repetitive form of work organization. It allows – makes possible – decentralization of production and distribution.

What we face today is a mismatch between productive capacity and demand, which could also be described as a mismatch between political and economic institutions, similar to that which the West faced in the interwar years. In the interwar period, it can be argued that Britain's pre-eminent political role skewed the international financial system and that domestic conservatism inhibited a growth of consumption. Today, the problem lies in the pre-eminent political role of the United States, which no longer reflects its economic dominance, and also in the composition of domestic demand. The failure of global demand to keep up with the global growth of productivity (which is a problem of distribution) explains the re-emergence of mass unemployment. At the same time, these traditional problems of capitalism have been overlaid by broader problems of industrialization shared by the socialist countries – the depletion of resources, the degradation of the environment, the atomization and powerlessness of the individual consumer.

The exhaustion of Fordism has also been accompanied by the breakdown of the Atlanticist political consensus both across the Atlantic and within Western societies. The advent of rightwing neo-liberal governments in both Western Europe and the United States in the early 1980s represented a decisive break with the postwar New Deal or social democratic domestic consensus. The advent of the 'New Cold War' launched by the Reagan administration also revealed a break with the consensus between the United States and Western Europe; West European governments were, for the most part, anxious to preserve détente. On the other side of the coin, the growth of peace and green movements constituted a major challenge both to the Cold War and to domestic political and economic priorities.

We are now in a period of transition in which important choices are being made about the future of international institutions and how these will shape global development. Broadly speaking, the West is poised in three directions. The first direction is the one described at the beginning of the essay. This is the attempt from within the institutions of the Cold War to ignore what is happening in the Soviet Union, or to treat the new changes as a victory for the West, a confirmation of past policies. It is possible that there could be a reversion to the Cold War, even if things do not go wrong in the Soviet Union. (And unfortunately, it seems quite possible that things could go wrong.) It is possible to envisage a new Cold War directed against China, perhaps, or alternatively, against some new threat, say Islamic fundamentalism. Whereas in Western Europe both government and public opinion benefit from a reduction of military spending and a redistribution of political power, this is not true in the United States. Military spending does sustain large parts of the American economy. It is true that military spending also undermines American competitiveness (Kaldor and Walker, 1988). But any reduction in military spending is likely to be extremely painful both economically and politically (for those whose lives have been vested in strategic analysis).

But reversion to Cold War cannot solve any of the current global problems – unemployment in advanced industrial countries, the environment, Third World poverty – for reasons suggested above. A second direction for international institutions would be a world of competing military blocs in which Western Europe and Japan became independent military entities. This could resolve some global economic imbalances with Western Europe and Japan reducing their trade surpluses through military spending and a new pattern of 'post-Fordist' or 'Fujitsuist' military technology with emphasis on space, smart weapons, etc. It is possible that some of the proposals for non-productive defence could be incorporated into this project. This approach would thus deal, at least in part, with the problems of capitalism, but not with the broader problems of industrialization.

Quite apart from the difficulty of reaching agreement within Western Europe, this prospect for international institutions does presuppose that democratization will not proceed too far in the socialist countries. Otherwise, what is the rationale for the militarization of Western Europe and Japan?

A third direction would be one which de-emphasized the role of force in international relations and sought to establish new institutions (like the Helsinki process) and reinvigorate existing institutions (like the UN or the European Parliament) which could provide new mechanisms for managing conflicts. In a sense, the Cold War suppressed conflict. Now all kinds of new and old conflicts are coming to the surface: ethnic conflicts, some of which may involve potentially dangerous border disputes as between Romania and Hungary, social conflicts, arising from the disastrous economic situation in many East European countries. Some conflicts may generate constructive change, others could lead to chaos. It would be important to seek ways of defusing ethnic conflicts and of resolving deep-rooted economic and social problems. In such a situation it would be possible to conceive of global redistribution through economic assistance rather than military spending, and domestic redistribution through environmental and social spending instead of military spending and private consumption.

The choice that is made between these different directions depends on the changing constellation of political forces in Western Europe and the United States. It depends on the changing balance of political institutions, between the European Community, the nation-state, NATO and so on. It depends on the changing balance among political parties (socialist, Social Democrat, Green, Conservative, Christian Democrat, for example) and between political parties and social movements. But it also depends on what happens in Eastern Europe. If the analysis is correct that Atlanticism and Stalinism were mutually reinforcing, then it could also follow that alternatives are mutually reinforcing.

At the beginning of this essay, it was argued that the changes in Eastern Europe and the Soviet Union had induced a kind of complacency among Western elites, a wait-and-see approach that could be self-defeating. At the same time, however, the changes in the socialist countries have transformed public attitudes towards the Cold War, especially in Western Europe. As was revealed by the debate about nuclear 'modernization', so long as democratization continues in Eastern countries, it will be harder for Western elites to obtain consent for tough policies. Hence those who favour the third direction, for political institutional change (a new set of democratic international institutions and less reliance on military threats) do have an interest in the democratization of socialist countries. Of course, reductions in military spending, less reliance on nuclear weapons, and alternative mechanisms for resolving conflicts, do not depend on democratization in socialist countries. This implication of the argument about the mutually reinforcing nature of Atlanticism and Stalinism is that the West would be in a much better position to criticize oppressive regimes in socialist countries and to engage in non-military forms of pressure if it were not also militarily threatening. But a tough NATO position combined with idealistic talk about human rights can be much more easily dismissed as cold war propaganda. There is an additional consideration. Western democracy has always been compared, obviously favourably, with undemocratic practices in the East. And this has provided a powerful argument for the status quo. Democratization in Eastern Europe could allow us to look critically at our own political and economic practices in the West. What we have experienced in the West is individual freedom. We can vote, join a union, demonstrate for our favourite cause, form a political party. But except perhaps in some of the smaller European countries (like those in Scandinavia or the Benelux countries) our ability to participate in decisions affecting our lives is much more limited. High levels of military spending and the way in which our identity as democratic nations has been defined by the Cold War are partly responsible for this lack of participation.

The roots of the Cold War, and by implication the arms race, are to be found not in the interaction of mutual threat but in domestic political and socio-economic conflicts within East and West. It follows that overcoming the Cold War is also a matter of domestic change. This is not simply something that is requested of governments, rather domestic changes can only be brought about through independent political groups or organizations which take responsibility for change or for negotiating change with governments. Just as democratization will be determined ultimately by internal struggles between old and new thinkers in socialist countries, so whatever replaces Atlanticism will be the consequence of our own actions in the West. Ultimately, new thinking in the West has to encompass a reinterpretation of our history which involves a critical reappraisal of our dominant political institutions. But new thinking in the West will be greatly strengthened by a dialogue with new thinking in the East. This is partly because alternatives to Atlanticism and Stalinism are mutually reinforcing. But it is also because East and West have for so long been divided and have experienced different cultures and different problems and different ways of seeing the world, so that we have a great deal to learn from each other.

REFERENCES

Alperowitz, Gar (1985), *Atomic Diplomacy: Hiroshima and Potsdam. The Use of the Atomic Bomb and the Confrontation with Soviet Power* (Harmondsworth: Penguin).

Anderson, Benedict (1987), *Imagined Communities* (London: Verso).

Aron, Raymond (1958), *War and Industrial Society*, Auguste Comte Memorial Trust Lecture, No. 3 (Oxford: Oxford University Press).

Archibugi, Daniele (1988), 'Peace and democracy: why such an unhappy marriage? The perpetual peace projects', unpublished MS, Consiglio Nazionale delle Ricerche, Rome.

Baran, Paul, and Sweezy, Paul (1966), *Monopoly, Capital*, (Harmondsworth: Penguin).

Buchan, Alastair (1966), *War in Modern Society* (London: Watts).

Evangelista, Matthew (1982–3), 'Stalin's post-war army reappraised', *International Security*, vol. 7 no. 3, pp. 110–38.

Freedman, Lawrence (1981), *The Evolution of Nuclear Strategy* (London: Macmillan).

Galbraith, J. K. (1967), *The New Industrial State* (Harmondsworth: Penguin).

Hyland, William (1987), 'Reagan–Gorbachev III', *Foreign Affairs*, Fall, pp.7–21.

Kaldor Mary (1990), *The Imaginary War* (Oxford: Blackwell).

Kaldor, Mary, and Walker, William (1988), 'Technologie militaire et dynamisme économique', *La Recherche*, October.

Kolko, Gabriel, and Kolko, Joyce (1972), *The Limits of Power, The World and United States Foreign Policy, 1945–54* (New York: Harper & Row).

Konrad, George (1984), *Anti Politics* (London: Quartet).

Michnik, Adam (1989), 'On détente' in M. Kaldor, G. Holden and R. Falk (eds), *The New Détente: Rethinking East–West Relations* (London: Verso).

Sabata, Jaroslav (1989), 'The politics of a new détente', in M. Kaldor, G. Holden and R. Falk (eds), *The New Détente: Rethinking East–West Relations* (London: Verso).

Scheer, Robert (1983), *With Enough Shovels: Reagan, Bush and Nuclear War* (London: Secker & Warburg).

Thompson, E. P. (1982), 'Notes on exterminism', in *Exterminism and the Cold War* (London: New Left Books).

Wolfe, Alan (1987), 'American domestic politics and the Atlantic Alliance: crisis and controversy', in M. Kaldor and R. Falk (eds), *Dealignment: A New Foreign Policy Perspective* (Oxford: Basil Blackwell).

Conclusion

War, Security and Strategy: Towards a Doctrine For Stable Peace

KEN BOOTH

International politics are experiencing a time of rapid and fundamental change. It may be some time before it slows down and gives
way to a plateau of stability, but when it does the characteristics
of the new period will be significantly different from those which
dominated the decades since the ending of the Second World War.
As this change is taking place, books on strategy and international
security have become out of date in the gap between writing and
publication. Clearly, the practitioners and observers of international
politics did not – and still do not – understand the world as much as
they would like to think.

One manifestation of our problem is the shortage of theories
about what might replace the foreign policy ideas, military doctrines and strategic infrastructure which are now out of their time.
This is not to say that there has been no new thinking to help the
transition through the interregnum described in the Introduction.
Previous chapters have suggested otherwise. But policy-making has
generally been dominated by the assumptions and prescriptions of
Doctrinal Realism, with the result that static thinking has clouded
policy-makers' ability to see the significance of the processes of
change. New thinking about security did develop through the late
1970s and early 1980s, but until Gorbachev it was marginalized on
the international stage. And even then there was scepticism, both in
the Soviet Union and among Western leaders. Consequently, new
thinking has still had only limited impact, and has not progressed
sufficiently to create great confidence that what we are witnessing is

more than a temporary and hopeful phase in international politics, to be replaced sooner or later by a familiar round of conflict and tension. Will disillusion quickly follow 1989, as it did 1789?

The essays in this book have attempted to identify the cracks that have developed across the foundations of establishment thinking about strategic studies, and to discuss the new ideas that have been taking shape. What has emerged is more than simply a set of critiques of conventional ideas; instead we can see the outlines emerging of a different approach to thinking about strategy and international security. At present it is more an attitude of mind than a set of concrete policies. The outline ideas will be identified and elaborated below, to further the discussion of what is needed to create a doctrine for stable peace. Some of the propositions will be more contentious than others, and not all the authors in the book would necessarily subscribe to every point, or even the general thrust of the argument. Nevertheless, none would dissent from the ultimate objective, namely the creation of a condition which Kenneth Boulding has labelled 'stable peace' (1979, p. 13). This is a condition in which war is unlikely not because of the threat of mutual annihilation ('unstable peace') but because of mutual satisfaction with the prevailing situation. It is peace based on positive relationships rather than on threats and fear.

If international politics are to be progressively moved out of the security dilemma, arms racing, tension and war onto a ladder leading towards stable peace, it is necessary to try to change the way people think about the game of nations. Images and behaviour are always intimately related in human interactions. The theme of this Conclusion is that by adopting the approach outlined below rather than old-style Realism a distinct bias would be introduced in favour of stable peace. New thinking could be interacting and reinforcing in a benevolent direction, just as, traditionally, the security dilemma and the Cold War were in reverse.

NEW THINKING ABOUT SECURITY

Anarchy does not preclude international security

The international system, in its condition of 'anarchy', has always and plausibly been described by Doctrinal Realists as one in which the threat and use of force is inevitable. The state system is believed intrinsically to be a 'war system'. Such a characterization was an accurate analysis of the past, but since the middle of this century several trends encourage us to question its appropriateness for the present and future.

War without doubt remains everywhere a 'possibility', but in important respects it plays a less prominent role than hitherto. In the northern hemisphere in particular, states have been running out of issues over which it is believed to be sensible to go to war. Increasingly, states will only fight if attacked, and there are fewer and fewer issues for which they will risk an attack. Defence-only forces are the logical culmination of this trend. So, while war remains a 'possibility', there is a growing bias against the institution of interstate war. The world remains a long way from having a 'peace system', but it is still too soon in history to declare dogmatically that the state system is immutably a 'war system'. If we accept this argument, then our understanding of the potentialities for the evolution of world society will change dramatically. To refuse to change is to disregard the extent to which the past was merely historical prologue, and to denigrate our evolutionary cultural potential.

The international system has typically imposed 'self-help' patterns of behaviour, but as the institutions, processes and units of the system change so will patterns of behaviour and the potentialities for security. Already, as the existence of 'security communities' suggests, the reality of developing a predictably non-violent but competitive international politics is empirically grounded. Security communities – without changing the nature of the international system from its 'anarchical' character – confront the analysis and prognosis of pessimistic Hobbesian Realism. There is a long way to go, of course, before these oases of stable peace spread to create a wider peacefulness, and this result is not a foregone conclusion. Furthermore, the outcome can never be one where non-violence is guaranteed or absolute, since our capacity for violence cannot be abolished. Even so, there should be significant differences in behaviour between those believing that interstate war is inevitable and those who believe that it need not be. We can predictably expect to live in an anarchical world, but 'anarchy' need not have the pessimistic connotations it invariably does have. 'Hobbesian' is not an appropriate label for the international system, and we can doubt whether Hobbes himself would have so described the system today (Hoffmann, 1965, p. 67; Holsti, 1985, pp. 20–1). This is one of several areas of international politics where the label no longer adequately describes the contents.

The conditions under which states now interact in a condition of anarchy are significantly different from those of the past. War is infinitely more costly, the reasons for states going to war have shrivelled, and the density and institutionalization of interdependence has grown markedly. Although these trends have been occurring at different rates in different parts of the world – and this is a major obstacle to building a war-free world – the major powers at least have been sensitized to those forms of behaviour that encourage or discourage international security. As the trends discussed in the Introduction proceed, and as the units and their interactions evolve, so will the character of the system. States will learn different patterns of behaviour as the logic of the system changes. Armed forces will obviously remain in being, but they will become less relevant as warmaking institutions. Increasingly their utility will be at low levels of violence – combating terrorism and drug–exporting, for example, or controlling migrations. At higher levels of violence their utility will be increasingly ritualistic, like a caveman's fire to scare away dinosaurs.

If this less war-prone world is the future, then our categories in international politics will have to change (our notion of a 'superpower', for example, will become less militarized). Another consequence is that the impact of the security dilemma will be mitigated. As states become less threatened, and so decreasingly less collectivities to deter and conduct external violence, so will the notion of the 'state' change. It will be defined less in military than in other terms. States will, as a result, revise the significance of the old adage 'Si vis pacem, para bellum'. Preparing for war will increasingly be seen to be counter-productive to the national interest.

Self-help will not work, because it breeds insecurity elsewhere, and insecurity breeds fear and fear breeds war. The security dilemma can be mitigated if the units in the system redirect their policies away from self-help and towards common security. If this is done, international anarchy will not be incompatible with international security.

Static thinking undermines long-term security

Before stable peace can be created in practice it is first necessary
to believe that it is conceivable in theory. This requires long-term
thinking, an approach which has been notoriously underdeveloped
by mainstream strategists. This is not surprising: the short term
is inherent in a Hobbesian view of the world. From the latter
perspective international politics are approached as a sports coach
might face a new season: the tactics and the opponents will change,
but the game remains the same. Similarly, despite its 'sophistication'
in so many areas, contemporary strategic thinking has been philo-
sophically static. This has been most apparent in the commitment
to nuclear deterrence.

Deterrence theory has inhibited strategists from thinking about
the long term and has offered no future for conducting international
relations other than more of the same, namely the balance of nuclear
terror. Unless we believe that this is the best of all possible worlds,
and that nothing can go catastrophically wrong – the operational
assumptions of pro-nuclear opinion – we need to define long-term
goals that are feasible so that we can identify the intermediate stages
necessary to achieve them, lay down an agenda from which to
choose priorities, and mobilize political support behind preferred
policies.

One of the major contributions made by alternative security
thinkers through the 1980s was their attempt to alert mainstream
strategists to the need to project their thinking into the far future,
instead of merely refining what they knew. The success rate was
low, but the prospects are now more hopeful. One aspect of the
attempt to project thinking forward rather than simply replicating
the past has been the attention given to the global dimension
of some threats. Ecological issues are an obvious case in point.
There are not only no quick solutions to such problems, but
there are also no traditional solutions. This is an obvious area
where security co-operation is imperative, since security through
self-help is impossible.

Long-term thinking gives a different perspective on many issues.
The nuclear weapons world, for example, seems far less comfortable if we consider the implications of widespread proliferation; likewise the problem of the environment, where we
have, literally, to re-adapt or decay. Human beings have the

potential of adapting consciously, if we analyse a problem correctly, think long-term and make the appropriate behavioural adjustments. But the danger is that we will fail to do this, and be caught out. Instead of conscious evolution we risk suffering the 'boiled frog' syndrome. (Ornstein and Ehrlich, 1989 p. 74). If frogs are placed in a pan of water, which is then slowly heated, they will not detect the gradual increase in heat; they will rest contentedly while deadly trends slowly threaten their very existence. This is the danger that confronts us both in the case of the nuclear challenge and environmental decay. Nothing less than a conscious shift in how we will deal with these global issues will have any hope of resolving them. Progress will vary with circumstances: successful adaptation requires boldness when the situation is propitious, and steady commitment in the face of disappointment. The present is a time for moving forwards.

'National security' is not enough

The theory and practice of strategy, and indeed the whole of the study of international politics, has been state-centric. The state has been the primary referent on matters of theory, and the maximization of its interests has been the primary object of practice. The state remains the major organizing unit for the daily business of the world, but as it declines in economic and strategic utility, and as interdependence grows, it becomes objectively necessary to adopt a less state-centric perspective. At the root of new thinking about security should be a reassessment of the relationships that do and should exist between nations, states, classes, economic structures, international organizations, groups of one sort or another (of nations and people) and individuals. The problem of national security must be considered in the context of the developing processes of a world society.[1]

A world society perspective is growing not simply because it should, but because it objectively must. Common problems transcend national boundaries (the arms race, overpopulation, pollution and so on) and the state system is maladapted to deal with them. There is a mismatch between the problems we face and the structures we have to deal with them. States for example have been slow to place on the agenda issues which growing numbers of people – arising out of their wants and needs – have demanded to be addressed: the call for peace and denuclearization in the East–West conflict, for more prosperity in the Stalinist economies of the East and the dependent economies of the Third World, and for greater environmental consciousness from green thinkers everywhere. In order to address these and other problems we need to think more globally in the allocation of resources.

The balance of danger in the lives of most nations is changing. The ultimate threat is less their neighbour's armies wanting to overthrow their political system *à la* Napoleon or Hitler, but the less obvious enemies of arms racing, debt, pollution, global warming, poverty, oppression and all the other elements preventing social justice. The security challenges most nations face are not as immediately catastrophic as those confronted by the adversaries in the Cold War, but they are interconnected, a matter of life and death, and their overcoming requires international co-operation on an unprecedented scale. Common threats demand to be met by common strategies.

If human needs are to be better satisfied, the theory and practice of international politics needs to change. We can argue about the present strength of world society, but for practical purposes it makes increasing sense to act as though a world society did exist or was in the process of being formed. If we do not deal with the global problems indicated earlier, they will some day deal with us.

Security is a 'holistic' phenomenon

It is becoming increasingly common (after Buzan, 1983), though not common enough, to conceive security as a holistic phenomenon. That is, it should be conceived (and practice should follow theory) at various levels of analysis. Consequently, the referent object of 'security' should no longer be almost exclusively the state (which emphasizes national military conceptions of security) but should also encompass the individual human being at the lowest level and world society at the highest. Thus the traditional strategic studies notion of security should become broader and synonymous with the peace research concept of 'positive peace'.

Provoked by the costly, dangerous and futile second Cold War of the early 1980s, with its extravagantly impotent nuclear machismo, increasing numbers of people were driven to ask: whose security are we talking about? The answer increasingly came back that it should be people and not just state machinery: it should be the global community of peoples and not just the state system. In the West growing numbers of people believed that the arms race had become a bigger threat to their lives and wellbeing, and those of the rest of the world (through the possibility of 'nuclear winter'), than the threat of Soviet military blackmail or occupation.

Not only was there seen to be a misconception as to what constituted the ultimate threat, but much attention was also focused on problems of economic opportunity costs: the arms race not only offered less than satisfactory security, it was also seen as swallowing up resources and human potential which could be more usefully employed. Meanwhile, those concerned with Third World rather than East–West issues argued that the security threat to most Third World peoples was less that of an adversary's *blitzkrieg* than that of 'structural violence'. The daily business of the world was ordered in such a way that the 'periphery' was systematically deprived of resources and opportunities, while the 'centre' of the world economy flourished (Frank, 1972; Galtung, 1971). The ideas which made up 'dependency theory' helped us to understand better how problems of politics and economics were also issues of security and justice. There was as a result a growing realization that security should be a broader concept than merely military strategy and that the way strategy had been conceived and practised during the Cold War was part of the problem and not, as traditionally thought, the most important part of solution (McGwire, 1985–6).

For security to be predictable over time requires both a vertical and horizontal perspective; the latter implies a global viewpoint while the former implies a willingness to operationalize the idea of security at various levels of analysis. In short, we should avoid both Eurocentrism and state-centrism. The security challenge must be met holistically. For people, states and the global community there will be no predictable peace without justice, no justice without security and no permanent security without peace.

Doctrinal Realism is a shop-worn ideology

As time passes, a progressively wider gap has opened up between books written from the Doctrinal Realist perspective (most strategy books) and what realistic observers see happening in many parts of the world. Doctrinal Realism no longer offers an adequate explanation of world politics. As was suggested in the Introduction, Realism did provide a reasonably accurate picture for an extended period, and was particularly persuasive because it offered what seemed sound analyses and prescriptions regarding the central issue of war. But since the 1970s Doctrinal Realism has become shop-worn. Its analyses and prescriptions are now inadequate. It is into this gap between our traditional theories and contemporary dynamics where new thinking needs to be injected.

Doctrinal Realism offers a static view of international politics. Nuclear deterrence, the jewel in the crown of postwar Realism, and Cold Warism have demonstrated this with particular clarity. Not surprisingly, the ideology of Realism, with its fatalistic view of politics among nations, obstructed our ability to see the very processes that overturned the cold war and brought nuclearism into crisis. The Realists have also exaggerated the extent to which the nuclear balance of terror created 'peace' and obscured the extent to which life on earth had been threatened by the nuclear arms race. The Realist hegemony, in addition, severely limited the potentialities of strategists to contribute to ideas about security co-operation, which in the late 1980s intruded increasingly onto the cold war agenda. As a result of the gap between world reality and the world of Realism, the latter must be regarded as an impediment to the development of a secure and ecologically sustainable world community.

Realism did its job during the Cold War, but it is now anachronistic in the general thrust of its ideas if not in all its particulars. War is still a possibility, for example, and military power can be useful. There are some regions, notably the Middle East, where its ideas still resonate. But a new philosophy of realism is required which is more generally appropriate for our changing circumstances. It is still being elaborated, and we do not know where it is leading in terms of the new institutions to replace the structures that are crumbling; but we do know where it is going from. Instead of a static and structurally dominated paradigm, new thinking is process- and future-oriented; it does not accept that established norms are 'natural' and immutable; it is open-ended about the potentialities for change, sees moral questions at the centre of politics and the individual at their end-point. In short, new thinking does not accept that this is the best of all possible worlds.

Contemporary security must be common security

Common security has emerged as a central theme under Gorbachev, but the idea was largely developed in the West. It was first given international prominence by the Palme Commission. According to the latter's report, because 'all nations would be united in destruction if nuclear war were to occur', there must be a recognition that this 'interdependence means that nations must begin to organise their security policies in co-operation with another'. The avoidance of war was said to be a common responsibility which depends on a mutual recognition of the need for peaceful relations, national restraint, and the amelioration of the armaments competition; 'co-operation will replace confrontation in resolving conflicts of interest'. The principles of common security identified by the report are that all nations have a legitimate right to security; that military force is not a legitimate instrument for resolving disputes between nations; that restraint is necessary in expressions of national policy; that security cannot be obtained through military superiority; that reductions and qualitative limitations are necessary for common security; and that linkages between arms negotiations and political events be avoided (Palme Commission, 1984, pp. 6–8). Subsequently, such ideas have been discussed, elaborated and reformulated by others.

Common security does not mean that states reject military power; rather, that military power is seen as only one dimension in the security equation. It also involves acceptance of the argument that military capabilities, doctrines and postures should be so organized as to maximize mutual rather than unilateral security. As a result, reciprocity, defensiveness, transparency, crisis stability, arms restraint and confidence-building are emphasized, while at the same time offensive capabilities, surprise attack potential and escalation and retaliation strategies are eliminated as far as possible.

Common security is therefore based on the idea that increases in one's own security cannot be attained by provoking insecurity in others. It gives due regard to the concept of the security dilemma by seeking to mitigate its worst features or even to escape it.

Empirically, the common-security programme is supported by the fact that the most dangerous periods in the postwar world have been when one or other superpower felt seriously threatened; the insecure are dangerous to those around, as the Berlin and Cuban missile crises showed. Proverbially, common security rests on the adage 'Fear the man who fears you'.

While nuclear weapons and long-range delivery vehicles exist and are targeted, their nature will ensure a degree of mistrust between their possessors. The corollary of this is that the prevention of nuclear war and the preservation of civilized life cannot be ensured without the co-operation (the political and military restraint) of the nuclear-capable or potential nuclear countries. True security is only possible on the basis of mutual understanding, trust and political accommodation. But it is not enough only to accept these ideas in principle. In the late 1980s, while some policy-makers and political analysts were moving towards common security, others were merely giving the idea a nod while hoping to continue with established ways. Common security will be no more than an empty slogan unless it is operationalized in procurement decisions, postures, negotiations and all the other processes of international life.

Security is a political and not simply military issue

One of the themes of new thinking is the idea that security policy should have political accommodation as a primary and persistent aim. This should not be regarded simply as a pious hope, while in practice security is still sought through the barrel of a gun. The adverse effects of identifying security almost exclusively with military strength was evident throughout the Cold War. This approach can be described as strategic reductionism, that is, conceiving security in a technical and mechanistic military way, as manifested in an obsession with the military balance, state-of-the-art technology, windows of vulnerability, orders of battle, and questions of inferiority and superiority.

Strategic reductionists take the politics out of strategy and reduce it to military accounting. The costs and dangers of such an approach to East–West relations was well chartered by one of the fathers of both Realism and containment, George F. Kennan (Kennan, 1983). President Eisenhower, in his famous farewell address, warned about the military-industrial complex and the danger of the 'insidious penetration' into American minds of the belief that all that mattered were missiles. Military preoccupations were even more powerful in the Soviet Union until Gorbachev. He has attempted to carry out a strategic cultural revolution against the traditionalist power-political approach which was forever encapsulated in the Stalinist question 'How many divisions has the Pope?'

Given traditional Soviet attitudes, it has been all the more remarkable that the lead in demilitarizing (and also de-ideologizing) the East–West conflict came from Moscow. Almost from the start Gorbachev stressed that political means were more important than military-technical factors in improving the security of the Soviet state. He argued that war is not a rational instrument of policy and that we live in an increasingly interdependent world. Instead of the old themes of systemic conflict and class interest, Gorbachev has stressed common humanity and common involvement in the problems of a smaller planet. In pursuance of these ideas, he set out to de-ideologize international politics (at a heavy cost to the authority of his party) and sought to settle problems that might lead to war. Crises lead to war and war is irrational. The new and positive Soviet attitude towards the United Nations and the settling of regional disputes can be seen in this light.

Military factors are certainly not unimportant in relations between some states (notably in the crisis-prone Middle East) but in East–West relations they came to have an exaggerated significance. As a result of this the future of civilized life on earth has been dangerously threatened by the state of Soviet–American military relations. The last and worst crisis of the Cold War, the Cuban missile crisis, largely arose out of the dynamics of their nuclear confrontation, not from the state of ideological or political relations. Strategists make a ritualistic obeisance to Clausewitz, but in much strategic thinking the politics gets in only through the cracks of military-technical doctrinal analysis.

Conflict resolution should become part of the strategists' concern, as should the whole area of 'security co-operation'. The latter is an underdeveloped idea, and international theory is of little help (George, 1988, pp. 3–17). At the heart of the problem is the need to achieve change without instability and violence. This requires the building up of non-military structures to manage conflict.

Here, the notion of international regimes, which attracted growing attention through the 1980s, is crucial. Stephen Krasner has defined regimes as

> sets of implicit or explicit principles, norms, rules and decision-making procedures around which actors' expectations converge in a given area of international relations. Principles are beliefs or fact, causation and rectitude. Norms are standards of behaviour defined in terms of rights and obligations. Rules are specific prescriptions or proscriptions for action. Decision-making procedures are prevailing practices for making and implementing collective choice. (1982, p.186)

Co-operation in a 'regime' is different from mere co-operation arising out of self-interest; it is distinguished, in Krasner's words, by 'the infusion of behaviour with principles and norms'. Regimes institutionalize and constrain international behaviour; they therefore direct behaviour away from the narrow self-interest of a 'state of nature' into the paths of order and ultimately community. Whether a comprehensive security regime can be established between the major military powers remains to be seen, but recent developments are encouraging, and should make even cautious supporters of a few years ago more optimistic (George, 1988, pp. 13–14). Undoubtedly there will be ups and downs but, as the postwar history of Western Europe suggests, if we change the principles, norms, rules and decision-making procedures of nations, we can significantly change the nature of their interrelationships. Regimes have redefined international politics in a traditionally war-torn continent.

Environmental degradation is a security issue

One of the problems of traditional ways of thinking about security has been its dichotomous character. There has been a tendency to separate strategy and politics, domestic and external affairs, military-technical and diplomatic issues, and the geopolitical North and South. There is now one crucial area where all these dichotomies overlap: this is the degradation of the world's physical environment. If the worst scientific forecasts come about, this problem could overturn all other predictions about the future.

Environmental issues bring together North–South issues and the domestic and external dimensions of policy in a particularly sharp focus. These boundary-crossing issues have contributed something towards creating a stronger sense of a shared planet earth, but they have also become the subject of disputes about what should be done and who should bear the burden. Further down the road, as some resources become scarcer and particular ecological dangers grow, the threat of open conflict ('eco-imperialism') cannot be ruled out. At present, it seems safe to predict that this is an area where matters will have to get much worse before they get better. One can have little confidence regarding the willingness of most existing governments to make farsighted decisions in this area, since they will impinge immediately on prospects for growth, and therefore electoral success. We can only hope, to paraphrase Hobbes, that the fear of ecological collapse will empower reason, and also the political will to act upon it.

The science and politics of the environment are complex, but from a global perspective what is happening is simply a case of massive mismanagement. This is not how it appears from many national perspectives, particularly those countries that continue to prosper. Agreeing upon and making global solutions effective will be difficult, since it requires, for example, the resolution of basic issues in the relationship between the North and South. Some nations export pollution; some import scarce resources; some destroy their environment to try to earn a living. People, as well as pollution, are on the move. States increasingly have direct interests in each other's environmental and economic policies. The objective conditions are thereby promoting a more global perspective, and are challenging traditional notions of an international society based on sovereignty and non-interference.

While ecological problems are becoming more obvious, so too are the obstacles to solution. Progress is hindered by the nature of the international system itself and by prevailing ideas about economic progress. Unfettered capitalism and a self-help world are incompatible with the needs of global ecological management. The latter directly threatens sensitive issues relating to sovereignty and standards of living. States guard the former as fully as they can, while the rich countries do not want to reduce their consumption and the poor want to consume more. In such circumstances it is not surprising that the study of international political economy is becoming an increasingly important sub-field in the study of international relations. It again reflects the need to conceive security in wider than simply military terms. If we do not bring the interrelated problems of climatic change, overpopulation and scarce resources under control within the next generation then all bets must be off regarding the prospects of an international community living in stable peace.

Security begins at home

Traditionally, the domestic dimensions of strategy have been neglected. At the start of the Vietnam War, for example, US policy-makers did not consider that the battlefield would include American cities and campuses, as well as the hills and jungles of South-East Asia. Any neglect of domestic factors will be worrying as our conception of security broadens.

Domestic considerations are obviously crucial in any strategy to minimize ecological degradation. Much could be achieved by the actions of individual states if, for example, the developed countries drastically reduced petrol consumption or the use of chlorofluorocarbons. But in democratic countries based on capitalist principles such actions are not likely to win elections unless remarkable international agreements have been made or there has been a marked rise in consciousness along the line of the Green imperative to think globally and act locally.

Domestic development in the Third World is another issue with security implications. In the late 1960s Robert McNamara, then US Secretary of Defense, made a much-quoted statement about the direct relationship between successful development and improved security. The remark is no less valid today, for there is an important correlation between domestic instability and international conflict (Luard, 1986). When it comes to international conflict, weak states are at least as much a problem as strong powers (Buzan, 1987). Nation-building and economic development in the Third World should therefore be conceived as an integral aspect of the security policy of Northern states. A secure international community will be one in which all or almost all the units are effective in meeting the basic needs of their people. Achieving this will obviously be a tall order, given the crisis of development, the human rights violations, and the unstable political cultures in many Third World countries. Furthermore, mitigating one problem may only exacerbate another, for development will increase pressures on resources, and further contribute to pollution.

Security issues in the Third World are far from being simply traditional strategic issues. Indeed, when it comes to military challenges, the threat most governments face is from their own armed forces rather than those of their neighbours, as the long history of military intervention attests. Similarly, the peoples of the Third World are more likely to be the targets of their own national forces, imposing 'internal security', rather than those of a neighbour invading to further its ambitions. What threatens the quality of life of most (though obviously not all) people in the Third World is not an external military problem – the traditional 'national security' issue – but the interplay of internal and global factors. The transcendant problem is that these states do not *work* as socio-economic organisms, not that they are inefficient fighting machines.

In the industrialized world the various domestic dimensions of military policy are becoming clearer. As the 1980s drew to a close the obvious relationship between economic wellbeing and political and military status attracted much attention (Kennedy, 1988). For the superpowers, the previous decade had brought home the lesson that military spending can be counter-productive: it is a heavy drain on even a superpower's economy, and rarely buys commensurate political leverage. The currency of power is decreasingly a matter of guns but of the power of currency.

Domestic factors can shape the way conflicts are perceived and evolve. It became apparent through the 1980s that the Cold War and the arms race were not simply a manifestation of geopolitical conflict, but had important domestic roots (Booth, 1990; Nye, 1984; Wolfe, 1984). There were constituencies in both superpowers which profited and gained status from the conflict; and these were symbiotically supportive. An obvious example of the latter were the military-industrial-defence intellectual complexes which fed off each other. Stable security co-operation requires that these forces be controlled. In the 1970s, when they were not, political efforts to build superpower détente were in part undermined by the pace and character of the 'technological push' of the military-industrial complex; as a result, military mistrust always outran political confidence-building. The Cold

War separated two philosophical systems, but it created some adversarial brotherhoods.

Both East and West were imprisoned by the Cold War. It had a corrosive effect on the political and social development of all concerned, though much more so in the East. The Cold War helped to compound (somewhat different versions) of old thinking about both domestic and external policy, and it was mutually reinforcing. New thinking is flowering across the old adversaries, but whether it lasts will depend on the struggles which take place in domestic political arenas. We are unlikely to see a stable and progressive international system until first we see modern democracies committed to social justice and ecological balance in their own territories.

Security is too serious to be left to the strategists

There have been serious problems in mainstream strategic thinking for many years (Booth, 1979). Much influential strategic thinking has been in the grip of four regressive mindsets that sustain an excessively militarized image of contemporary international politics. These are ethnocentrism, Doctrinal Realism, ideological fundamentalism and strategic reductionism. Together, these mindsets shaped and were shaped by the Cold War. They now threaten to perpetuate old thinking about international politics in general. There has been some improvement in aspects of strategic thinking; the strategic community is not as ethnocentric as formerly, though in some cases lip-service is paid rather than real attention. But the strength of regressive mindsets has been evident in the slowness with which even the most sophisticated exponents of mainstream thinking have responded to notions such as common security and denuclearization. There was undue scepticism in responding to the Gorbachev revolution, as a result of which much precious time was lost.

For most of the postwar period the answer to the question 'who are the experts on security?' was straightforward: it was 'the strategists', and especially the new breed of nuclear strategists in the United States. Their intellectual dominance was challenged in the 1980s in what became the 'crisis of nuclearism' as the result of the rise to prominence of an alternative body of thinkers about security. The defence debate broadened, with the setting up of new organizations, the salience of new authorities and a range of different perspectives. A variety of new groups and individuals made particular contributions, such as the women of Greenham Common taking direct action, West German theorists of non-provocative defence, American defenders of the ABM Treaty, Scandinavian theorists of alternative security schemes and British organizations disseminating information questioning official analyses.

The 1980s showed that public opinion can have a positive effect on defence policy. There were several successes: arms control was kept on the agenda despite the hostile instincts of Reagan, Thatcher and Kohl; anti-nuclear slogans evolved into the policy options of alternative defence; the language of common security and alternative defence spread across Europe; the desirability of détente was kept alive during a period of East–West sabre-rattling; limits were maintained on the extreme military and political ideas of the strategic fundamentalists in the United States; President Reagan was kept from temptation in such areas as intervention in Central America, the development of the MX-missile, the breaking out of the SALT II limits, or embarking full-steam ahead (and damn the ABM Treaty) on Star Wars; Western public consciousness was raised on nuclear issues to an unprecedented level; in West Germany popular opinion discouraged Kohl from stopping the progress towards an INF agreement in deciding to keep the Pershing IA missile; an INF agreement was pursued and then welcomed by the major Western governments; at a time when confrontation and boycott were the preferred official postures towards the East, the dissatisfaction of many people led to a great expansion of 'personal diplomacy'; advocates of 'civil society' in Eastern Europe challenged the fist of totalitarian regimes; and peace movements everywhere led the way in seeing the problem of European security from an all-European perspective, and thinking about security with a view to the long term (measured in decades) rather than year to year.

This body of opinion did not achieve a critical mass in electoral terms but it did have an enormous impact. It helped to raise the level of debate on defence matters by challenging official orthodoxies; it kept the ideas of arms control and détente alive through inauspicious times; and it eventually contributed to the creation by the late 1980s of a superpower agenda that was radically different from that of only a few years earlier. All these successes were achieved by public opinion in a period when the international atmosphere was inclement. These results should be better publicized. If successes could be achieved in bad times, what cannot be achieved now, when the conditions are brighter, there are positive results to build upon, and alternative security ideas are being taken seriously?

For new thinking about security to succeed and prosper, broader participation, better accountability and freer information are crucial. For too long there has been a cult of experts on defence. The ending of the Cold War should help to change this, since it imprisoned most minds as well as some bodies. The Cold War demanded great secrecy on both sides and the suppression of criticism. The 'experts' should not now be defined so narrowly. After all, if it all went wrong, we would be equal in victimhood. Pressure from military-industrial complexes and militaristic ideas should be kept at bay not only in the cause of civilized politics at home but also in the interests of international peace.

One of the most interesting features of the defence debate in the 1980s was the questioning of cold war/pro-nuclear norms by a growing number of individuals who were specialists in defence. Former 'insiders' (political and military) criticized established policies. This helped to legitimize alternative defence ideas. The importance of such a trend should not be minimized. The alternative security case will gain confidence and supporters from these authorities, while the latter will offer increasingly sophisticated ideas and policy options to doubters, don't-knows and young people yet to think about it. The experts on military strategy are now far from being all on one side of the debate, that of the pro-nuclear pro-big-defence Doctrinal Realists (Booth and Baylis, 1989, pp. 42–61).

Although street demonstrations by peace movements had declined markedly by the late 1980s, this did not represent a victory of old over new thinking. Indeed, those who now want to reform the way we think about security are more extensive than those who march, and their influence is spreading. The main prize of alternative security thinking was the invasion and capture of the mind of the Kremlin. After 1985 Gorbachev and his supporters echoed and magnified the concerns of Western alternative security thinking, and the Soviet leader placed the new agenda on the table of East–West negotiations. In the Soviet Union itself Gorbachev and his supporters struggled with old orthodoxies, but alternative voices to the traditional defence establishment were brought in, and this led to a willingness never seen before to recognize the security problems of other nations, and to see security in common terms. Even if Gorbachev does not survive long, as a result of the enormous domestic problems he faces, it would not be easy for any successor to return to traditional militaristic gigantism.

The role of academic strategists remains important. They can help to establish the general framework of ideas, and contribute to the language within which the debate takes place. But the rise of different voices has been important and has led to a change in the tone and character of the debate about security. At the same time there has been a call in several countries to broaden the concept of 'security issues' and make them more accountable. The call has not yet been satisfactorily met, but again, the search for peace and the search for democracy and human rights are simply different arenas of the same struggle.

NEW THINKING ABOUT WAR

War is a cultural phenomenon

As with most of the other ideas to be discussed in this section, the proposition that war is a cultural phenomenon is not new. Margaret Mead, for one, wrote about it a half of a century ago (Mead, 1968). However, the implications of this insight have not been acted upon by the strategic studies community; it has been left to peace researchers to explore.

Periodically, the concept of war has altered. As with any attempt to understand human phenomena, we must avoid parochialism of time as well as space. Different people at different times have had different pictures in their heads when confronted by the question: what is war? War is not an objective fact on the world's surface, like a mountain range. Rather it is a social tradition, a cultural construct. As such it is changeable. Different cultures have constructed somewhat different conceptions of 'reality'. As a result, although violence between groups has taken place since the beginning of time, the character of war has changed. Its 'nature' has been determined by how we have conceived it, and how we have conceived it largely determines the way we have prepared (or not) to fight (Clausewitz, 1968).

The idea that war is a cultural phenomenon confronts the Realist correlation of international politics with a Hobbesian state of nature. There have been times when such a characterization was correct, but human institutions do change, and we now seem to be at a significant turning point. To date the history of war has seemed to be a remorseless testimony to Brecht's brilliant line in *Mother Courage*, in which he wrote that war 'is like love, it always finds a way'. Man has been a truly inventive animal, always thinking of new things to fight about; but some of the reasons why men laid down their lives in large numbers now appear to be quite bizarre. Who in Europe today would kill and be killed in order to procure a bride for a royal prince, or to ensure that foreign ships dipped their flags in salute? Our forebearers – surely no less imbued with the potential for wisdom or generosity than ourselves – once did.

Although war has been a persistent feature of the human story, it is neither necessary nor inevitable; nor on balance has it had positive social value (Luard, 1986, conclusion). To begin to overcome the war system we must begin by recognizing that war is a cultural not an objective phenomenon; what can be learned can also, perhaps with difficulty, be unlearned. It is still too soon in human history to conclude, as Realists have, that the international system is immutably a war system.

Interstate war is becoming obsolete

On the face of it, with figures pointing to over 135 'wars' since 1945 and over 20 million casualties, it looks foolhardy to describe interstate war as becoming obsolete. According to Luard, it is probable that war results in the deaths of a large number of people each year, and an even larger proportion of the world's population, than in any earlier period (1986, p. 395). But these calculations include internal strife as well as interstate wars; most of the wars that have taken place since 1945 have been internal (coups, civil wars and so on) rather than external, have been between small rather than great powers, and the numbers do not look as significant if we consider the permutations of possible belligerents in a state system whose members have trebled since the late 1940s.

An immediate distinction can be made between the North and South in war-proneness. In many parts of the South war still has its Clausewitzian connotations. But even here war-proneness is not as great as conventional wisdom suggests. There has been abundant internal violence in the Third World but interstate war has been the exception. There have, nevertheless, been some brutal struggles, as the Iran–Iraq war shows. Aggression still occurs, but it has been substantially delegitimized. Few leaders today, even in the grisliest regions of the Third World, could get away with the public declarations about territorial aggression which were made by Frederick the Great.

One of the most significant features of the post-1945 scene has been the stability of the traditionally war-torn continent of Europe. This has partly been the result of the growing costs of modern war, conventional as well as nuclear, but also of other factors: war-weariness, unprecedented prosperity, settled nation-state boundaries, the clarity produced by two tightly organized superpower-dominated alliances, relative domestic tranquillity, the spreading belief (since the First World War) that war is not a rational way to settle conflicts, and a certainty about the loss that would result from any massive breakdown in European security. These factors together have diminished the attractiveness and utility of major war. They have given Europe a significant degree of stability, regardless of nuclear weapons.

All the major powers believe that war between them can no longer serve as an acceptable instrument of policy, and so their disputes have either to be lived with or settled by alternative means. There are still some dangerous possibilities, but the likelihood that they will end in war is lower than ever before in history. International politics between the major powers have entered a post-Clausewitzian era.

For the foreseeable future states will maintain armed forces as badges of sovereignty and independence, to remind potential intruders that a price will have to be paid for aggression. Violence is not about to disappear from the international scene – but the history of war has reached a watershed. Hobbesian state-of-nature imagery is more likely to be applicable to domestic settings than to the state system as a whole. There will be fewer interstate wars, but no shortage of low-level conflict within states. Just as most violence is committed in the home rather than in the streets, so people are more likely to suffer from their own government's forces than those of foreign powers.

Nuclear war cannot be regarded as a rational continuation of politics

The invention of nuclear bombs decisively broke the ends–means relationship in strategy. The idea that nuclear war is fundamentally un-Clausewitzian has now achieved general acceptance. Even so, it is worth reminding ourselves that it is less than a decade ago since US nuclear strategy was looking towards surviving and prevailing in nuclear war, while the idea of 'victory' was long promulgated by sections of the Soviet military establishment. Unless it is guarded against, no doubt such irrational ideas could again resurface. Whatever the declaratory positions now adopted by the superpowers, the nuclear infrastructure of the Reagan–Brezhnev years remains essentially in place, is being modernized, and still represents a threat to civilized life which is quite unrelated to the political differences presently existing between the Soviet Union and the United States. Total war is a physical possibility, but it can no longer be regarded as a rational instrument of policy, as it could even up to the Second World War. Wars which would be mutually destructive would be politically pointless. There would be no winners and few survivors, and would those survivors, in Herman Kahn's brilliant question, envy the dead?

We live in a world of rapid obsolescence, when even our words do not work as they formerly did. The words at the very heart of our subject – 'war', 'strategy' and 'weapons' – still resonate with Clausewitzian implications of reasonable instrumentality. Our collective strategic imagination is blinkered when the adjective 'nuclear' is placed before them; this word decisively changes their meaning, so that these phrases at the heart of our subject become oxymorons. Nevertheless, many policy-makers have sought to handle the apocalyptic problems of the present with the Clausewitzian concepts of the past. The words 'war', 'strategy' and 'weapon' are deeply embedded in the way we think about the game of nations, even though in the nuclear context any reasonable relationship between ends and means has been destroyed. If we cannot abolish our Clausewitzian language, we need to learn that the adjective 'nuclear' undermines whatever follows: nuclear war is therefore irrational, nuclear strategy impossible, and nuclear weapons are not weapons. If these non-weapons cannot be used rationally, can they wisely be threatened? If they cannot wisely be threatened, what then is this thing called 'nuclear deterrence'?

Nuclear war remains the ultimate threat

Nuclear war remains the greatest threat not only to states but also to people's lives at the individual level and to the global community as a whole. Although at present the risk of nuclear war appears small, proliferation remains a danger, there are many other morbid symptoms, and we depend on the eternal absence of madness, miscalculation, accident and bad luck. In the timespan of centuries, this looks a poor bargain.

It is encouraging that we have avoided nuclear war for over forty years, but the recent past is only a limited guide for the long-term future. Denuclearization and nuclear risk reduction must therefore remain a priority. The very existence of nuclear systems – their offensive character and intercontinental range – feeds the security dilemma. It is difficult to conceive the growth of security communities within and between regions while nuclear weapons and long-range delivery systems exist. But what can be looked forward to at present is the progressive irrelevance of nuclear weapons in the affairs of the major powers. For this process to spread to the near or quasi-nuclear powers it is essential that the non-proliferation regime be strengthened.

Nuclear weapons are the ultimate threat to security because of the speed and scale of their destructiveness. This point does not need labouring. Many would argue that too many babies are being born. Almost all accept that too much pollution is being discharged and that too many resources are being consumed too quickly. These problems represent threats to the quality of life on earth, and in some cases have profound security implications. But these crises do not threaten the instant destructiveness of nuclear weapons. Of all the threats facing the future of civilized life on the planet those imposed by modern weapons must be of particular concern. They threaten instantly and literally to blow us back into the dark ages. Reducing, each year, the risk of nuclear war should therefore continue to be a crucial test of statesmanship.

Even if, in the end, it were to prove impossible to secure global nuclear weapons elimination, it is important to act as though we can. To do otherwise is to legitimize proliferation and the belief that there is no stronger basis to human coexistence than genocidal fear. At some point in the future such minimalist thinking is likely to prove a recipe for disaster.

Military force is declining in utility

The costs of maintaining and using armed forces have risen for all societies. Direct economic costs have soared, while everywhere there is a new sensitivity to opportunity costs. When it comes to the use of military force for acquisitive purposes, the costs (economic, moral, diplomatic) have risen while the benefits (territorial control, bases and so on) have gone down (Knorr, 1966).

The declining utility of force for acquisitive as opposed to defensive purposes is the result of a mixture of changing costs and attitudes. Large-scale intervention has been affected as well as war between major powers. The record suggests that the recent reluctance of the superpowers to become embroiled militarily in Third World issues is not merely a matter for the immediate future, but is more deep-rooted. Although the capabilities will remain, large-scale intervention in Third World countries looks decidedly less likely than ever in the past. Projection forces will be employed at lower levels of violence – drug control, migration/refugee interception, blockade, the protection of nationals – but the era of traditional great power military intervention seems past. Future attacks by superpowers against Third World states will be on the scale of Grenada and Panama rather than Vietnam and Afghanistan. It is rash to predict that large-scale interventions will never take place, as long as the capabilities exist, but the historical trends suggest that the end is in sight. The militarily powerful have all blundered, so it is unlikely that Suez (Britain and France), Vietnam (the United States) and Afghanistan (the Soviet Union) will be repeated. Reruns of more successful projections of large-scale force (Korea, Hungary, Czechoslovakia) are equally unlikely, because of the special circumstances which surrounded the originals.

What is more predictable are large-scale conventional wars between Third World countries. Several tense regional conflicts exist in which there is not the same war-weariness, fear of high casualty rates and massive destruction that have characterized European history, and there is more scope for ambition as a result of national claims and artificial boundaries. War is still in its Clausewitzian phase. Outside powers may be invited in a supportive capacity, but are unlikely to choose offensive interventionary roles. But as we argued earlier, even in the Third World it is easy to exaggerate the war-proneness, though not the violence, which exists. Some parts of the Third World, notably South America, have remained distinctly free of interstate war.

It is evident that war is not the rational answer to political problems that it formerly was. For the past two centuries the major powers have operated on the basis of the Clausewitzian 'political philosophy of war', the idea that war is or should be rational, national and instrumental (Clausewitz, 1968). But fewer and fewer exercises of force can be so regarded, and those that can be tend to be at a lower end of the spectrum of violence. The argument here is not that military force is useless in all circumstances. Defensive force still has utility: there were, after all, local winners as well as superpower losers in Vietnam and Afghanistan. Furthermore, military power is still needed in varying amounts to signal a determination to defend national territory. But the use of force for acquisitive purposes continues to decline: this is a matter of cost/benefit calculations, changing attitudes and the preference for alternatives. There is no sign that this will change. It again logically points to the evolution of 'defence only' armed forces.

Major war is more likely to be inadvertent than deliberate

If war is decreasingly rational and instrumental, it follows that outbreaks are more likely to be inadvertent – the result of miscalculations, madness or accident – than deliberate. If this is so they will by definition be outside the bounds of deterrence theory. Deterrence, therefore, is not enough for security. More attention must be given to reassurance, crisis prevention and conflict resolution, as will be discussed later.

War remains the central issue in the study of international relations and attitudes towards it – its roles, likelihood, causes and potential eradicability – have implications for particular issues in security and strategy. Our verdicts on the present historical status of war will colour our perspectives about the future evolution (or not) of world society. An appropriate attitude for new thinkers, based on empirical observation, was summed up in the early 1970s by Bernard Brodie, a political Realist and nuclear strategist, but a fundamentalist in neither:

> We can predict over the long term a much lesser inclination than in times past to take for granted the periodic recurrence of war . . . We can predict also much greater earnestness about searching for alternatives to war . . . that violence should continue indefinitely to take the specific institutional form known as war . . . is now decidedly questionable. This could be wishful thinking, but we are not obliged to deny important visible changes simply because they happen to be in a direction we like. (1973, pp. 274–5)

War and the threat of war still dominate the theory and practice of international relations, but the second half of the twentieth century suggests that this will not always be the case. Even some Realists have glimpsed the possibility of international politics without interstate war.

NEW THINKING ABOUT STRATEGY

Strategic doctrine should reflect common security consciousness

It is not enough to accept common security intellectually. If we are to move to a new level of security it is also necessary that strategic doctrines be operationalized according to common security principles. Actions speak louder than words. This involves, above all, the pursuit of military policies that exhibit sensitivity to the implications of the security dilemma.

Operationalizing common security will face major obstacles as reform challenges traditionalist approaches to security. It is not simply policies that need changing, but strategic cultures, and these, by definition, are not easily altered (Jacobsen, 1990). Gorbachev has discovered this, in his struggle to bring about a Soviet strategic cultural revolution. Nevertheless, beliefs, even basic beliefs, can change, especially when old ideas are seen to be dysfunctional. A growing body of opinion believes that major reforms are necessary in the structure and arrangements for European security; meanwhile, the major military establishments are claiming that their own deterrent efforts have 'worked' and that it is unwise to try to fix what 'ain't broke'. But despite traditionalist resistance, there are signs of change in both the Soviet Union and the West, as mental and material adjustments are slowly made to post-Clausewitzian realities.

Strategic postures reflecting common security consciousness will be guided by a desire to avoid digging the trap of the security dilemma any deeper than is unavoidable. Such postures will emphasize reasonable sufficiency, arms restraint, defensive intentions, confidence-building strategies, multi-faceted transparency, mutual reciprocity and a lower or zero reliance on nuclear weapons. If common security is operationalized, major states will still have considerable military power, but its character would create a radically different military security environment from that with which we have been familiar. Asymmetries will be reduced, the most threatening doctrines will disappear, and there will be a significant reduction in manpower and weaponry. Reforms will take place in equipment, doctrines, organization, training manuals and philosophy. It needs to be stressed that common security is not simply a matter of reducing troops and weapons; it matters how the reductions take place. This is where restructuring along the lines of non-provocative defence (to be discussed below) is so valuable, since it promises to mitigate the security dilemma by promoting arms control, crisis stability, non-provocation in peace and non-escalation in war. Reductions without restructuring can be destabilizing.

Common security strategies represent varieties of confidence-building. As it happens, the internationalization of economies, culture and communications in the northern hemisphere will have a major impact on the character of the interactions between societies which were formerly enemies. They will in future be increasingly open towards each other. This in itself will assist military confidence-building. But the more directly military dimension of confidence-building still deserves considerable attention, since there is much mistrust to overcome. In this respect a slow but promising start has been made in the CSCE process. It has established a framework for pan-European negotiations on security, embracing military, economic and human-rights dimensions, and it has also helped to promote the idea of peaceful change and a continent-wide consciousness. Not least of its achievements, the CSCE process has given small, medium and neutral and non-aligned states a voice. This is important, to remind the larger powers that they are not the only actors in the game, and that they do not have a monopoly of wisdom. Much more can be done under the CSCE umbrella, as the strategic map of Europe evolves, in terms of developing codes of conduct, conflict resolution procedures and the promotion of mutual confidence.

Nuclear deterrence is easy

The record of the 1980s strongly suggests that what Bundy (1984) labelled 'existential deterrence' has won the nuclear debate. In one word, that of Buzan, deterrence has been found to be 'easy' (1987, pp. 163–72). The empirical evidence for this is the way the superpowers are now winding down their superabundance of nuclear weaponry, amassed during the 1970s and 1980s. The Reagan administration, in its first worrying years, proved to be the last round-up for those who believed that nuclear deterrence was 'hard' and that nuclear overkill could be translated into political leverage. By his nuclear extravagance, in words and weapons, Reagan proved that nuclear *strategy* did not work.

The 'easy' school, according to Buzan, assumes that the magnitude of the possible cost of any war overawes considerations about the degrees of risk (1987, pp. 168–9). At the same time this school assumes that 'fanatical zeal for aggression' is the exception rather than the rule in international relations. Opportunism, on the other hand, is widespread, but opportunists are calculating: they are 'more likely to be impressed by the possibility of infinite costs than are zealots'. Nuclear deterrence is also easy if the earlier argument is accepted regarding the growing obsolescence of war. It does not take much to deter what nobody wants to happen.

We can argue how many tens or hundreds of nuclear systems are necessary to deter a potential adversary, but the last few years have seen virtually the whole strategic community in the northern hemisphere decide that it was desirable to revise downwards their estimates of what is safe. Fewer is better because minimum deterrence undermines dangerous ideas about nuclear warfighting and it sends positive political signals to one's adversary. The main role of nuclear weapons will increasingly be that of the basic deterrence of attacks on the homeland, but also, in some cases,

the continued identification of 'vital interests' through extended
deterrence. But the practice of extended deterrence has long been
under strain as a result of the problem of credibility and now the
changing character of certain hitherto nuclear-underpinned 'vital
interests'.

Nuclear strategy is a contradiction in terms

Since the early 1980s alternative security thinkers have argued
that nuclear strategy is a contradiction in terms. The idea then
spread to a significant number of insiders and people who formerly had been satisfied with nuclear policies. The catalyst for
the change was the introduction of cruise and Pershing II missiles into Western Europe; this left increasing numbers of people asking what would happen if deterrence failed. The result
was an upsurge of anti-nuclear opinion which rather spectacu-
larly eroded the former pre-eminence of nuclear 'strategy'. As was
suggested earlier, the Clausewitzian concept of strategy implies
reasonable instrumentality, but this has been abolished by nuclear
technology.

Nuclear 'weapons' are not weapons in the traditional sense
(Bundy, 1988; Halperin, 1987). Not only did the 1980s witness their lack of political utility, as the superpowers failed to
translate overkill into leverage, but investigation also showed
that nuclear threats, whether implicit or explicit, had never been
as significant as they had once been thought. Despite early
(and reasonable) expectations about the massive implications of
the nuclear revolution, it has actually proved to have only
limited impact on the character of international relations. It
reinforced the historic trend towards the irrationality of war
between major powers, but otherwise its effects have been mar-
ginal. Nuclear threats disappeared after the early 1960s, and
even before then they had never been as significant as conventional wisdom believed. This is not to say that in some
future crisis nuclear threats will not be made; but it does suggest that such threats will be both unlikely and lacking in
utility.

Most if not all decision-makers recognize the irrationality of
nuclear war, and therefore, increasingly, have come to accept the
unacceptibility and incredibility of nuclear threats. The nuclear

'taboo' is powerful and an increasingly long tradition of non-use and no-threat is evolving. Some still talk and act as if nuclear 'weapons' are 'weapons' but, as with all doctrines/ideologies/theologies, when behaviour and reason grow apart it is to be expected that those in positions of 'responsibility' and those 'authorities' with stakes in the old ideas will cling on. Paradigm collapses can occur suddenly, as happened in Eastern Europe in 1989.

Nuclearism went into crisis in the early 1980s. This crisis, created by the peace movement's response to Reaganite-Thatcherite nuclearmania, proved to be not merely 'artificial', as was claimed by pro-nuclear opinion, but to be fundamental. The pro-nuclear case is now badly dented. Confidence about the rationality of nuclear doctrine has been shaken, and there is now a pronounced anti-nuclear tide, evident in the support for the 'third zero' and minimum deterrence. We do not know how to get rid of all nuclear weapons, and many people do not want to, but their centrality and perceived utility in international relations has been radically undermined when compared with the nuclear fundamentalism of the early Reagan years.

The irrationality of nuclear strategy is evident in the posture of 'first nuclear use', which has always been central to NATO doctrine. Former insider critics like Lord Carver and Robert McNamara explained that the implementation of the 'strategy' could not with any confidence be expected to lead to success; on the contrary, the risks of escalation meant that its implementation would have been suicidal. The credibility gap between threat and implementation is also evident in the increasingly threadbare posture of 'extended deterrence'. This became obvious to (almost) all in the convolutions associated with the INF issue. At first there was the urge to deploy these weapons to strengthen US–West European coupling; then came the stress on their necessary role in creating a 'seamless web' of deterrence; finally there was the scrapping of these same weapons which, until the day before, had been deemed to be essential for extended deterrence. Despite the crisis of nuclearism, inertia is powerful, and there is a long way to go before policy implementation will match changing ideas. Even so, it looks as though it will become increasingly difficult in the years ahead for defence establishments to justify what have previously, and erroneously, been called nuclear strategies.

Arms reduction is a precondition for security

One aspect of common security consciousness must be a commitment to arms reduction. Arms reduction in itself is not a panacea, as old disarmers believed, but it is an important part of the solution. Controlling and reducing arms – formally and informally – cannot be ignored by those who wish to ease the mistrust that exists between states. This has been recognized in recent years as the WTO and NATO have begun to address each others' fears. Several extraneous trends are assisting the prospects for success, particularly economic pressures for reasonable sufficiency, demographic trends and the growth of transparency in most societies. Other developments – the collapse of the WTO and the unification of the two Germanys – are, on the other hand, creating new complexities.

In approaching arms restraint it is important to consider unilateral as well as multilateral approaches. To avoid doing so is to invite disappointment. The multilateral approach received a boost towards the end of the 1980s, with the signature of the INF Treaty and the progress in START and CFE, but in the short term the results have not been remarkable. No warheads were destroyed by the INF Treaty, while it was seen by some defence planners and politicians as a challenge to devise ways of compensating for the missiles destroyed.

Multilateral arms control has always been a cumbersome process. Excessive hopes have sometimes been encouraged, and disappointments have been correspondingly great. As at the present time, when so much is expected, multilateral forums can easily be overstrained. If agreement is long delayed, there is always the risk of the negotiations being overtaken by military innovation, or by unhelpful linkages with developments outside the arms control framework. After the immobilism of the early 1980s we are probably now expecting more from the formal talks than they can deliver. This being the case, unilateral tactics are as necessary as multilateral approaches. Such tactics have been greatly vindicated since Gorbachev came to power, and used them to show sceptical Westerners that he was serious about arms reduction. This encouraged a more accommodating Western approach, even from deeply anti-Soviet leaders. In the complex times ahead reciprocal unilateral action may well be more productive than overloading the multilateral processes. A judicious mixture of both unilateralism and multilateralism is probably necessary for success.

Improving security is not only a matter of arms reduction, it is also a matter of how the reductions are organized. In some scenarios, force postures at lower levels can appear to be more destabilizing (for example, lower force: space ratios on the side of the defence can make an aggressor's task easier). It is here where non-provocative defence can come into its own as a philosophy around which to restructure forces at lower levels. On NATO's side a mixture of deep cuts and the maintenance of the pro-nuclear flexible response doctrine will merely produce a ragged and unstable posture, characterized by stretched area defence and an overemphasis on heavy armour, nuclear first use and high-tech deep-strike systems. In the first instance, conventional arms control should address the threat of offensive conventional forces (the possibility of surprise attack and large-scale offensive operations) and then work towards comprehensive restructuring in the direction of defence-only postures, as will be explained below.

Arms control is an idea which has been so exhaustively examined over the past thirty years that it would be surprising if any significantly new ideas were to emerge on how it might better be done. What is new about the present is the seriousness with which it is being approached and the shift of emphasis from the competitive cold war arms control of the past (for propaganda and unilateral gain) to the mutually beneficial arms control of the present. Among the hopeful approaches are the recognition given to CBMs, the belief that unilateral as well as multilateral tactics are useful and the understanding that stability at lower levels is a matter not just of cutting but of restructuring the forces concerned.

Arms reduction is not only important for countries in the old East–West confrontation; it could also be helpful in mitigating some conflicts in the Third World; Europe will find it difficult to remain a stable ship of peace if the rest of the world becomes a more dangerous place. In this respect it is important that serious efforts are made to keep alive and strengthen the non-proliferation regime and to inhibit the further spread of ballistic missiles, and the now surplus arsenals of the northern hemisphere. To achieve results, the major military powers will need to set examples, and not just deliver exhortatory words. And arms suppliers will have to give up business. In arms control as in other dimensions of security, the perspective must increasingly be internationalist, and there will be an economic cost.

Non-provocative defence is the soundest basis for military détente

Of all military doctrines, none reflects common security consciousness better than non-provocative defence. It is the only strategy now available that attempts to mitigate the old problem of the security dilemma and meet the new needs of security interdependence.

Surprise attack has always been a particular anxiety for military planners. It was burned into the Soviet military mind by the experience of June 1941 and has been a controlling fear for NATO as a result of the Soviet Army's looming military might. But one of the premises of non-provocative defence is that such fears – and all the pressures towards mistrust – could largely be removed if opposing sides agreed on structural limitations on their offensive capabilities. Mutual threat perception – implicit or explicit – is at the heart of the security dilemma. The only military way of escaping from the trap is by reducing the major asymmetries between adversaries, addressing each other's main fears, and moving towards defence policies based on non-provocative principles. The result would be a growth in both national and international security.

The postwar record shows that increases in Soviet security did not translate into increases in Western security (and vice versa). Indeed, the opposite was the case. If 'power politics' is the game, one state's security is often another's insecurity. In a world of complex interdependence, however, security is also an interdependent dilemma which promotes mistrust and countervailing military efforts. Instead of relying on order based on fear – a balance of terror – we can work towards peace based on mutual defensive supremacy. That is, we can replace the idea that attack is the best form of defence with the idea that defence is the best form of security. Non-provocative defence seeks to maintain a level of deterrence against aggression but to do so in such a way that arms competition would be slowed, crisis stability increased, arms reduction encouraged and political accommodation improved.

States cannot expect to have political détente over a long period without military détente. The military and political agenda must go hand in hand. The problems that arises when they are out of phase were evident in the 1970s. The military agenda pressed ahead, threatening modernization, innovations and action–reaction matchings. These developments all undermined the parallel attempts to achieve political détente. The arms competition between the superpowers was not the only factor explaining the end of détente, but it was a major one. Political and military détente should therefore proceed in parallel and there is no better concept for military détente than non-provocative defence.

The argument that denuclearization will simply leave the world safe for conventional war is mistaken. The fact is that in modern conditions a general conventional war between industrial societies cannot be won in a meaningful sense. This was apparent with the Iran–Iraq war, and the devastation involved in a conventional war across Europe would leave little left of the countries which were being defended or occupied. Conventional wars between major powers now risk too much unacceptable damage to be considered 'safe'.

Crisis prevention is preferable to crisis management

A great deal remains to be developed in the theory and practice of non-provocative defence. There is not a consensus among supporters about which model(s) of it to adopt. Further discussion and public education is necessary, but it nevertheless represents a hopeful route to follow, since it promises a more secure military basis for the pursuit of political co-operation between states. Among its advantages, it promises to be crisis stable.

Crises, as some Soviet writers have stressed, are paths to war. It is therefore desirable that crises be prevented altogether rather than confront policy-makers with the uncertain task of managing them. It may not always be possible to prevent crises, however, for some national leaders will go too far, inadvertently or by design, and then the risk will need controlling.

Because of the danger inherent in crises, it is desirable that military planners give more attention to crisis stability. As the sense of East–West threat declines and the utility of war decreases, it is only logical that choices about weapons, force structures, tactical and strategic doctrine, and command-and-control arrangements emphasize crisis stability over surprise attack and offensive operations. History shows that the mutual fear of attack can create a spiral of tension such that an actual decision for war comes to be seen as the rational option; fighting begins, although nobody necessarily 'wants' war.

For the most part, since the early 1960s the superpowers have been relatively restrained in their military behaviour, so far as the risks of direct confrontation have been concerned. Some efforts were made in the 1970s to devise 'rules of the game' for bargaining, decision-making and operational conduct; but this did not progress far. It is therefore a route that needs further exploration. Europe is now a more confusing place, and some low-level violence looks predictable as a result of ethnic and other disturbances. In these circumstances the desirability of developing crisis prevention schemes, with institutions for conflict resolution, is obvious. The attempts in the 1970s to create albeit primitive crisis-prevention rules and structures failed in face of superpower competition in the Third World and then the new Cold War; but these efforts did produce some lessons and ideas. In the second half of the 1980s, interest was shown in reviving the idea of crisis prevention, as was evident in the high profile given to so-called 'regional issues' in superpower summits.

The strange Reagan era encouraged a healthy anxiety about the dynamics of the Sarajevo crisis, and this replaced the self-congratulating obsession of some strategists with the management of the Cuban missile crisis. The theory of crisis management advanced accordingly, while the formalization of East–West exchanges again began to be explored. The result should be improved channels of communication and, perhaps, even improved understanding. There is now more confidence regarding the stability of US–Soviet relations, but questions still arise as a result of the danger of instability in Eastern Europe and the Third World. There are grounds for believing that more concern will be shown to crisis prevention in the 1990s, as is evident in the growing interest in security regimes and, in the military field, in crisis stable non-provocative defence postures.

Strategic studies should be broadened

In addition to the problems caused by regressive strategic mindsets, as epitomized by the Committee for the Present Danger, strategic studies have suffered from too narrow a focus. Were a Committee for Future Security to be established today its agenda and outlook would be very different from those of the strategic fundamentalists of the Reagan era. Strategic studies needs to be conceived more broadly. The subject has a focus – the military dimension of international politics – but no boundaries should be placed around it. The question of objectives, for example, which is traditionally taken for granted by strategists, must become a concern.

A restrictive military-technical definition of strategic studies will place fences, even if small ones, around our minds. It will cut us off from important and interesting intellectual developments elsewhere; this has long been a problem with strategic studies, as has been evident in the divorce from history and area studies; without these, strategic thinking is largely in a void. Fences discourage the asking of the hard questions. As a result, mainstream strategic studies has frequently ignored the phenomenon of war. In this sense so-called strategists have simply been deterrence theorists. The question 'what if deterrence fails?' has rarely been asked. Instead the paradigm sin of war planners through the ages is committed: it is assumed that it'll be all right on the night. The awkward questions have only been asked and answered, however inadequately, by the war-fighting school on the one hand and the peace movement on the other. The former have worried about targeting, while the latter have sought to replace nuclear deterrence. Despite such efforts to grapple with the hardest questions, the so-called hawks and the so-called doves have often been defined out of the 'real' debate by the self-professed 'owls' who have dominated the subject. Owls it should be remembered invariably work in the dark.

There has been an innate conservatism in strategic studies. Our job is to explain the world, strategists often say, not to change it. But that is not a real choice, because how we explain something very much shapes our prescriptions, while our explanations are shaped by our values. Explanation in practice is often a rationalization from a nationalistic point of view. Edward Luttwak has made a virtue of such an approach. He has written that strategic studies is not a neutral pursuit; its only purpose is to strengthen one's own side in the contention of nations (Luttwak, 1985, p. xiii). It should go without saying that the idea of strategic studies as a loyalty test does not fit well with the traditional idea of academic life.

The 1980s saw the emergence of a debate about paradigms in international relations. This subject, once largely unified in its assumptions, has become increasingly fragmented (Holsti, 1985). One trend, however, was an attempt to look at the whole rather than the parts. As interdependence flourished, and global problems grew, the world-society perspective drew more attention. Strategic studies should reflect this, giving a greater prominence to the system as a whole. The appropriate organizing concept would be a broader concept of security. In addition, it would be helpful in thinking about strategy to revive the classical notion of politics as an open-ended subject belonging to the realm of ethics. Within this conception of politics, strategy can be seen as a continuation of moral philosophy with an admixture of firepower.

One hopeful sign of the broadening of strategic studies has been the tendency to converge with peace studies. There is still not enough of the 'real' world in peace studies for strategists, while strategic studies are too static and state-centric for peace researchers. But some of the differences between the two approaches have been exaggerated. Peace research, for example, has often been criticized on the grounds of its being a 'campaign'. But the ostensibly more 'apolitical' strategic studies is no better; it has only had better public relations, and hidden its values more effectively. As convergence grows there are areas where peace research and strategic studies could profitably co-operate, as in the field of security co-operation or developing ideas of defensive supremacy.

Following the so-called Golden Age of contemporary strategic theorizing, there was a sense that all the important strategic issues had been settled. What was left was merely the writing of footnotes to Brodie, Kahn, Schelling and so forth. This, more than ever before, is an untenable position. There is still much to be done: new reconceptualizations, silences to be filled, richer history, broader perspectives, fewer ethnocentric ideas, dynamic rather than static theories, more sophisticated critiques and the exploration of alternative models of security. The first generation of strategic studies, which shaped and was shaped by the Cold War, is dead; the second generation, strategic studies for the age of complex interdependence, is being created. If strategic studies continue in a narrow technical sense, the subject will become less and less relevant to the daily business of the world. Those strategists and organizations that do not try to become part of the solution will increasingly become part of the problem.

CONCLUSION

International relations are undergoing an interregnum, in both practice and theory; we are moving from the kingdom of the Cold War and political Realism to one whose landscape and Big Idea is not yet clear. It is hoped that this book will provide some guidance through the unfamiliar security terrain of the post-cold-war world. Naturally, it will not be possible to get everything right at once, any more than it was possible at the start of the Cold War. There is a danger that new thinking will become rigidified into New Thinking, or that ideas like common security will become mere clichés in the writing of academics or buzzwords in the mouths of politicians. To avoid this, thinking about security could benefit from the intellectual leavening of Critical Theory. Unlike traditional Realism, which takes the world as a given, naturalizes it and creates sub-branches like strategic studies to practise problem-solving, Critical Theory encourages openminded thinking directed towards reconceptualizing the security predicament. The status quo is not seen as immutable; and it is assumed that we have potentialities to change the world. Since there is an intimate relationship in human behaviour between image and reality, we must first reshape our images. Developing a new philosophy of security should be part of our self-conscious cultural evolution. If military, security and foreign policies were to be based on the propositions and assumptions discussed in this Conclusion, then a distinctly different bias would be introduced into international behaviour. The 'nature' of the system would be changed because of the changed conceptions – strategic cultures – of the units.

Changing strategic cultures is not easy. A critical mass of opinion favourable to the ideas identified as new thinking has not yet evolved. Much official and public opinion believes that alternative ideas are neither practical nor desirable. But growing numbers do now believe that alternative security conceptions provide the basis for a shared practice and theory of coexistence between nations. The traffic in international politics is moving at an astonishing pace and the present is one of those periods when conscious evolution can take place, when a determination to act will be rewarded.

Can new thinking develop into a new orthodoxy about security, or will it just be a blip on a screen dominated by traditional Realism? Behind the widespread optimism identified with the end of the Cold War there are many morbid symptoms, as was indicated in the Introduction. The wind is not set fair for a trouble-free future; indeed, Hobbesian pessimists are rubbing their hands and predicting a speedy return to a pre-1939 world, with an unstable Europe, an isolationist United States, a troubled Soviet Union, an upsurge of nationalism, and a Third World characterized by turmoil and intervention. Despite these possibilities, the potential for benevolent change have not been better this century. Crises are longer apart and there is a growing sense of global awareness.

The importance of the relationship between our images and the 'reality' of world politics has been stressed: in this sense the significant division in the world today is less between different national perspectives as between old and new thinkers in each country. Nevertheless, new thinking about strategy and international security will not give ready answers to precise issues, such as what should be done about a united Germany or how can a new European security system be organized; but the principles, ideas and guidelines discussed earlier will help us to contemplate a post-cold-war, post-Realist world with a more hopeful sense of direction. By rethinking world politics we can help to reshape international relations in ways that better fulfil human needs. If we get the processes right, the structures should look after themselves.

There is much about world politics which is characterized by unreason. But there is always some scope for conscious choice. Reason has liberated societies from regressive ideas and inhuman behaviour in the past. There is no reason to suppose that it cannot happen again. Applying reason to international politics involves nothing less than attempting to reshape world politics in the human interest, rather than replicating the past by applying Doctrinal Realism. The study of international politics may be in disarray in some important respects but it is still the cockpit for the most intriguing and significant issues of our time. In trying to tackle these issues, we will play a part in setting the world's agenda for the start of the next century. And if, by new thinking, we can mitigate the security dilemma – thus providing greater safety at less cost – we will free both energy and resources to try to deal with all the other pressing problems the future is bound to dump upon us.

NOTE

1 The world-society approach confronts the state-system approach, which almost exclusively posits states as the primary referents in international politics. Rather than concentrating upon states, the world-society approach focuses on the global community, emphasizes the plurality of actors (firms, ethnic groups and so on) among which nation-states are one, examines human needs (material wellbeing and fulfilment) and not just national interests (the maximization of state prosperity and security), and analyses all significant interactions (conflictual and co-operative), not only those of interest from a power-political perspective. The world-society approach is explicitly value-orientated, as opposed to the traditional state-system approach, which is implicitly so. It emphasizes the importance of ideas, images and ideological preferences, as opposed to 'facts' whose validity is questionable. The world-society approach recognizes that we live in a multi-cultural world, but believes that there is a slowly growing sense of common destiny. It rejects the idea that this is the best of all possible worlds, as Realists assume, or that the future is guaranteed, as deterrence theorists assume. On the contrary, survival is believed to be problematic unless priority is given to the future, to non-violent change, to ecological balance and to the progressive satisfaction of the needs of the individuals who ultimately make up the global community.

REFERENCES

Booth, Ken (1979), *Strategy and Ethnocentrism* (London: Croom Helm)

Booth, Ken (1987), 'New challenges and old mindsets: ten rules for Empirical realists', in Carl G. Jacobsen (ed), *The Uncertain Course: New Weapons, Strategists and Mind-Sets* (Oxford: Oxford University Press/SIPRI).

Booth, Ken (1990), 'US perceptions of the Soviet threat: prudence and paranoia', in Carl J. Jacobsen (ed.), *Strategic Power USA/USSR* (London: Macmillan).

Booth, Ken, and Baylis, John (1989), *Britain, NATO and Nuclear Weapons* (London: Macmillan).

Boulding, Kenneth (1979), *Stable Peace* (Austin, Tex.: University of Texas Press).

Brodie, Bernard (1973), *War and Politics* (London: Cassell).

Bundy, McGeorge (1984), 'Existential deterrence and its consequences', in Douglas Maclean (ed.), *The Security Gamble* (Totawa, NJ: Rowman & Allanhead).

Bundy, McGeorge (1988), *Danger and Survival: Choices about the Bomb in the First Fifty Years* (New York: Random House).

Buzan, B. (1983), *People, States and Fear. The National Security Problem in International Relations* (Brighton: Wheatsheaf).

Buzan, B. (1987), *An Introduction to Strategic Studies: Military Technology and International Relations* (London: Macmillan).

Clausewitz, Carl Von (1968), *On War*, ed. Anatol Rapoport (Harmondsworth: Penguin).

Frank, A.G. (1972) 'The development of underdevelopment', in James Cockcroft, André Gunder Frank and Dale L. Johnson, *Dependence and Underdevelopment* (New York: Doubleday).

Galtung, J. (1971), 'A structural theory of imperialism', *Journal of Peace Research*, vol. 8, pp. 81–117.

George, Alexander L., Farley, P. J., and Dallin, Alexander, (1988), *US–Soviet Security Cooperation. Achievements, Failures, Lessons* (New York: Oxford University Press).

Halperin, Morton H. (1987), *Nuclear Fallacy. Dispelling the Myth of Nuclear Strategy* (Cambridge, Mass.: Ballinger).

Hoffmann, Stanley (1965), *The State of War: Essays on the Theory and Practice of International Relations* (New York: Praeger).

Holsti, K. J. (1985), *The Dividing Discipline. Hegemony and Diversity in International Theory* (Boston: Allen & Unwin).

Jacobsen, Carl G. (ed.) (1990), *Strategic Power USA/USSR* (London: Macmillan).

Kennan, George F. (1983), *The Nuclear Delusion* (New York: Pantheon).

Kennedy, Paul (1988), *The Rise and Fall of the Great Powers* (New York: Random House).

Knorr, Klaus (1966), *On the Uses of Military Power in the Nuclear Age* (Princeton, NJ: Princeton University Press).

Krasner, Stephen D. (1982), 'Structural causes and regime consequences', *International Organization*, vol. 36, No. 2, pp. 185–206.

Luard, Evan (1986), *War In International Society* (London: Tauris).

Luttwak, Edward (1985), *Strategy and History. Collected Essays*, vol. 2 (New Brunswick, NJ: Transaction).

MccGwire, Michael (1985–6), 'Deterrence: the problem – not the solution', *International Affairs*, vol. 62, (No. 1, pp. 55–70.

Mead, Margaret (1968), 'Alternatives to War' in Morton Fried, Marvin Harris and Robert Murphy, (eds), *War: The Anthropology of Armed Conflict and Aggression* (Garden City, NY: Natural History Press).

Nye, Joseph S. (ed.) (1984), *The Making of America's Soviet Policy* (New Haven: Yale University Press).

Ornstein, Robert, and Ehrlich, Paul (1989), *New World, New Mind* (London: Methuen).

Palme Commission (1984), *Common Security. A Programme for Disarmament* (London: Pan).

Wolfe, Alan (1984), *The Rise and Fall of the Soviet Threat* (Boston, Mass.: South End Press).

Contributors

Roy Allison is a Lecturer in Soviet Defence Policy and International Security at the Centre for Russian and East European Studies, University of Birmingham. He was previously Research Fellow at St Antony's College, Oxford, and Senior Research Fellow at the University of Southampton. He has written various articles and book chapters on Soviet defence and arms control policy, and recent books include *The Soviet Union and the Strategy of Non-Alignment in the Third World* (1988) and *Superpower Competition and Crisis Prevention in the Third World*, edited with Phil Williams (1988).

Ken Booth is Professor of International Politics in the Department of International Politics at the University College of Wales, Aberystwyth. He was the first Scholar-in-Residence at the US Naval War College and was a Senior Research Fellow at the Centre for Foreign Policy Studies, Dalhousie University, Canada. His books include *Navies and Foreign Policy* (1977), *Strategy and Ethnocentrism* (1979) and *Law, Force and Diplomacy at Sea* (1985); he is joint author of *Contemporary Strategy: Theories and Policies* (1975 and 1987) and *Britain, NATO and Nuclear Weapons: Alternative Defence v Alliance Reform* (1989).

Barry Buzan is Reader in International Studies at the University of Warwick, Chairman of the British International Studies Association, and a Research Director at the Centre for Peace and Conflict Research in the University of Copenhagen. He has written widely on the conceptual and practical aspects of international security, and his books include *People, States and Fear. The National Security Problem in International Relations* (1983) and *An Introduction to Strategic Studies: Military Technology and International Relations* (1987).

Michael Clarke is Director of the Defence Studies Centre, London University. He has written on the politics of alternative defence and on NATO's conventional strategies and is presently completing a study on British foreign and defence policy-making for the Royal Institute of International Affairs. He has recently co-edited *Britain and the World* (1990) and *European Defence Cooperation in an Anglo-American Context* (1990).

David J. Dunn is a Senior Lecturer in the Department of International Relations and Politics at Staffordshire Polytechnic. He has written several articles on the evolution of peace research and, more recently, has written about naval arms control and naval collaboration. A member of the International Institute for Strategic Studies and the Conflict Research Society, he is currently working on a book on *War, Peace and the Study of International Relations*.

Lawrence Freedman is Professor of War Studies at King's College London. Before that he held research positions at Nuffield College, Oxford, the International Institute for Strategic Studies and the Royal Institute of International Affairs. He has written extensively on arms control, strategic theory and East–West relations. His books include *US Intelligence and The Soviet Strategic Threat* (1977), *Britain and Nuclear Weapons* (1980), *The Evolution of Nuclear Strategy* (1981 and 1988), *Atlas of Global Strategy* (1985) and *The Price of Peace* (1986).

Eric Herring is a Lecturer in Politics at the University of Bristol. He was previously a Social Science Research Council-MacArthur Foundation Fellow in International Peace and Security at the Institute of War and Peace Studies, Columbia University. His primary research interests are deterrence theory and crisis diplomacy. He is presently working on a research guide to strategic studies.

Adrian G. V. Hyde-Price is a Lecturer in the Department of Politics Southampton University. Previously, he was Research Fellow on the International Security Programme at the Royal Institute of International Affairs (Chatham House). He undertook post-doctoral research at the Humboldt University in Berlin (GDR), and was a Lecturer in Government and Politics at the University of Manchester.

Mary Kaldor is a Senior Fellow of the Science Policy Research Unit at the University of Sussex. Her books include *The Baroque Arsenal* (1982), *The Disintegrating West* (1978) and *The New Détente: Rethinking East–West Relations* (1988), co-edited with Gerard Holden and Richard Falk. She was a founder member of European Nuclear Disarmament and, for several years, was editor of the *END Journal*.

Colin McInnes is Defence Lecturer in the Department of International Politics, University College of Wales, Aberystwyth. He was formerly a Lecturer in the Department of War Studies and International Affairs, The Royal Military Academy, Sandhurst. He is joint editor with G. D. Sheffield of *Warfare in the Twentieth Century*, and author of *Trident: the Only Option?* and a number of articles on strategy and military doctrine. He is currently working on a project on the future of European security.

Hugh Miall read Modern History at Merton College, Oxford, and obtained his doctorate in Peace and Conflict Research at the University of Lancaster. He is currently Research Director of the Oxford Research Group and Secretary of the Conflict Research Society. He is author of *Nuclear Weapons: Who's in Charge?* (1987).

John Roper is Director of the Institute for Security Studies, Western European Union, Paris. Before this he was Head of the International Security Programme at the Royal Institute of International Affairs, taught Economics at Manchester University and was a Member of Parliament with particular interests in European and defence issues.

Jane M. O. Sharp is presently a Senior Researcher at the Stockholm International Institute for Peace Research. Before that she held various research positions in the United States, including the George B. Kistiakowsky Visiting Scholar of the AAAS, Peace Fellow at the Bunting Institute and Director of the Warsaw Pact Project at Cornell. She has written widely on arms control and European security and is editor of *Opportunities for Disarmament* (1978) and *Europe After An American Withdrawal: Economic and Military Issues* (forthcoming) and is co-editor of *The Warsaw Pact: Alliance in Transition* (1984).

Caroline Thomas is a Lecturer in International Relations at Southampton University. She has a special interest in Third World security, and is currently co-ordinating with Saravanamuttu a MacArthur-funded project on South Asian security. Her publications include *New States, Sovereignty and Intervention* (1985) and *In Search of Security: the Third World in International Relations* (1987). Most recently she has edited with P. Saravanamuttu *The*

State and Instability in the South (1989) and *Conflict and Consensus in South/North Security* (1989).

Phil Williams is Professor of International Security in the Graduate School of Public and International Affairs, University of Pittsburgh. He was formerly in the Departments of Politics at Aberdeen and Southampton Universities, and Head of the International Security Programme at the Royal Institute of International Affairs 1988–9. He is author of *Crisis Management, The Senate and US Troops in Europe,* and co-author of *Contemporary Strategy, Superpower Détente: A Reappraisal* (1988) and *Contemporary Strategy* (1975 and 1988). He is also a co-editor of *Soviet and American policies in Central America and the Middle East* (1987) and *Superpower Competition and Crisis Prevention in the Third World* (1988).

Index